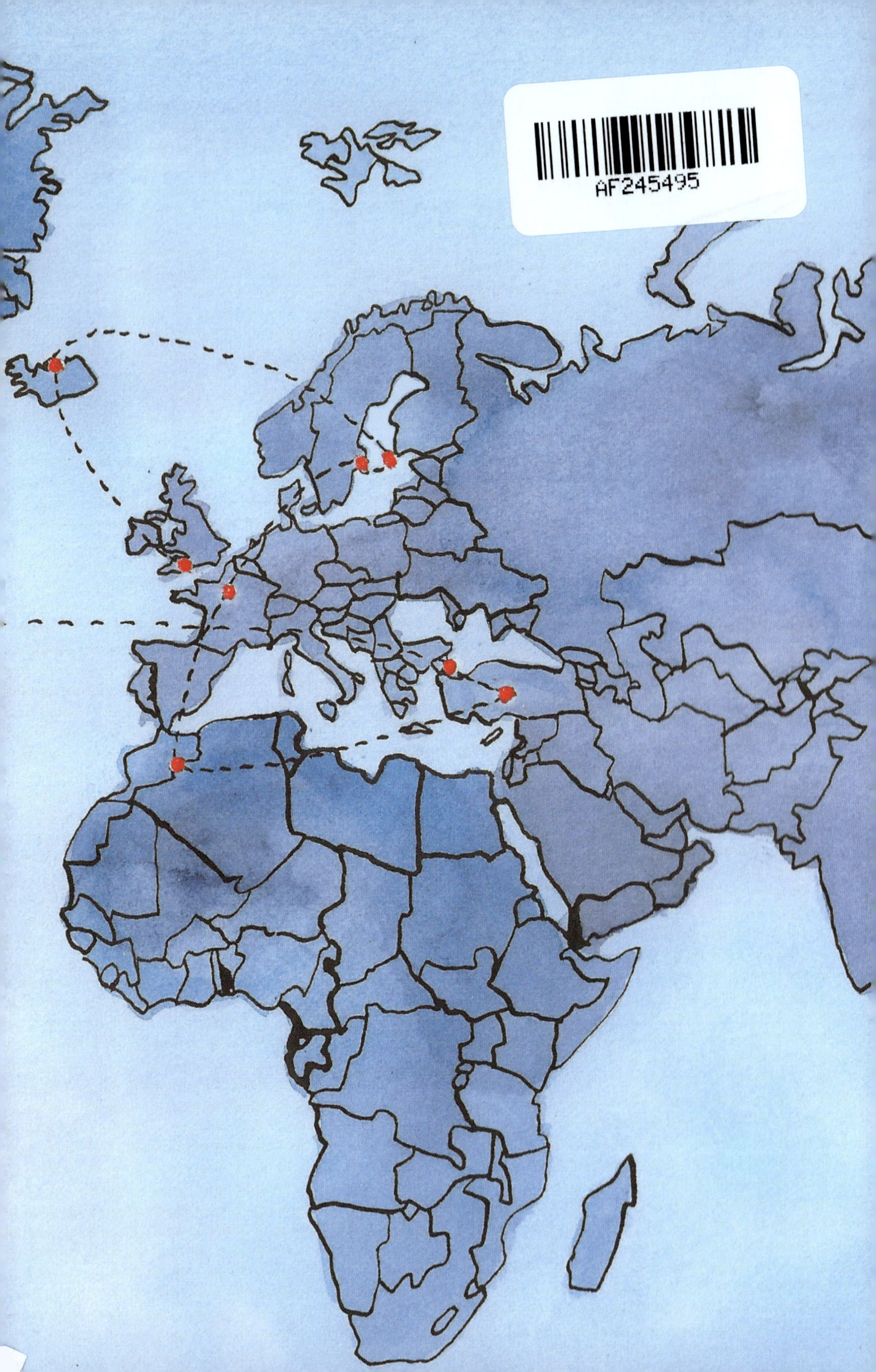

AF245495

The Traveling Artist
A Visual Journal

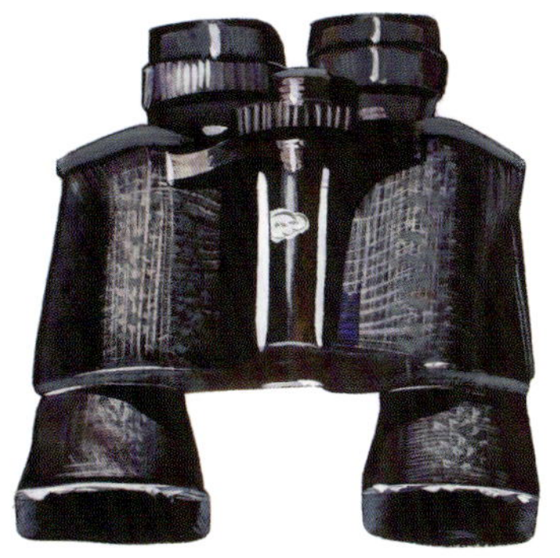

Missy Dunaway

G EDITIONS

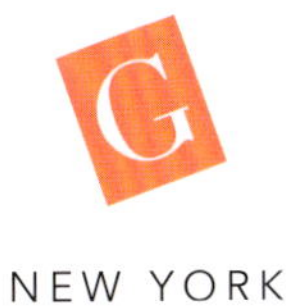

NEW YORK

For my mother,
whose love, friendship, and sound advice made this book
and the memories recorded herein possible.

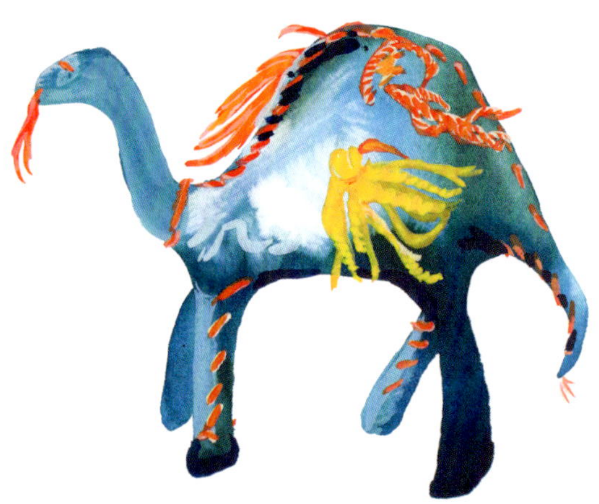

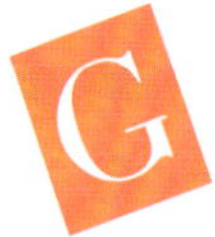

G Editions
www.geditions.com
media@geditions.com

Artwork on pages 18, 19, 24, 25, 26, 27, 46, 47:
From *A World Of Artist Journal Pages* by Dawn DeVries Sokol.
Compilation copyright © 2015 by Dawn DeVries Sokol
Used by permission of Harry N. Abrams, Inc., New York. All rights reserved.

First edition, 2021

Library of Congress Cataloging-in-Publication Data is available from the Publisher.
Hardcover edition ISBN: 978-1-943876-18-1
Limited edition ISBN: 978-1-943876-19-8
Design: Fay Graphic Design
Printed and Bound in China

10 9 8 7 6 5 4 3 2 1

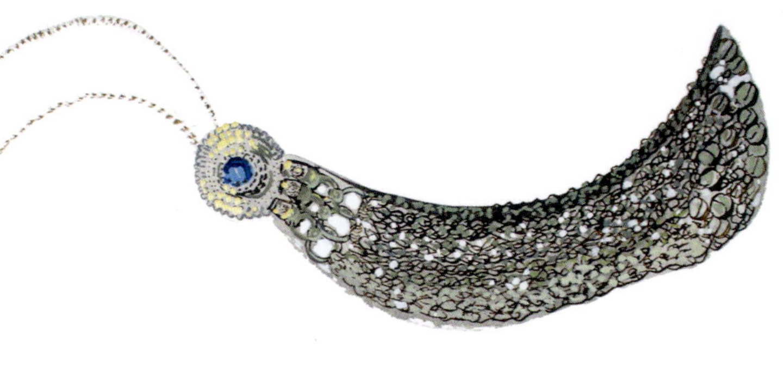

Contents

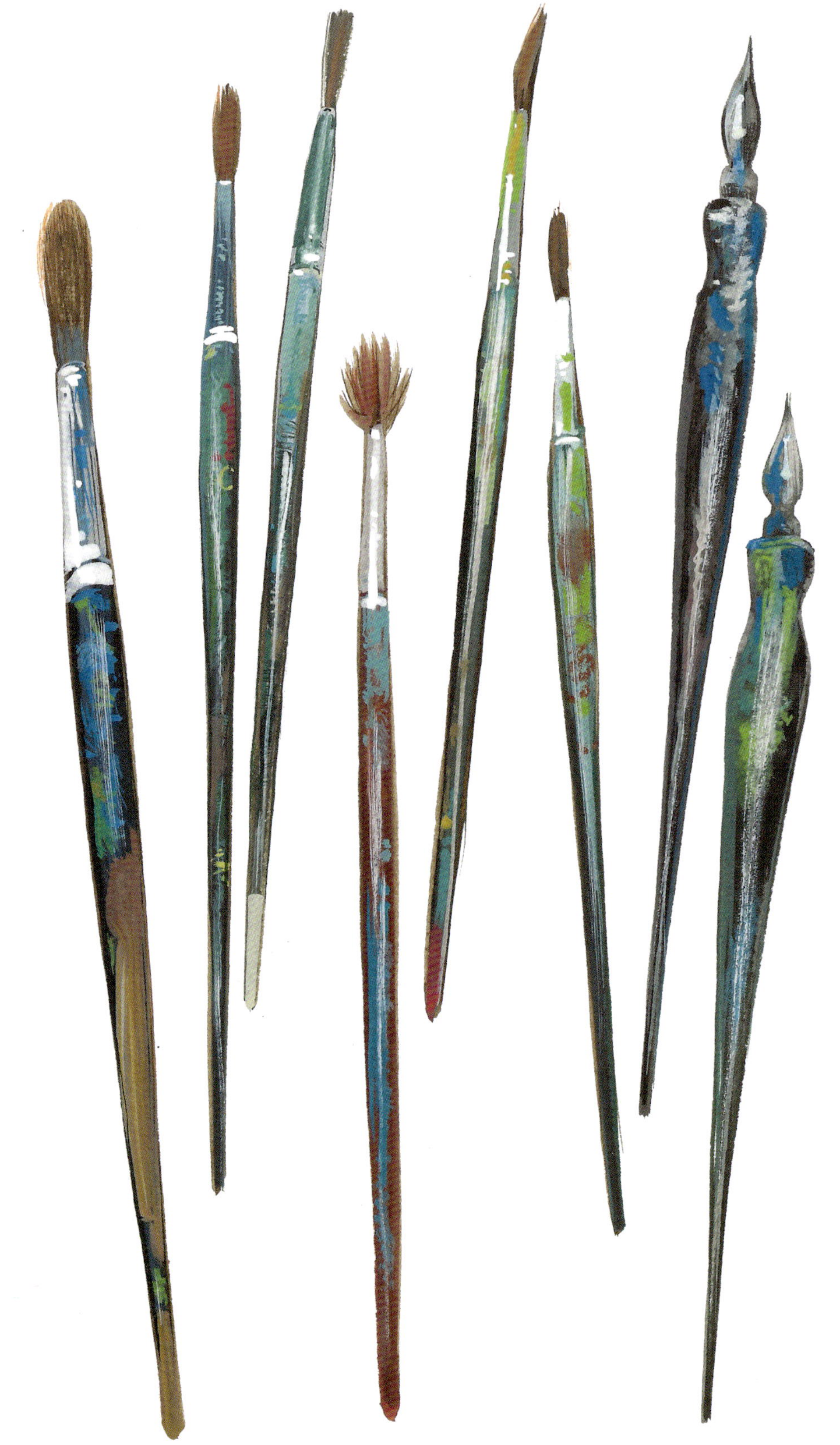

Introduction

I like to compare painting to alchemy. As an artist, I take colored mud ground from earthly materials, brush it across a surface, and somehow render life. I transform something basic into something valuable. It's magic.

When I travel, I fully see this alchemy at work. I encounter many things I want to take home but can't. Maybe they are too big, expensive, or abstract, like atmosphere and feeling. Painting is a gentle and innocuous way for me to capture it all. Through painting, I can transform a place into a tangible thing I can keep that is free, portable, doesn't take from others, or challenge the environment.

As art shifts to digital formats, as cameras capture scenes in fractions of a second, as hours of my day are increasingly occupied by computers, I've found it's essential that I still create with my hands. Painting by hand takes more time, but as a nostalgic person, it's a satisfying process. Painting a memory allows me to return there, if only in my mind, to spend several hours in a moment that brought me joy. I consider every detail as I recreate it line by line, plane by plane. I focus on what I appreciate about the place and, in doing so, I fall more in love.

Although I may snap hundreds of photos per day when I'm traveling, I rarely look back at them. I am not a gifted photographer, nor do I have professional equipment. Colors are washed out, details are lost, and scale is diminished. All of these elements can be corrected— or exaggerated—with a paintbrush. Something is lost when I take a photograph, and painting allows me to recapture its essence by emphasizing how a scene felt, not just how it looked. When I transform a memory into a painting, it is distilled into its purest form.

The artwork continues to morph because, as you may expect, painting in a bound format is a messy process. Ink seeps into the centerfold and spills onto previously completed pages, damaging them. If I close the book while a painting is not completely dry, I have to pry the pages open later, ripping off flecks of paint. Despite these challenges, I choose to paint inside a book, so I accept that the medium is subject to wear and tear. I find these changes add character.

In your hands is a selection of eighty paintings that document four of the most adventurous years of my life. The scenery spans New York, Turkey, the Sahara Desert, France, Sweden, Finland, Iceland, and England. Instead of a static photo album, this is a peek into how my journeys felt moment to moment. While this book is about my personal voyage, both inside and out, I believe it touches upon emotions felt by all.

Beginnings

I suspect my wanderlust is rooted in a childhood of constant movement, the consequence of having a father in the Navy. To provide stability and a creative outlet, my parents enrolled their two daughters in art classes wherever we were stationed. Those were the constants in my childhood—art and travel—and it's still very much the same in my adult life.

I was eleven when my dad retired from the military, and we stopped moving to settle in Annapolis, Maryland, but by then the travel bug was under my skin. It wasn't long before the desire to explore beckoned: first as a high school exchange student in Italy, then as a college junior studying abroad in Barcelona, and then a move to New York City after I graduated college in 2010.

I discovered acrylic ink in art school, and it is still my preferred paint medium today. It is a rich and forgiving substance that, as it seems to me, is not as widely used or as well-known as it deserves. As the name suggests, acrylic ink is a mixture of ink and acrylic, and takes the best qualities from each media. Like ink, it is fluid, graceful, and vibrant. Like acrylic, it dries quickly and can be layered, allowing the artist to paint light over dark and cover mistakes. Once dry, paintings are lightfast and water-resistant.

As a student, and in the years following graduation, my artwork was large-scaled, highly detailed, and aimed to demonstrate technical skill and academic research. I used painting as a tool for learning, and projects indulged my curiosity in the natural sciences, literature, and material culture. The most significant example of this inclination came in 2012, when I began studying and painting carpet designs.

Textiles have been a lifelong curiosity, thanks to my parents. Our home was decorated with knotted pile carpets from a myriad of countries, and I wanted to better understand the historical and cultural weight of an art form that enriched my adolescence. Inspired, I applied for and was given a Fulbright Fellowship in Istanbul, Turkey. This nine-month grant allowed me to research and make paintings of the oldest examples of Anatolian weaving, to explore their deep heritage and study how they visually portray their culture of origin.

Goodbye, New York City

Receiving my Fulbright acceptance letter was a bittersweet event. I was about to embark on an adventure but another one neared its end. At the time, I was living in New York and my departure would surely end an already disintegrating five-year relationship. I desperately needed a way to process my feelings, and my research projects were of little help.

For the first time, I focused my art inward. I opened a Moleskine sketchbook, a few jars of acrylic ink, and reached for my sturdy, supple Kolinsky sable-hair watercolor brushes.

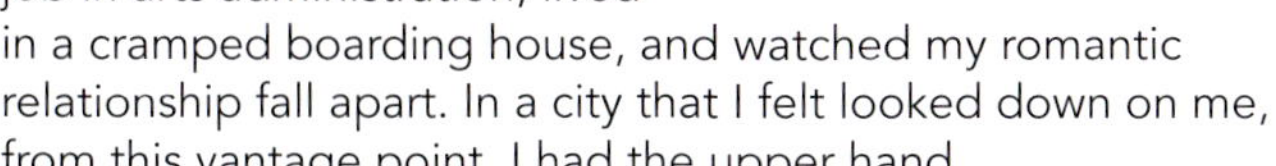

I painted the view from my street in Brooklyn, standing between Greenwood Cemetery and an electrical park. This spot was a stone's throw from the highest topographic point in the five boroughs. I visited often for its sweeping perspective of Manhattan and could even see the Statue of Liberty. While living in New York, I worked a stressful job in arts administration, lived in a cramped boarding house, and watched my romantic relationship fall apart. In a city that I felt looked down on me, from this vantage point, I had the upper hand.

In that first painting in my sketchbook, I flattened trees, buildings, and streetlamps into dark silhouettes. I wanted shadows to surround the viewer, but for the sky to feel open and inviting. I scrawled a single sentence on the page: "I walk home without you." Those words contained all the sadness I felt for the city and relationship I was leaving, while also conveying a quiet confidence that I could continue on alone.

Until this day, I had loosely kept a sketchbook to practice drawing techniques, copy images from the internet, and scribble favorite lyrics. But this painting was different. It was the first page in a new book and a new chapter in my life. From this painting onward, I vowed to fill my sketchbook with scenes from my life and to write my own poetry.

With only one summer left in New York, I used my sketchbook to document the city, discovered hidden parks and streets, reveled in moments of light and shadow, and came to terms with the shifting landscape within me. I developed a rhythm of jotting down poems and snapping reference photos with my phone. Each poem was a variation of how I felt at the time I took the picture, adding context, exaggerating mood, and providing visual interest to the image.

Even though I lived there for two years, I realized I hadn't fully experienced New York until I painted it. My renderings paid homage to smaller treasures that might have fallen away had I left them to memory. My sketchbook asked me to focus on what enchanted me, and in doing so I appreciated the city more deeply.

My sketchbook tapped into a well of emotion that sprung up in between larger, academic projects. It was a small practice I kept on the side, but I sensed its potential. To make my big paintings, I had to lay a piece of Masonite across my bed to fashion a wide desk. Painting in a small sketchbook was far more agreeable. I'd unwittingly stumbled upon the perfect creative project to maintain while living out of a suitcase for the next year.

Merhaba, Istanbul

When I landed in Turkey, my senses were overwhelmed with the unfamiliar. I drove into Istanbul for the first time, speeding past primary-colored cargo barges on the Marmara Sea, while new melodies flowed from the radio, drifting on sea breezes that eased the lingering motion sickness from my flight. I was intoxicated by change. There were no reminders of my life in New York, and I liked that.

I was eager to dive into my project and hit the ground running. Within a month of landing, I found an apartment, enrolled in Turkish language classes, and filled my schedule with lectures at the American Research Institute in Turkey. I resolved to fix myself in the present and open my eyes to the beauty of Istanbul, but while painting in the quiet of night, I couldn't help flipping back to earlier pages and thinking of New York. I did not paint about it again, though those memories occasionally colored how I interpreted my new environment.

While attending a wool-dyeing demonstration at the Crimea Memorial Church, I met a master weaver who offered to give me weaving lessons in his private atelier. A few streets behind the Blue Mosque, in a tiny Sultanahmet workshop swathed in skeins of indigo, chamomile, and madder-dyed silk, I learned how to knot the pile carpets and flat-weave kilims like the ones that were scattered across the floors of my childhood. My instructor and I wove side-by-side and were kept company by Turkish soap operas, an Istanbul constant, much like the street cats that joined us for morning coffee, or kahve, before lessons.

By daylight, I explored Istanbul. Rather than perch on one street corner absorbed in onsite, plein air painting, I preferred to spend afternoons wandering an entire neighborhood, studying patchwork architecture, smelling briny fish pulled from the Bosphorus Strait, tasting sesame-crusted simit pretzels from street vendors, and testing my Turkish by eavesdropping on pleasantries exchanged between neighbors.

Each evening, I sat at my desk to reflect on my day, reworking a page until it became my favorite yet. Moments that inspired me were spontaneous and fleeting—like catching a glimpse of the Sulemaniye Mosque as I ran to catch a bus or watching seagulls flock past the window as I dozed on the Prince's Islands ferry.

My paintings became increasingly complex and vivid. I stopped calling it "my sketchbook," because it had evolved well beyond an assemblage of preparatory drawings. It was a collection of therapeutic, autobiographical paintings: my visual journal.

Villages in Turkey and Morocco

When I emerged on the other side of my grant period, I had no obligations and nowhere to be. I made a list of potential next steps: pursue a graduate degree, return to my former job in New York, or attempt to support myself on art sales and part-time work. I looked over these options with sober interest. In the evenings, I continued to lose myself in the pages of my journal. I realized this small book was more precious to me than my larger portfolio and research. I wanted to add more pages to it, and for that I had to keep traveling.

I attended one artist-in-residence program in the past, shortly after graduating college and before I moved to New York. I was 22, one of the youngest residents at Vermont Studio Center, unsure how I would navigate the art world. One reason I applied to the residency was to meet artists more experienced than me and to seek advice. There, I encountered artists who made a living by bouncing from one residency to the next. Trying my best to imitate their system, I combed websites that listed art residency calls-for-artists.

The programs varied widely: some invited artists to engage with the local community and collaborate with each other, while others promised solitude. Some offered financial support, and others asked for tuition. Even unsuccessful applications were productive because they were good practice. I compared successful applications with ones that failed, reusing language and themes, and shaving off what hadn't worked.

I let curiosity guide me in choosing locations. I searched countries I had fantasized about since childhood, like Morocco. I also applied in countries I had little interest in, like Iceland, knowing that sometimes the best experiences happen when you least expect them. I recalled another artist who said her favorite place in the world was Finland, and I wanted to see what made it so special. At the same time, I submitted my portfolio for gallery representation, fine-tuned my website, and set up an online print shop. I secured gallery representation and booked commissions. Finally, my first acceptances rolled in: one for an art residency in Cappadocia, Turkey, followed by another in the Moroccan Sahara Desert, as well as a grant to fund my journeys.

That spring, I spent six weeks in a small village in Cappadocia, a region of central Turkey famed for its hot air balloons and cave dwellings. In this tight-knit community, news of a visitor traveled fast. Neighbors approached to ask, "Missy, resimci?" Missy, the artist? Making introductions was easy when I could open my journal and share an illustrated record of who I was and where I'd been. Utilizing my intermediate Turkish, I expressed that I was interested in textiles, and before long I was back in weaving lessons and admiring local textile treasures.

My living space was a century-old stone house with relief sculptures carved into its walls and a cool underground studio. My first day there, I unpacked my acrylic inks: two variations of each primary color, plus three to four jars of white. Counting an earth tone here and there, I had a total of twelve jars. Unfortunately, I discovered a bottle of turquoise had loosened in transit, staining my sandals, paintbrushes, blouse, and hands. Luckily, acrylic ink can be lifted from most surfaces with soap, water, and aggressive scrubbing.

En route to my next art residency in Morocco, I took precautions to avoid more spilled ink. I tightly screwed the caps on my ink jars, stacked them into a large container, taped it shut, and wrapped it in a trash bag. This time, my ink survived damage, but my journal did not. My overnight coach was caught in a surprise rainstorm and the bus was forced to wade through deep pools of water as we lumbered south from Fes to Erfoud, a seven-hour trip. My precious journal—the one you hold now—was tucked in my backpack and stowed in the undercarriage of the bus, where it was soaked through. When I arrived at the small Berber village of

Tissardmine, I emptied my waterlogged luggage, seized the journal, and placed it on a windowsill in my resident bedroom. Its pages fluttered in the dry Saharan breeze while I set up my art studio in a perfect cube formed by dried mud. This traditional Berber structure had a single window that looked onto the Algerian border a few kilometers away.

The studio was completely empty except for a small table and single chair: the only supplies I needed for my craft. After I arranged my inks in rainbow order, I gathered my courage and surveyed the damage to my book. Miraculously, none of the paintings were altered, and the book survived without scars.

In the next month, my sight was overwhelmed by orange: sand, dunes, light, even camels. After sunset, I climbed to the roof of my art studio to practice yoga as stars appeared, one by one, amidst the respite of a deep blue sky.

Paris

Between my residencies, I spent four months in Paris, where I let myself fall for the city and a new lover. Days passed leisurely in the sixteenth arrondissement as I made breakfast in bed, admired brightly clothed teenagers idling by the turquoise Seine River, and dared myself to walk into the empty, aged crypts of Passy Cemetery.

Since my visual journal was essentially my diary, it might seem like an obvious place to elaborate on my romantic relationships. However, I blurred details and removed specifics. In my paintings, I referenced "you" and "they" but rarely identified people by name or by face. I have always been uncomfortable using words, which often felt too loaded and direct, when talking about emotions. I preferred painting and poetry to express myself because my story was communicated in an oblique way.

This decision to intentionally obscure or omit figures helped me respect the privacy of people with whom I had intimate relationships and even strangers I passed in the public sphere. When I traveled, there were times that I was between housing and had to relax in public out of necessity. I loitered in airports and bus stations, daydreamed to mentally escape crowds, and overstayed my welcome inside cafés to access internet. I thought of how often people take their private lives into public spaces due to circumstance, because of long-term displacement, or in small, temporary ways like I did.

It was in Paris that I began thinking about having a home in one location

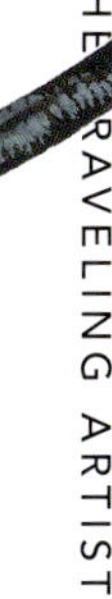

11

instead of moving from place to place. My quiet, domestic tenure in the sixteenth arrondissement was soothing, and I was sad knowing that I would inevitably have to leave. As my relationship in Paris came to its natural end, I found myself thinking of the small towns and villages that were the backdrop of my residency experiences, where local residents had known each other their whole lives. I slowly realized that I too wanted friends who don't move away, relationships that I didn't leave, and a house in which I could invest.

I decided it was time to establish my own landing pad, rather than continuing to crash with lovers and friends. No matter where I settled, I established a "one residency a year" policy to satisfy my wanderlust.

The dream scenario was to support myself with my art, which by now provided a modest income. I lived without health insurance and narrowly covered my bills, but in exchange I painted often and traveled whenever I desired. I couldn't afford to live this way in a big city, so I looked for somewhere smaller. I consulted friends, read online forums, weighed pros and cons, and chose Portland, Maine.

Within three months of moving to Portland I found a small apartment, a flexible part-time job, and the man I would eventually marry. I also secured two residencies: one on an island in the Finnish archipelago for 2016, and another island destination off of the northern coast of Iceland for 2017.

Islands and Coastlines of Finland, Sweden, Iceland, and England

I remember places in color. New York is greys with flashes of neon; Paris is steely blues; Cappadocia is yellow ochre. Finland's Korpo Island I remember as an entire rainbow.

The islands of the Finnish archipelago burst with vegetation and blossoming plants, which I witnessed from my bicycle seat. I zipped through fields of blossoming flowers and let the sunlight embrace me inside greenhouses filled with smiling pansies. On nearby Utö Island, I counted shades of blue as they rotated hour by hour with the changing light. My living and studio spaces on Korpo Island were inside a red-and-white striped building that formerly housed ferry pilots.

While painting, I utilized my artistic training to understand objects in space and to organize perspective, assisted by crude references taken with a digital camera. I consulted the photos: Exactly how tall was Utö's lighthouse compared to surrounding cottages and pine trees? Was there a bushel or just a handful of birch branches resting in the glow of the sauna?

Technicalities addressed, I broke free and relied on memory. Yes, the scene looked like my photo, but how did it feel? Was the atmosphere bright and crisp, or thick and humid? What color was the light: gold, violet, pink, or all three? The nuances in Finland's color spectrum were lost in

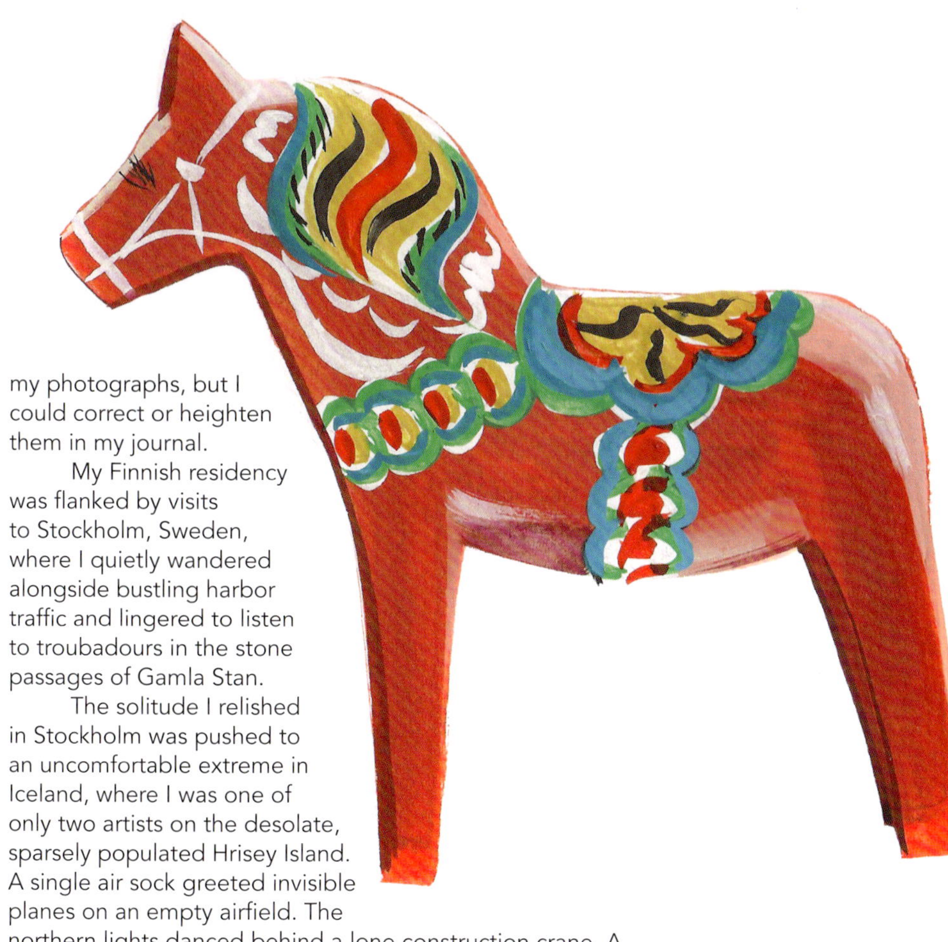

my photographs, but I
could correct or heighten
them in my journal.

My Finnish residency
was flanked by visits
to Stockholm, Sweden,
where I quietly wandered
alongside bustling harbor
traffic and lingered to listen
to troubadours in the stone
passages of Gamla Stan.

The solitude I relished
in Stockholm was pushed to
an uncomfortable extreme in
Iceland, where I was one of
only two artists on the desolate,
sparsely populated Hrisey Island.
A single air sock greeted invisible
planes on an empty airfield. The
northern lights danced behind a lone construction crane. A
solitary lighthouse floated on the horizon, dwarfed by the
enormous rock below it, and even more immense sky above.
I felt myself becoming one of these fixtures; a single vertical
structure on an empty flat plane.

After so much time alone, I was grateful to spend
time in Devon, England. The county is famed for its dreary
landscape, but I was kept warm by the company of friends
old and new as we rambled through heather-filled moors,
disheveled greenhouses, and windswept beaches.

My Journal and Me

I feel that my journal is a
continuation of my body, as
our appearances seem to
mirror each other. I turned thirty in Iceland and my journal
turned five, and we show our ages. The lines around my eyes
are the result of years of laughter, and the book's damage is
evidence of its extraordinary journey.

Keeping a journal taught me to feel comfortable alone.
When I painted, I was at ease and at home. Bare studio
spaces and generic hotel rooms meant nothing to me until
I utilized them to create artwork. The process helped me
work through feelings of loss, allowed me to say farewell

to old loves and ways of being, pushed me to find beauty in the new and unusual, and guided me in taking comfort in the wildness around me.

My journal is my best and favorite travel companion. As a woman venturing alone, I was cautioned that the second I let my guard down would be when catastrophe found me. Despite these warnings, I hitchhiked in Cappadocia and Iceland, rode more overnight buses than I can count on two hands, and arrived at my destinations in Morocco well before dawn with no one to greet me.

In moments that invited danger, I was approached by strangers who asked if I needed assistance and shepherded me to where I needed to be. As we made introductions, I revealed that I was an artist, and a personal connection was formed. Everybody knew an artist, was an artist, or in the very least appreciated art. I could build upon this connection with a visual aid because my journal was always by my side.

Yes, there were difficulties when I traveled, but they did not outweigh the thrill of discovering my independence and experiencing the kindness of strangers. My journal was met with wonder and love—qualities that defined my trips and are captured in its pages.

Here you hold a treasured possession; a visual diary of my most intimate memories. I hope that these paintings prompt you, dear reader, to recall your own adventures in greater detail—and to imagine with eager anticipation those that still await you.

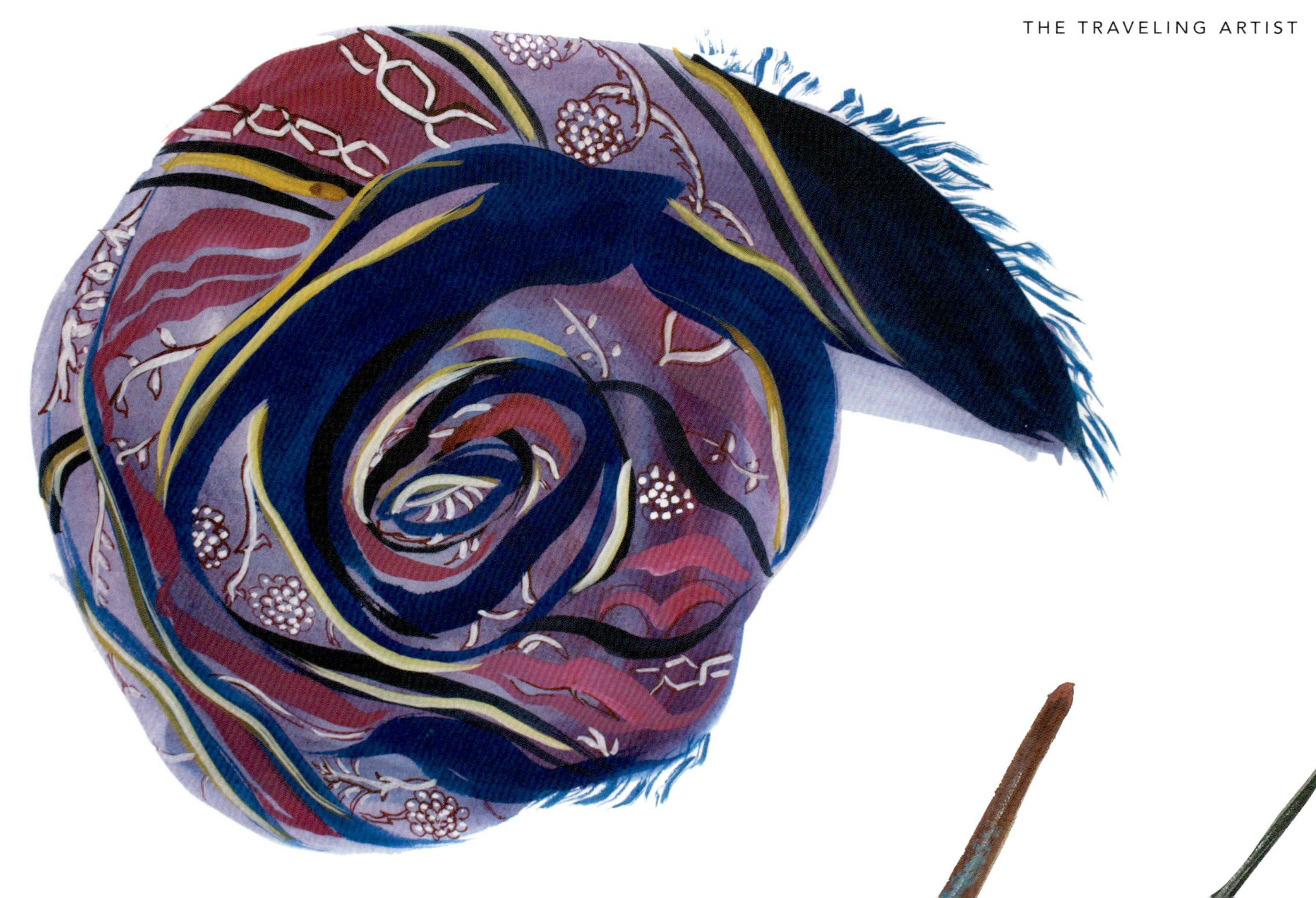

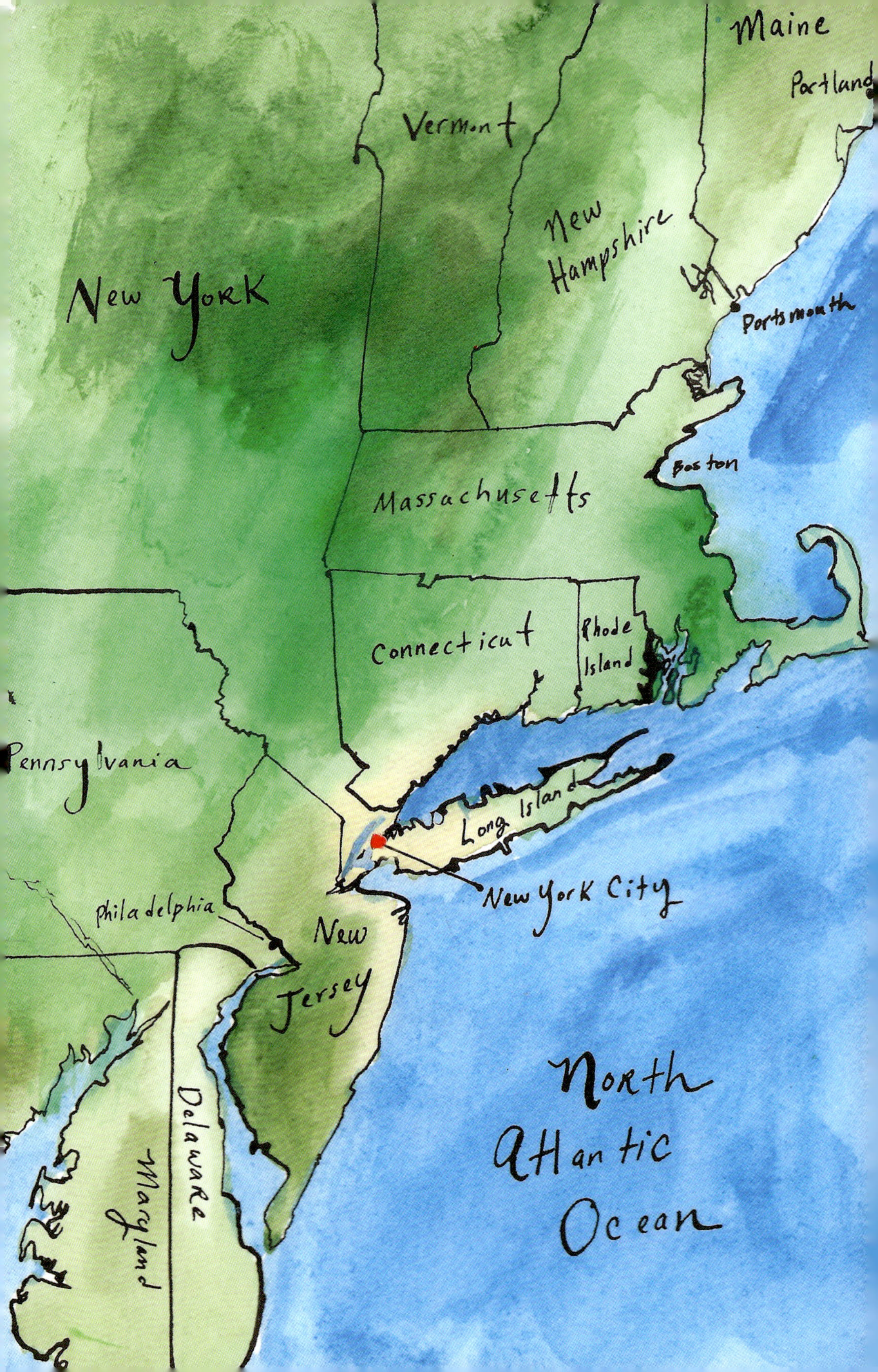

Maine
Portland
Vermont
New Hampshire
New York
Portsmouth
Boston
Massachusetts
Connecticut
Rhode Island
Pennsylvania
Long Island
New York City
Philadelphia
New Jersey
Delaware
Maryland
North Atlantic Ocean

I ♥ New York City, USA

August 21st, 2013

Two years in New York, the biggest thing to have happened to me since graduating college, and I didn't realize how long I've had my head down. I feel like I've been treading water, keeping focused on work and routine. This summer will be my last one here, and every day I remind myself to keep my gaze lifted. I want to take in the city's subtler charms, and am already feeling nostalgic for what I'll soon leave behind.

I will miss the hidden, inconspicuous parks the most. I've happened upon so many by accident. It's a relief to know silence can still be found in a dense city. I always pause my evening walk to savor the Greenwood Cemetery and the skeletal shell of the McGovern Weir Greenhouse. As if the arch to enter Greenwood wasn't opulent enough, it's also the favorite perch for monk parakeets. They decorate the façade like lime-green ornaments.

colors:

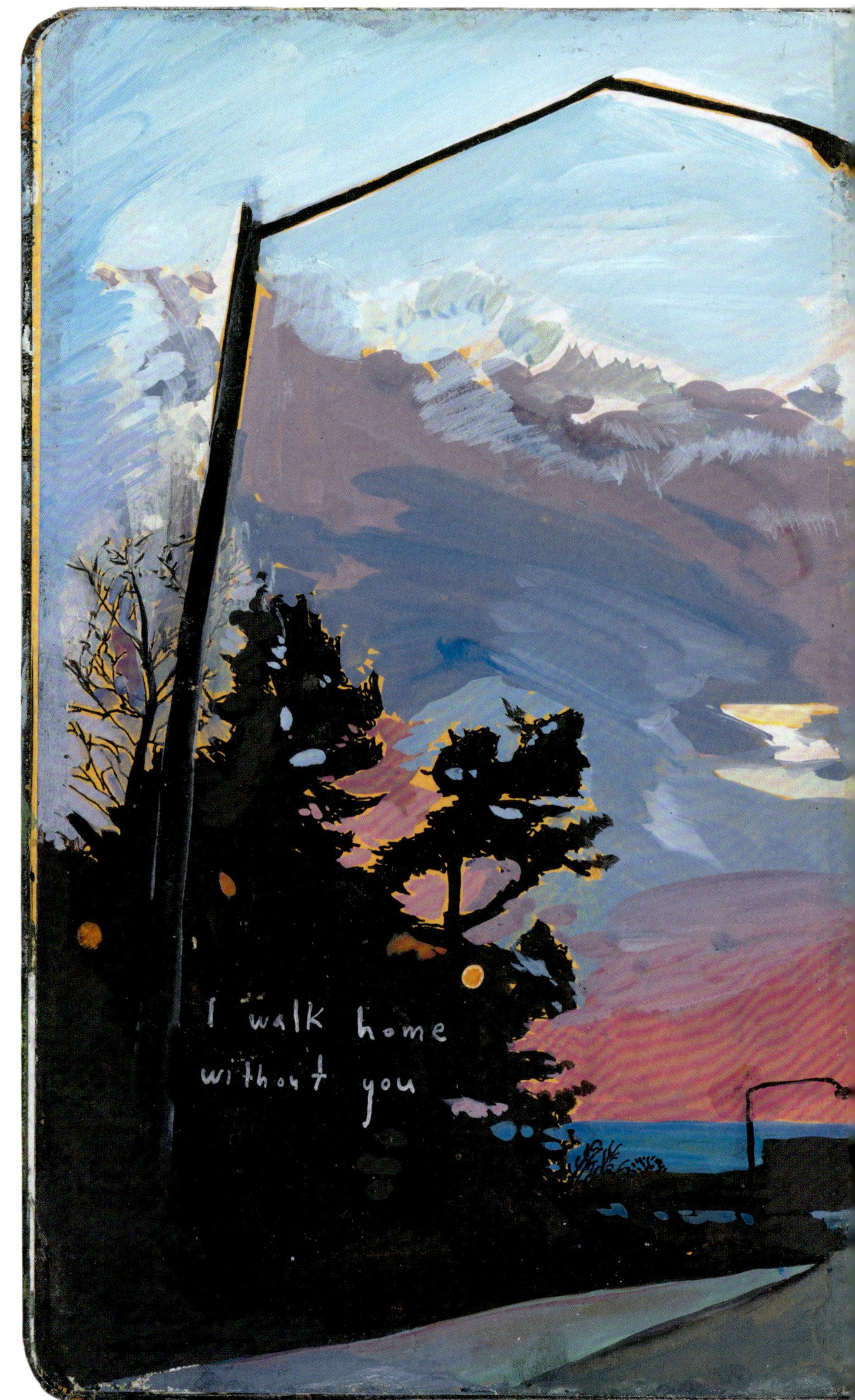

I walk home
without you

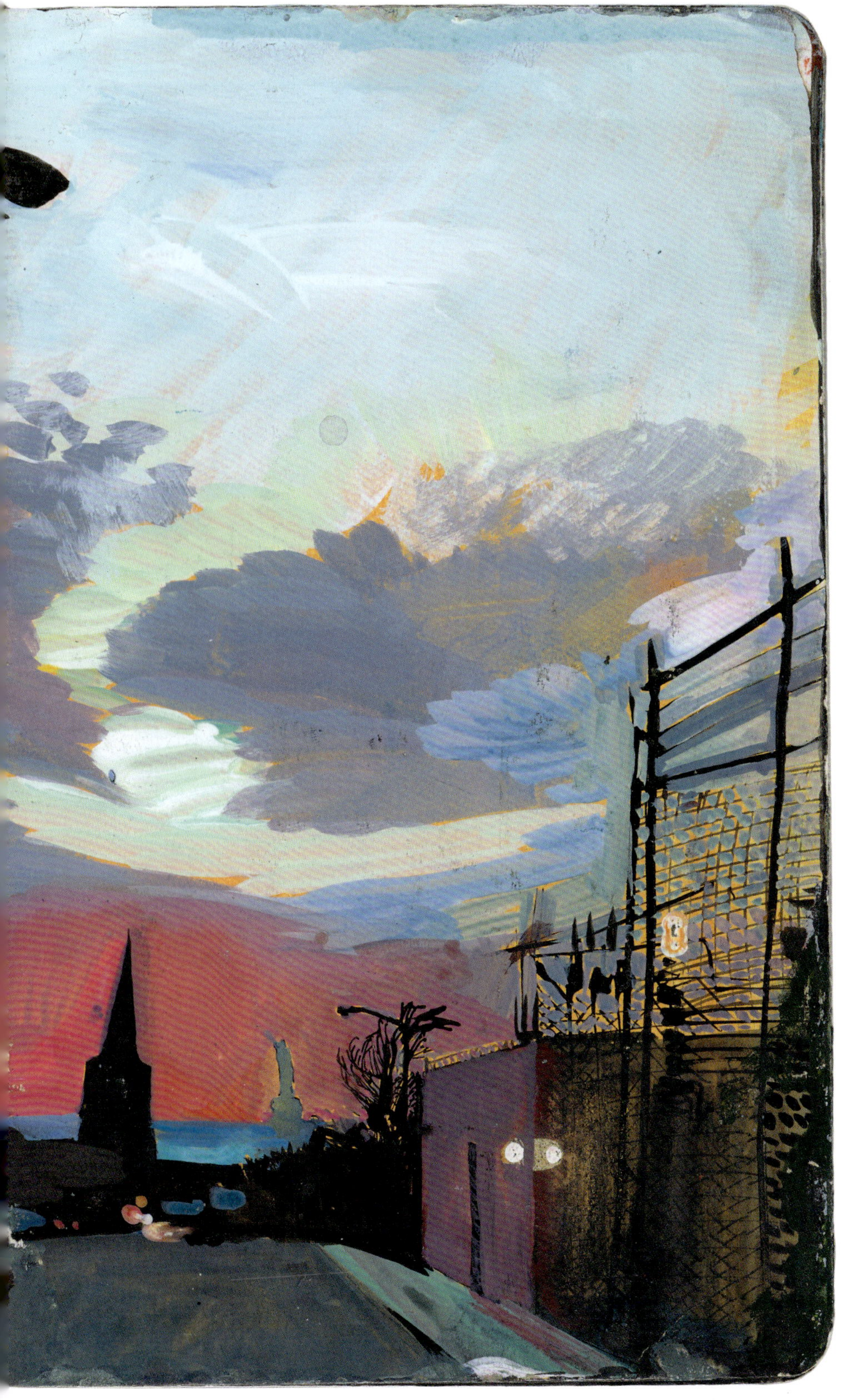

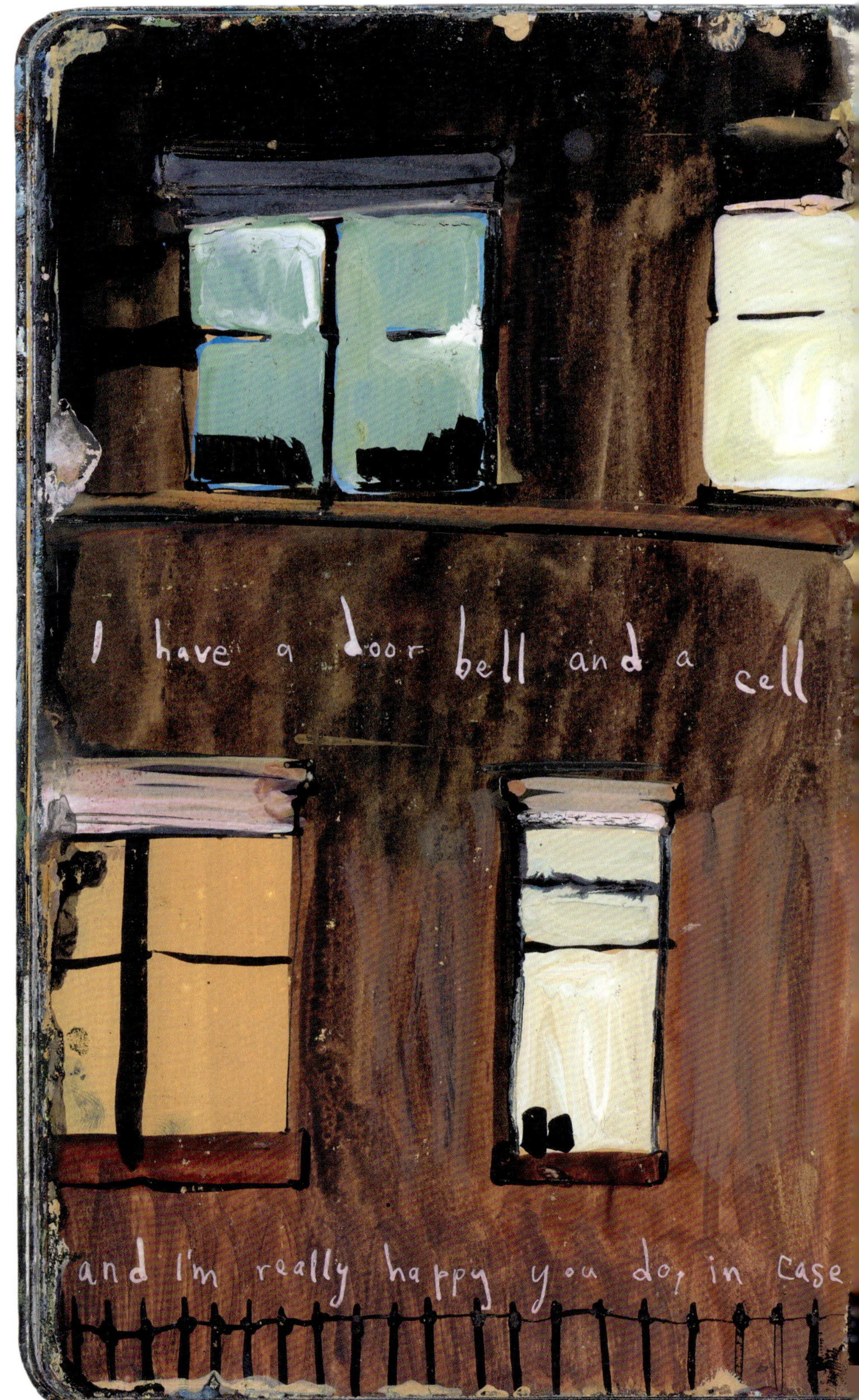

I have a door bell and a cell
and I'm really happy you do, in case

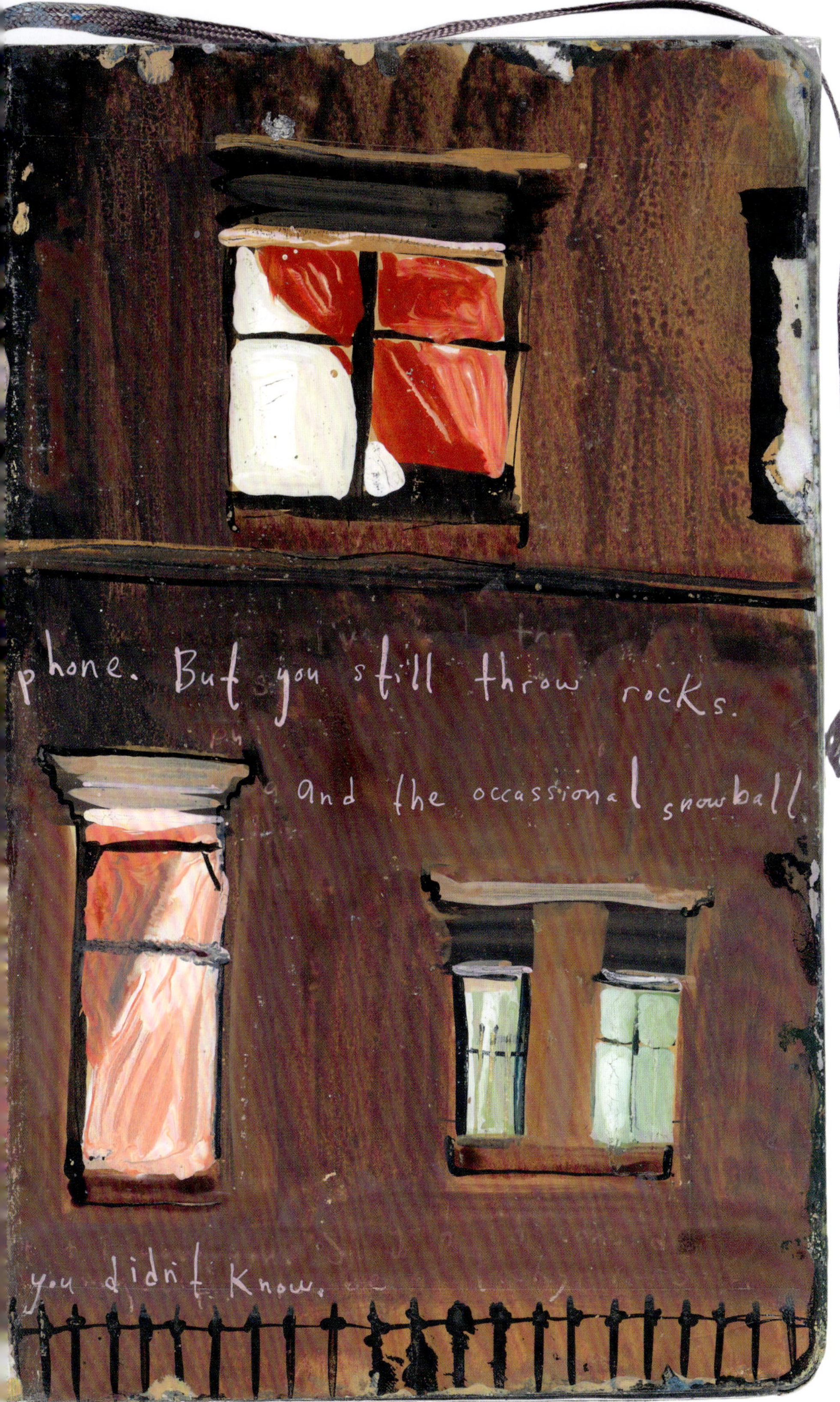

phone. But you still throw rocks.

and the occassional snowball.

you didn't know.

we walked down the opposing stairs, t
trains, to take us in opposite directions.
had no service. I wanted to call out to you
tracks. So we stood there, directly across fron
each other like strangers.

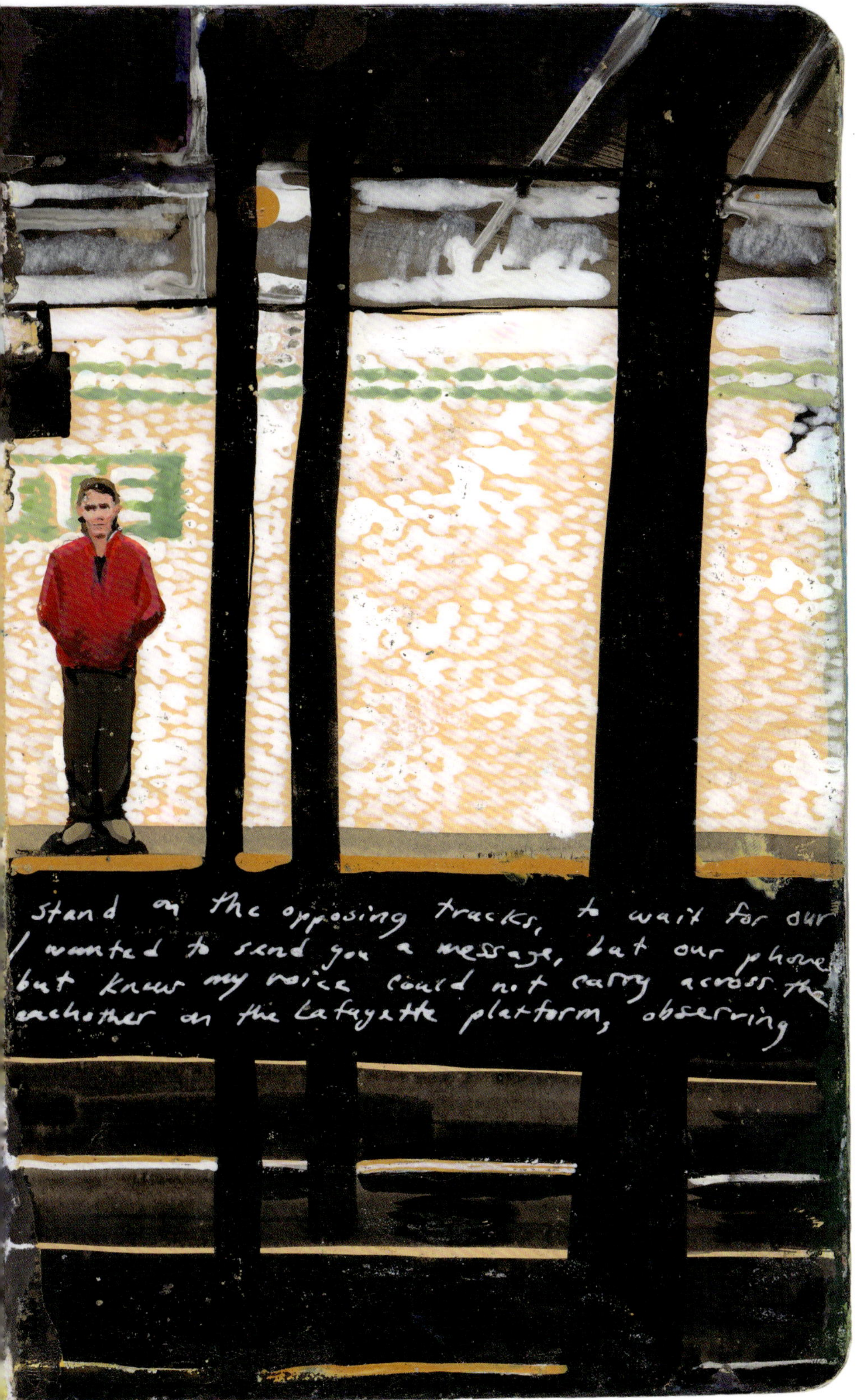

stand on the opposing tracks, to wait for our
I wanted to send you a message, but our phone
but knew my voice could not carry across the
eachother on the Lafayette platform, observing

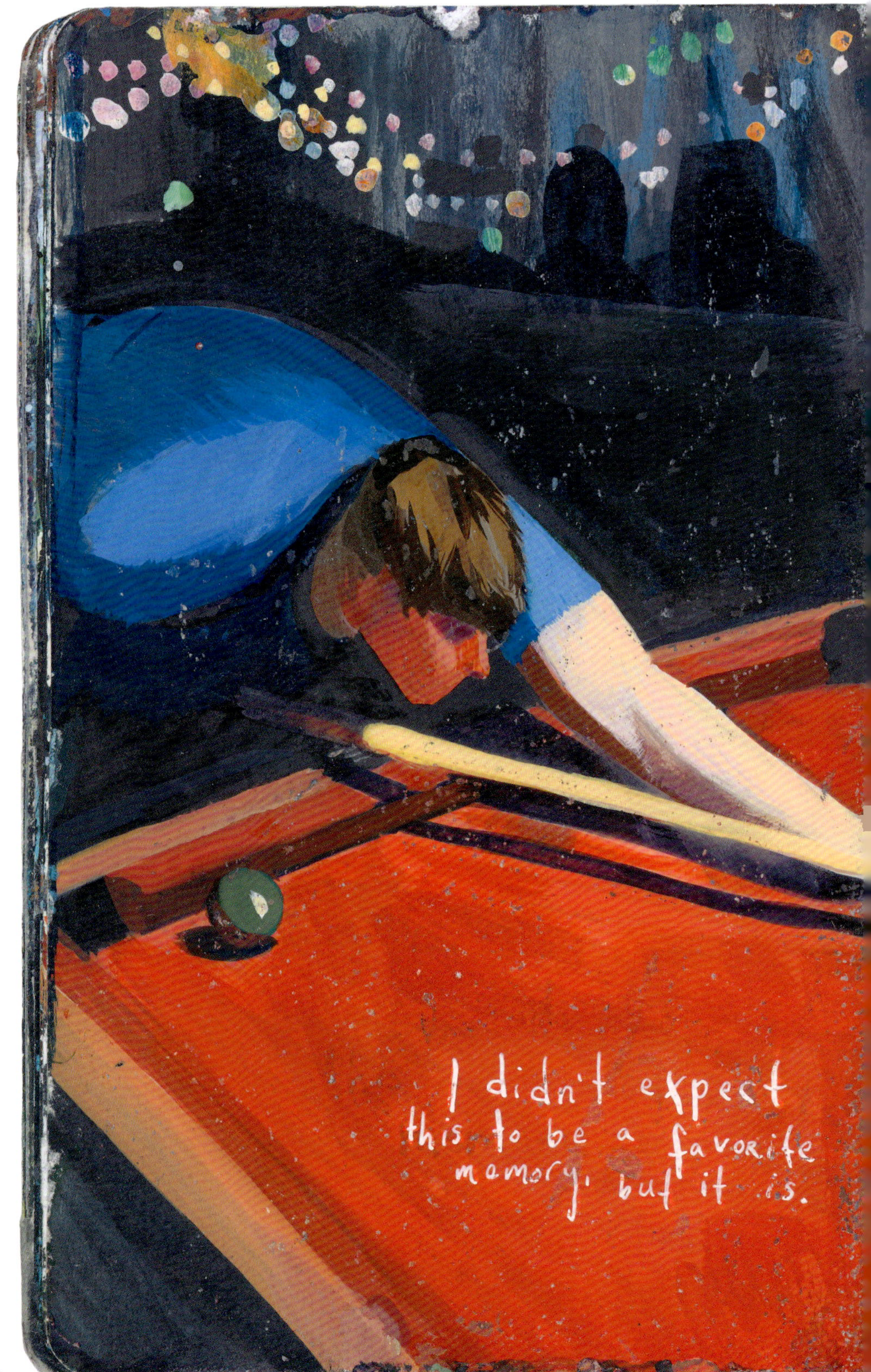

I didn't expect
this to be a favorite
memory, but it is.

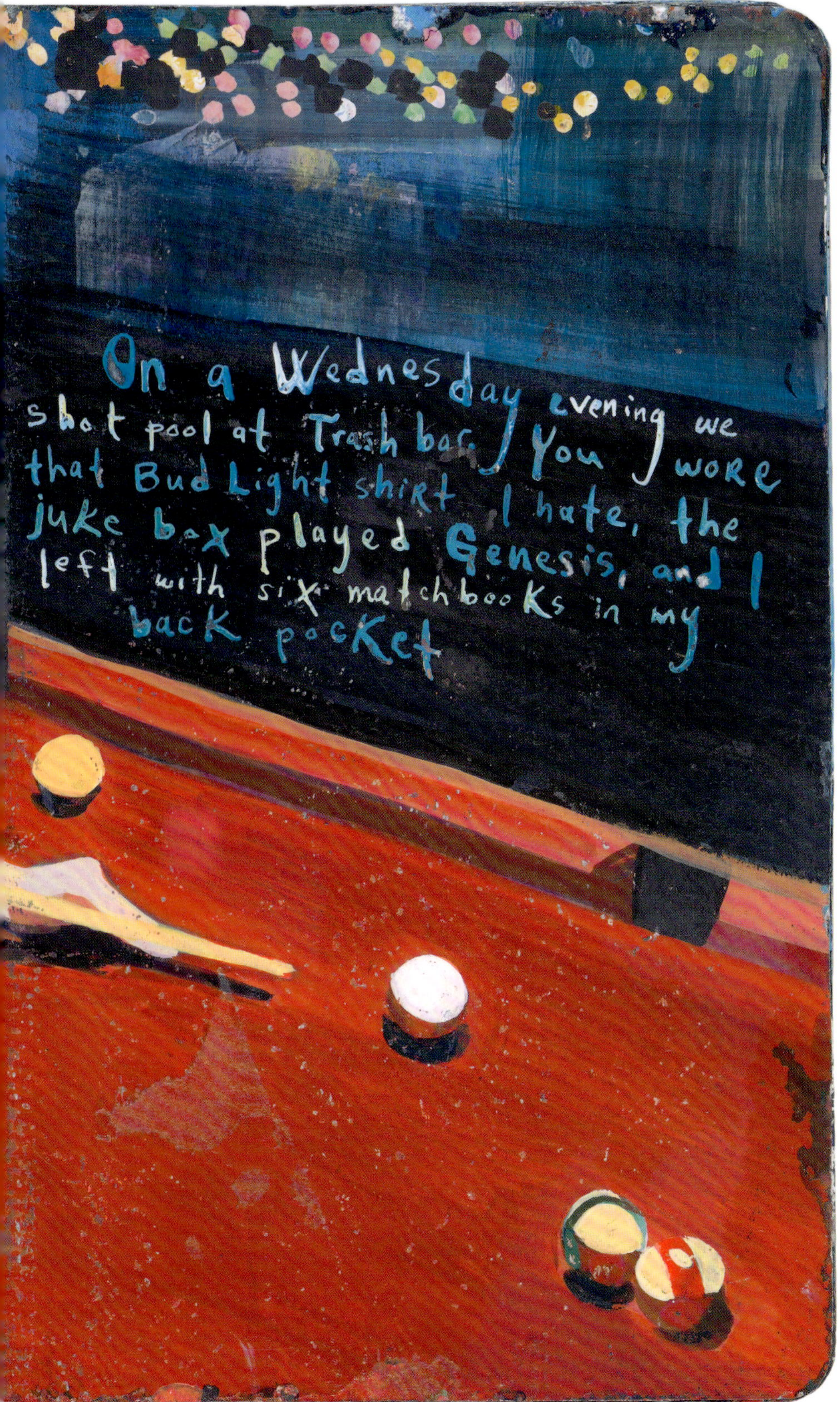

On a Wednesday evening we
shot pool at Trash bar. You wore
that Bud Light shirt I hate, the
juke box played Genesis, and I
left with six matchbooks in my
back pocket

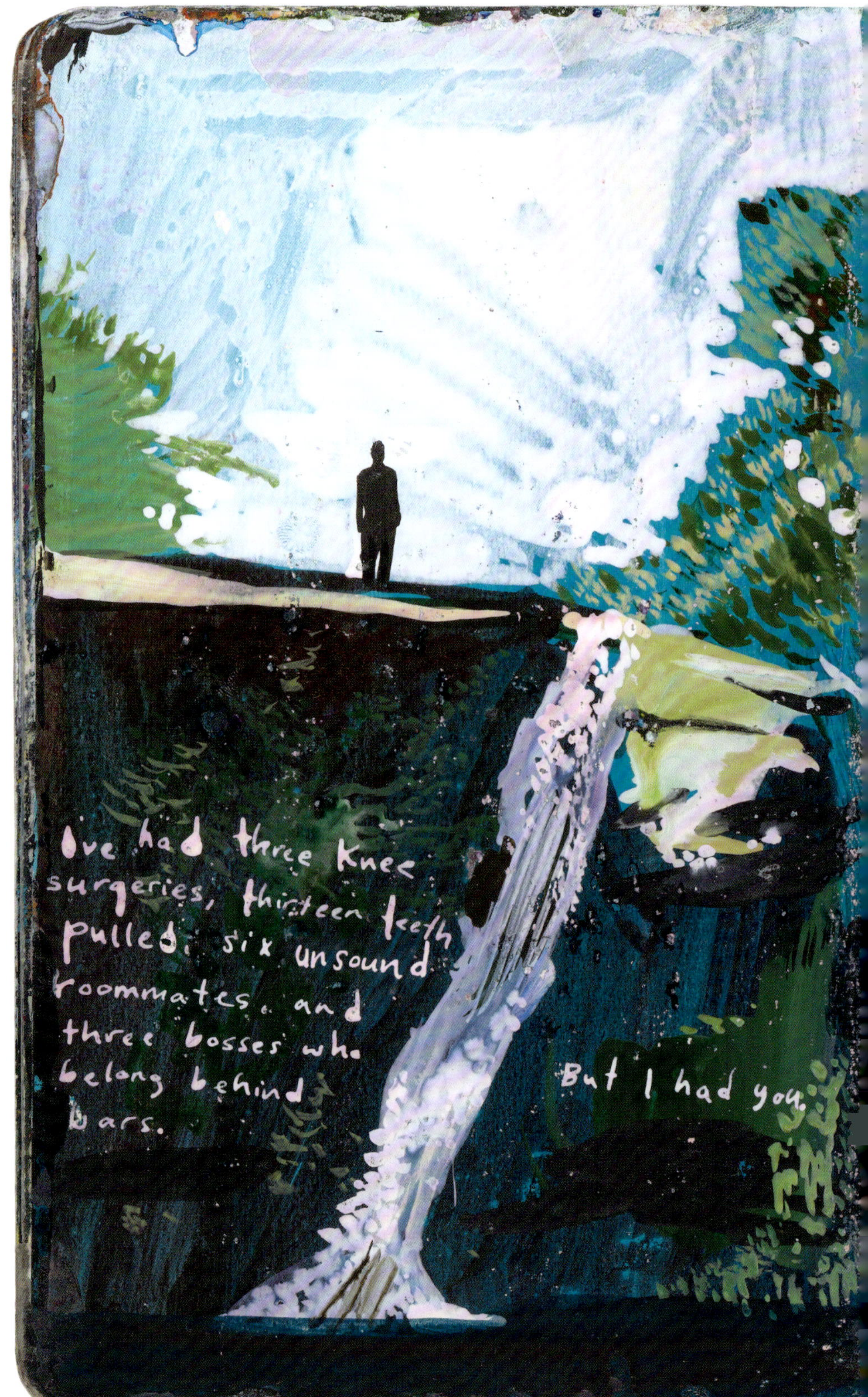
I've had three knee
surgeries, thirteen teeth
pulled, six unsound
roommates, and
three bosses who
belong behind
bars.

But I had you.

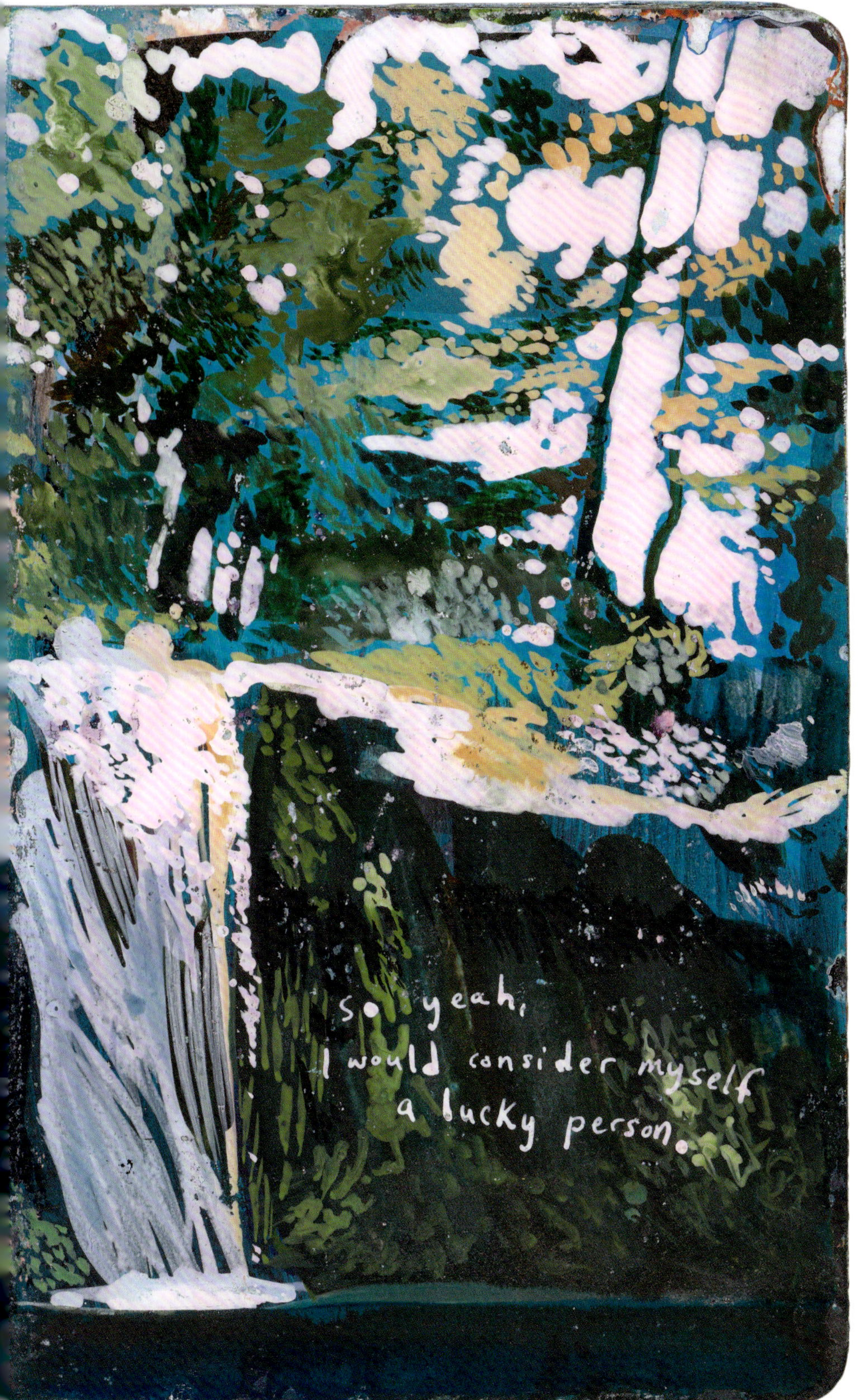

so yeah,
I would consider myself
a lucky person.

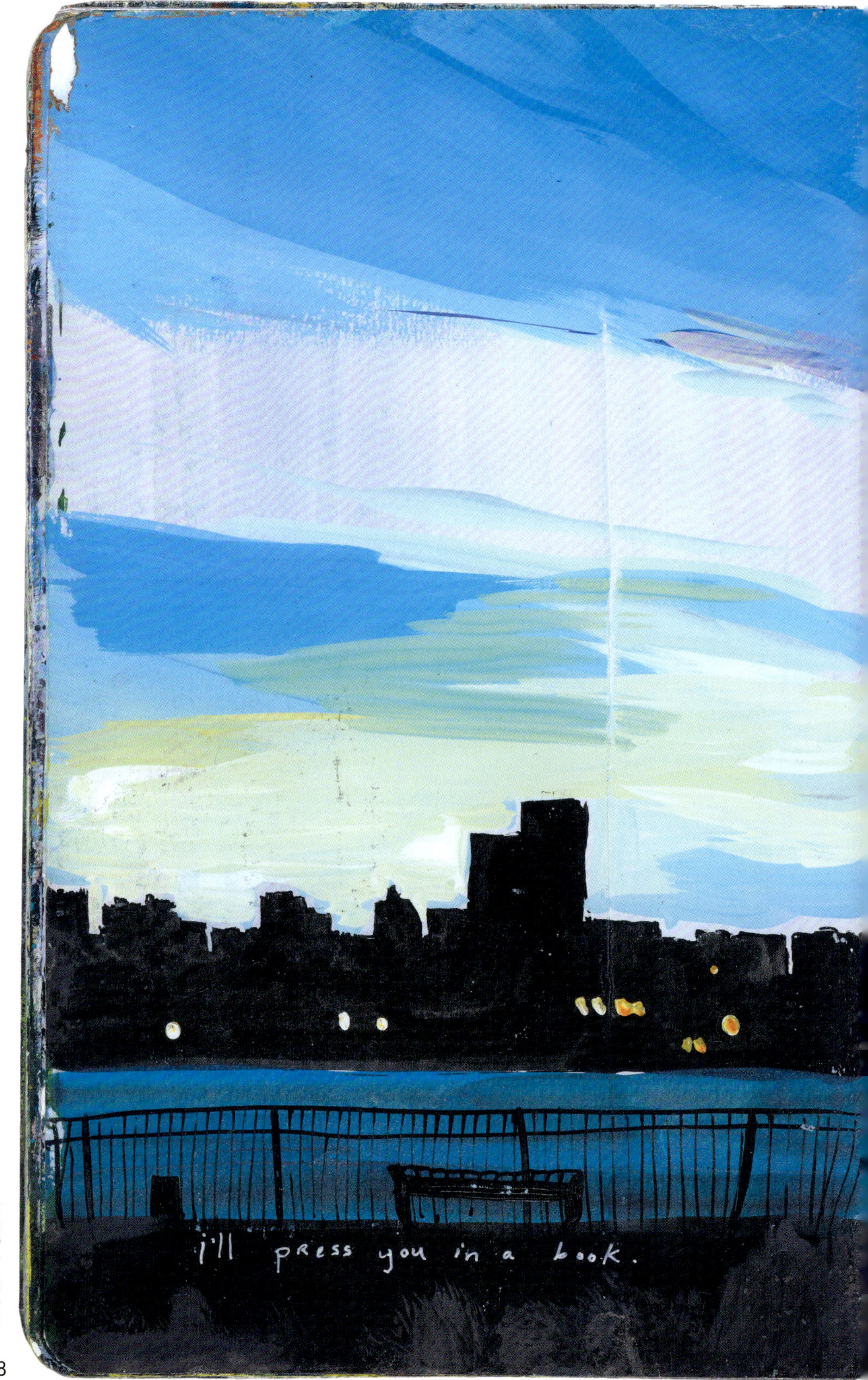

i'll press you in a book.

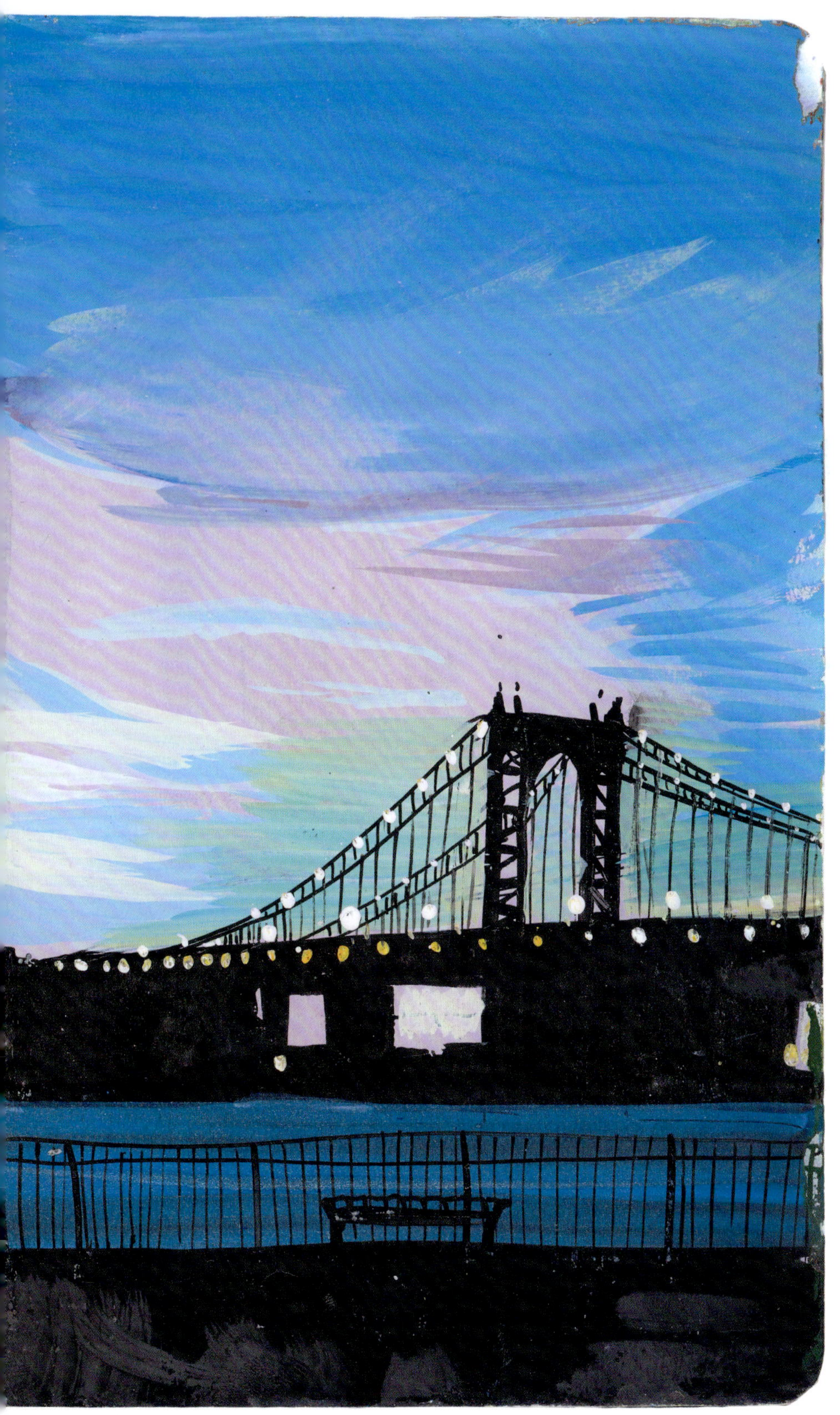

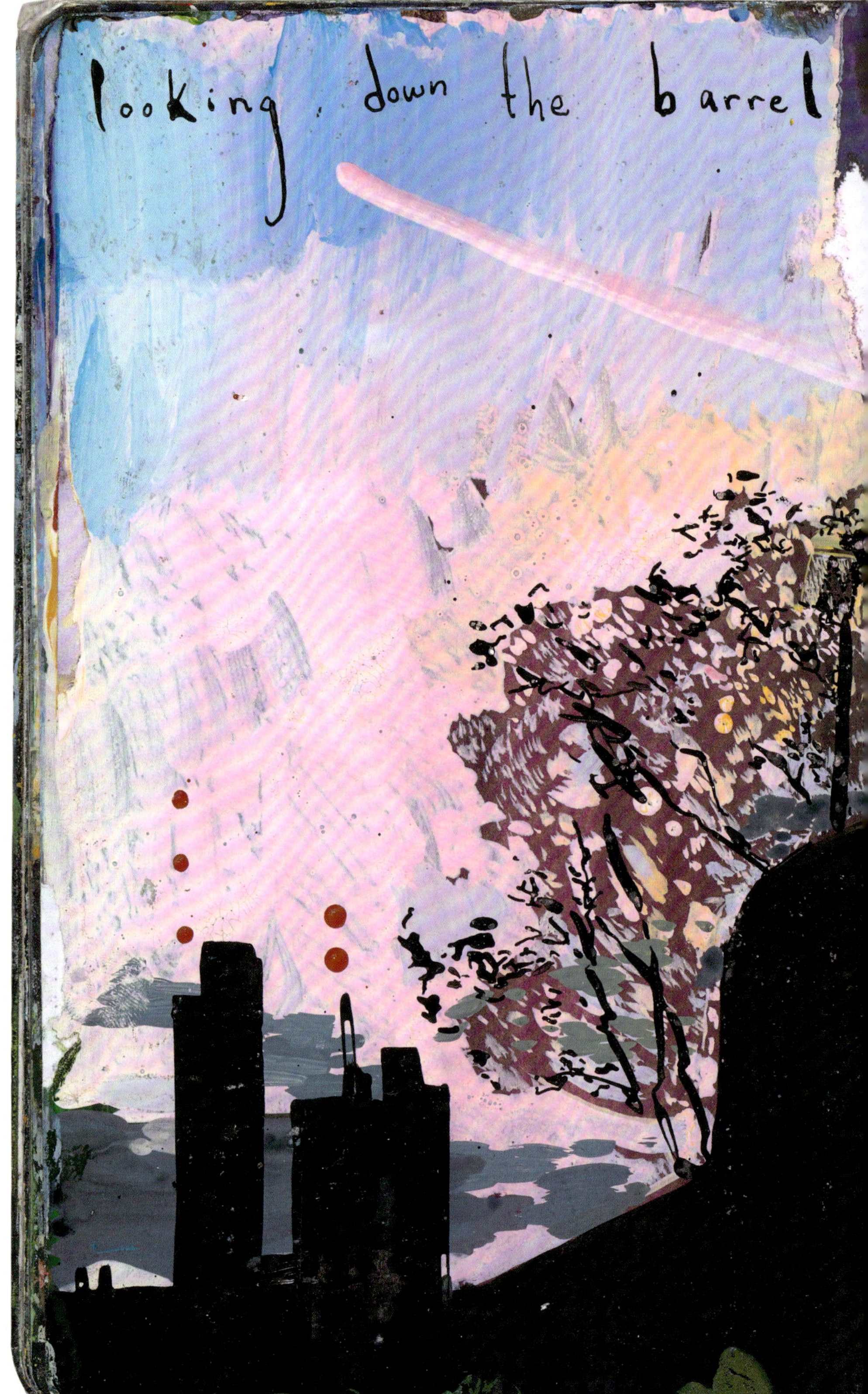
looking down the barrel

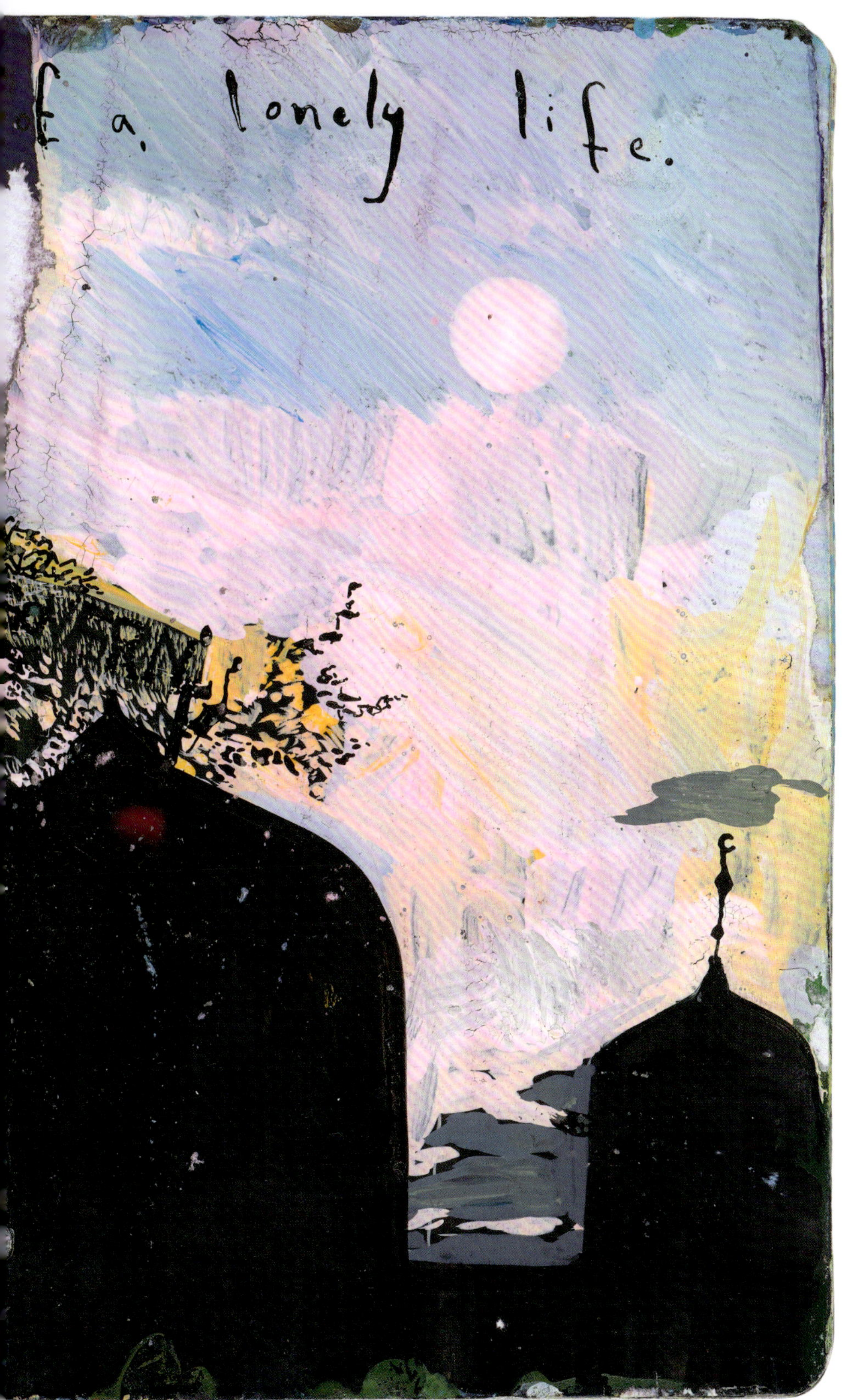
of a lonely life.

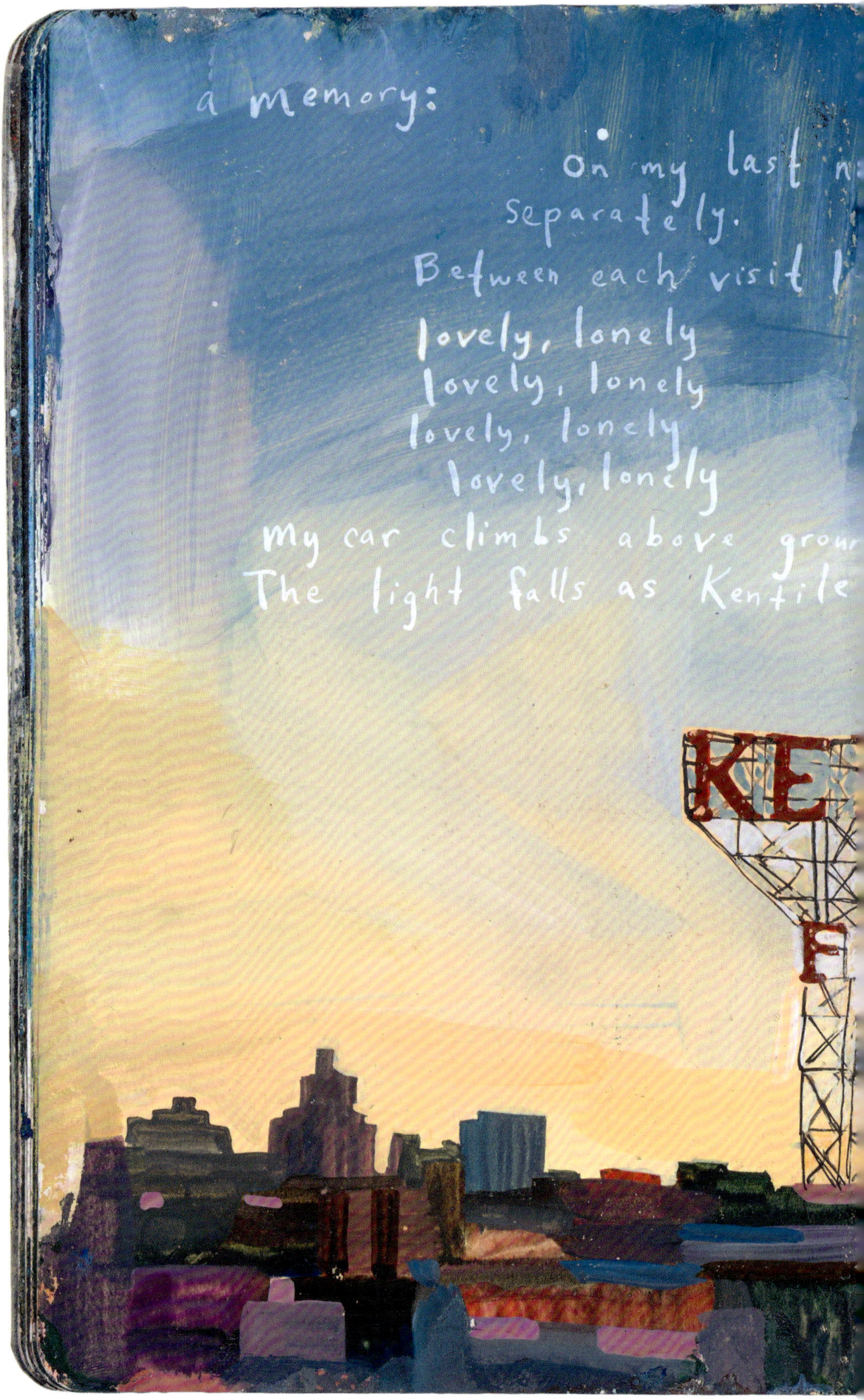

a memory:

On my last n
separately.
Between each visit I
lovely, lonely
lovely, lonely
lovely, lonely
lovely, lonely
My car climbs above grou
The light falls as Kentile

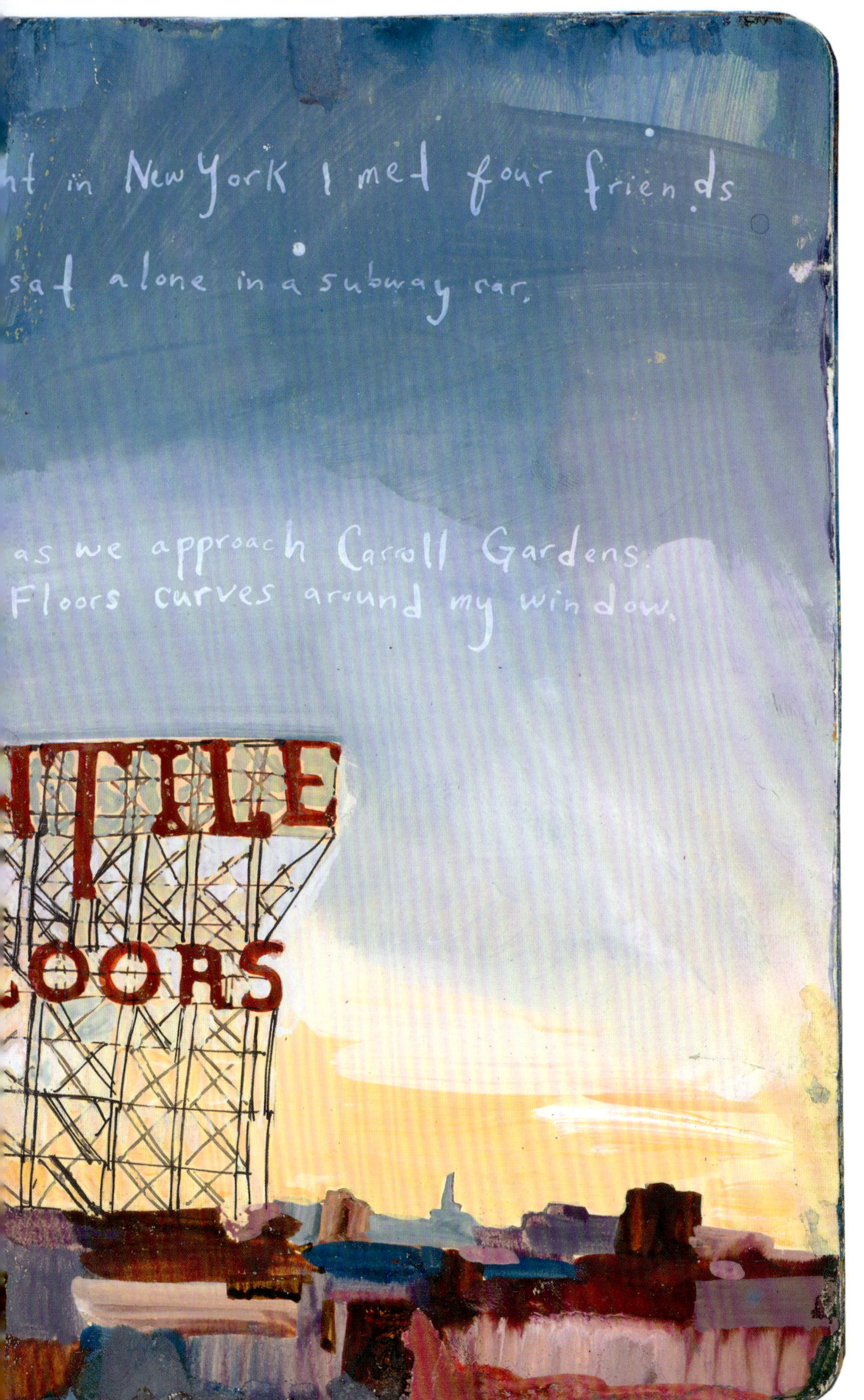
ht in New York I met four friends
sat alone in a subway car,

as we approach Carroll Gardens.
Floors curves around my window.

TILE
LOORS

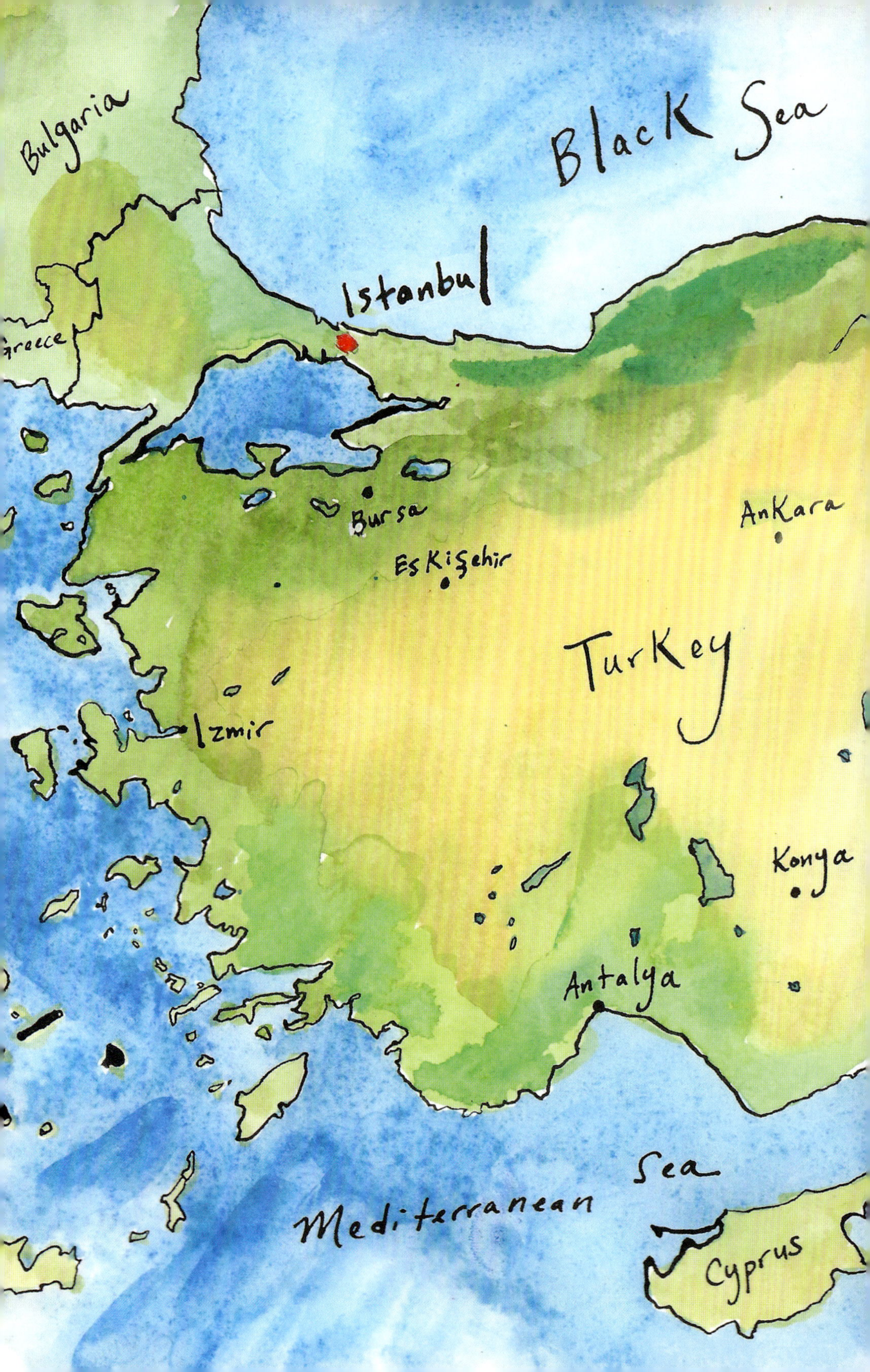

Bulgaria
Greece
Black Sea
Istanbul
Bursa
Eskişehir
Ankara
Turkey
Izmir
Konya
Antalya
Mediterranean Sea
Cyprus

II
Istanbul, Turkey

October 1st, 2013

My flat in Turkey is atop one of the many hills that make up the 20-million strong metropolis of Istanbul. The Harbiye neighborhood that spills down the streets below has a dozen mosques, each projecting the "ezan", or Call to Prayer, through megaphones five times a day.

I was mopping the caramel wood floors with all of my windows open when the ezan blasted in for the first time. I found myself mesmerized by its haunting almost-melody, by its power. Moving to Istanbul had been a dream for so long and, in that moment, it sank in that I am finally here, learning Turkish and studying Anatolian weaving and textiles at the source. I am in awe of how unpredictable life can be, and how far away it has taken me.

colors:

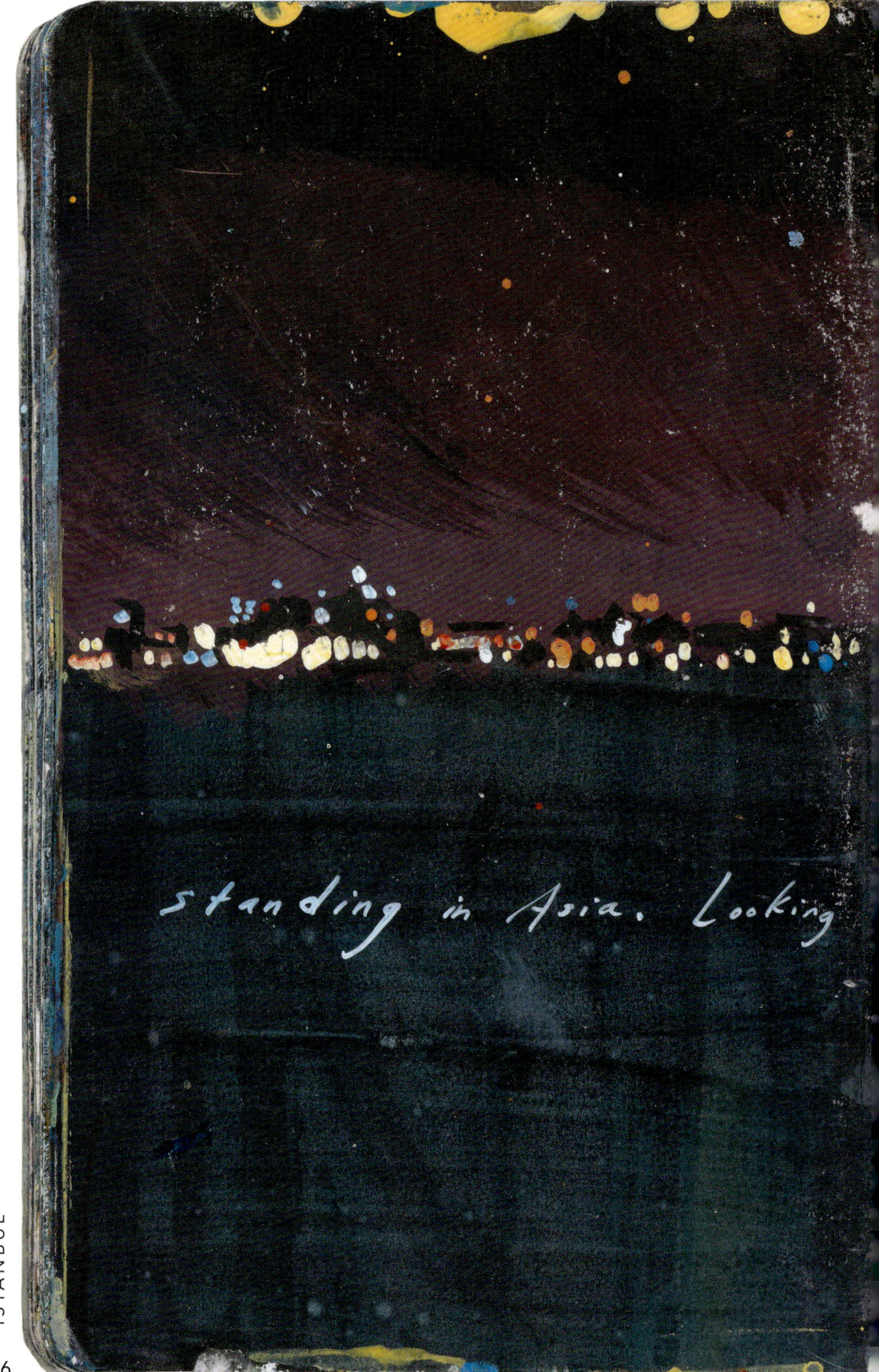
standing in Asia, Looking

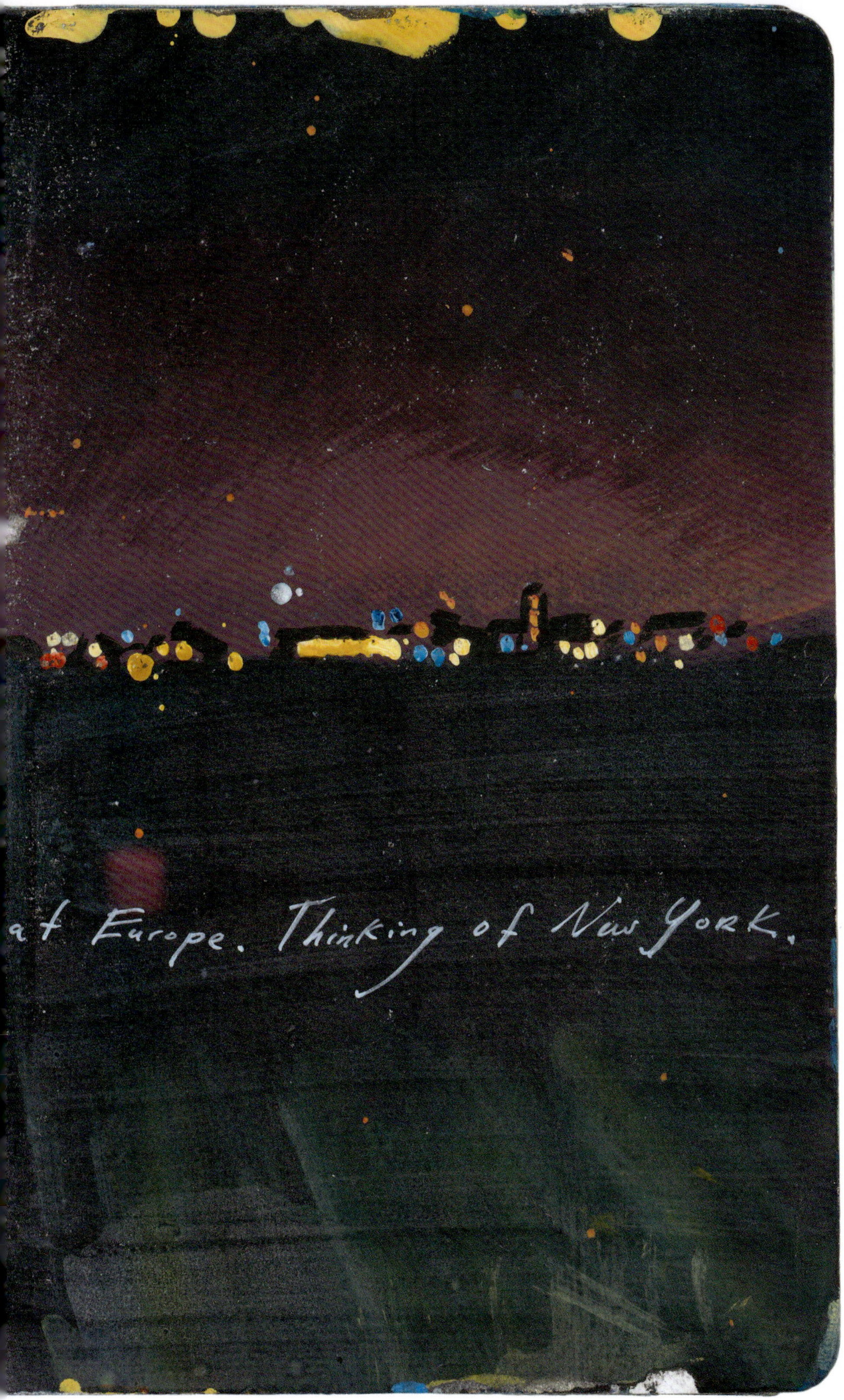

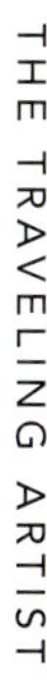

at Europe. Thinking of New York.

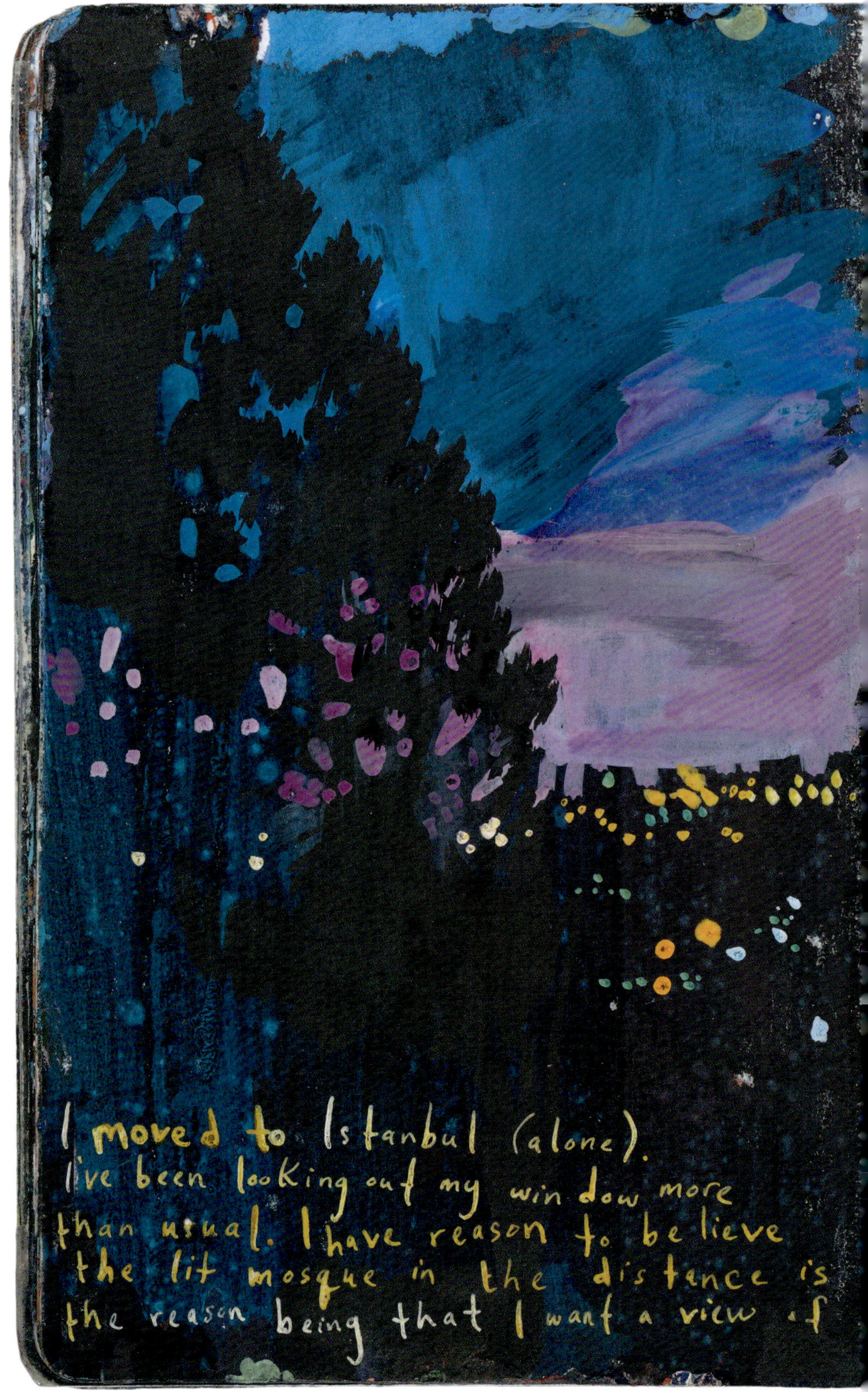

I moved to Istanbul (alone).
I've been looking out my window more
than usual. I have reason to believe
the lit mosque in the distance is
the reason being that I want a view of

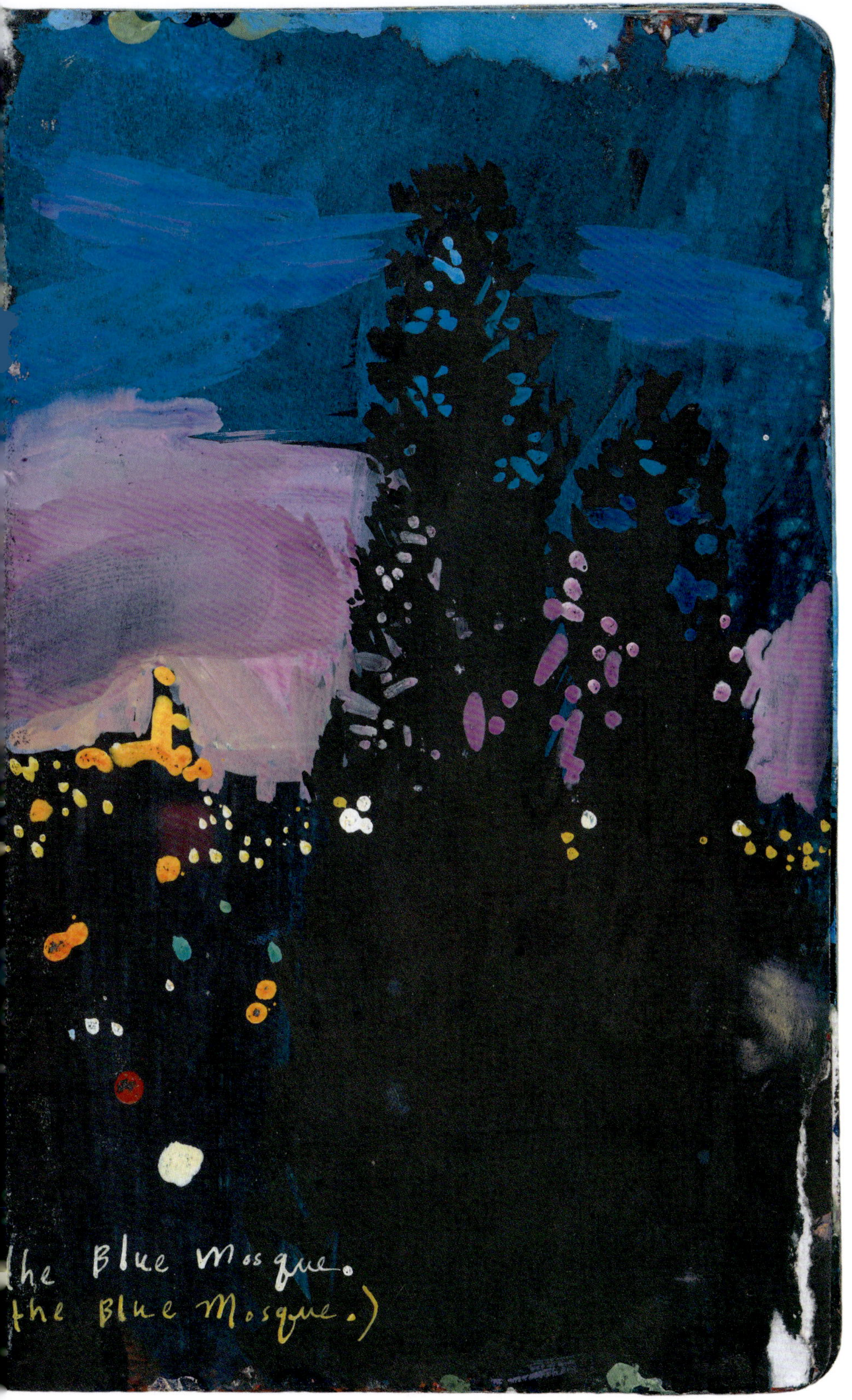

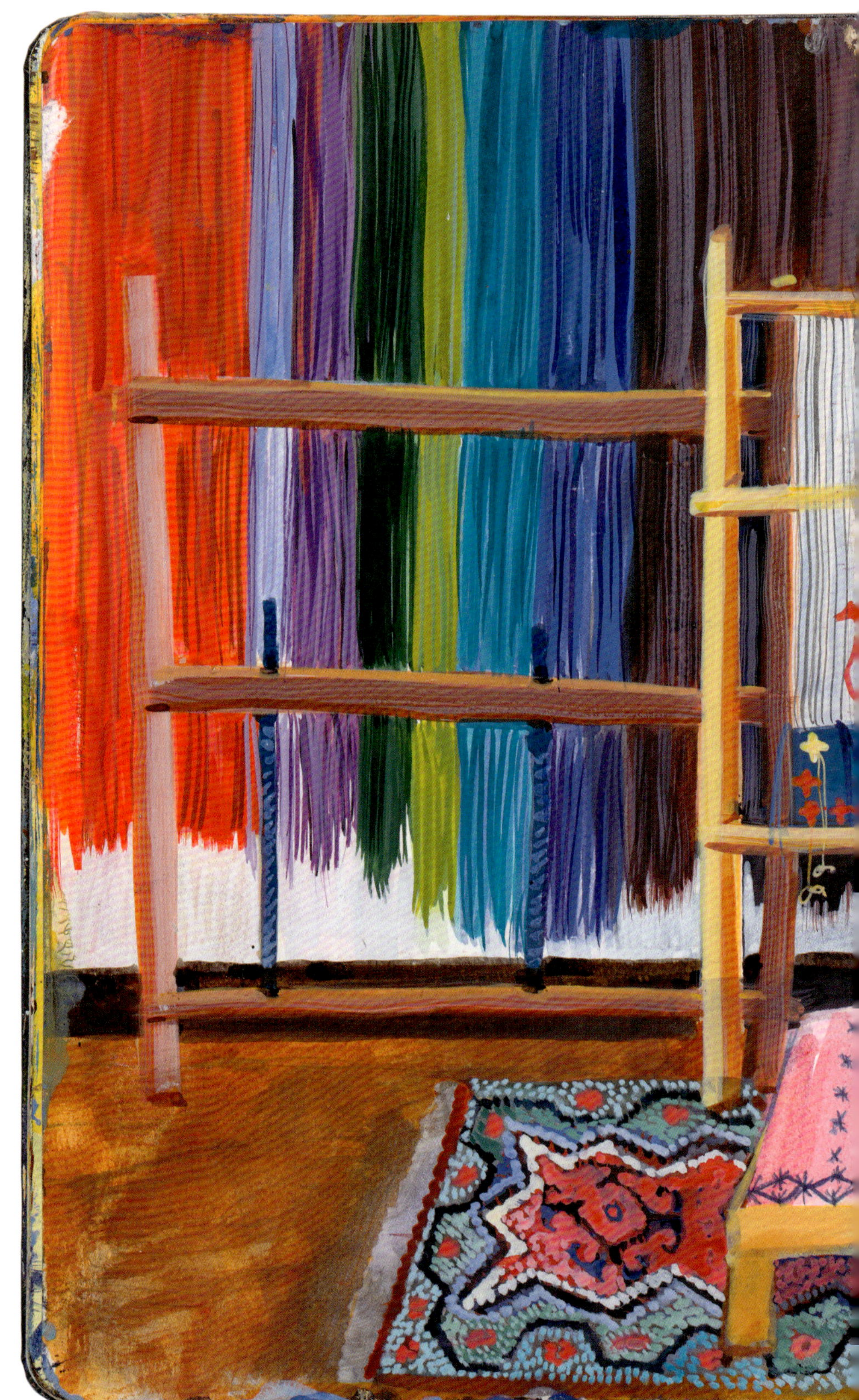

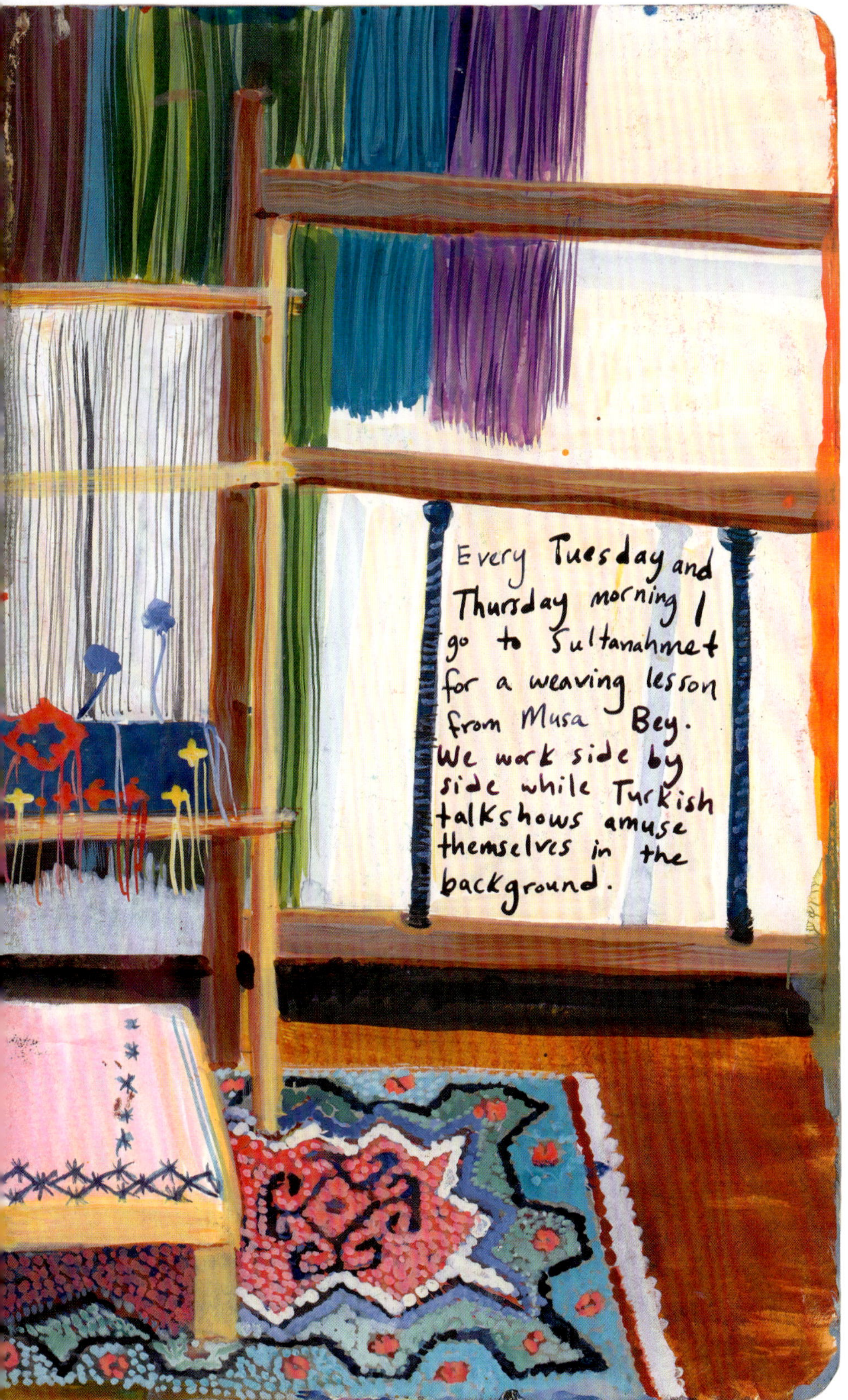
Every Tuesday and
Thursday morning I
go to Sultanahmet
for a weaving lesson
from Musa Bey.
We work side by
side while Turkish
talkshows amuse
themselves in the
background.

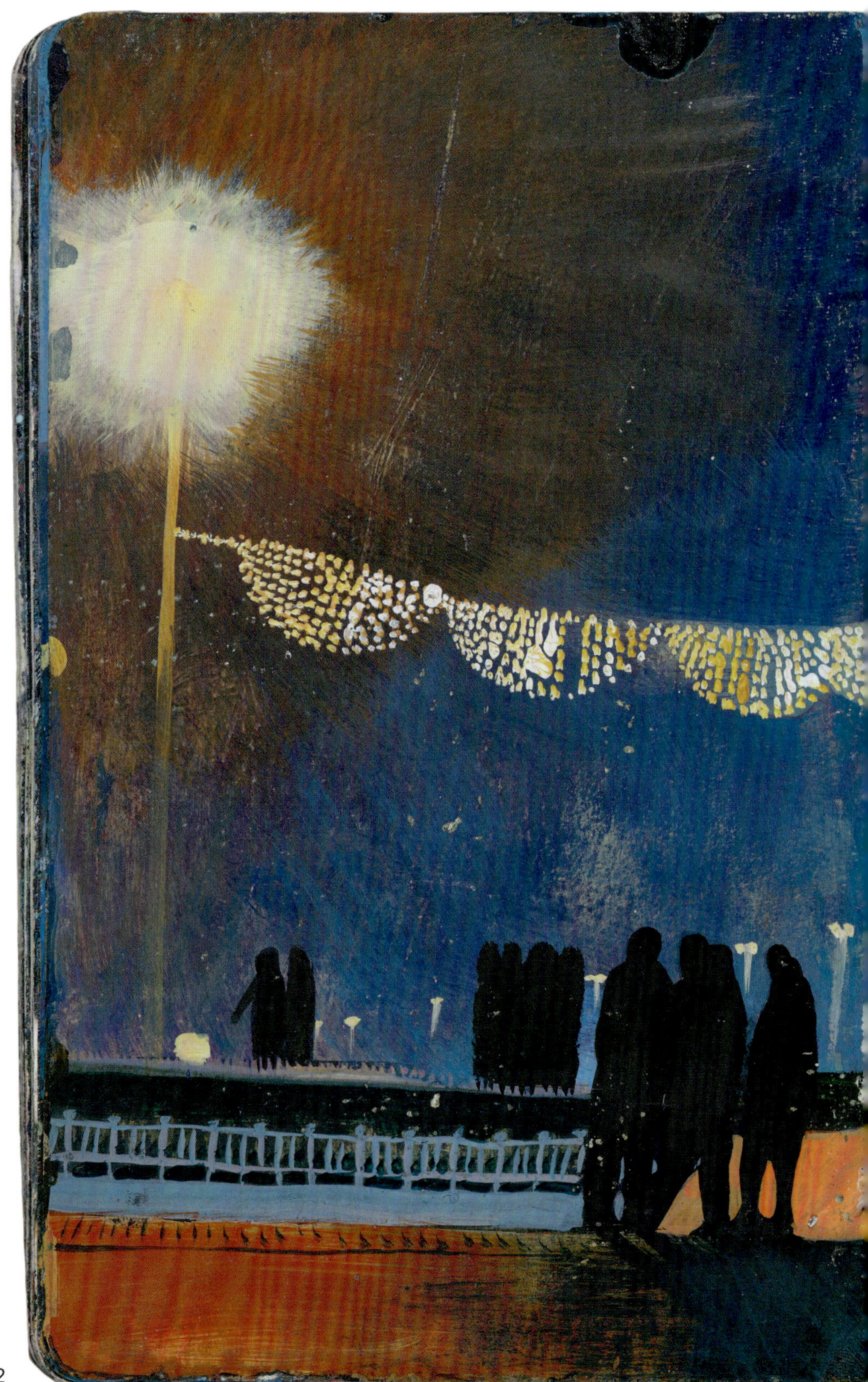

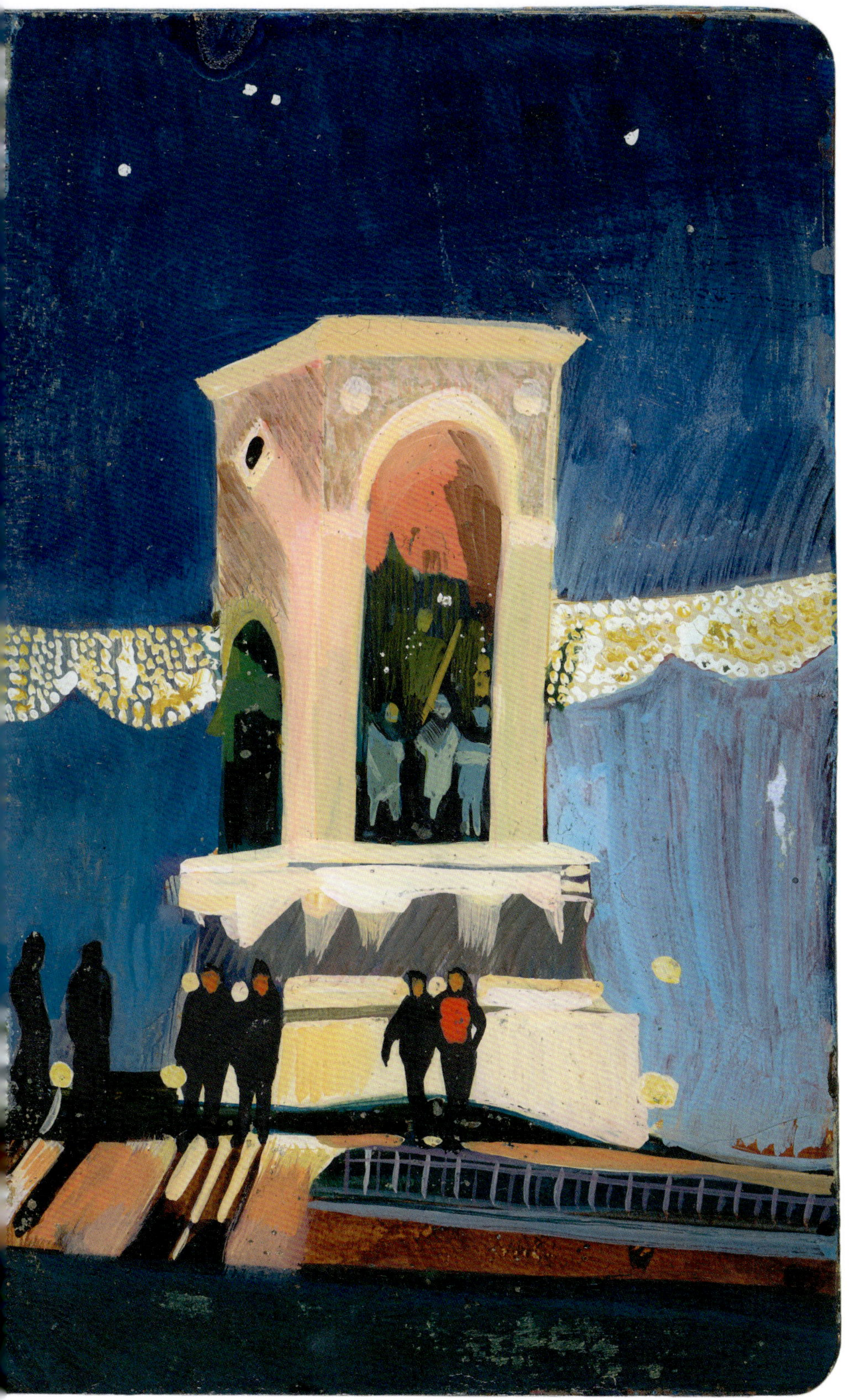

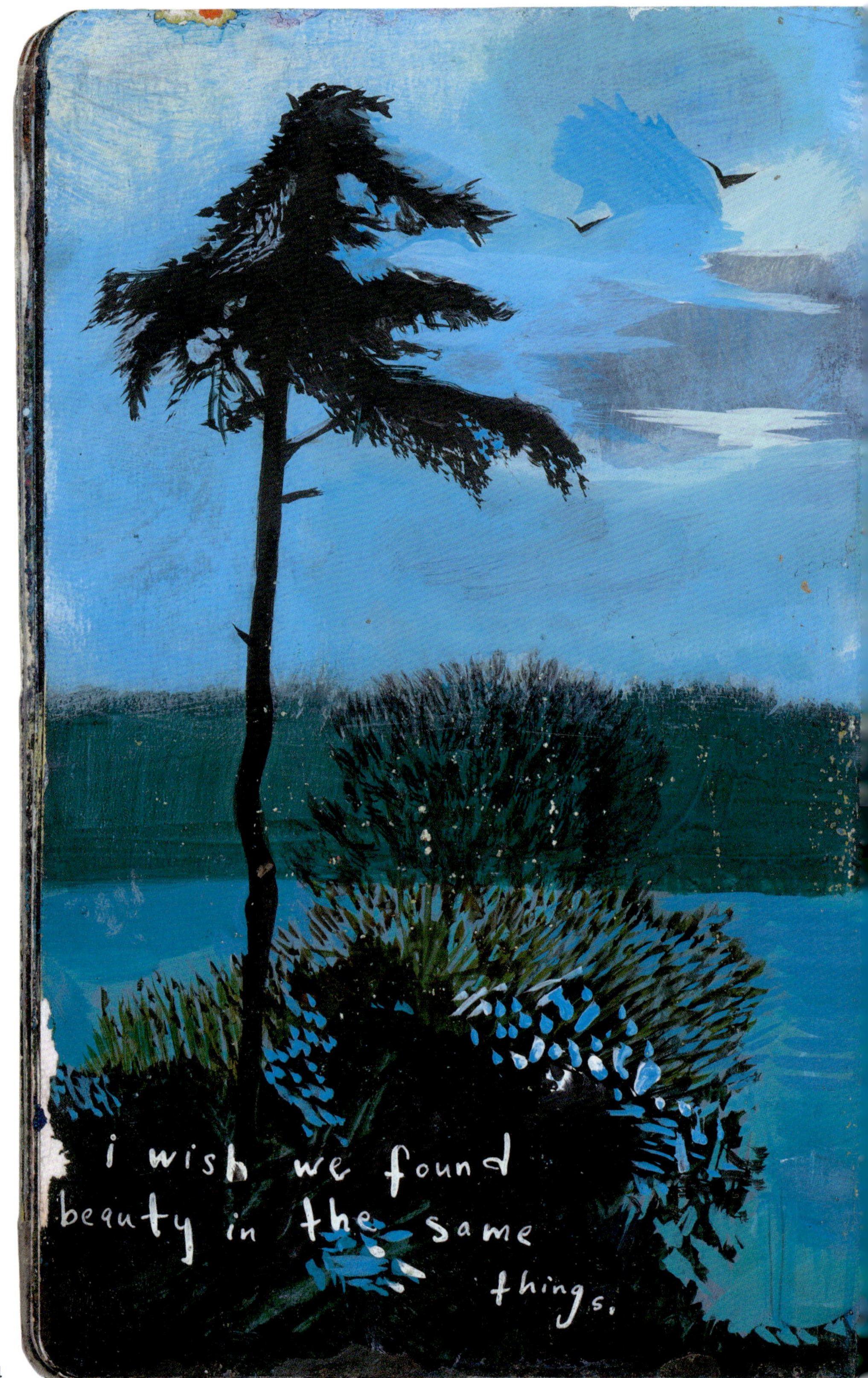

i wish we found
beauty in the same
things.

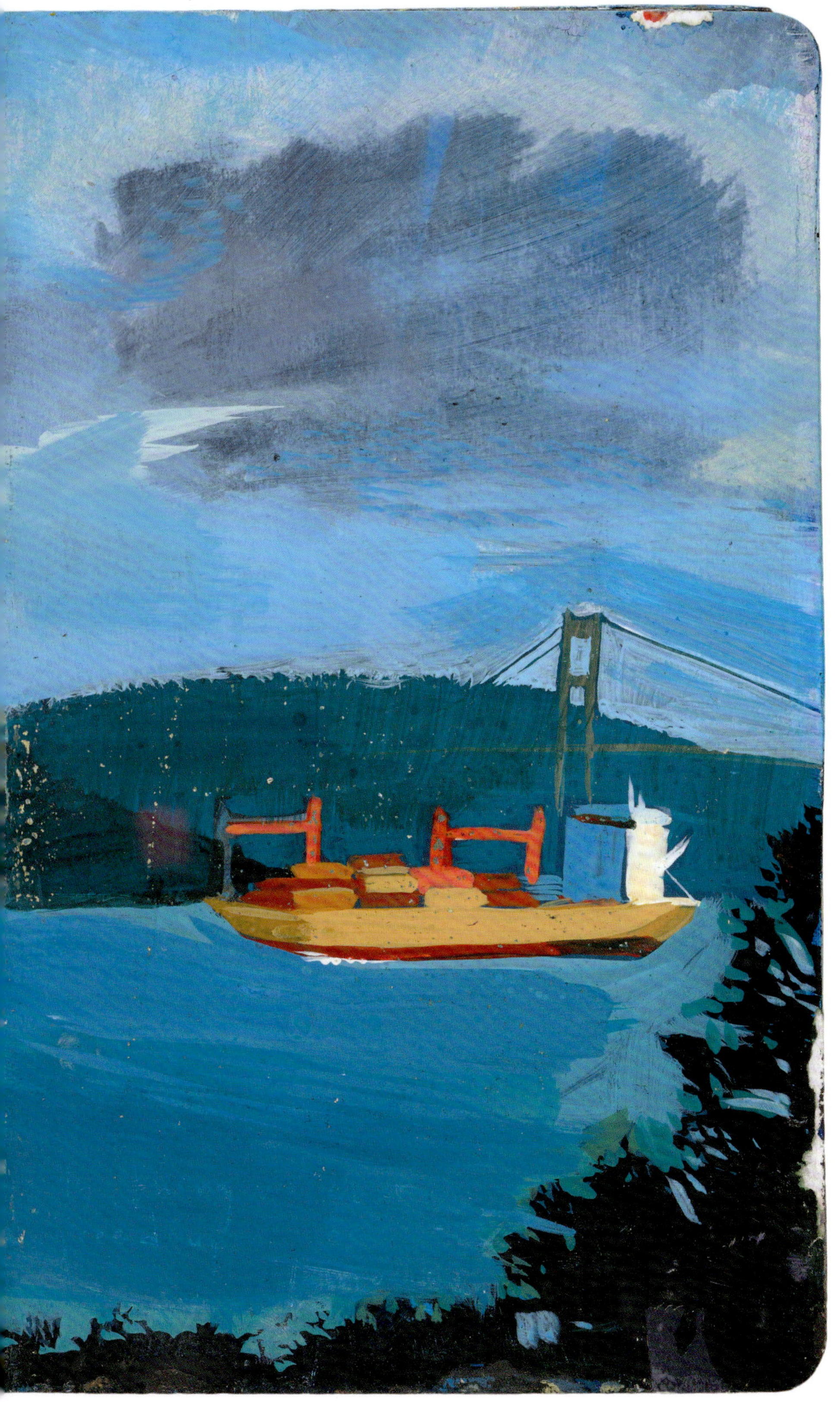

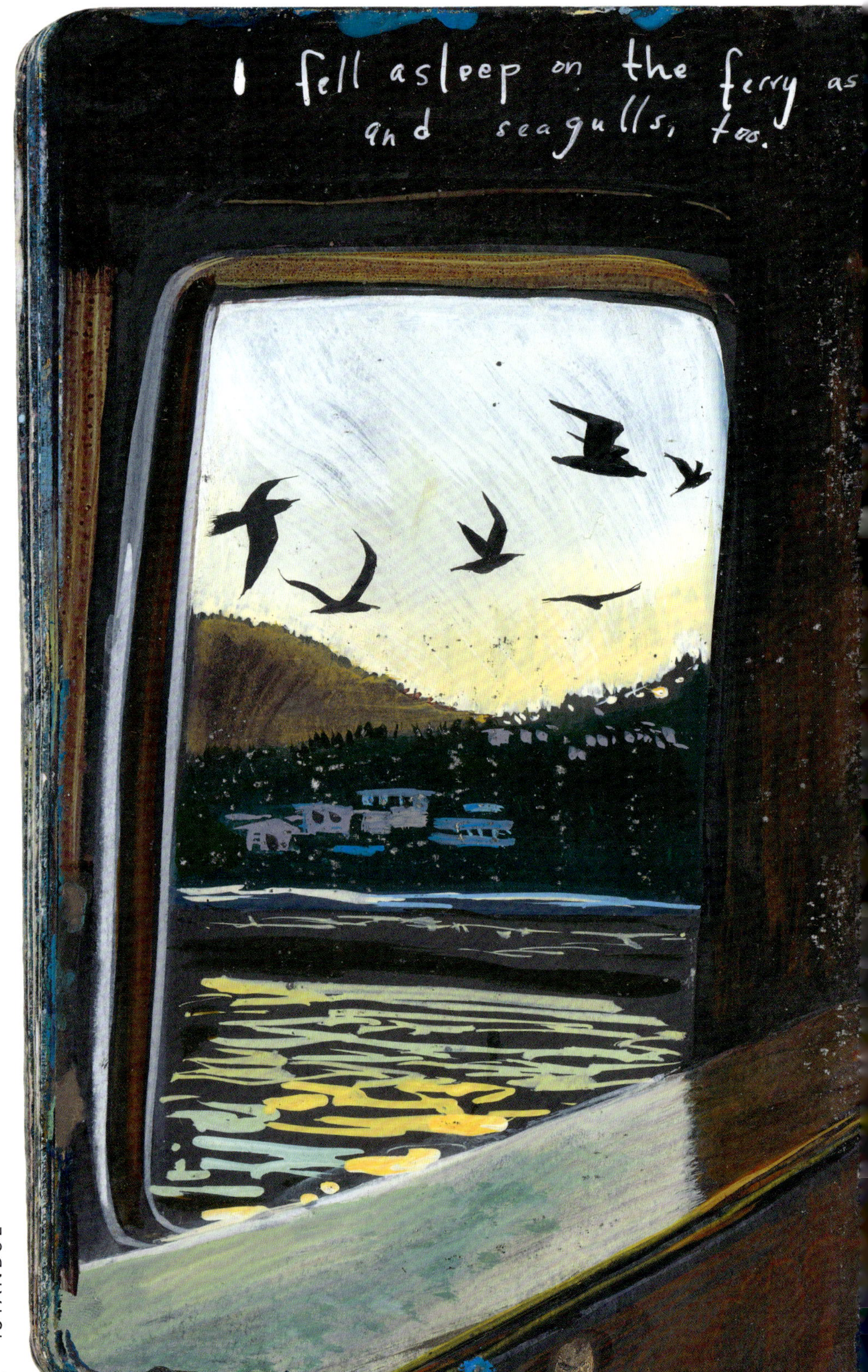
I fell asleep on the ferry as
and seagulls, too.

Prince's Islands passed by,

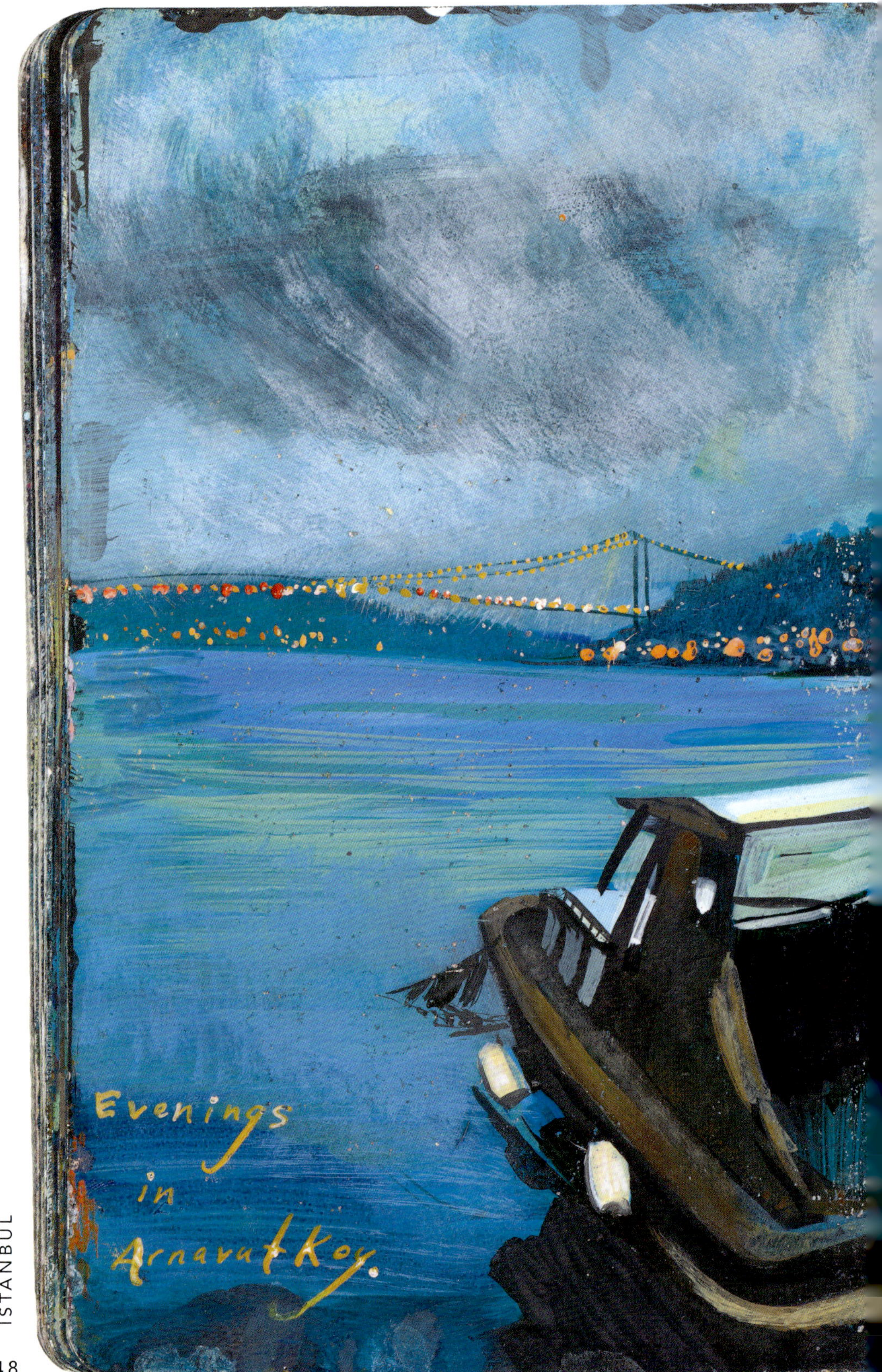

Evenings
in
Arnavutköy.

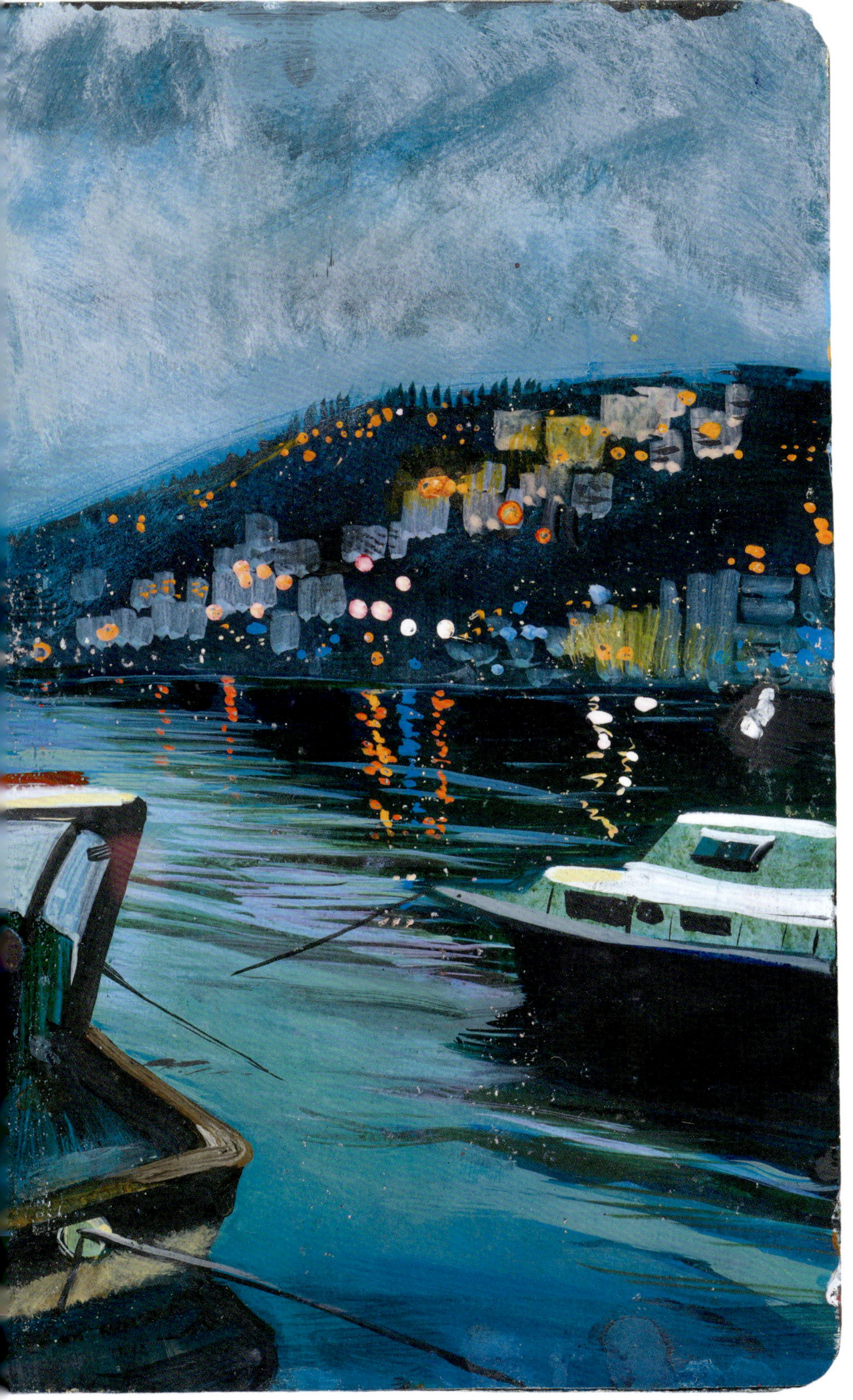

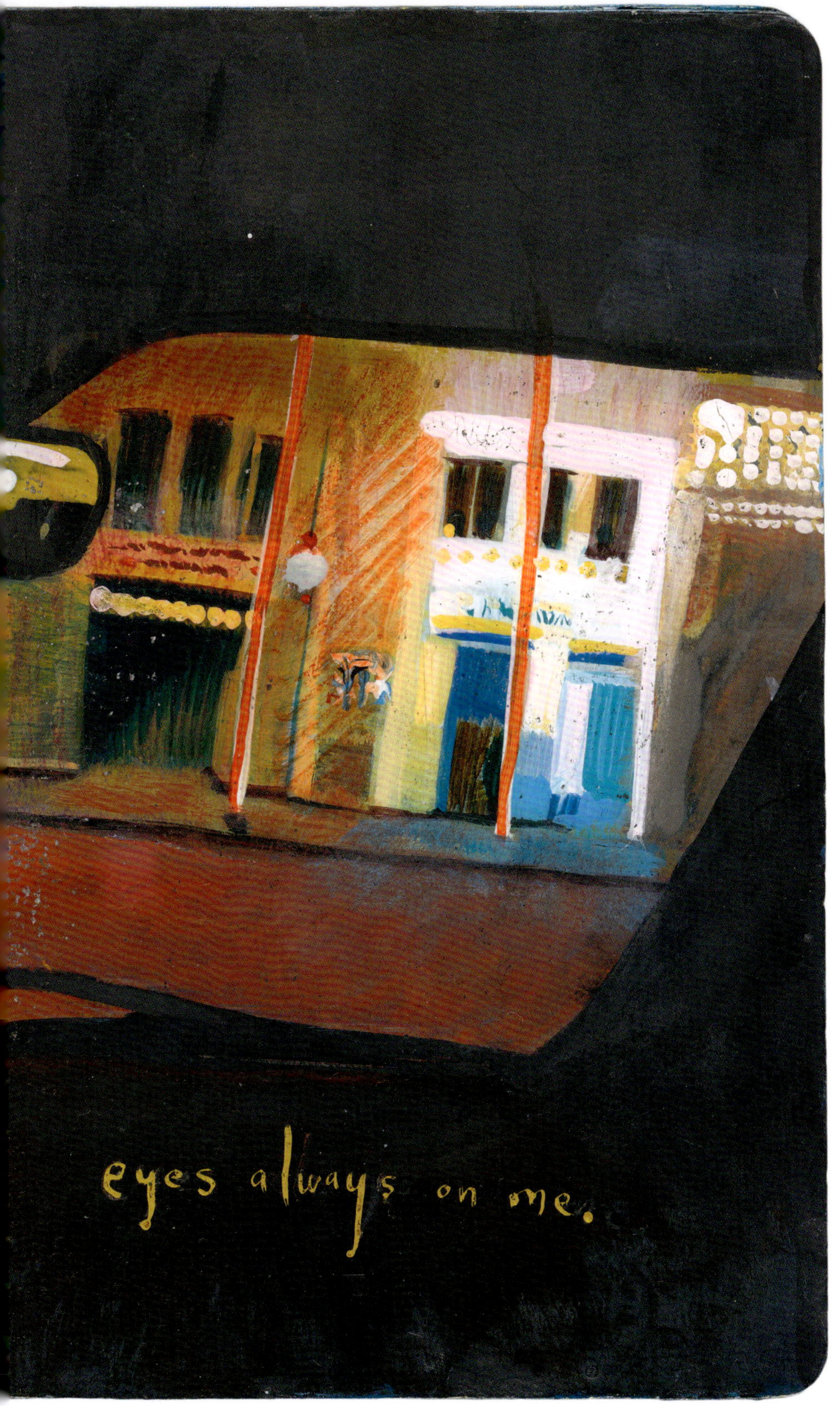
eyes always on me.

I explained the term "burning
and her eyes widened and glitte
"Yes, that's exactly what I mean
That's what we'll do.
We'll burn our bridges."

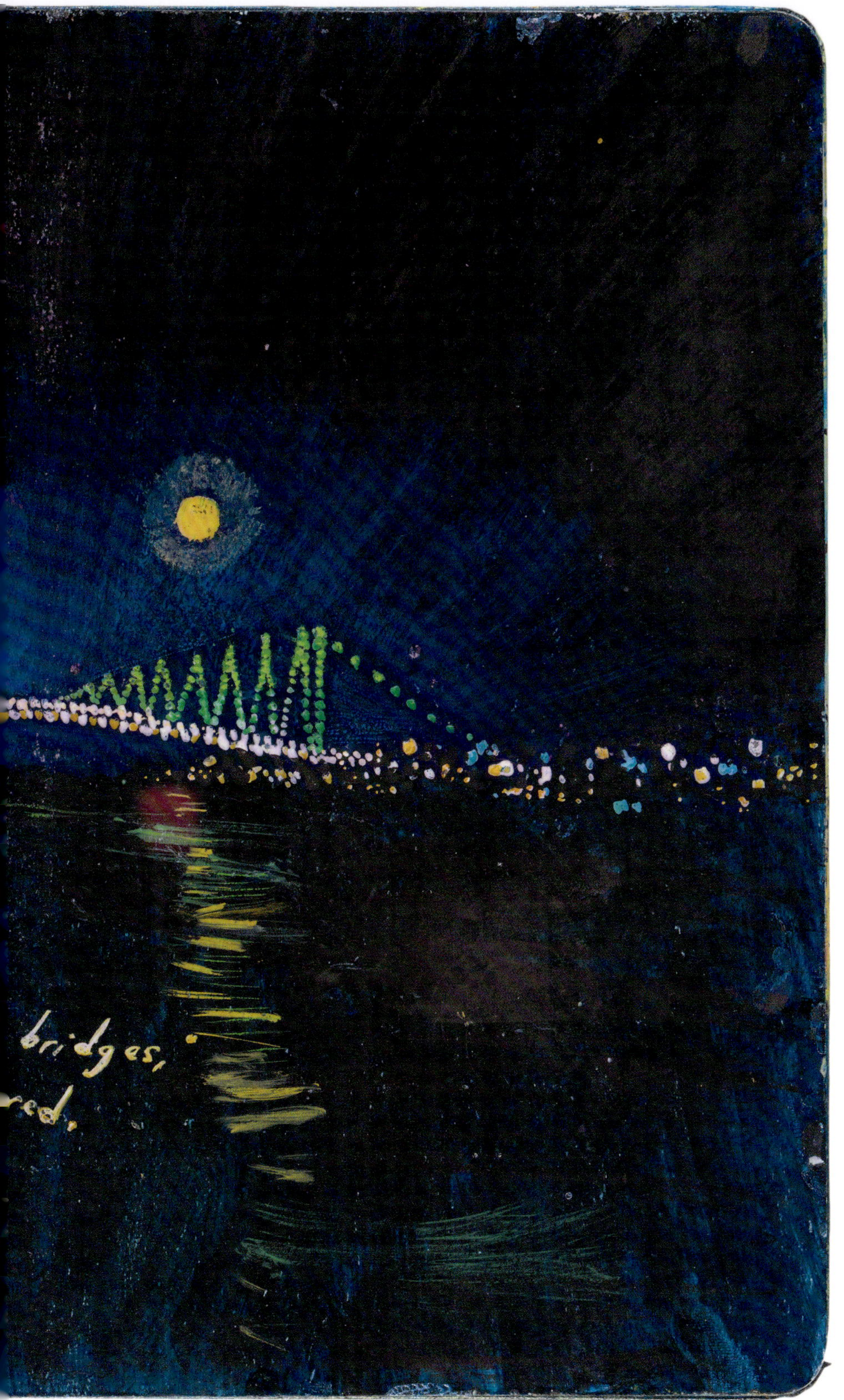

bridges,
red,

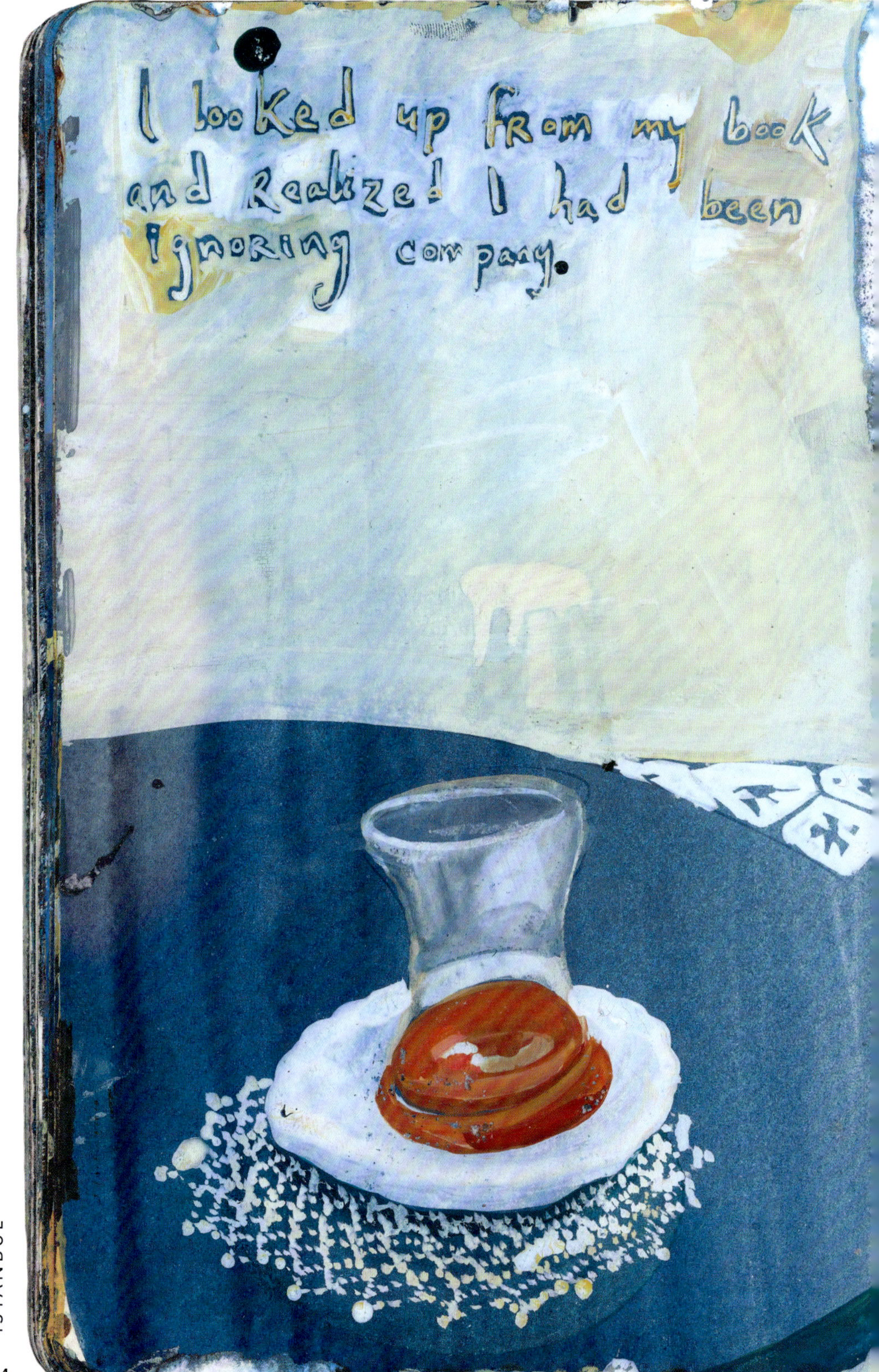
I looked up from my book
and Realized I had been
ignoring company.

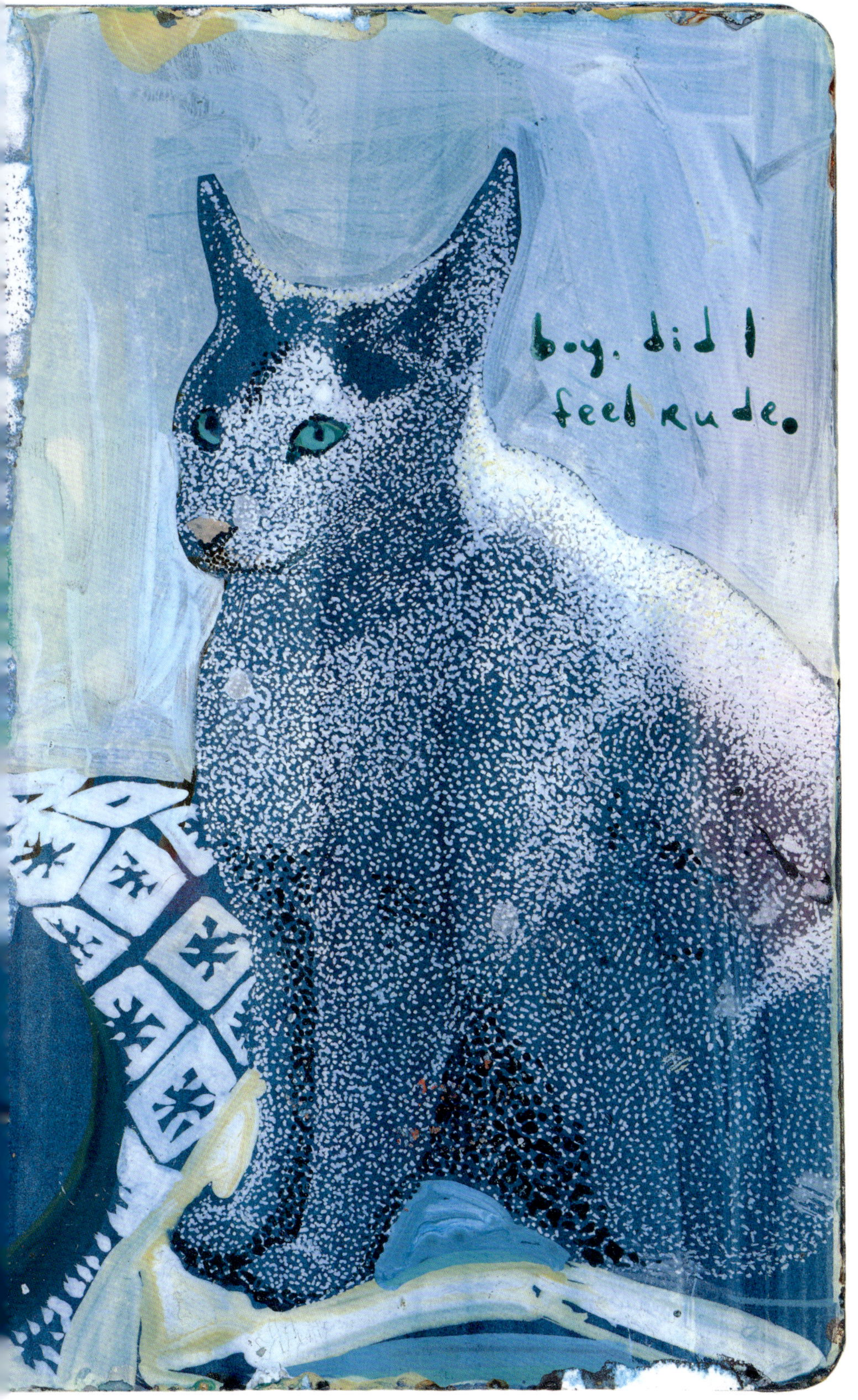

boy. did I
feel rude.

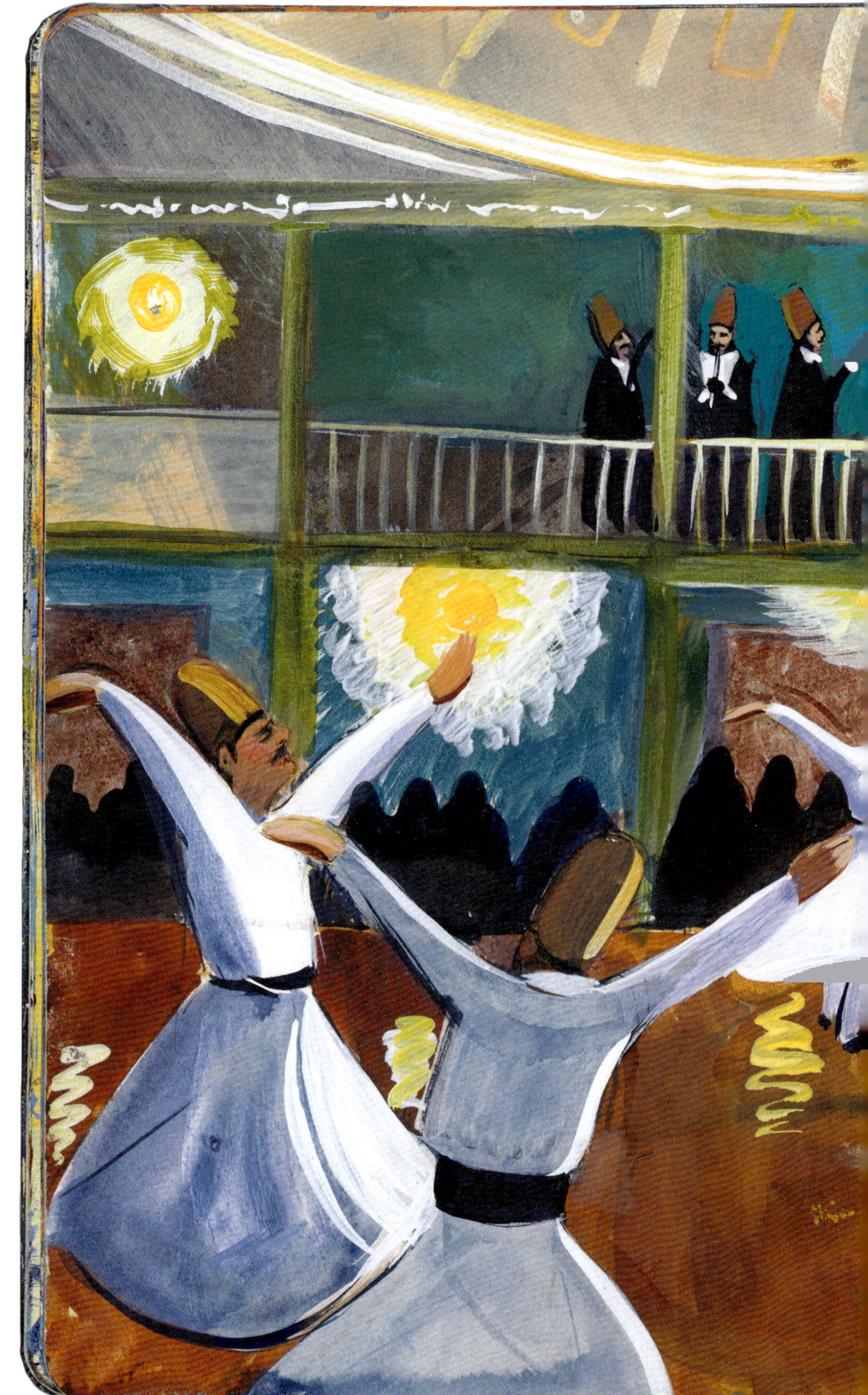

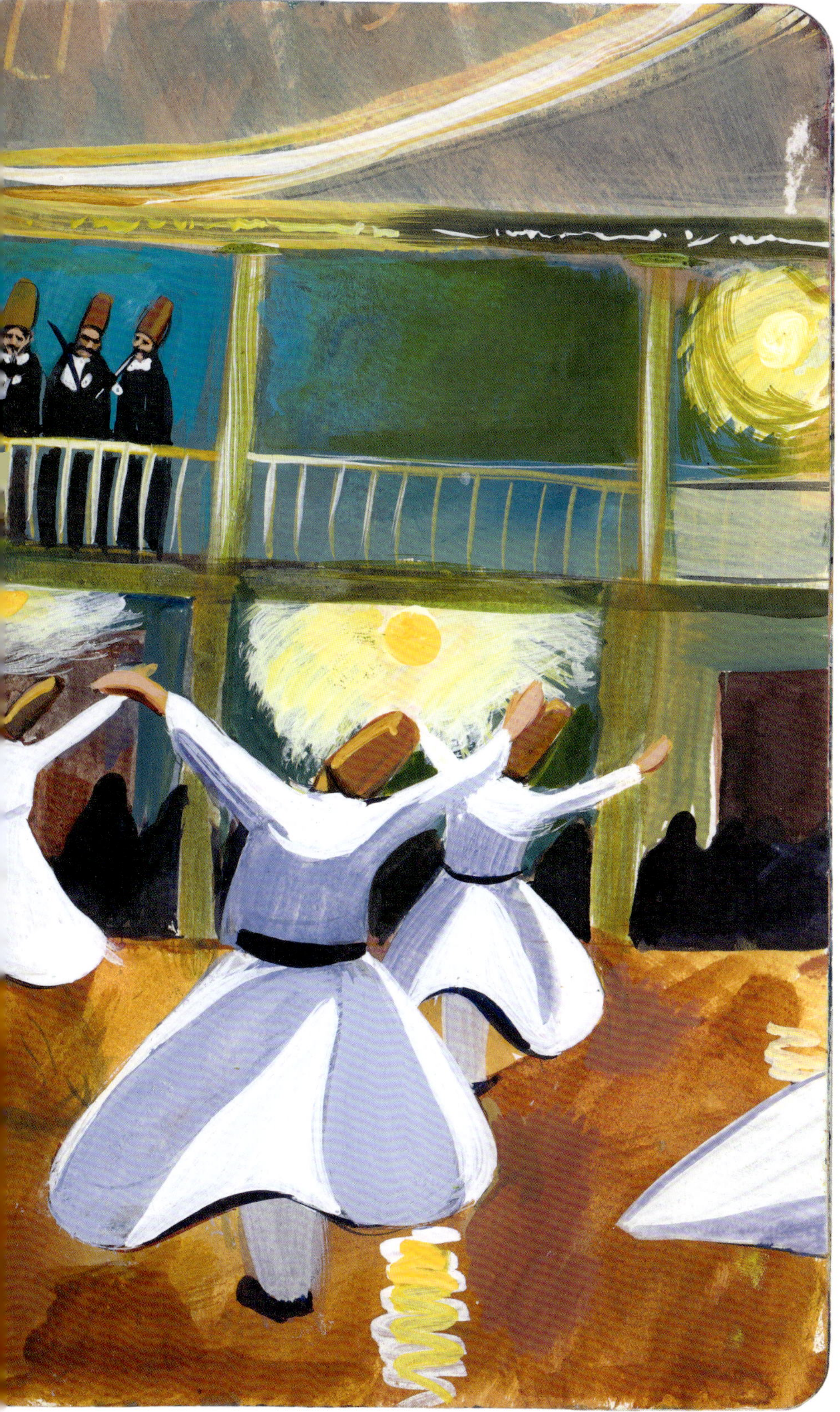

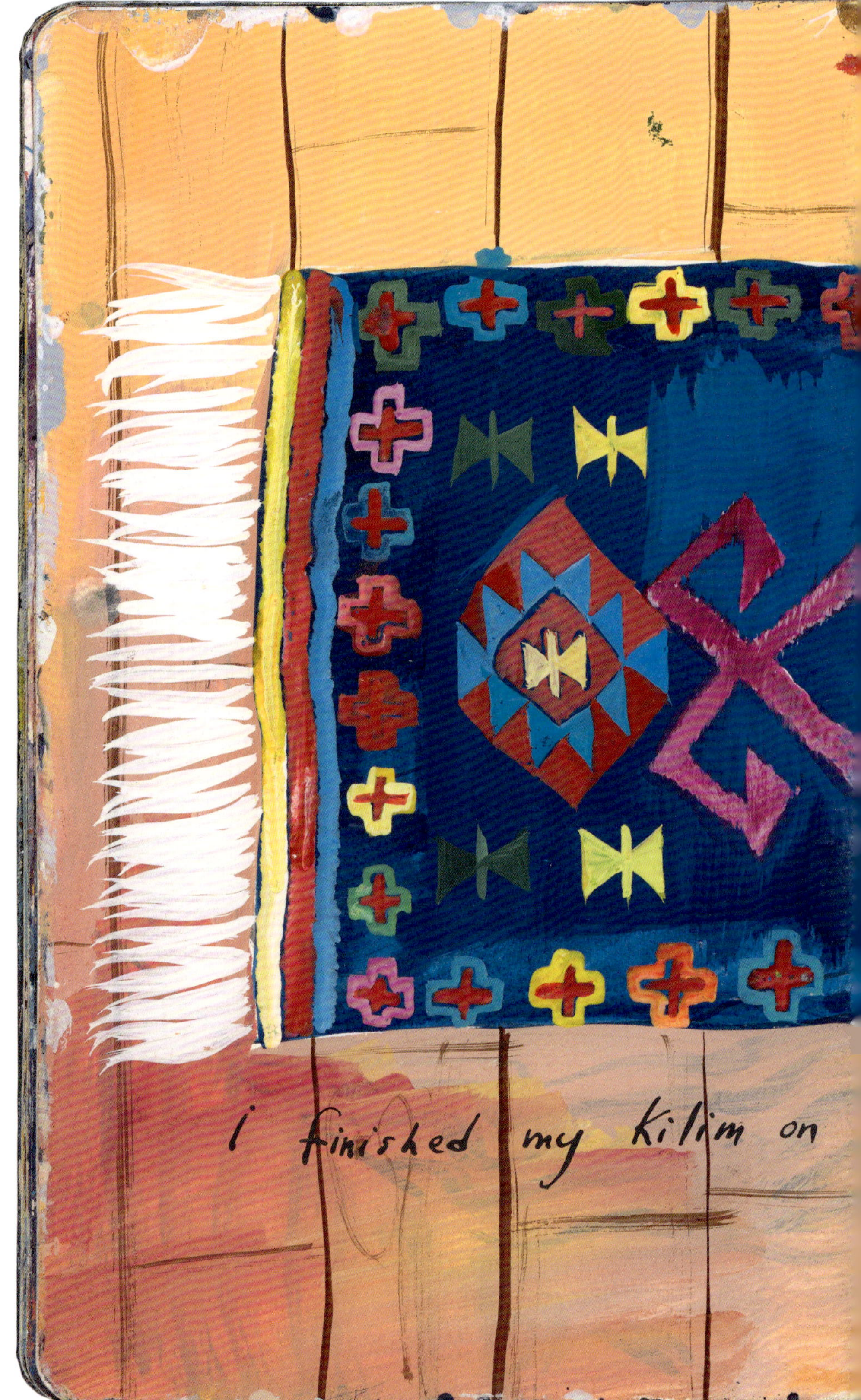

I finished my kilim on

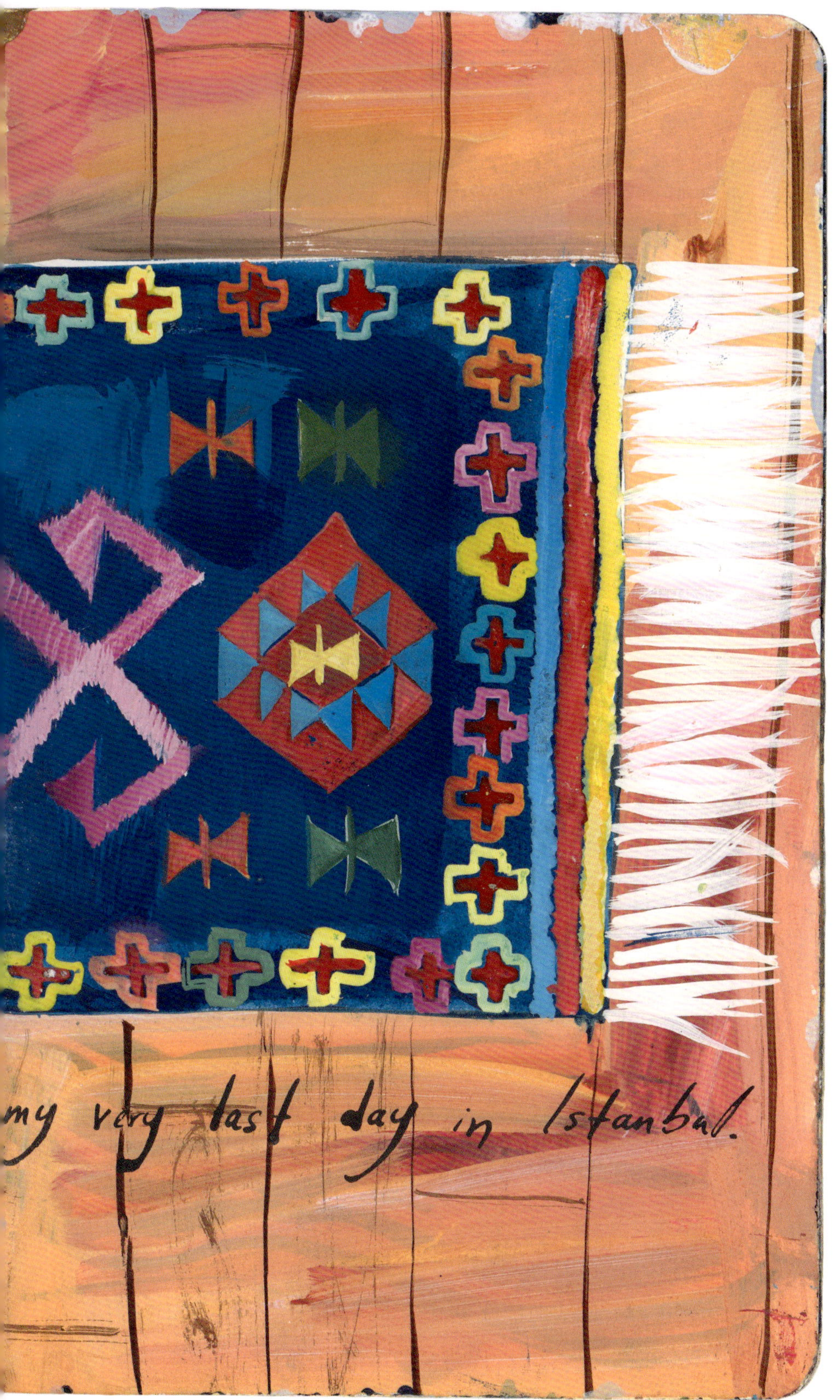

my very last day in Istanbul.

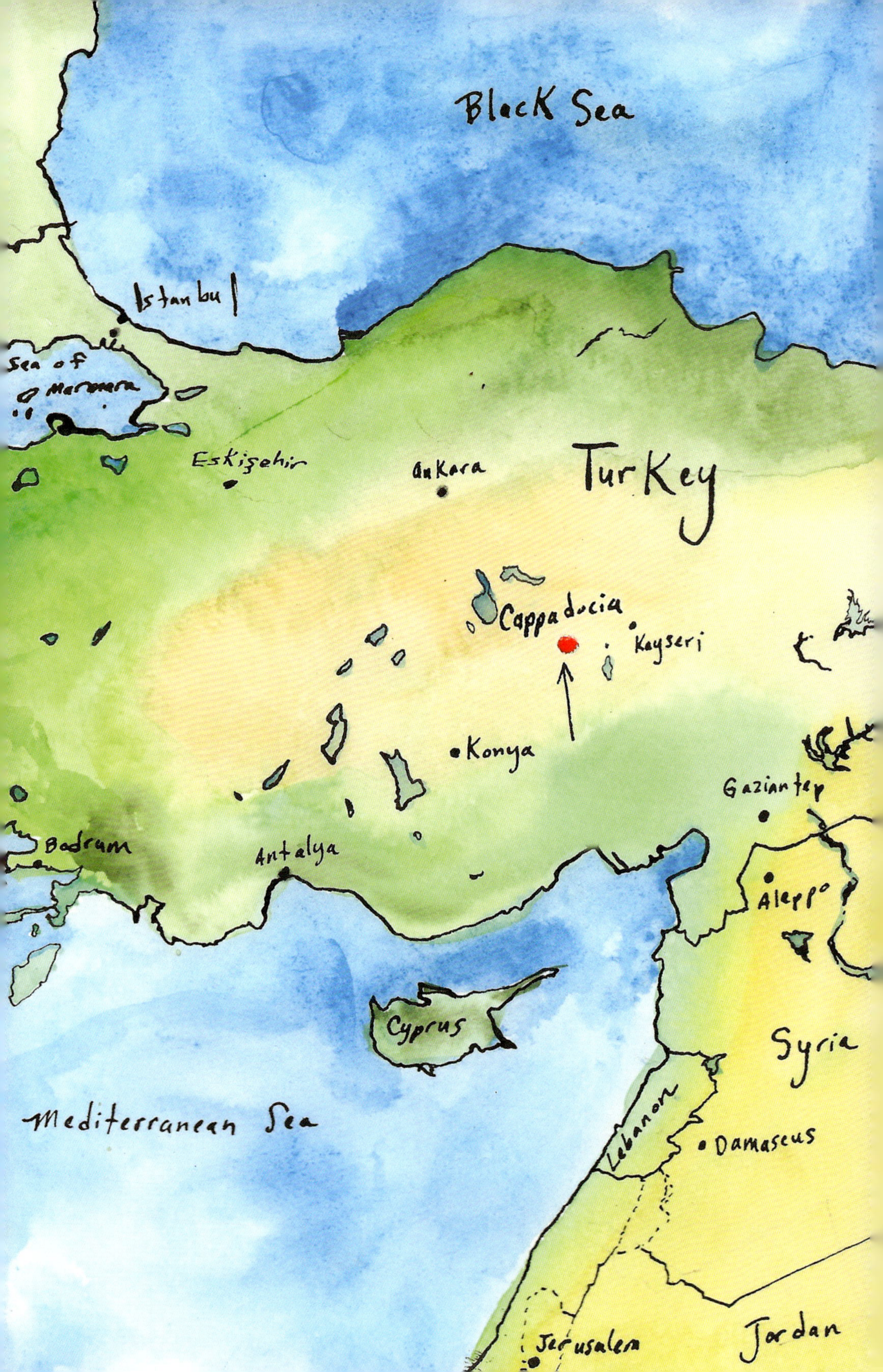

Black Sea
Istanbul
Sea of Marmara
Eskişehir
Ankara
Turkey
Cappadocia
Kayseri
Konya
Gaziantep
Bodrum
Antalya
Aleppo
Cyprus
Syria
Mediterranean Sea
Lebanon
Damascus
Jerusalem
Jordan

III

Cappadocia, Turkey

June 14th, 2014

I've had three words in the back of my mind since I heard them two years ago: cave art residency. Cappadocia is known for its sunrise hot air balloon rides, rock formations, ancient underground cities, and cave dwellings. As an artist-in-residence, I was given the choice to live in a cave or a large stone house. But given how long I'd fantasized about this residency in a cave, I surprised myself and chose the house. As it turns out, caves are very dark, and I quite enjoy light!

Tonight, my neighbor invited me to a wedding in the village. I sat among the women on the lawn, and male guests watched from the rooftops above. A man rose from the crowd and pointed a thick silver handgun to the sky. He shot it off with a deafening boom, catalyzing a cacophony of celebratory bullets from the male audience. Different family groups took turns dancing with the newlywed couple as bullets whizzed into the night sky.

colors:

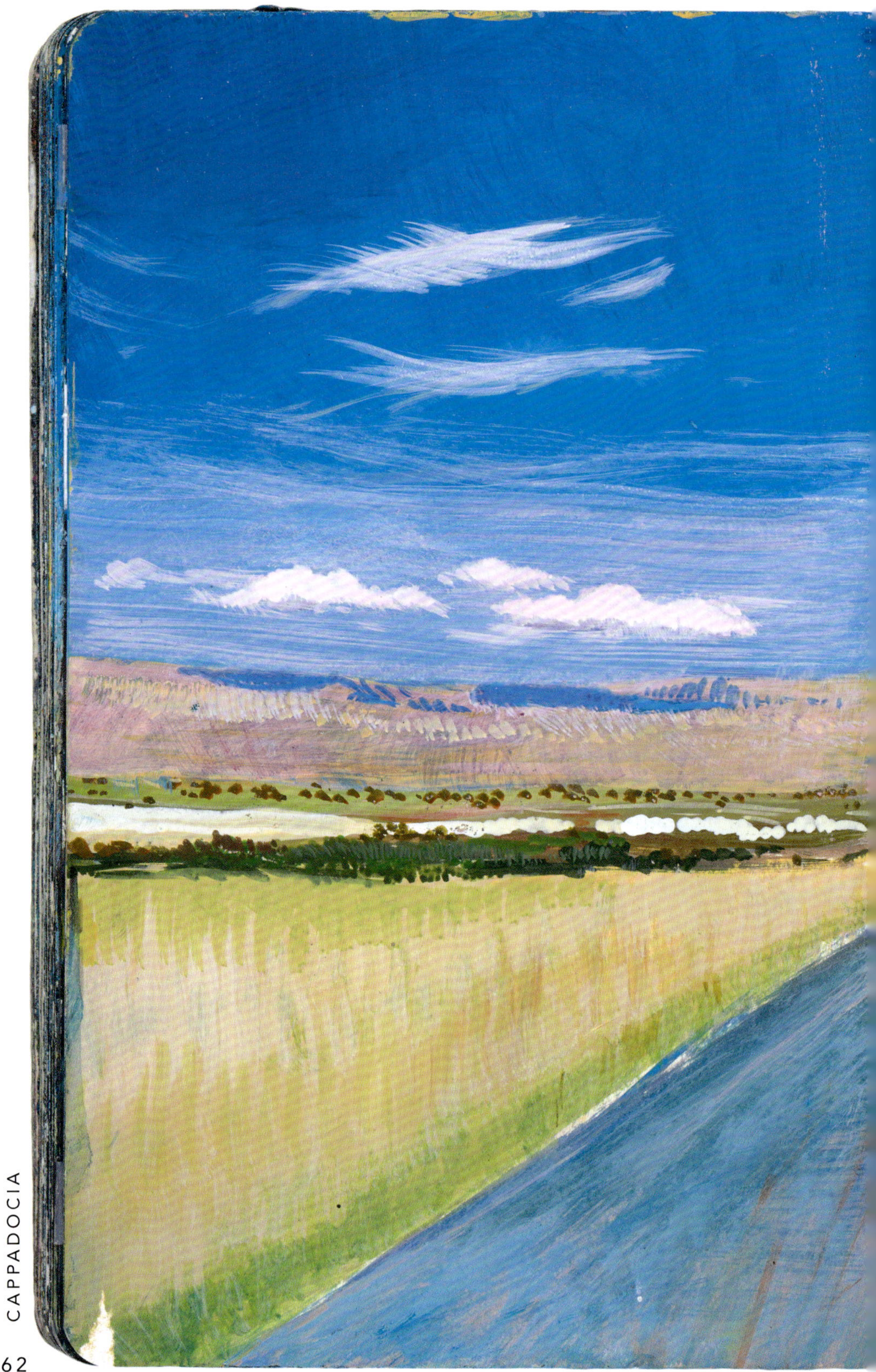

CAPPADOCIA

i moved to Cappadocia.

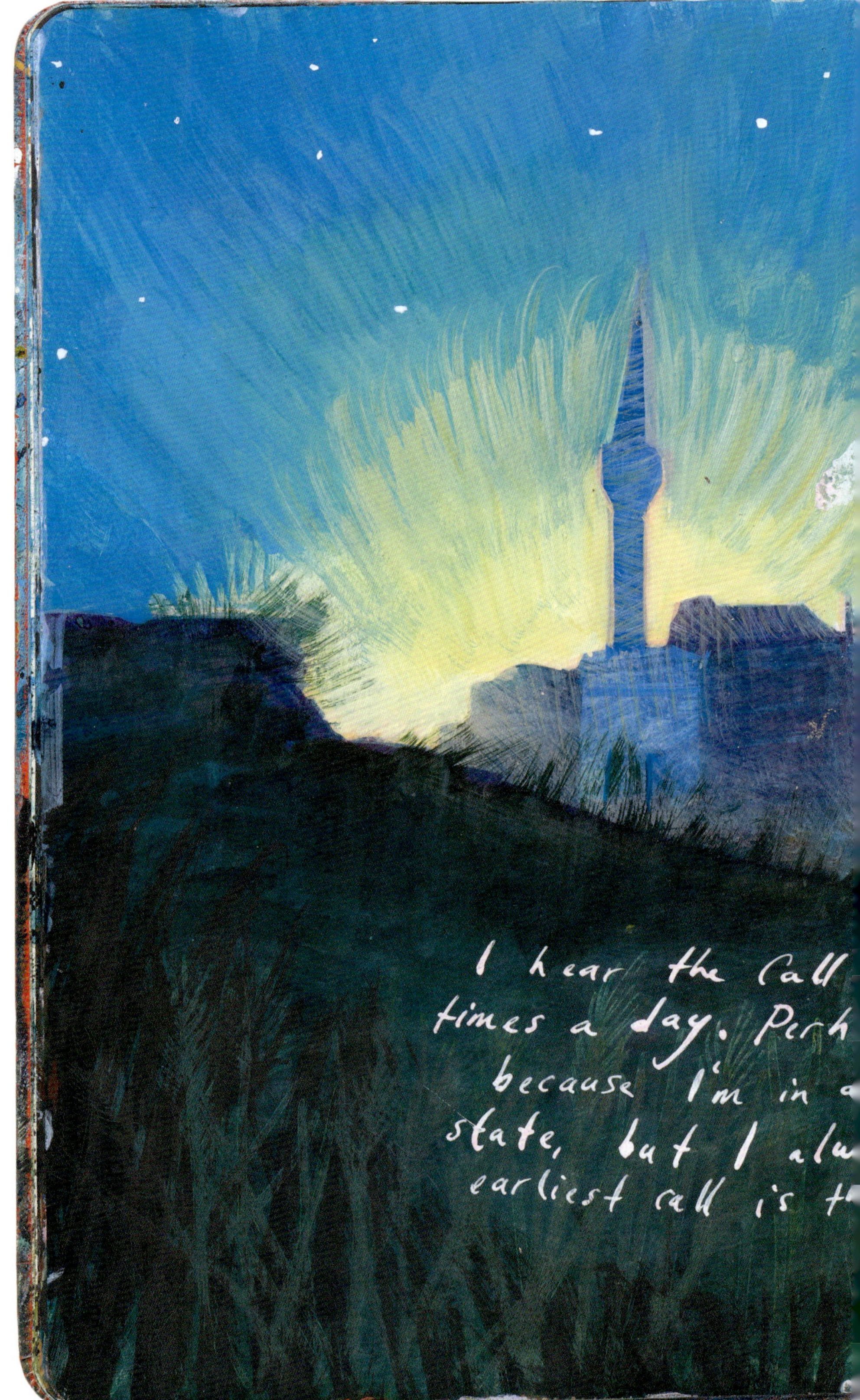
I hear the call
times a day. Perh
because I'm in a
state, but I alw
earliest call is t

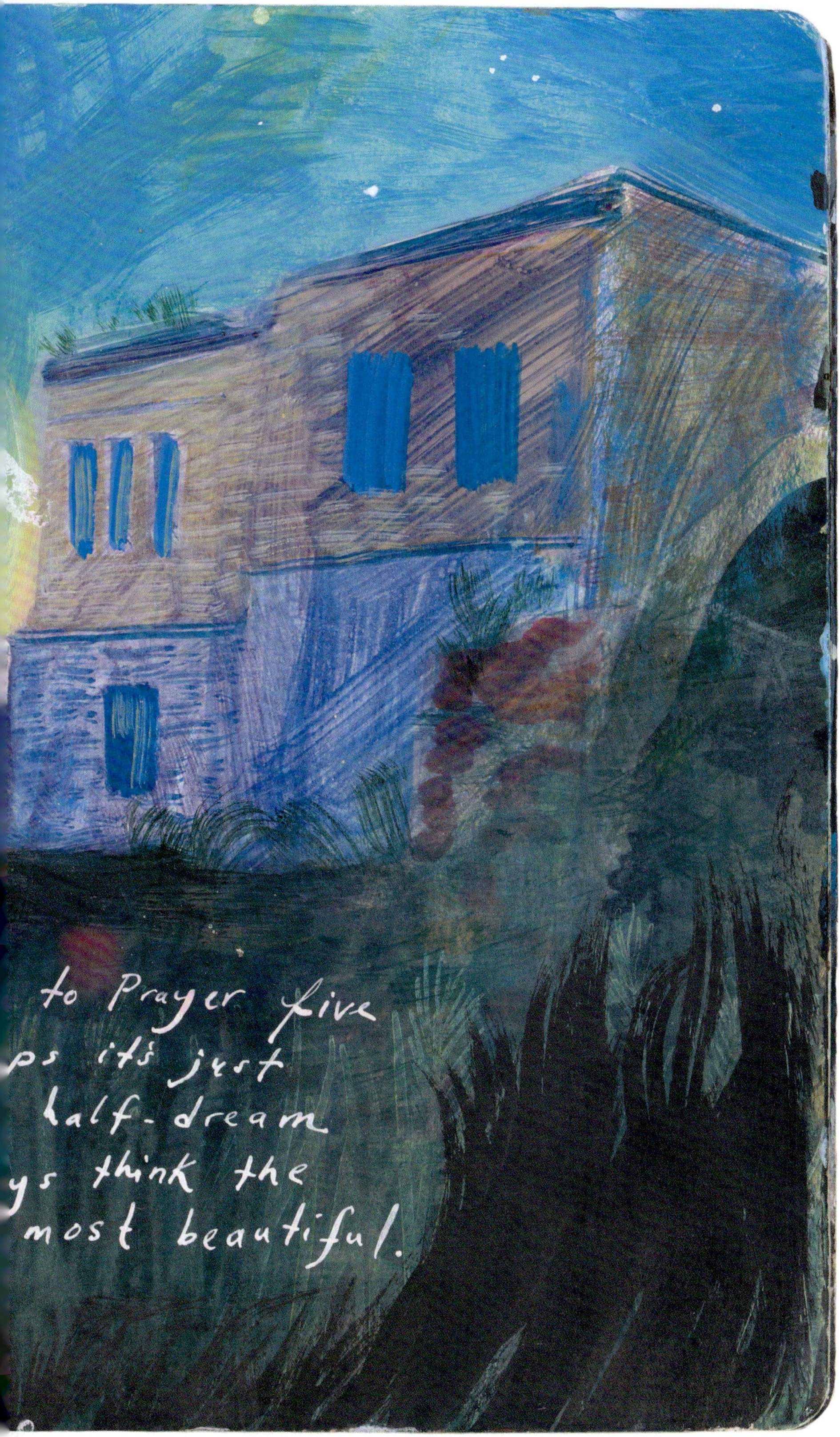

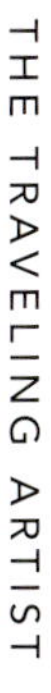

to Prayer five
ps its just
half-dream
ys think the
most beautiful.

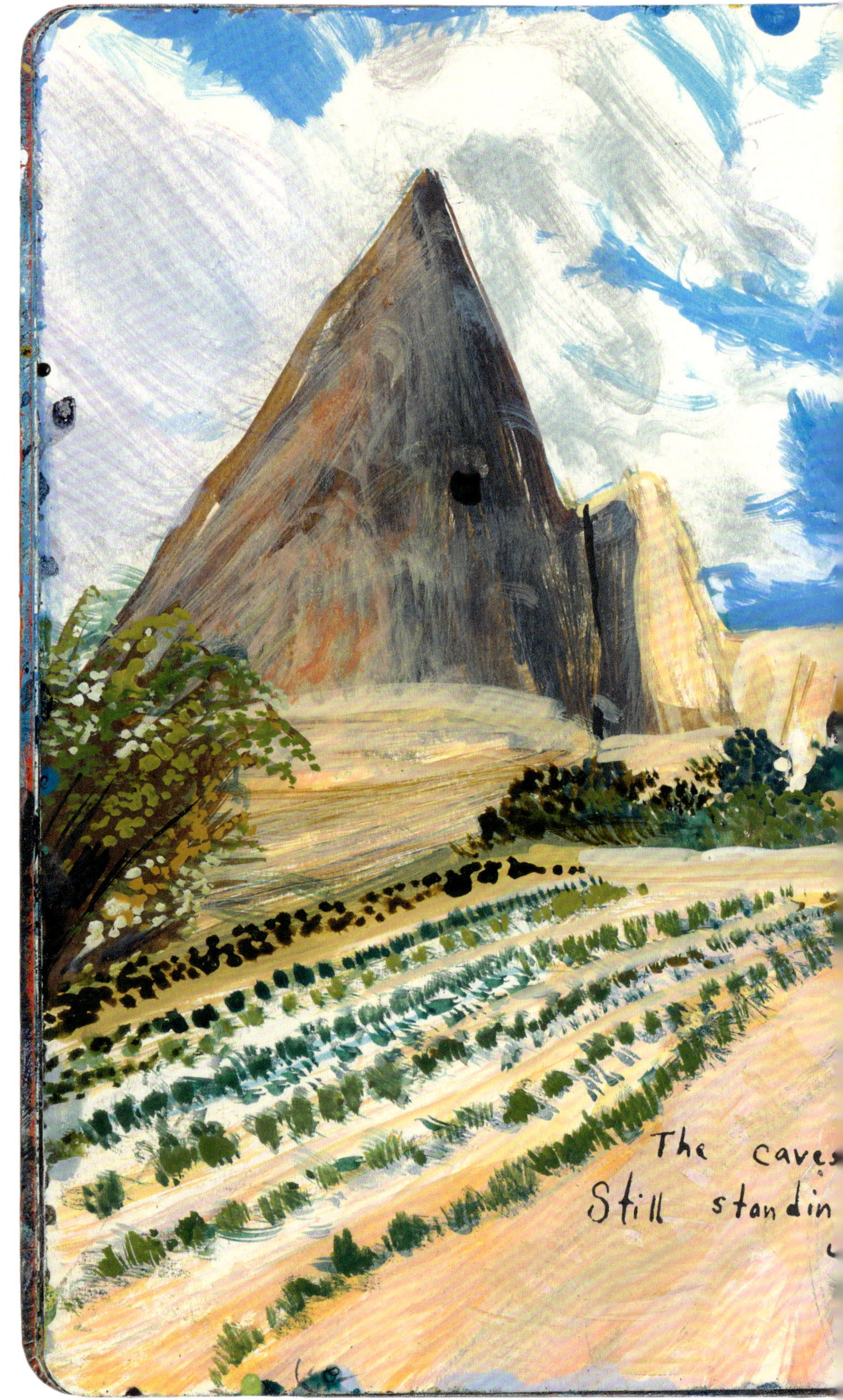
The caves
Still standin

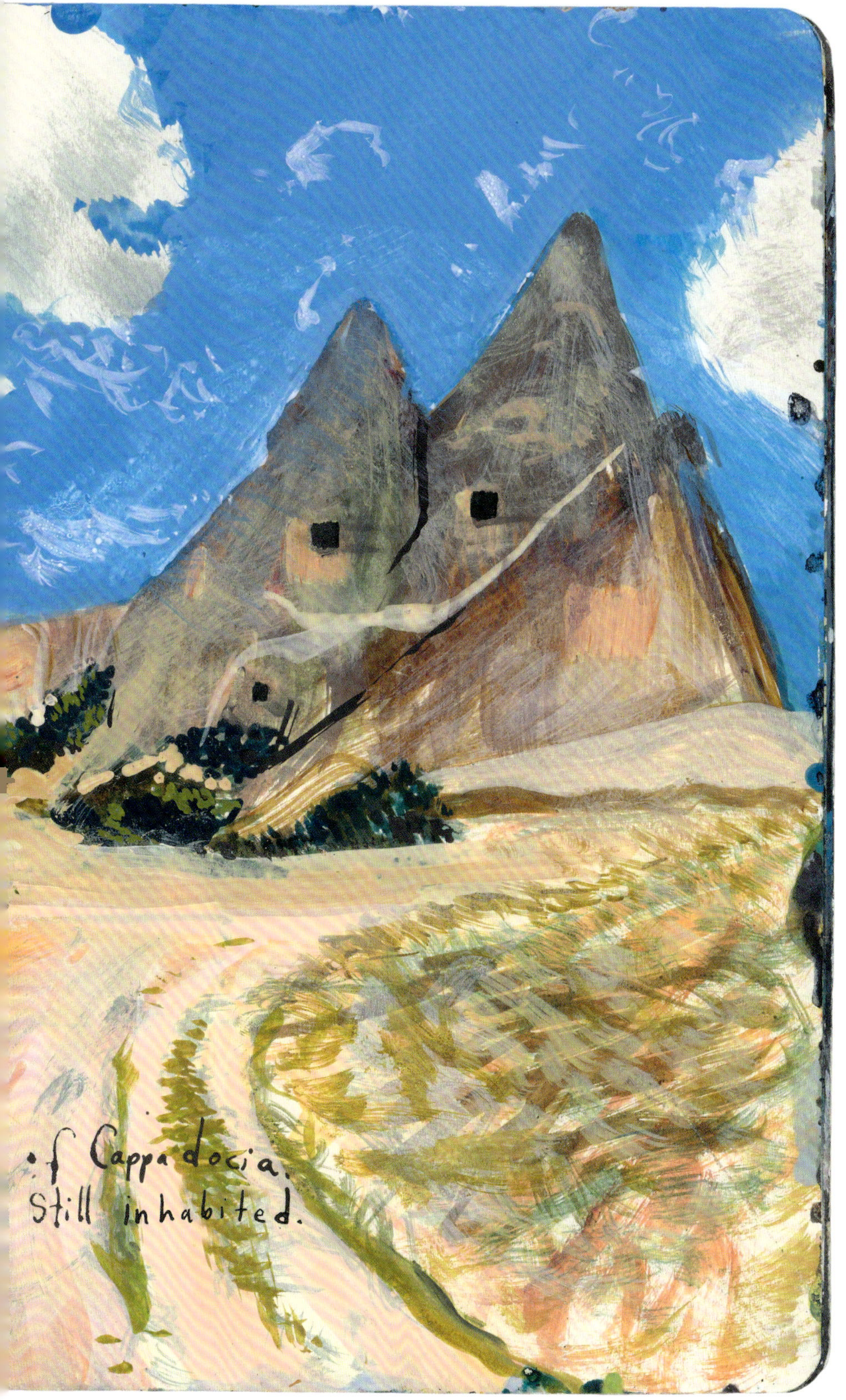
·f Cappadocia.
Still inhabited.

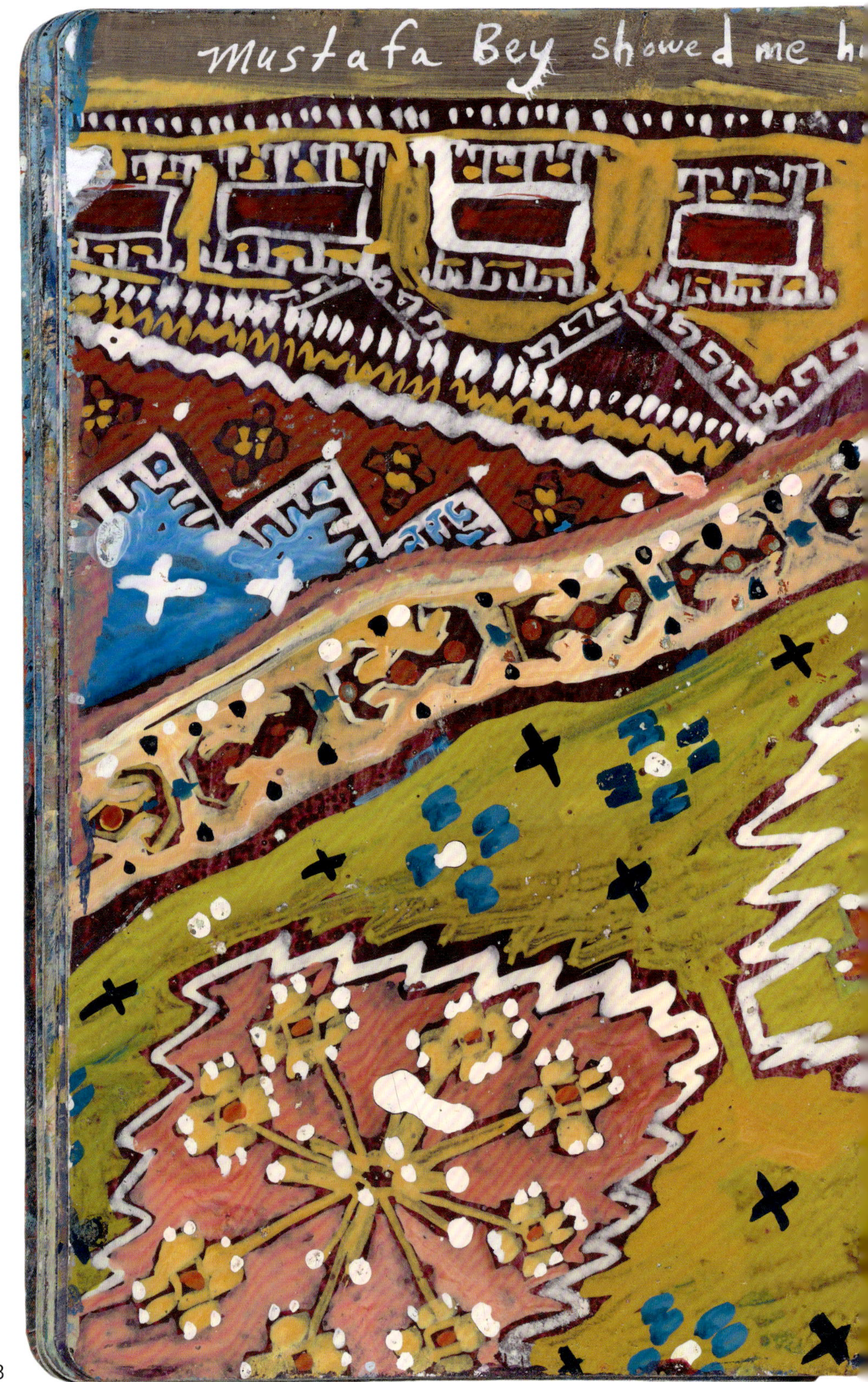

mustafa Bey showed me hi

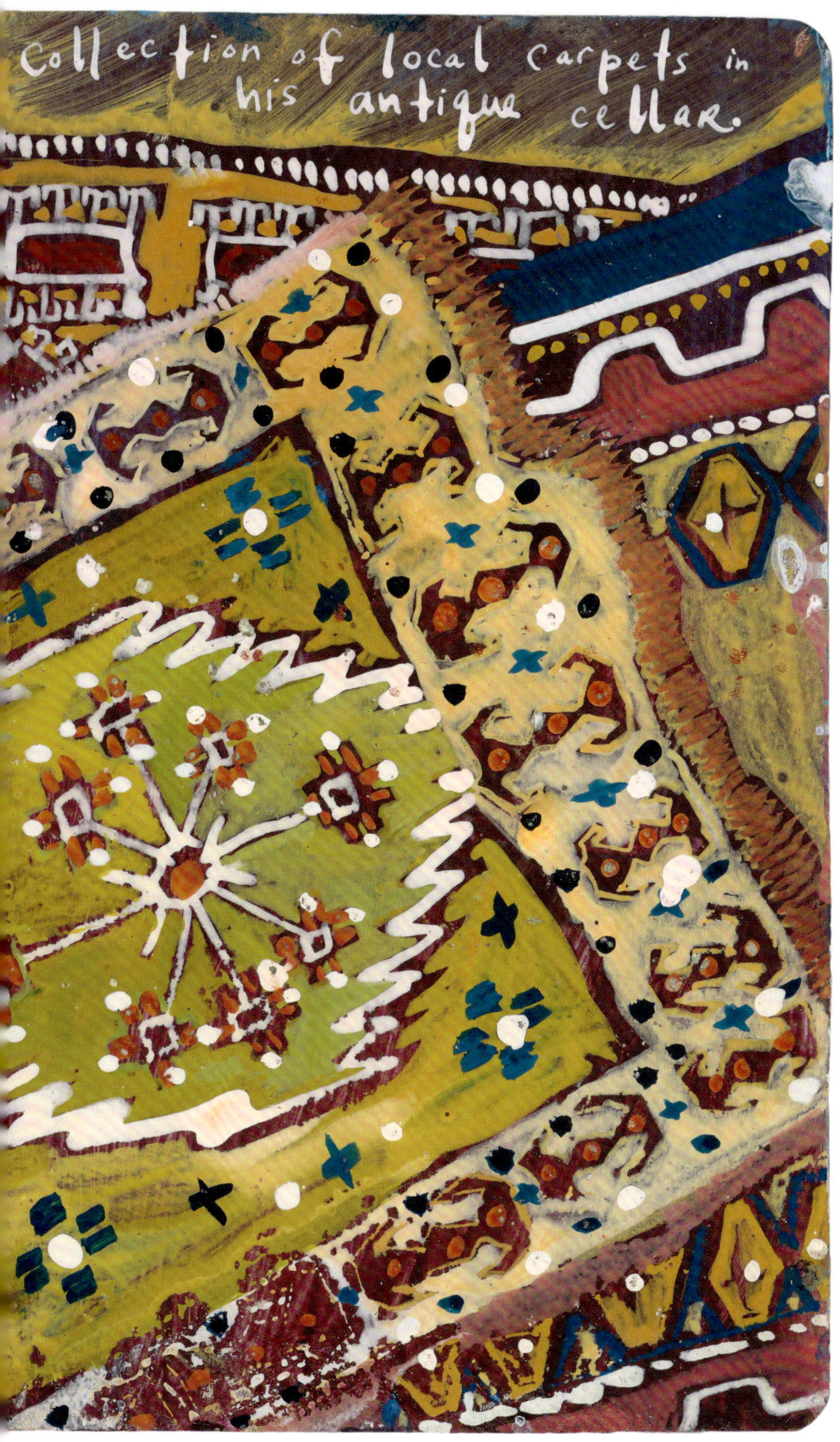

collection of local carpets in his antique cellar.

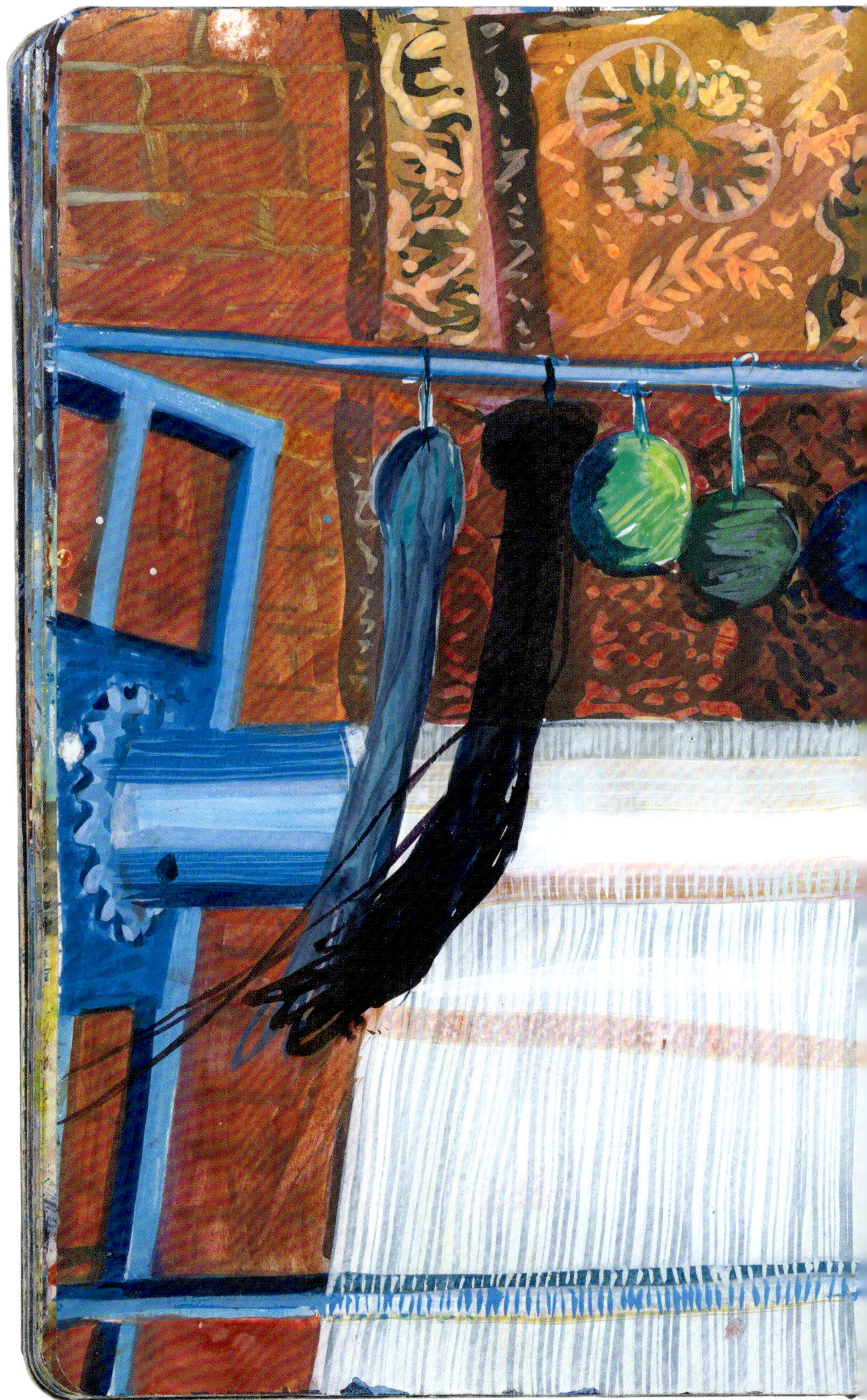

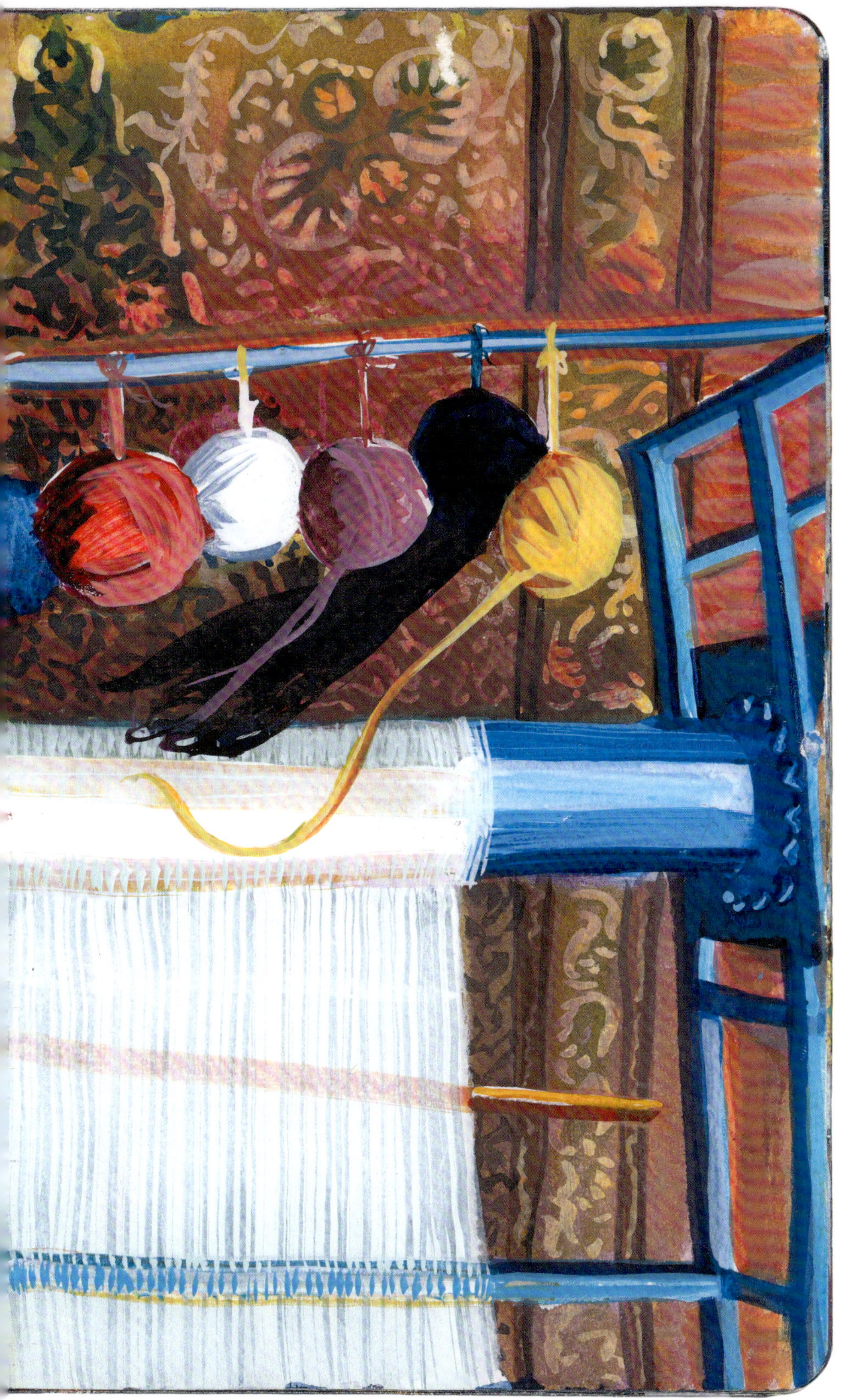

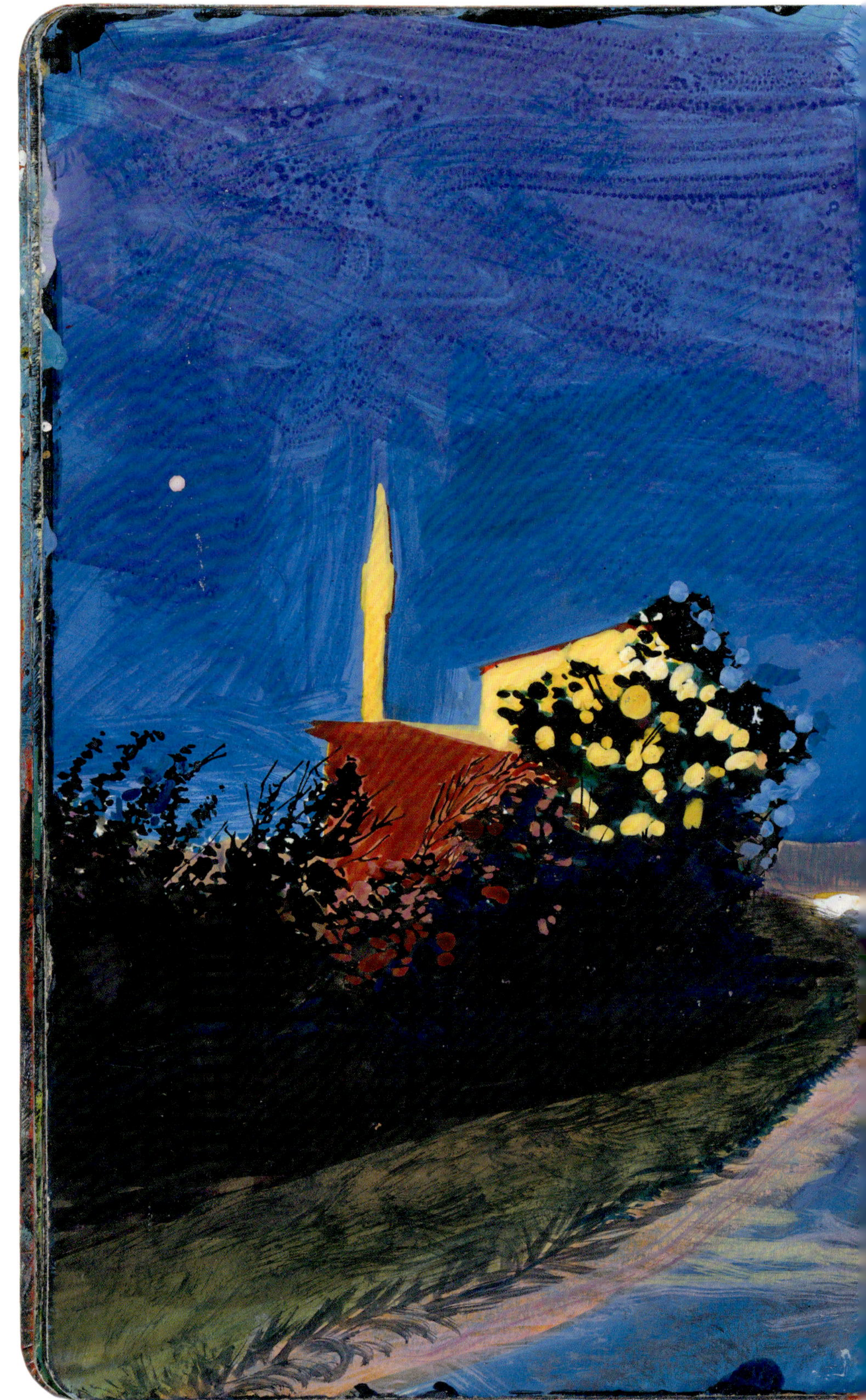

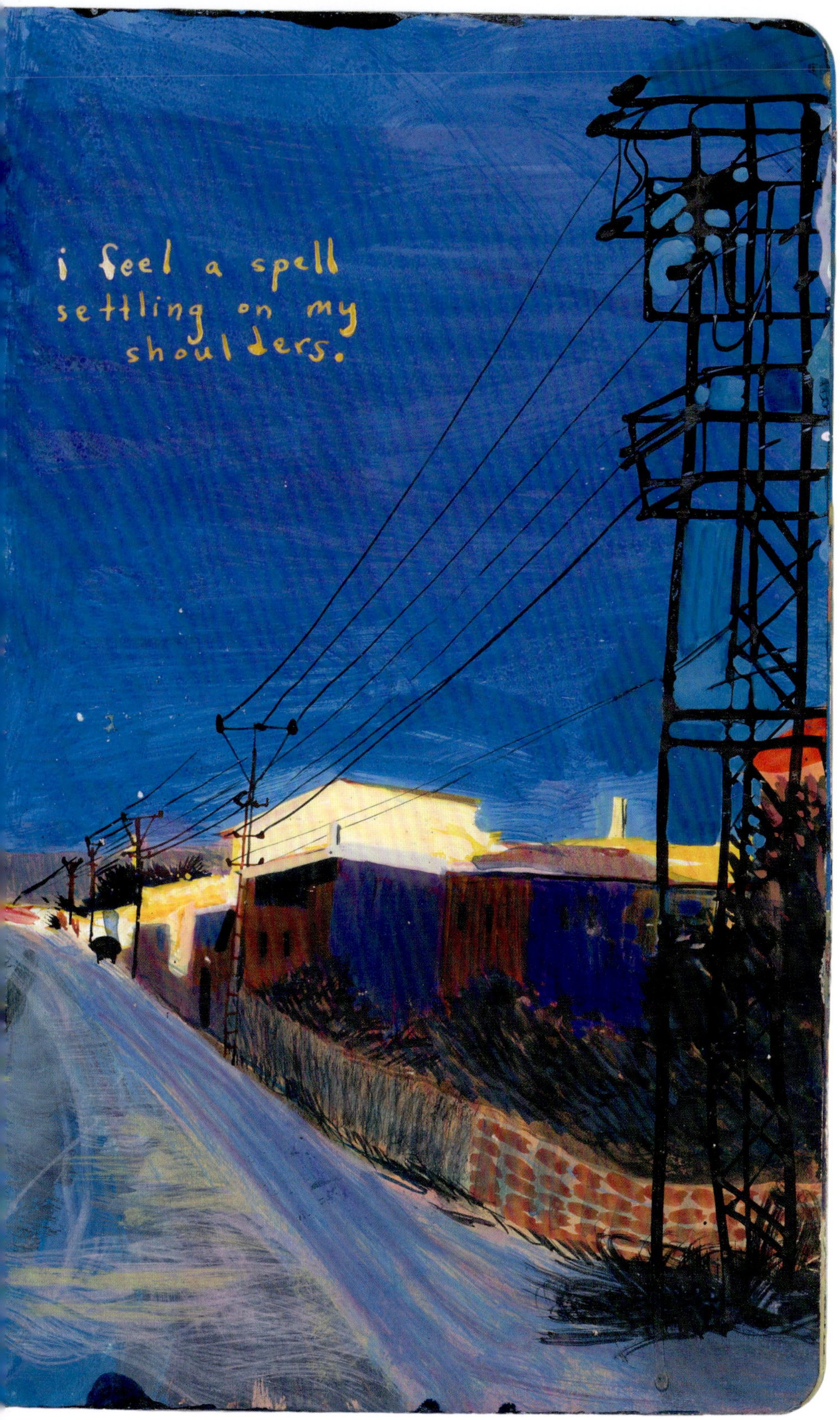
i feel a spell
settling on my
shoulders.

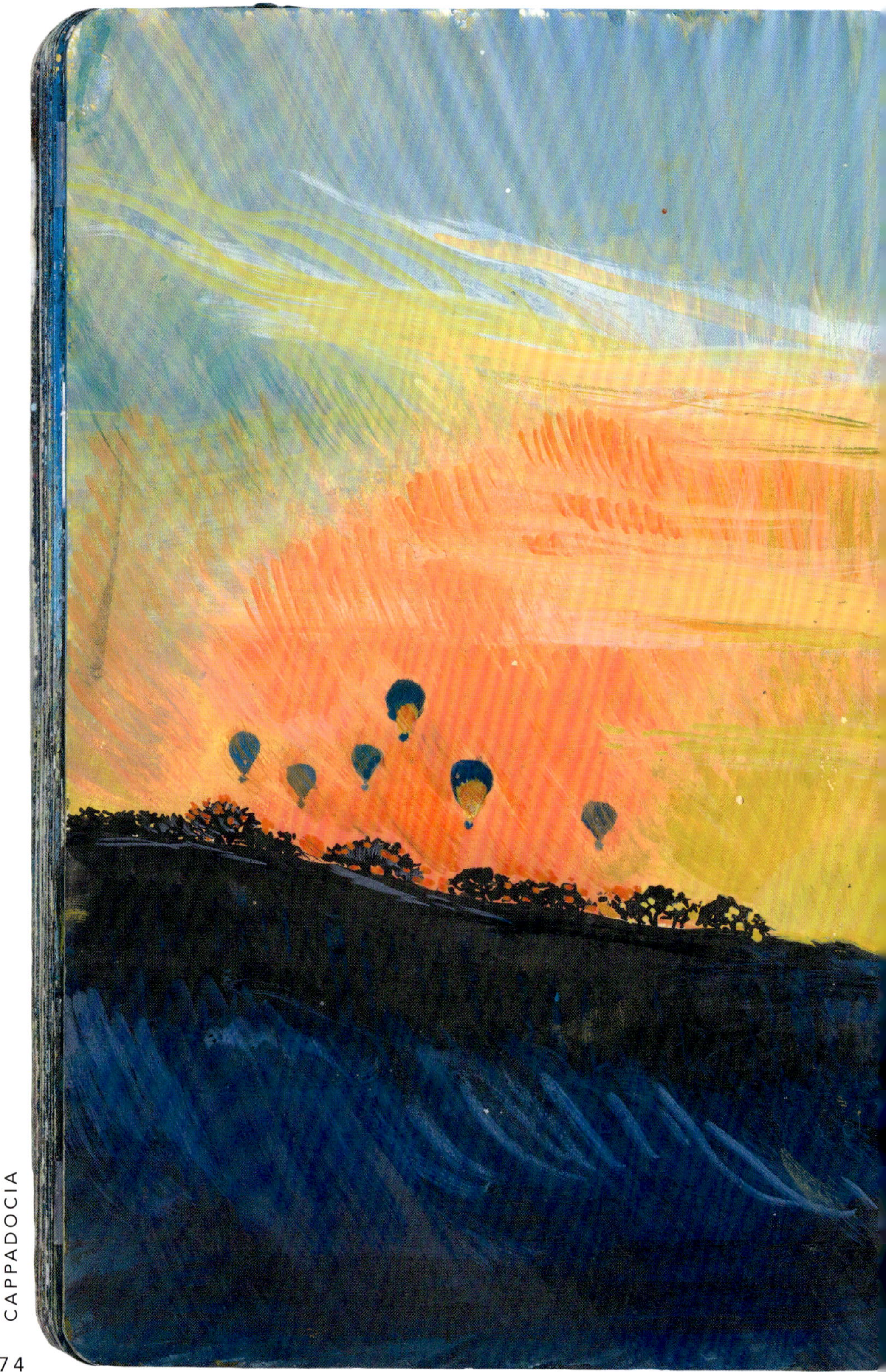

CAPPADOCIA

i met someone.

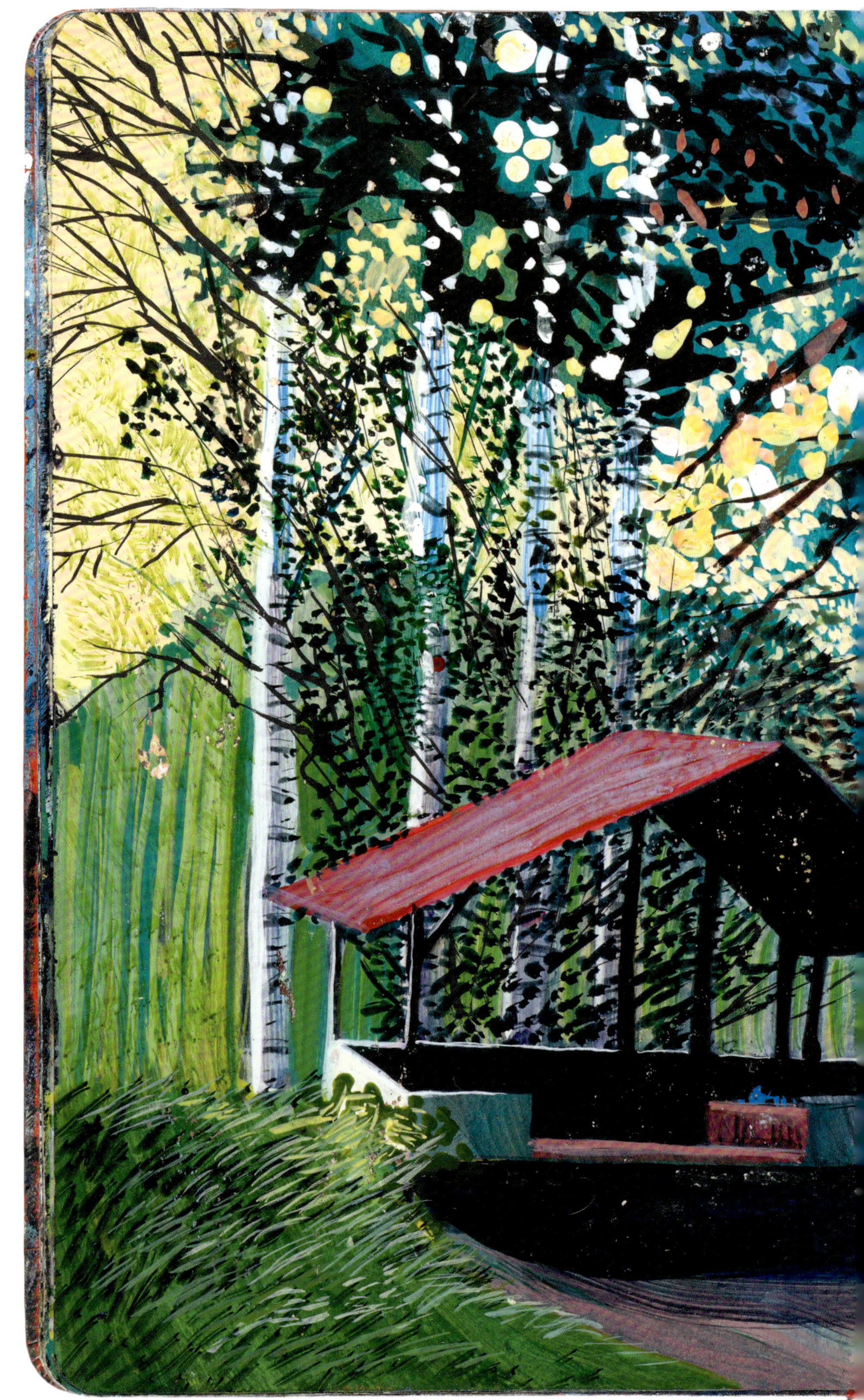

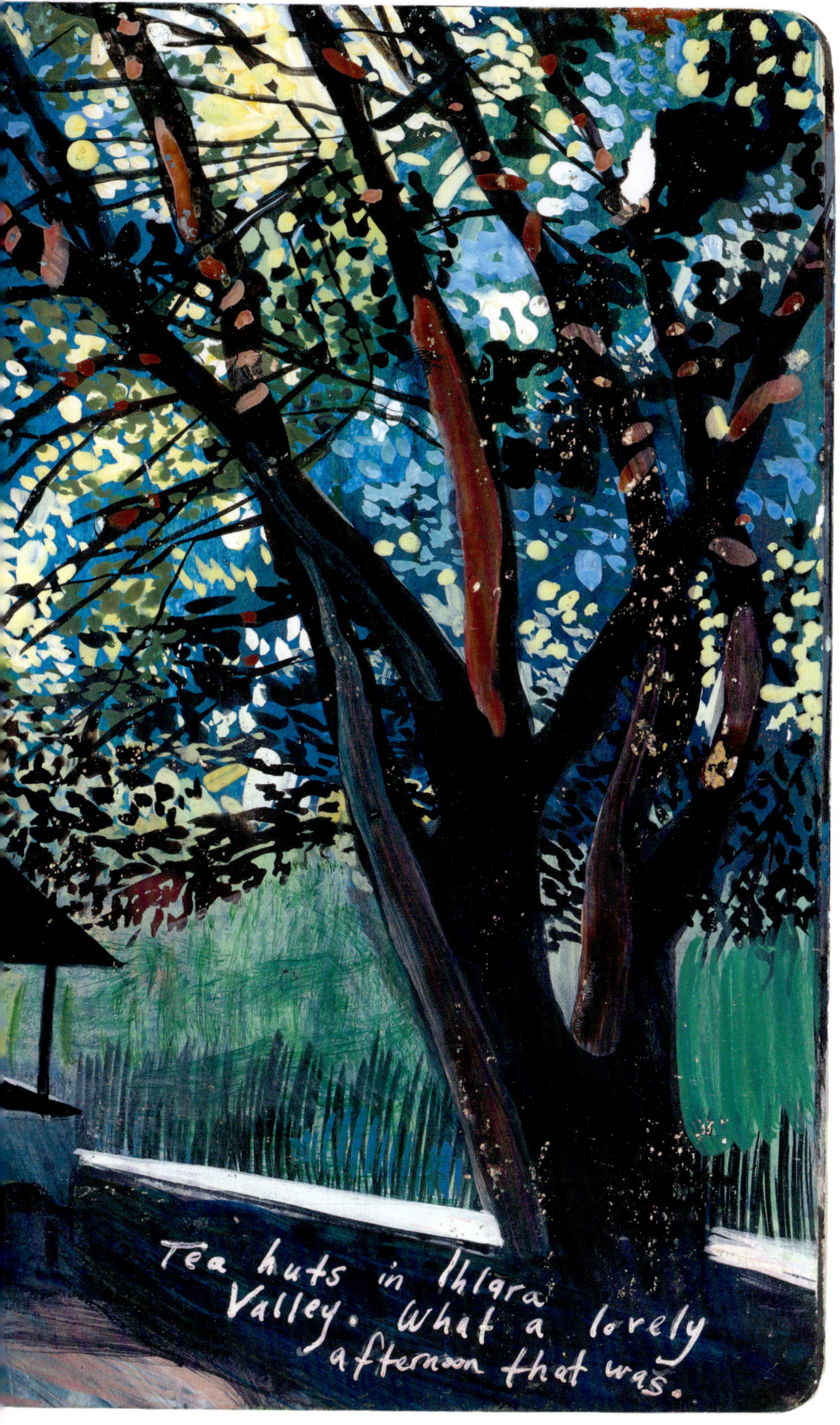
Tea huts in Ihlara Valley. What a lovely afternoon that was.

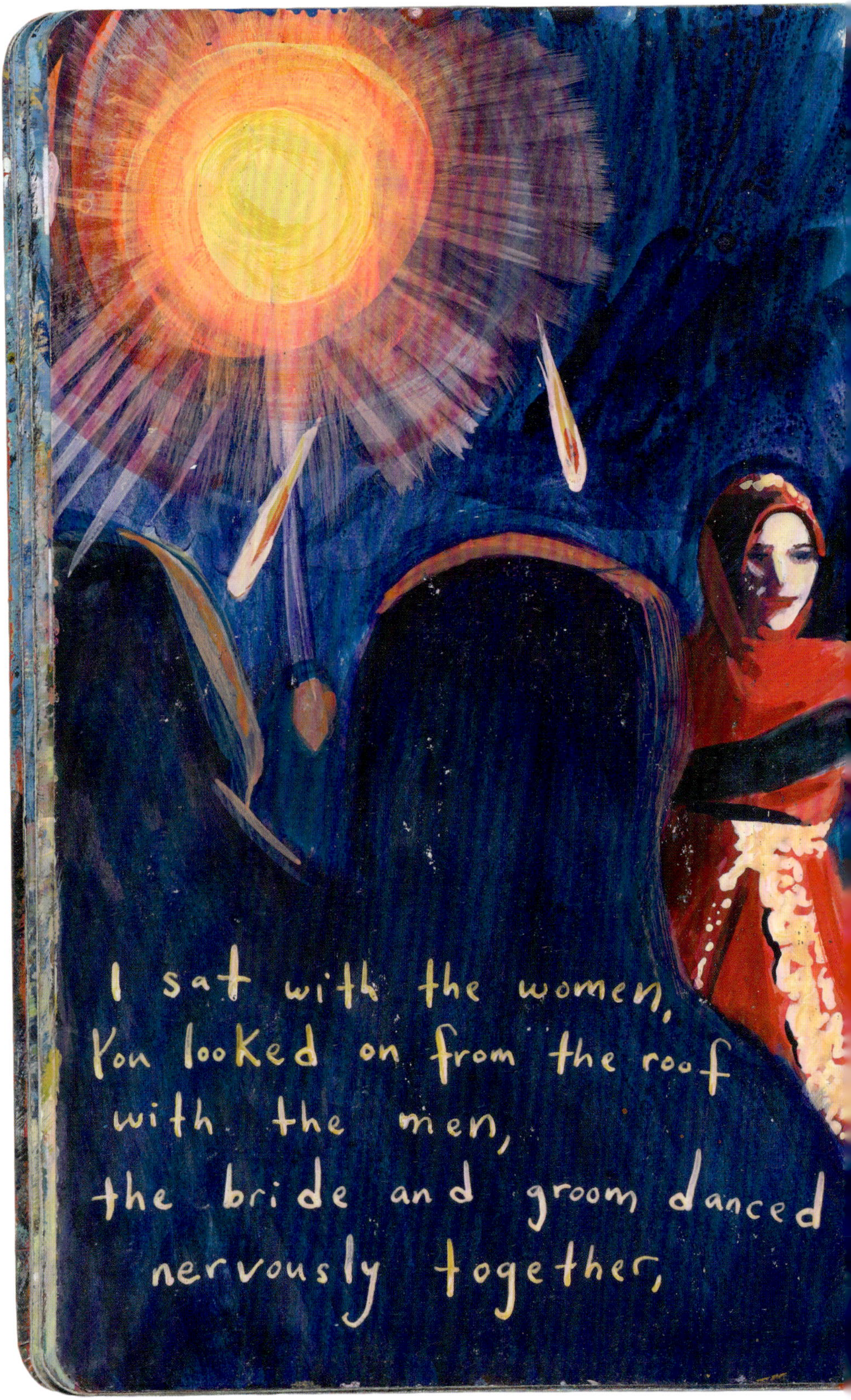

I sat with the women,
You looked on from the roof
with the men,
the bride and groom danced
nervously together,

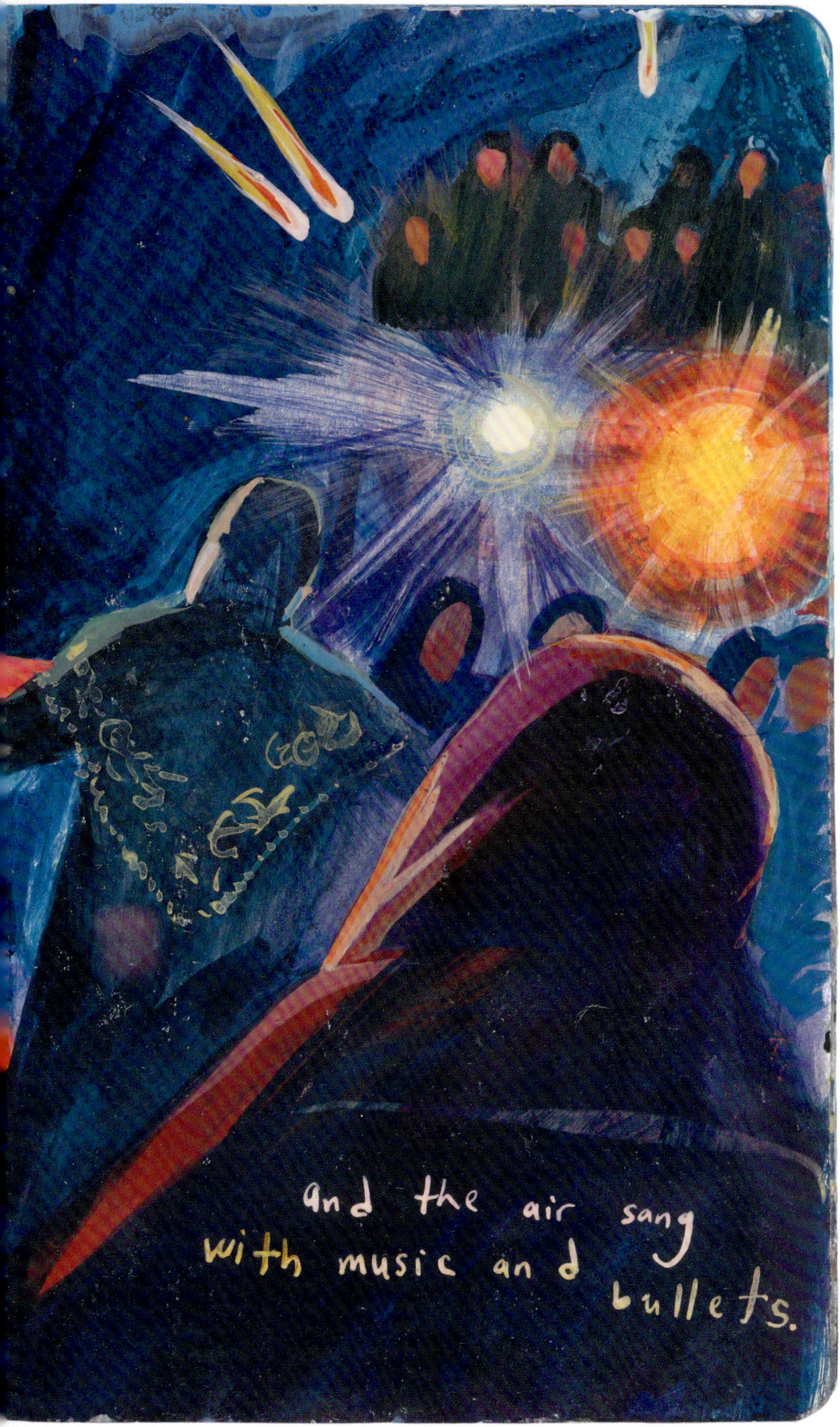

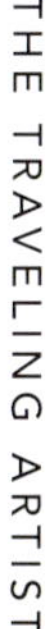

and the air sang
with music and
bullets.

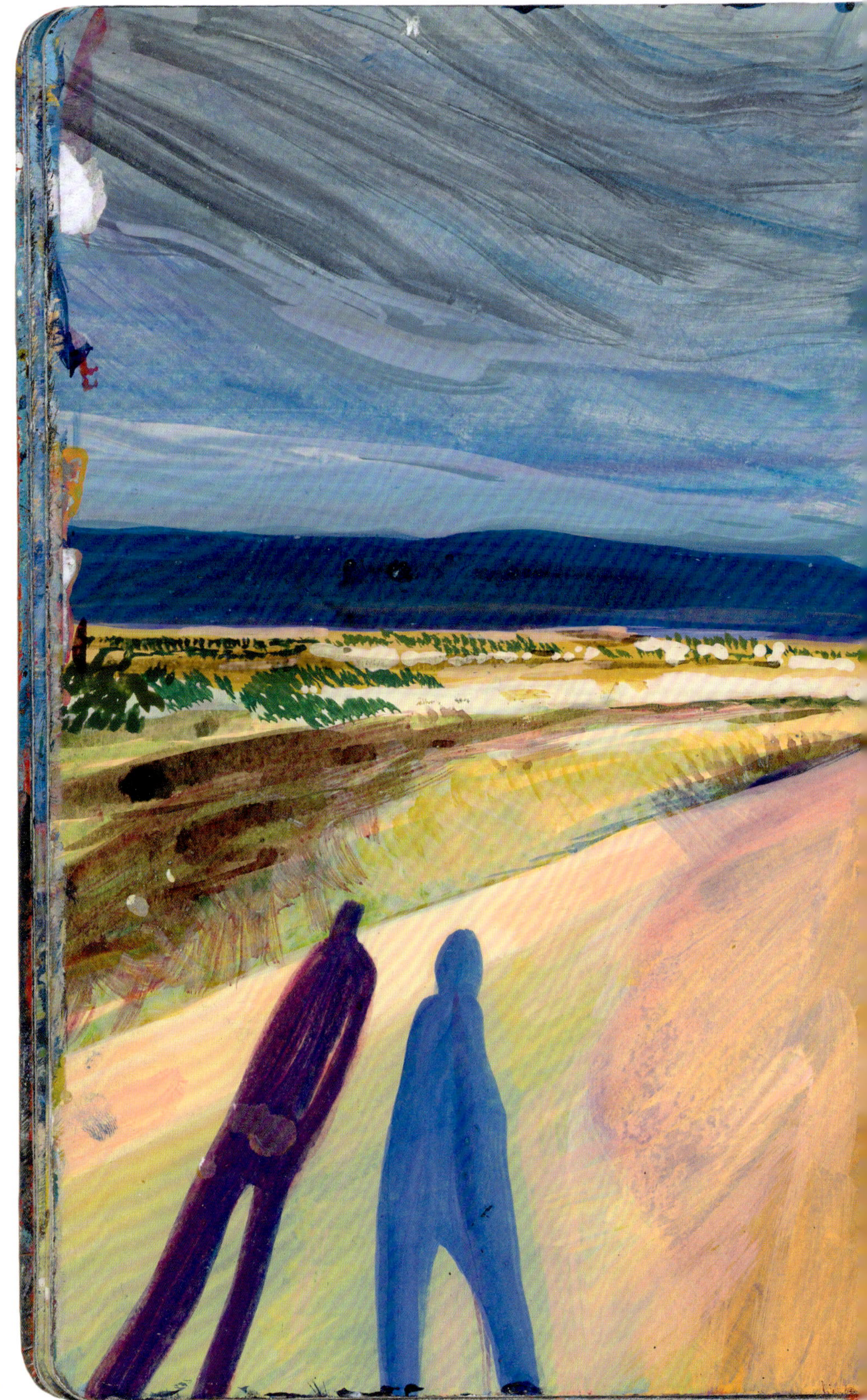

CAPPADOCIA

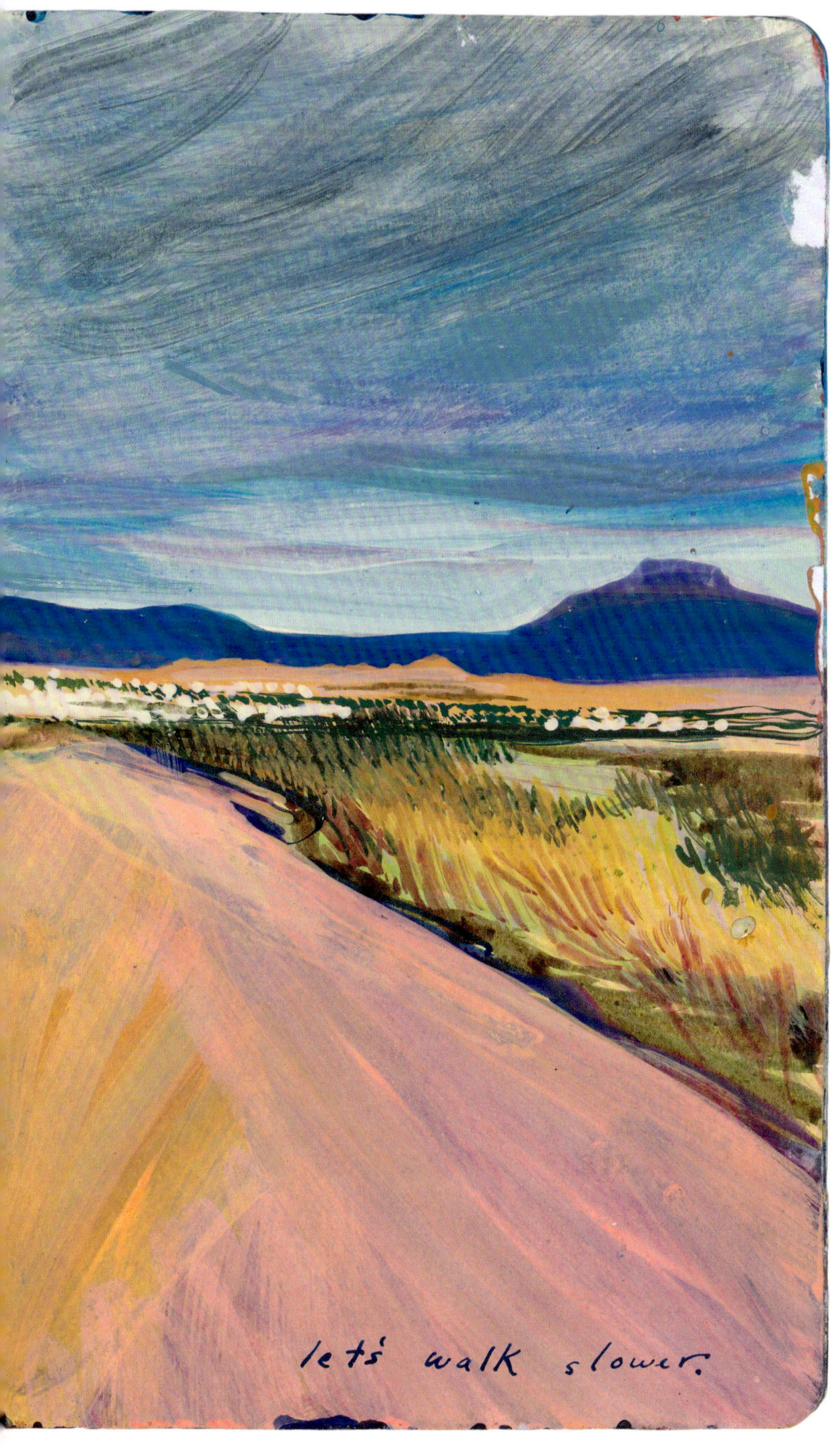
let's walk slower.

I have heard 1,290 calls to Prayer.
Each day five are distributed
evenly through the daylight.
Telling time will feel very
different when I return
to the United States.

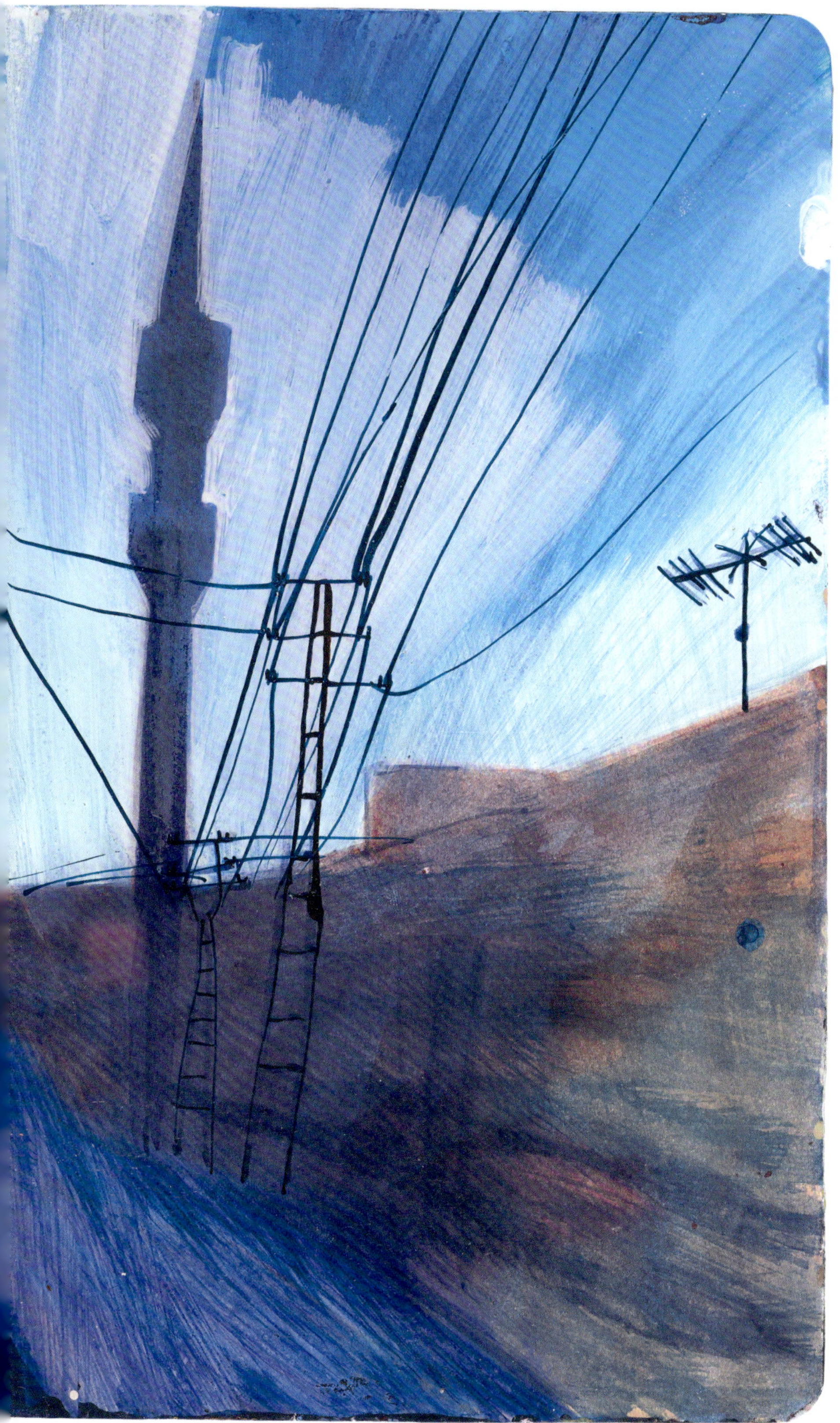

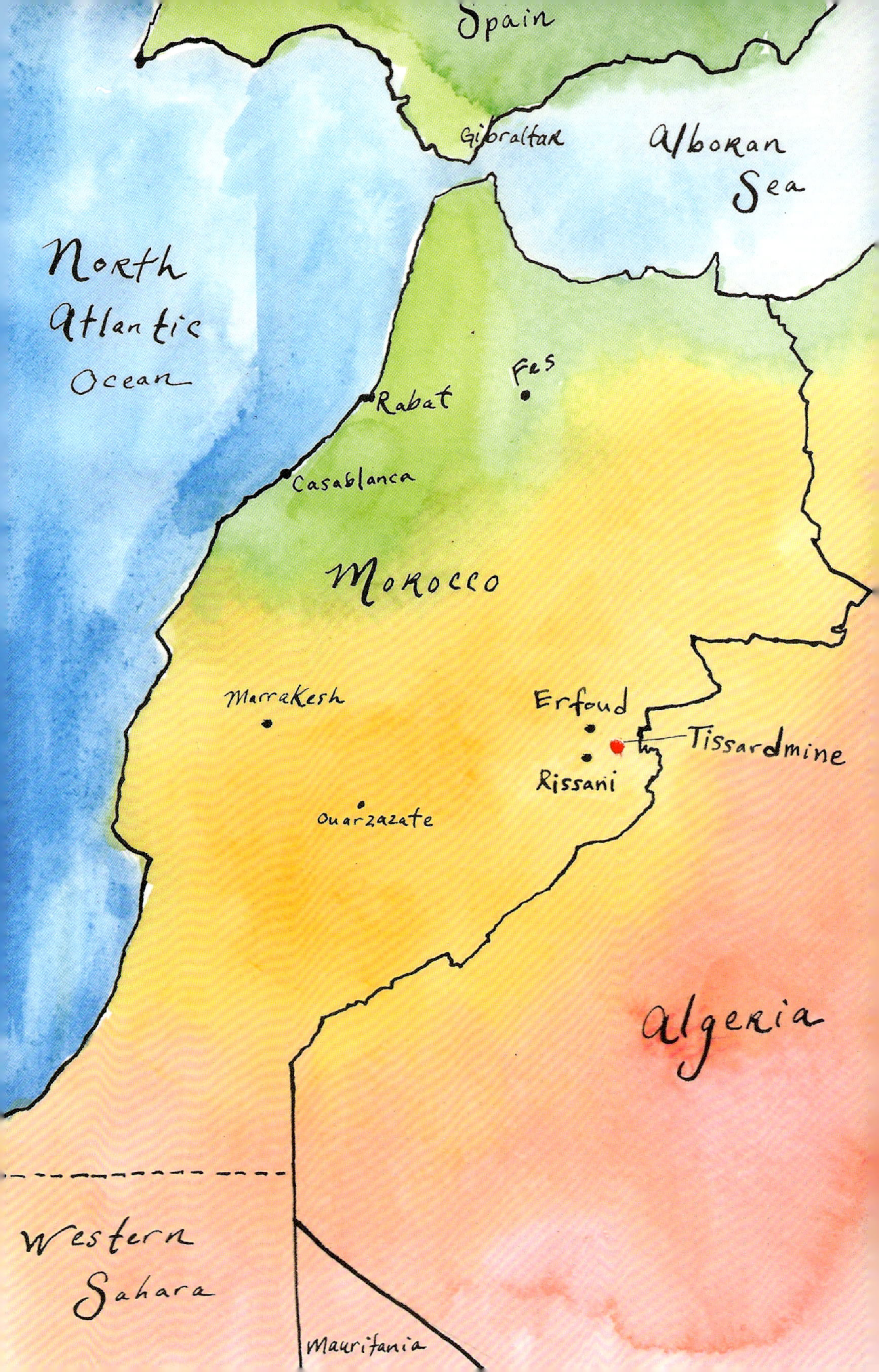

Spain
Gibraltar
Alboran Sea
North Atlantic Ocean
Fes
Rabat
Casablanca
Morocco
Marrakesh
Erfoud
Tissardmine
Rissani
Ouarzazate
Algeria
Western Sahara
Mauritania

IV

Jissardmine, Morocco

October 13th, 2014

    I've traveled to another art residency, this time in Morocco. I love complementary color combinations, like blue and orange, so I knew the Sahara would delight my eyes.

    Yesterday, I joined an excursion into the Erg Chebbi dunes on camel. We climbed dune after dune until the landscape was a disorienting sea of sand. The light dimmed and the air became quiet and still. Our guide called back in his elegant Tashelhit-tinged accent, "Don't worry, we'll be okay!" Behind us was a sandstorm as tall as a tsunami, tumbling forward at breathtaking speed. I clenched as the wave took us, but was surprised by a blast of cool air and soft dust. Our guide explained sandstorms are destructive on flat land but, when they enter Erg Chebbi, the sand is absorbed into the dunes, leaving only a quick-moving fog.

colors:

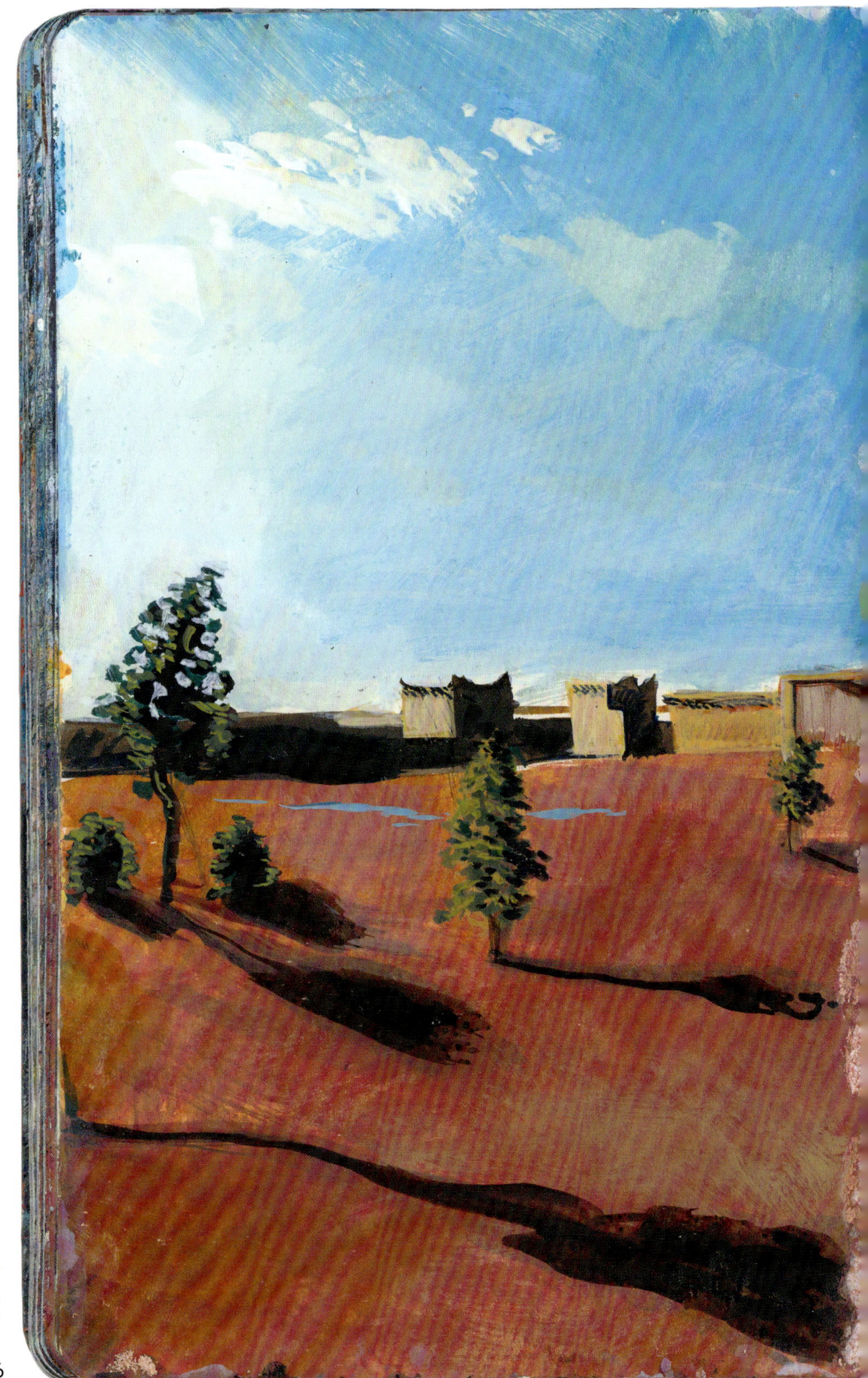

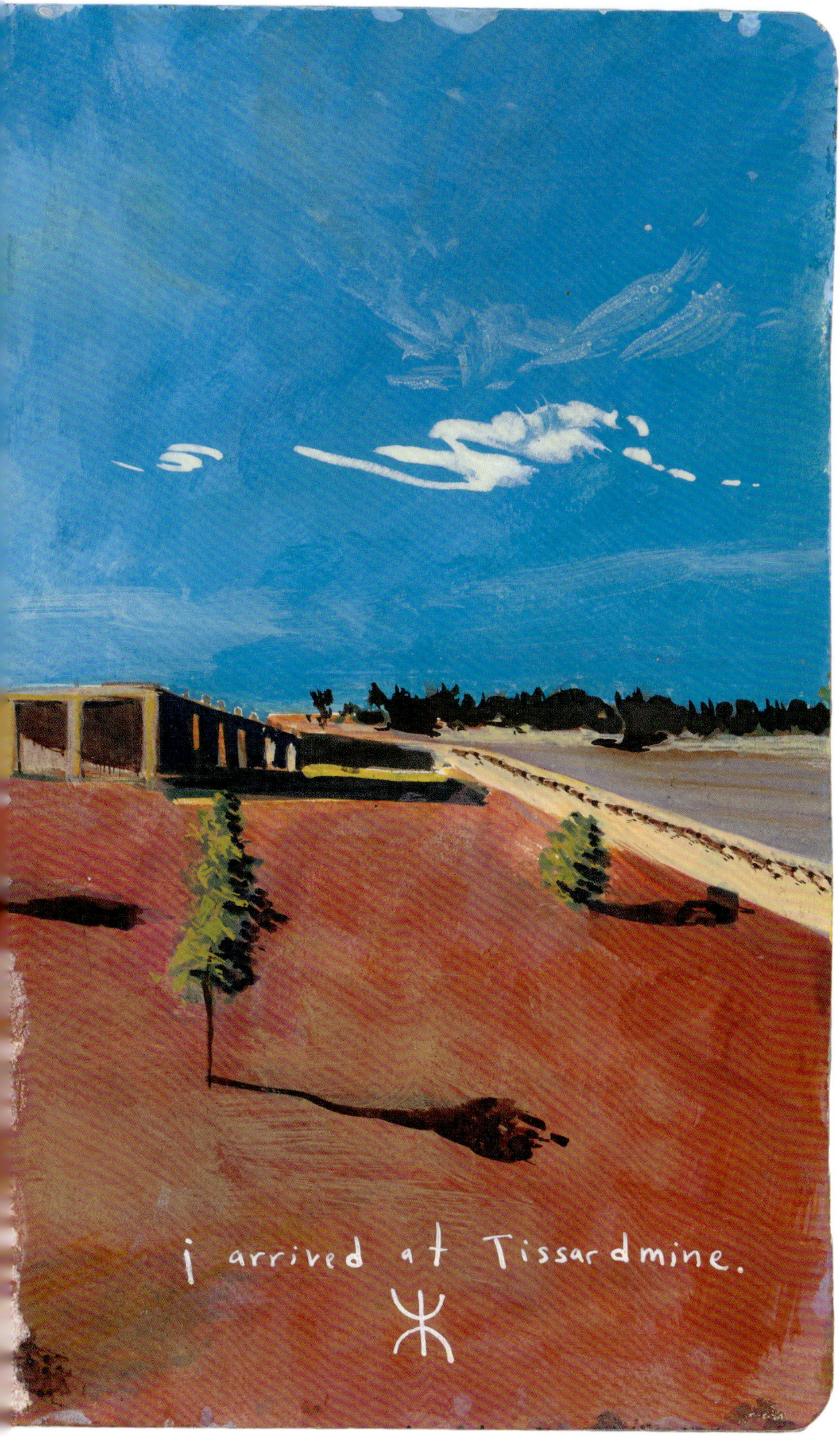

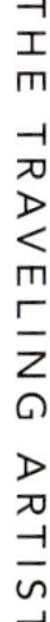

i arrived at Tissardmine.

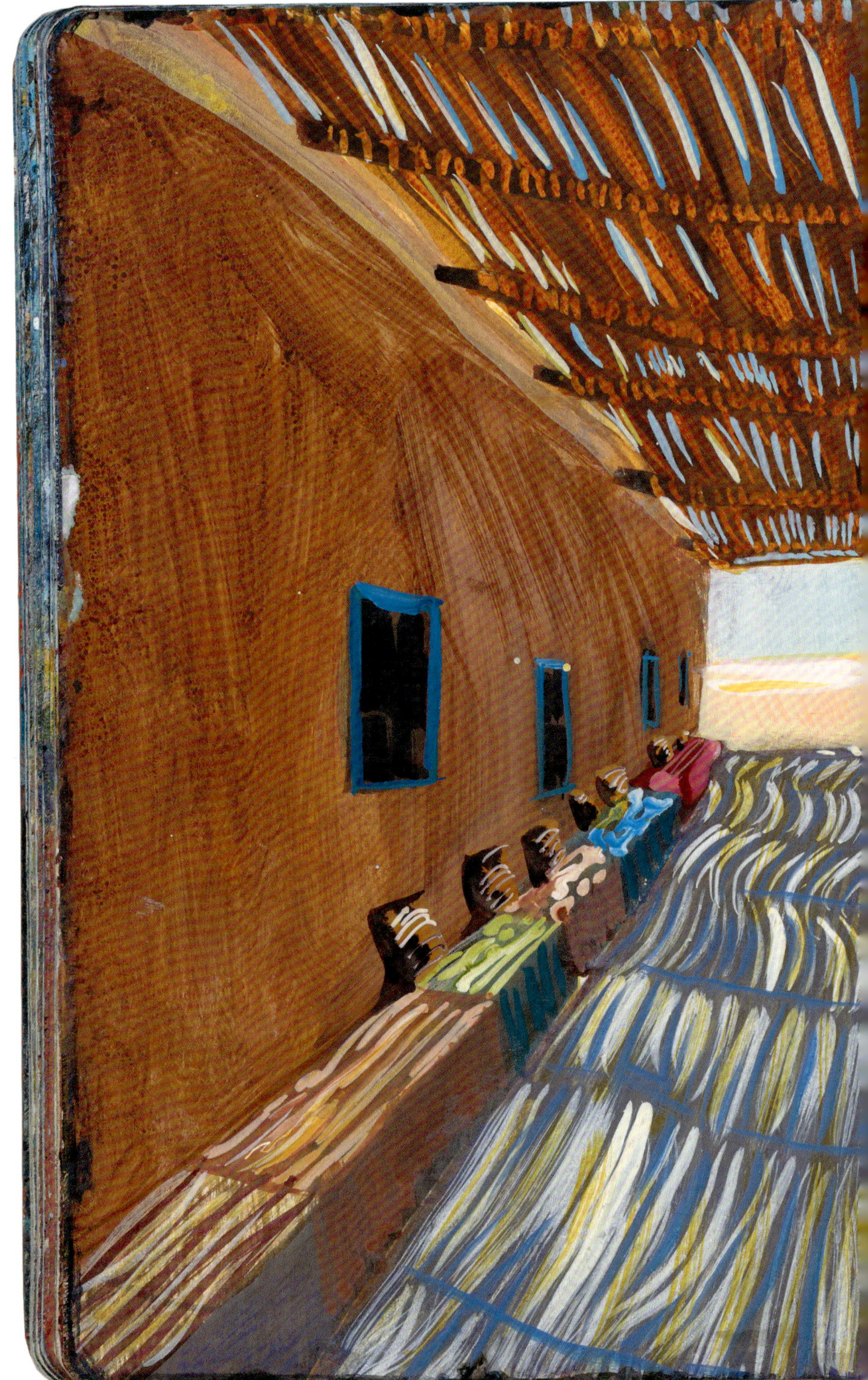

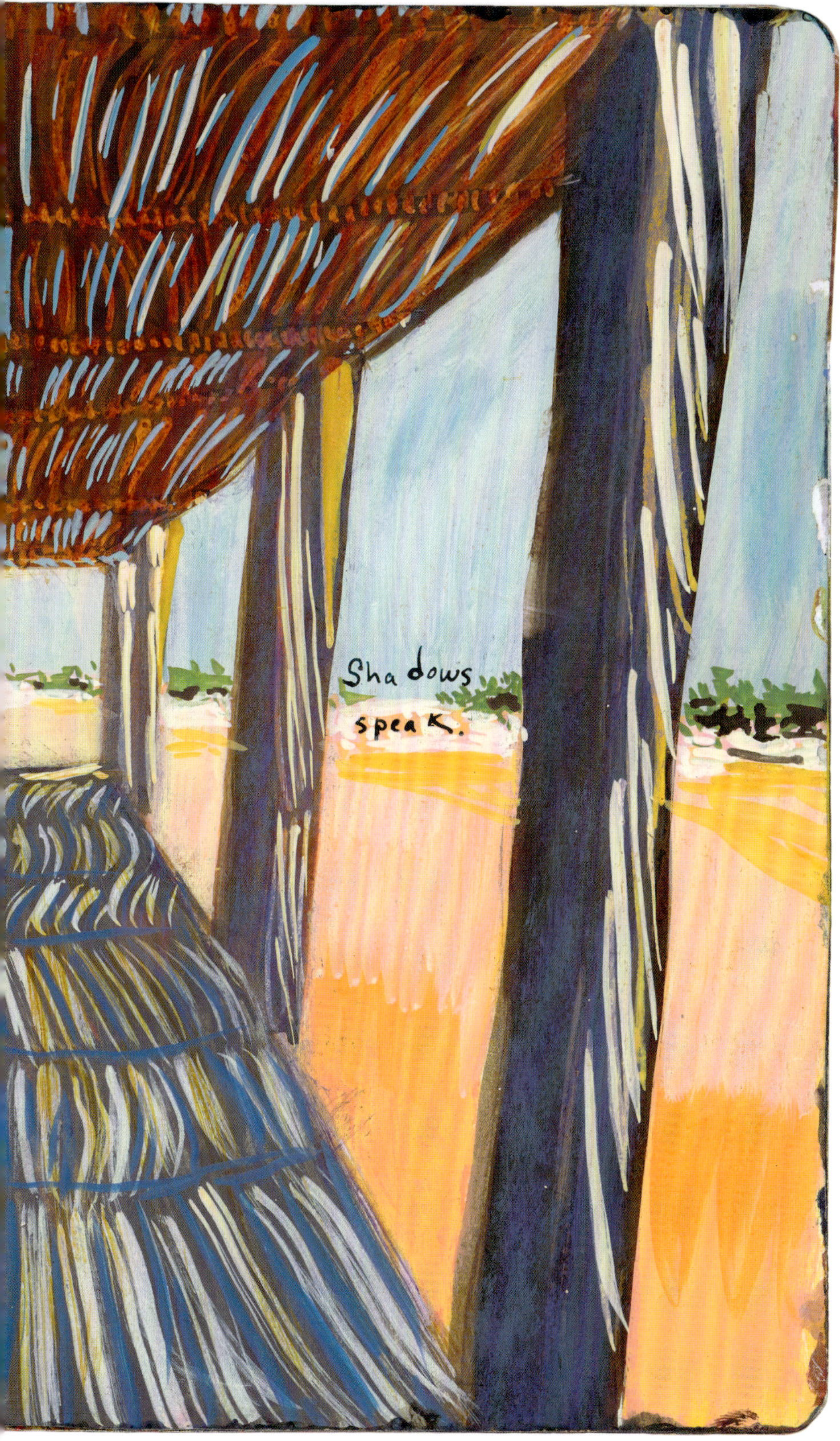

Shadows
speak.

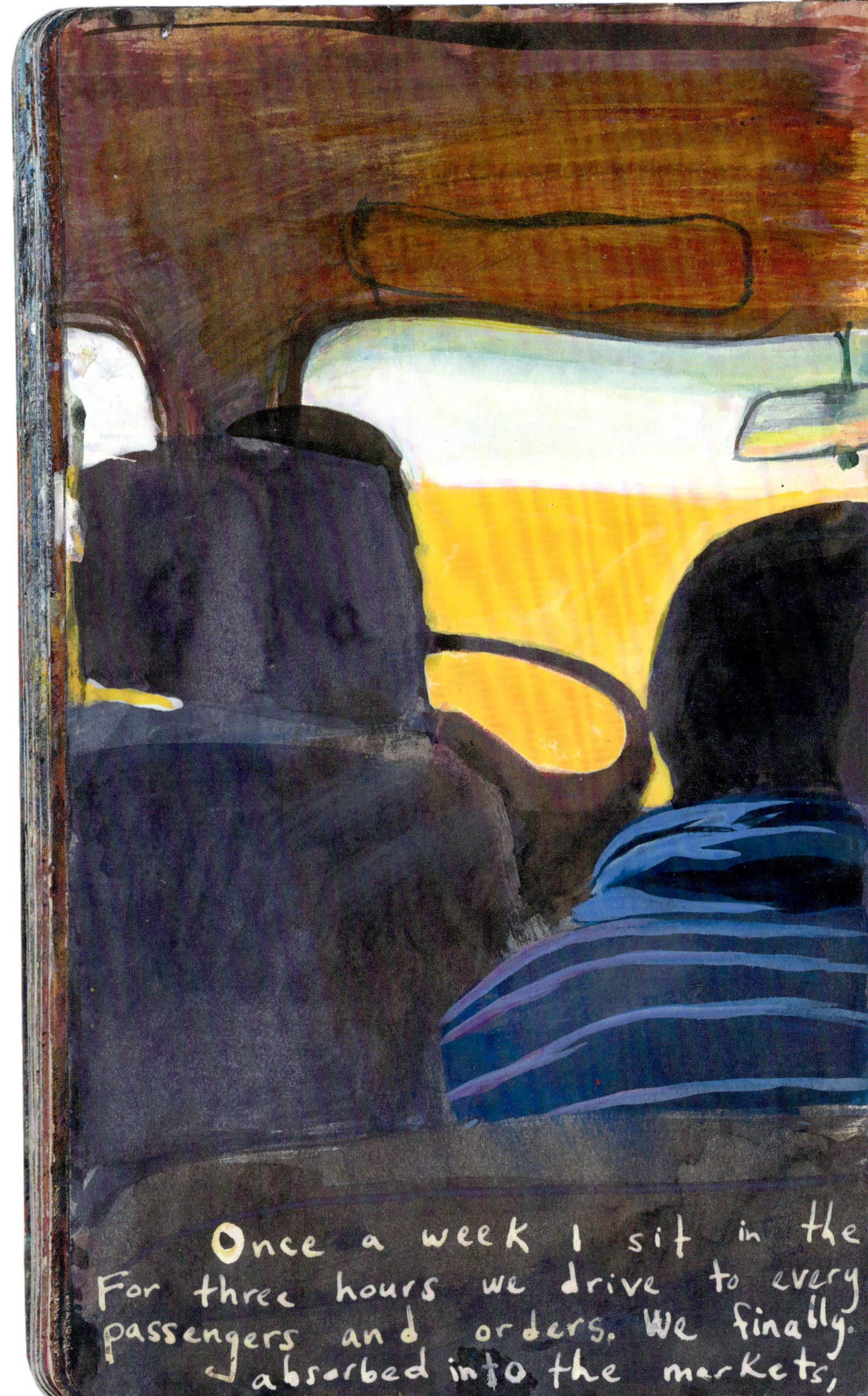
Once a week I sit in the
For three hours we drive to every
passengers and orders. We finally
absorbed into the markets,

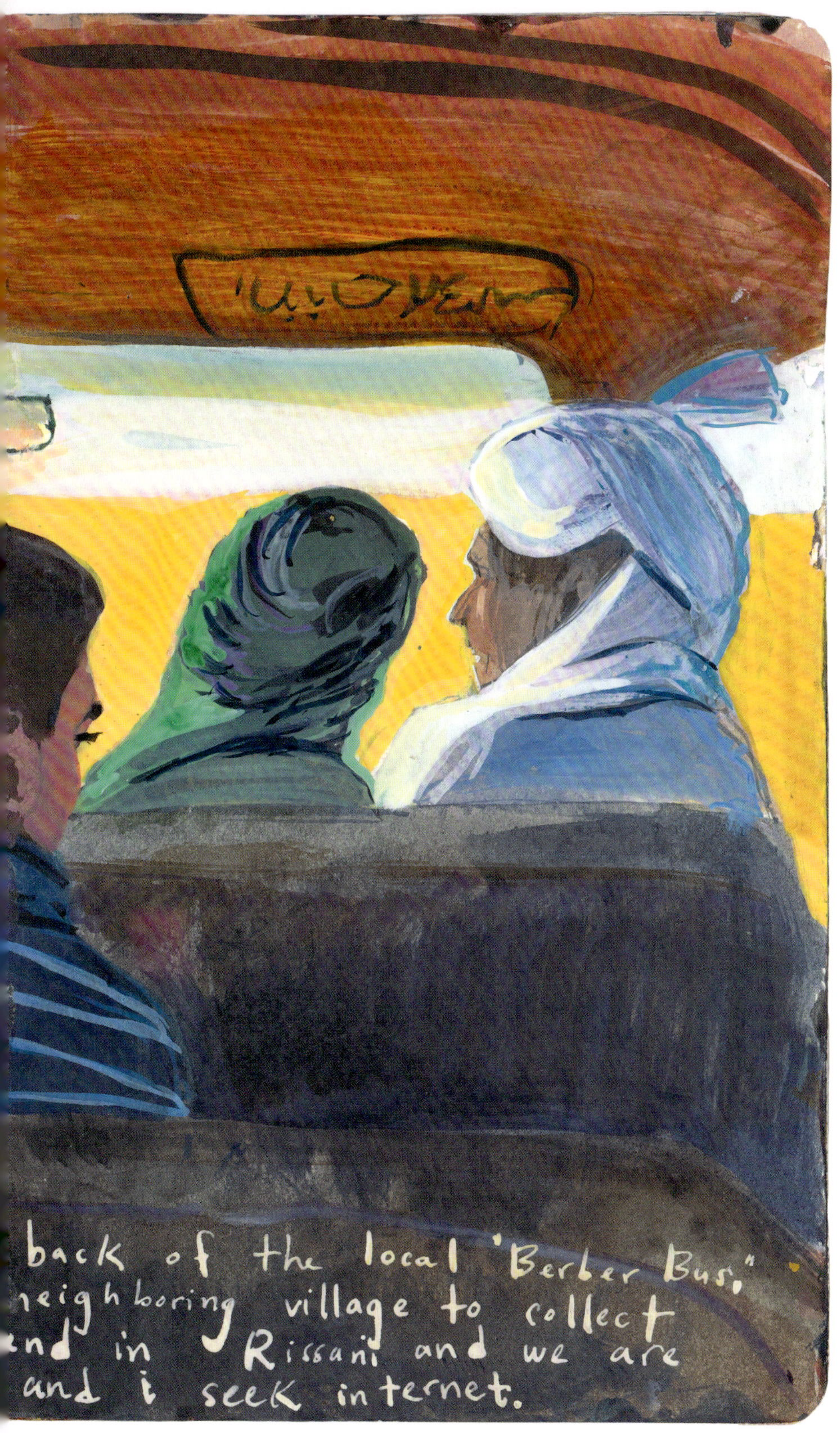
back of the local "Berber Bus,"
neighboring village to collect
nd in Rissani and we are
and i seek internet.

Our camels rested in the fog.

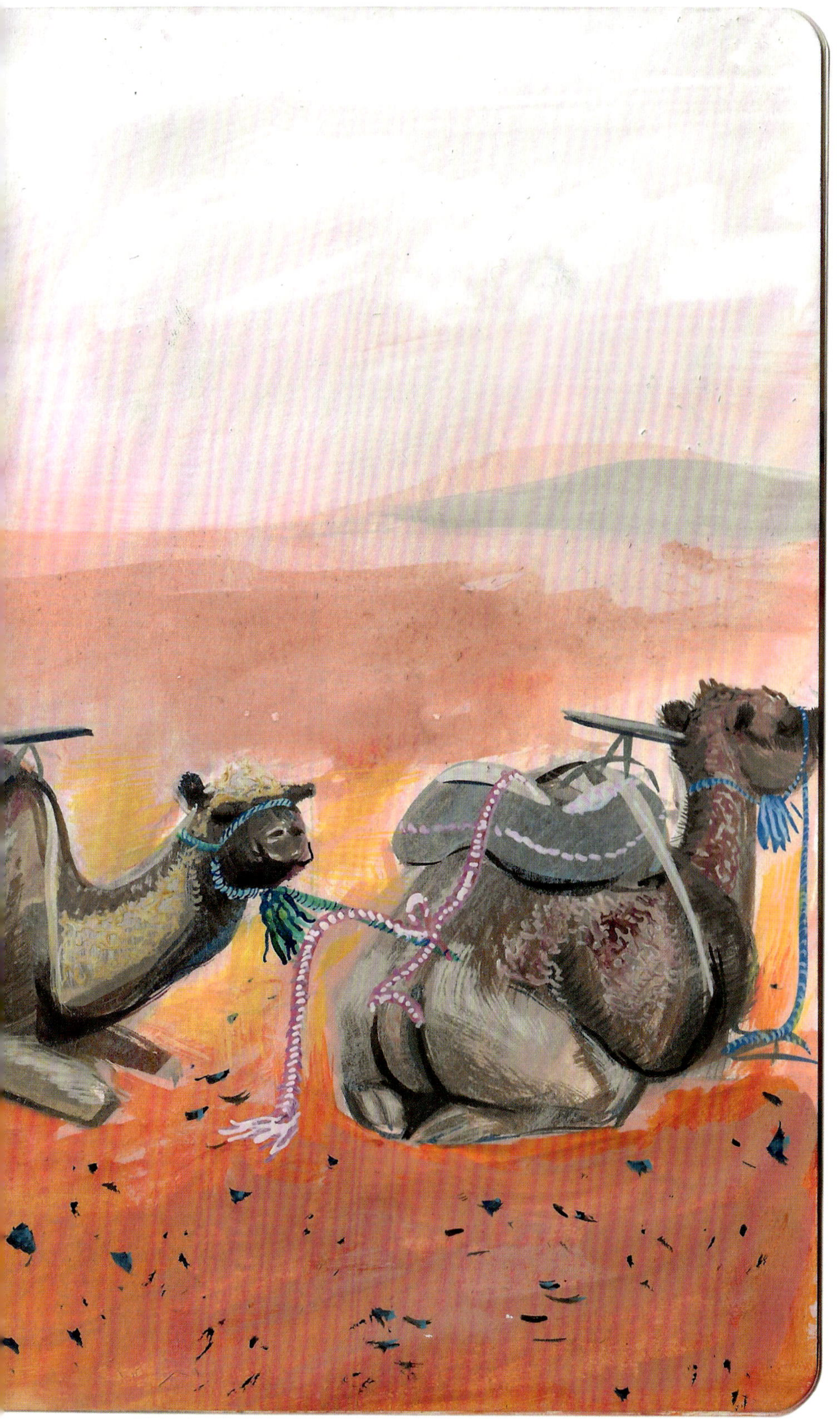

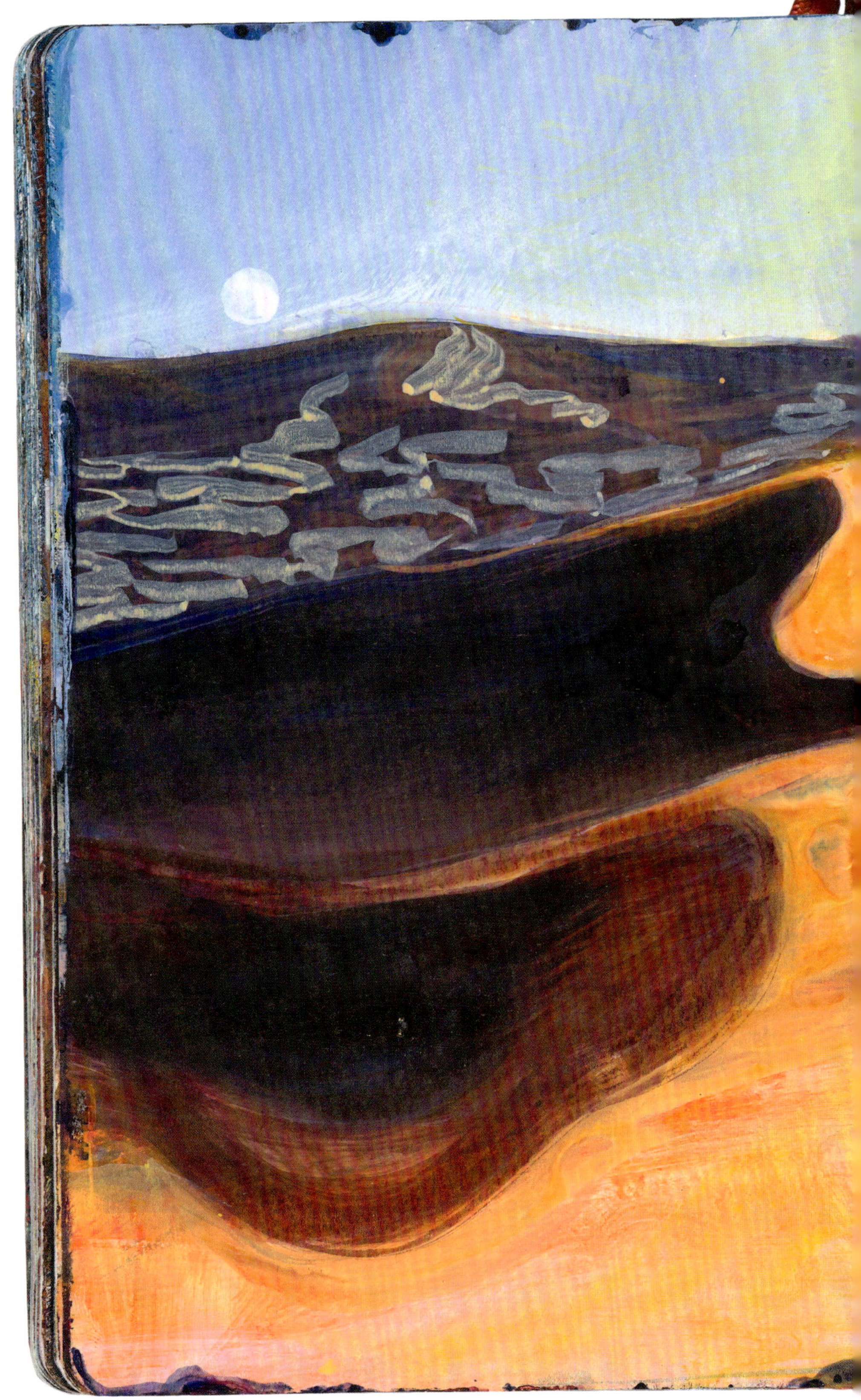

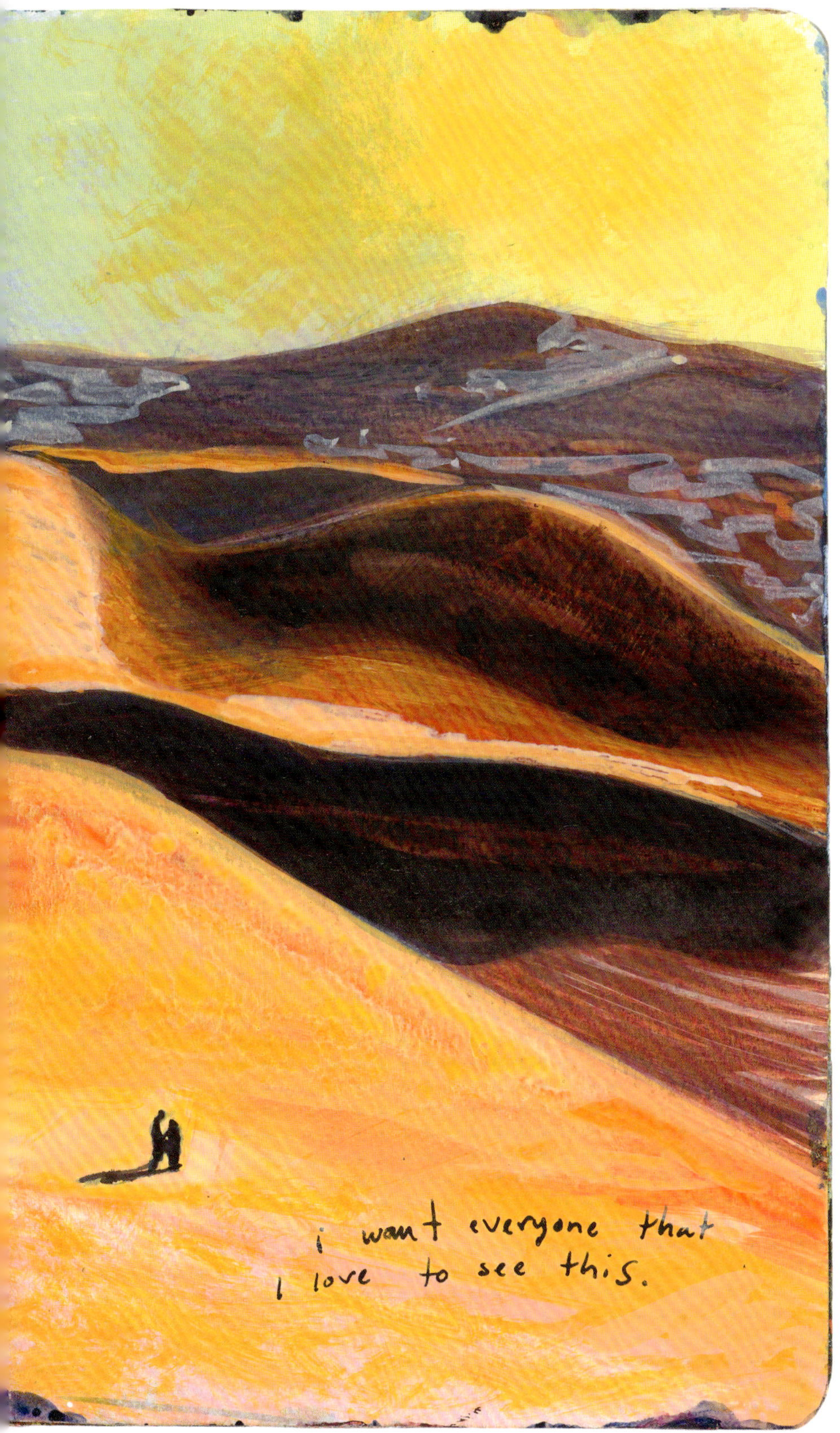
i want everyone that
i love to see this.

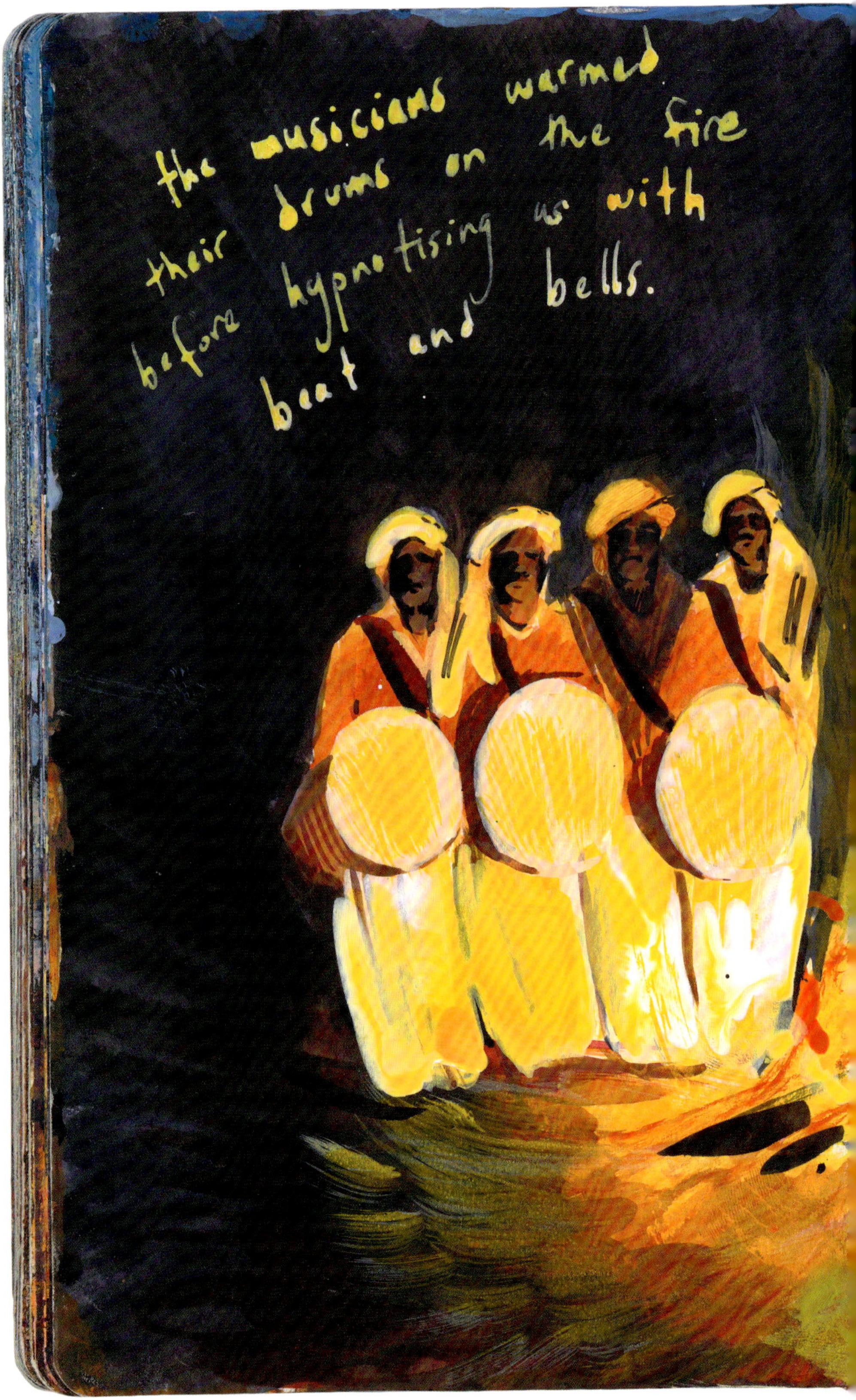

the musicians warmed
their drums on the fire
before hypnotising us with
beat and bells.

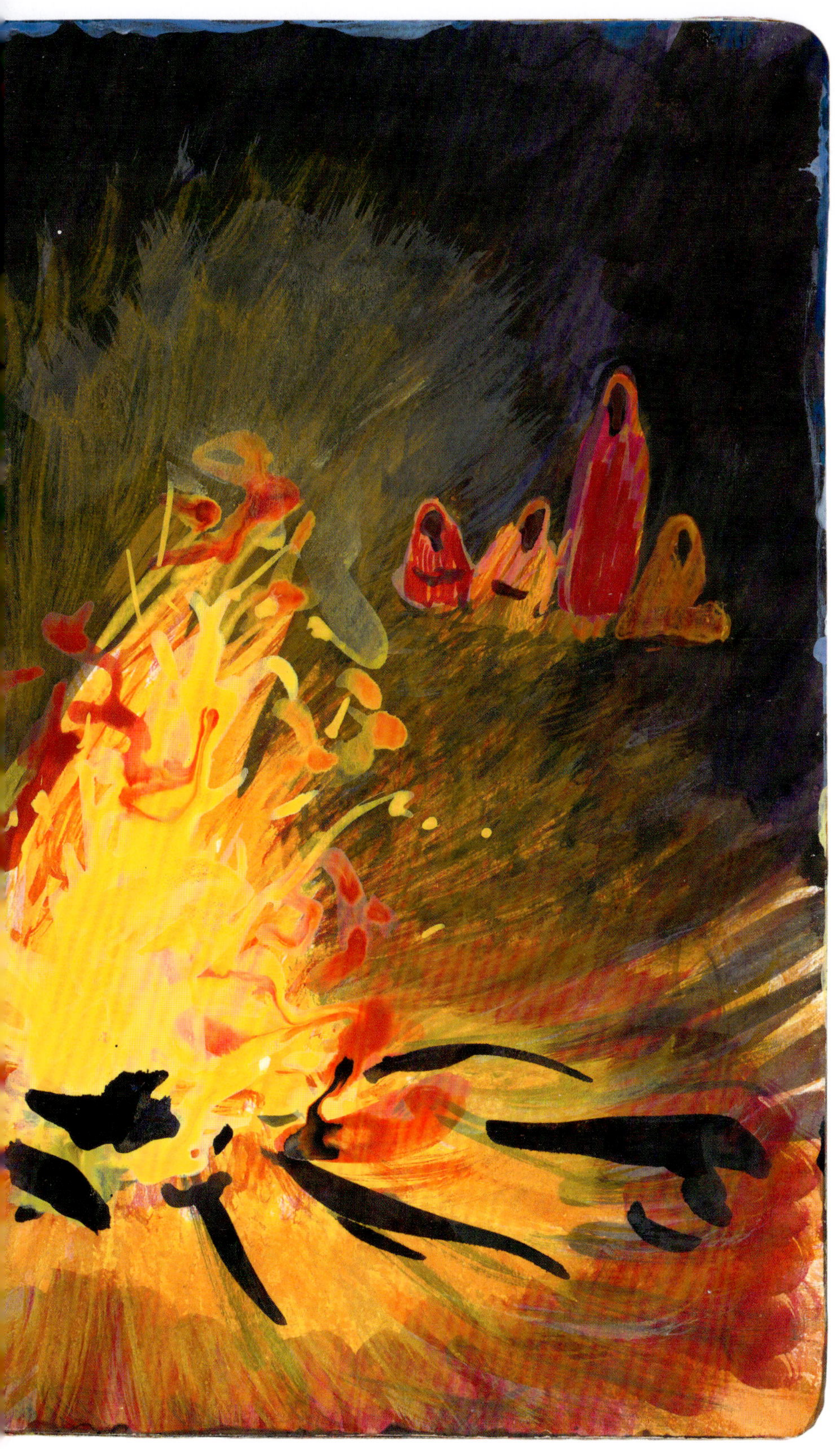

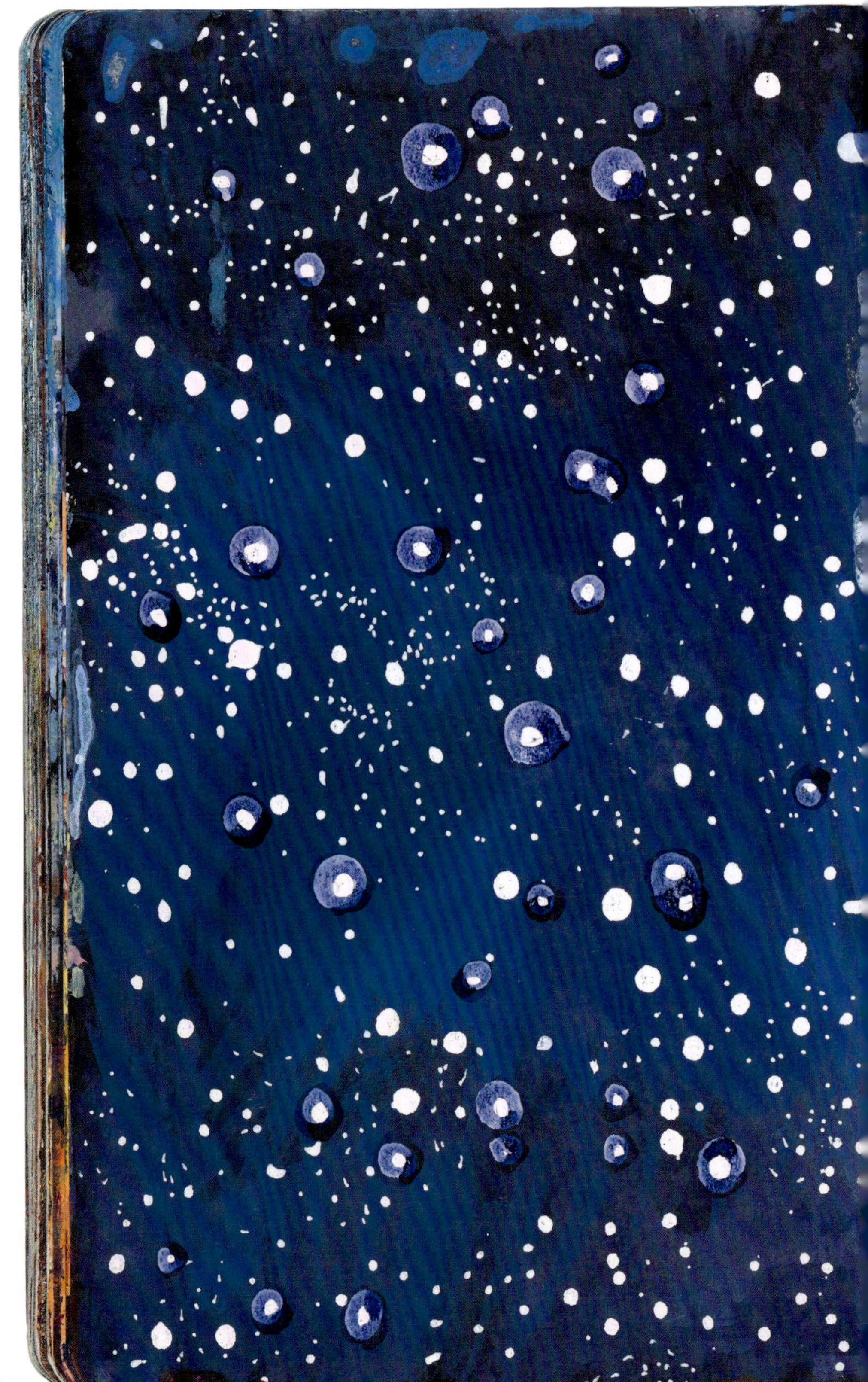

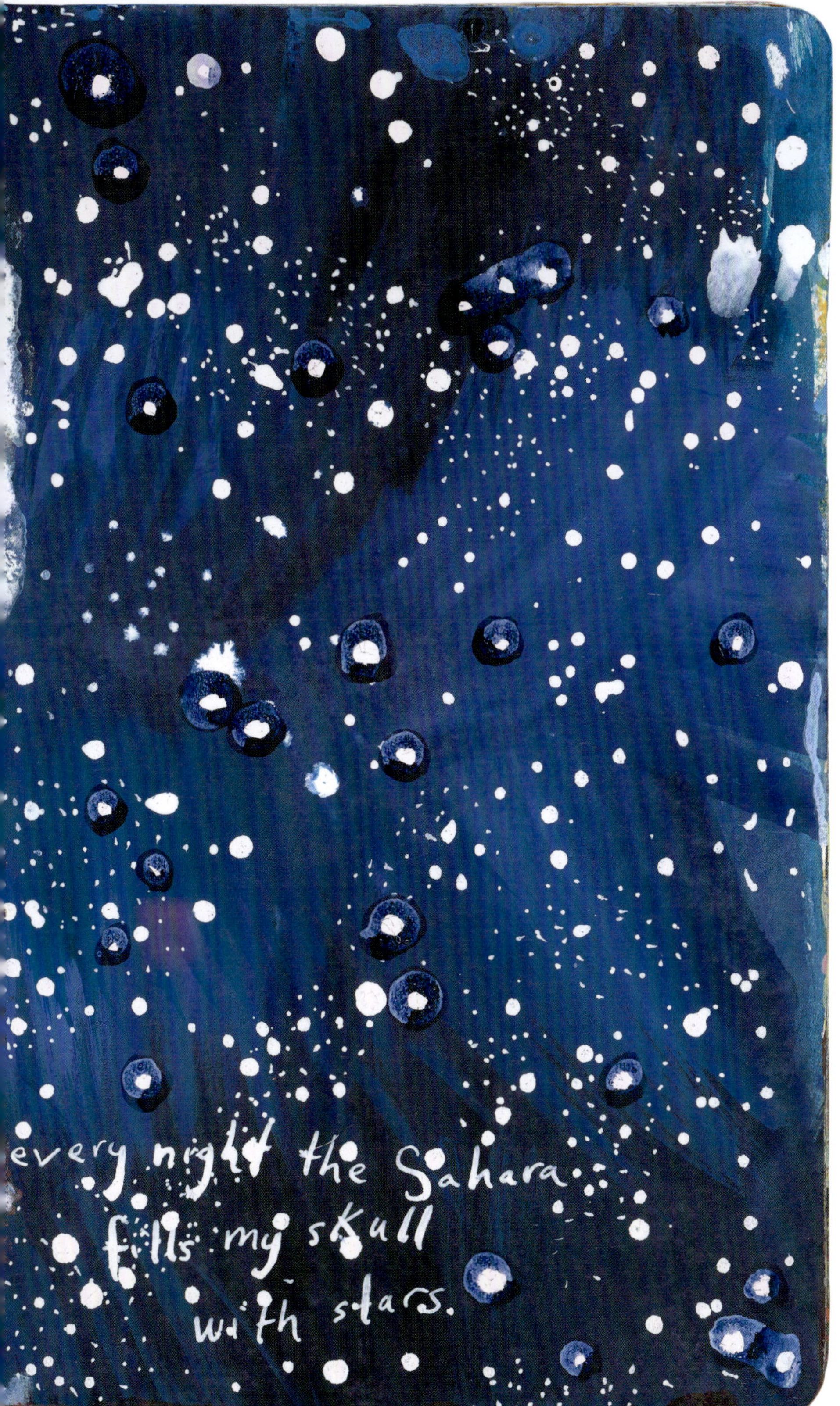
every night the Sahara
fills my skull
with stars.

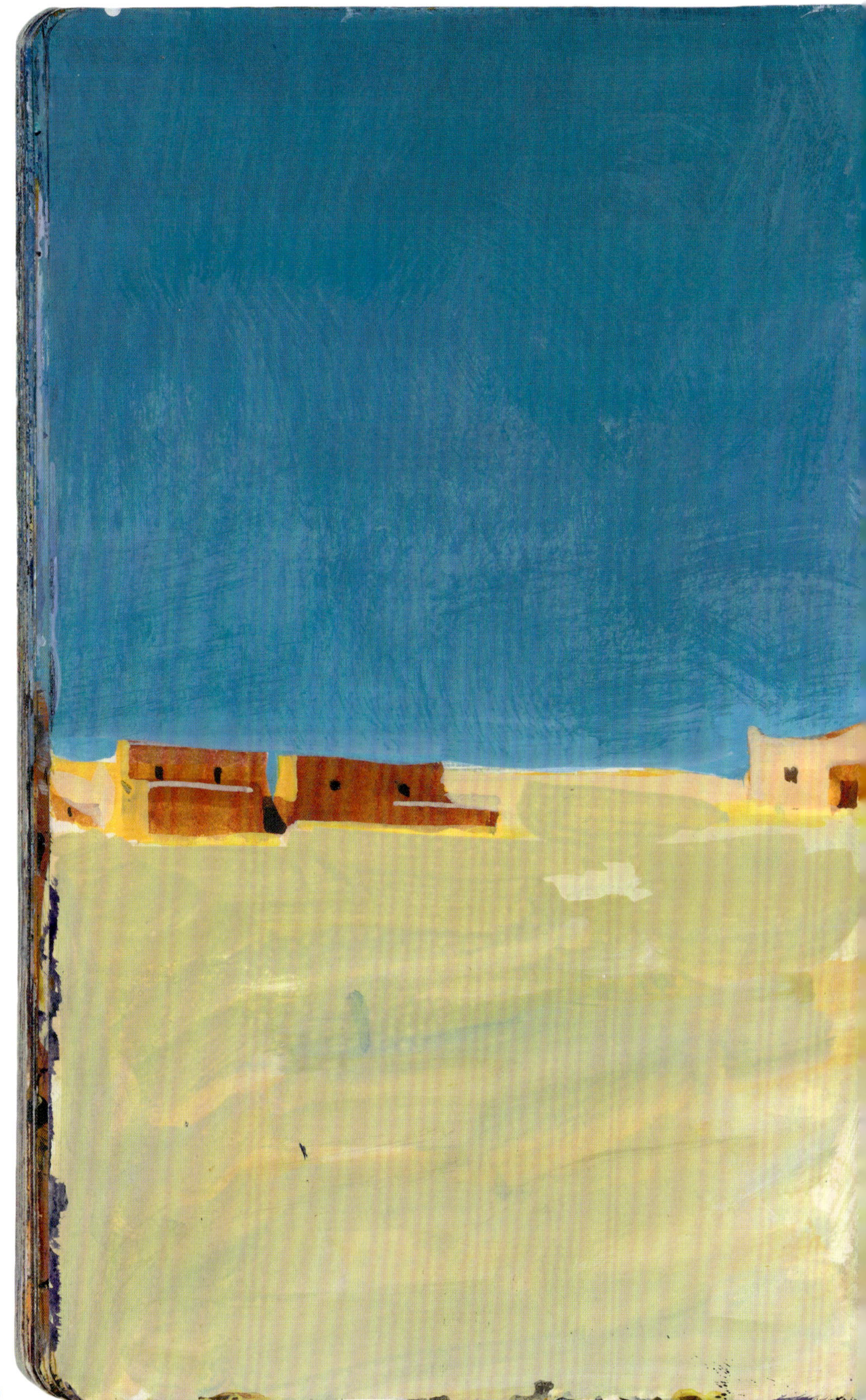

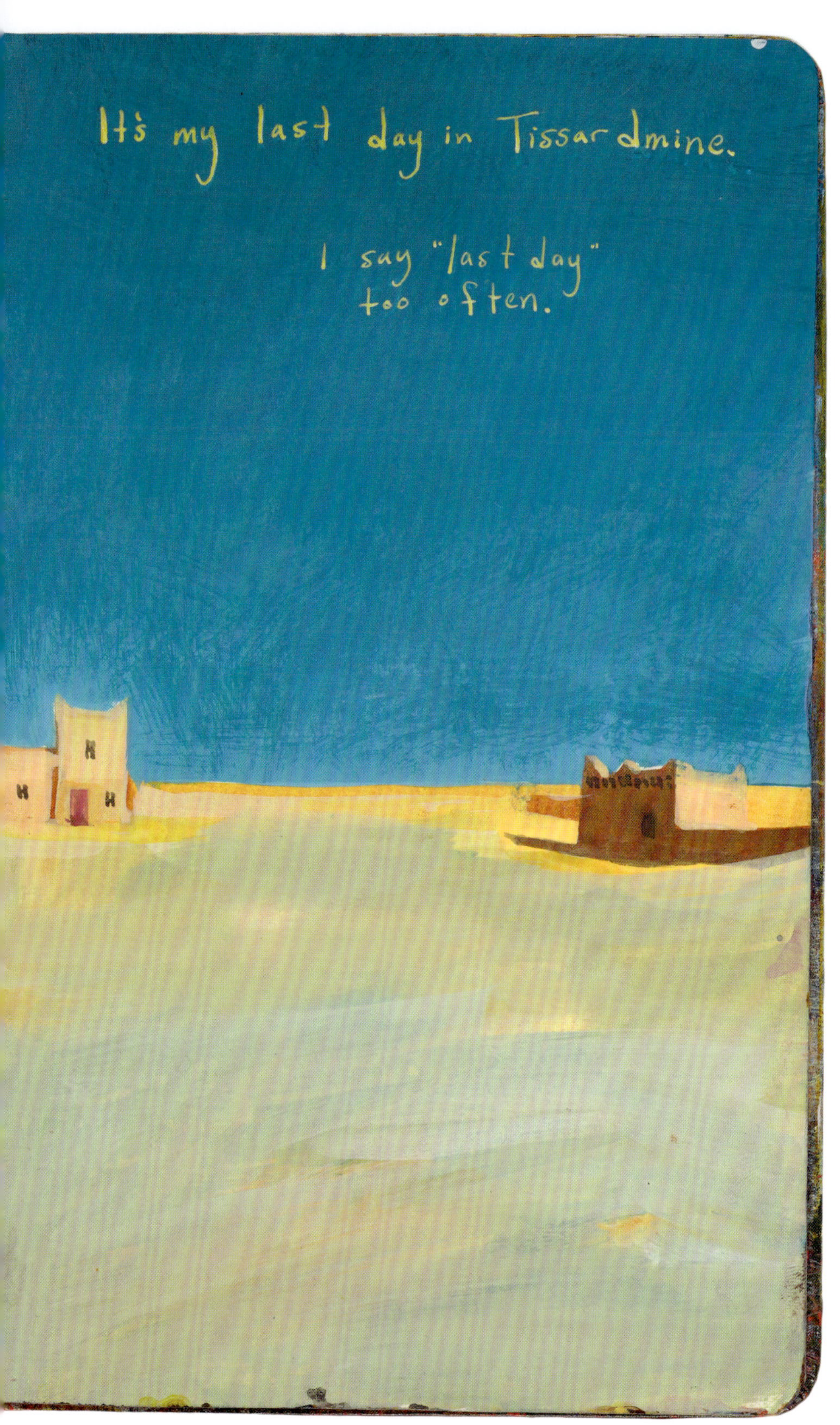
It's my last day in Tissardmine.

I say "last day"
too often.

It's my last day in Tissardmine.

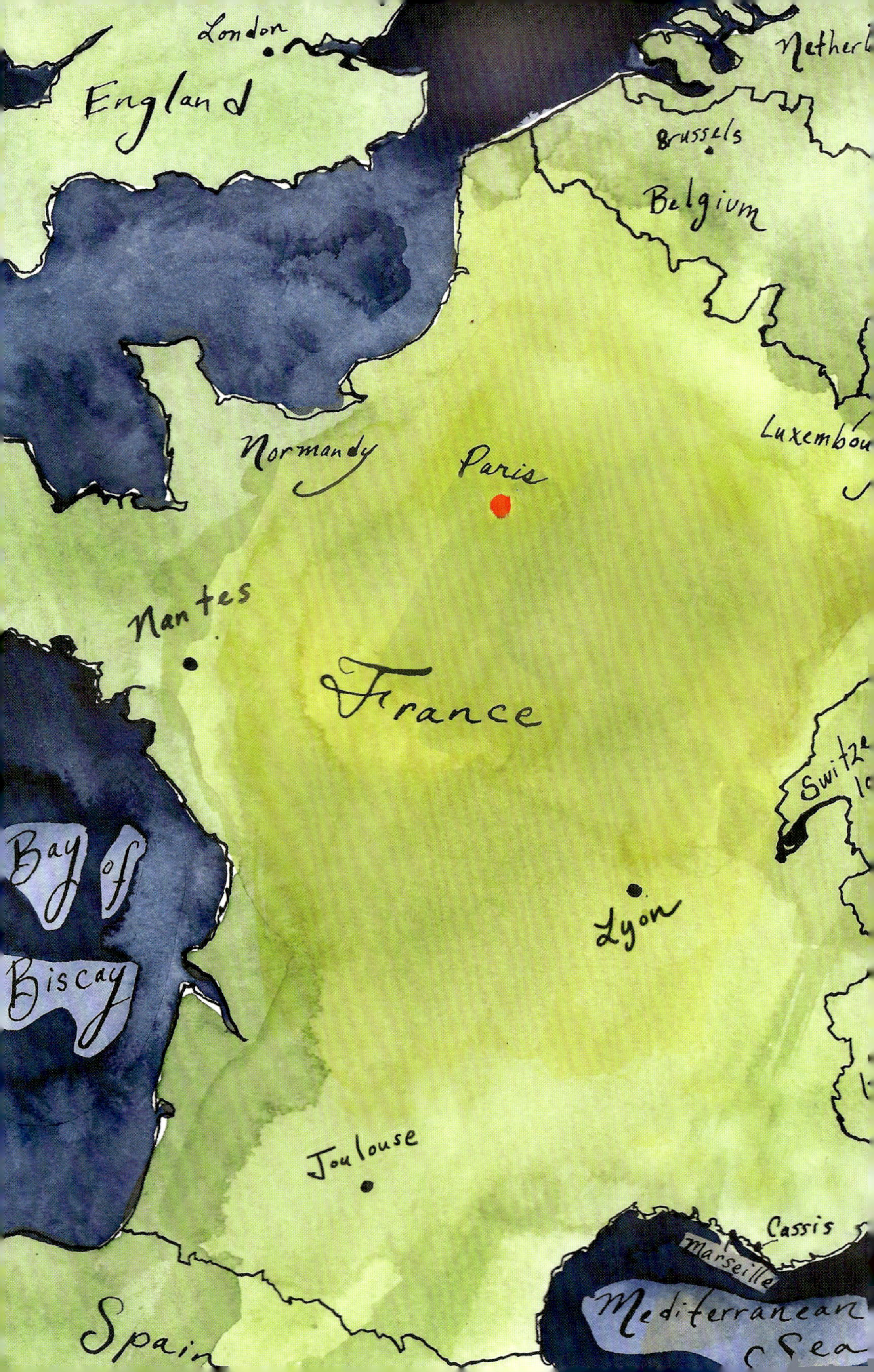

London
England
Netherl
Brussels
Belgium
Luxembou
Normandy
Paris
Nantes
France
Switze
lo
Bay of Biscay
Lyon
Joulouse
Cassis
Marseille
Mediterranean Sea
Spain

V
Paris, France

March 12th, 2015

"If you've romanticized Paris your whole life, it will disappoint you. If you're indifferent to the idea of Paris, it will blow you away." That's what my new lover told me when he invited me to stay with him in France's capital. I'd never had an interest in visiting Paris before dating a student at Sciences Po, but he was right: I'm blown away.

The closest cemetery to our apartment is Passy Cemetery. The doors to several underground crypts are swung ajar, beckoning visitors inside. One mausoleum has placed an ominous, dusty chair beside a sarcophagus, in case you want to stay a while for a conversation. I have returned to this mausoleum four times, daring myself to descend underground and take a seat. I get halfway down the staircase and chicken out every time, terrified that the mausoleum door will close and an apparition will appear.

colors:

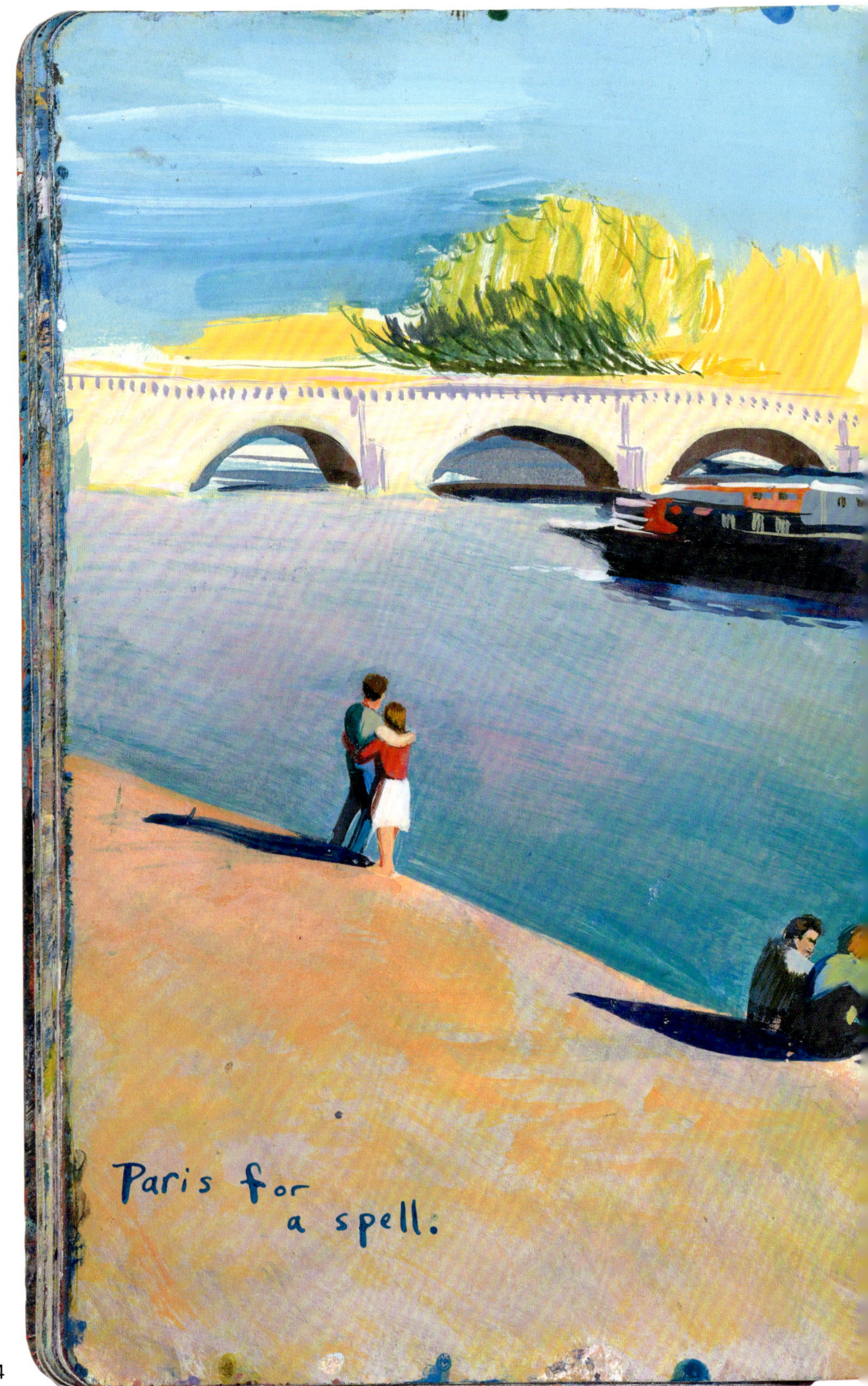

Paris for
a spell.

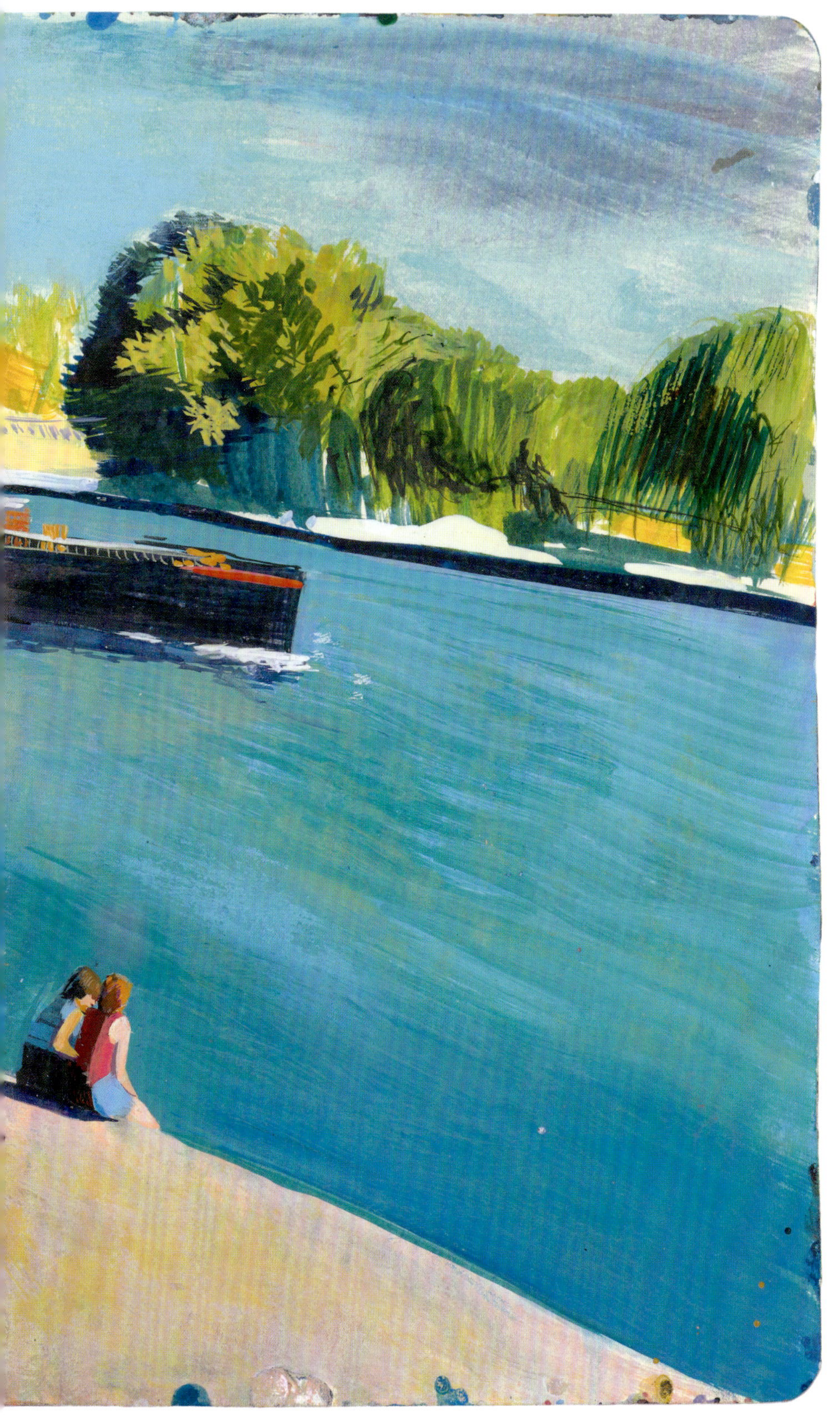

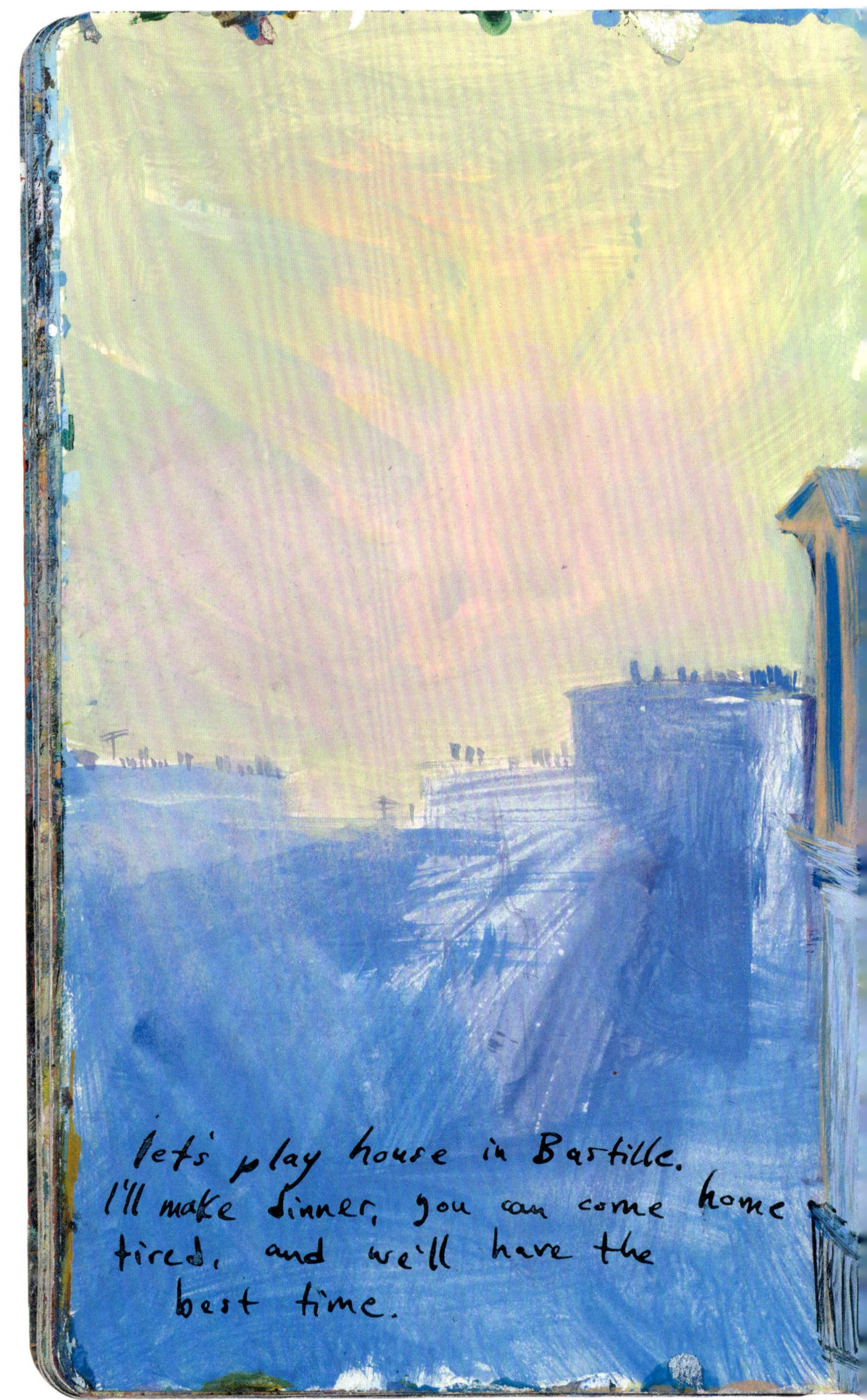
let's play house in Bastille.
I'll make dinner, you can come home
tired, and we'll have the
best time.

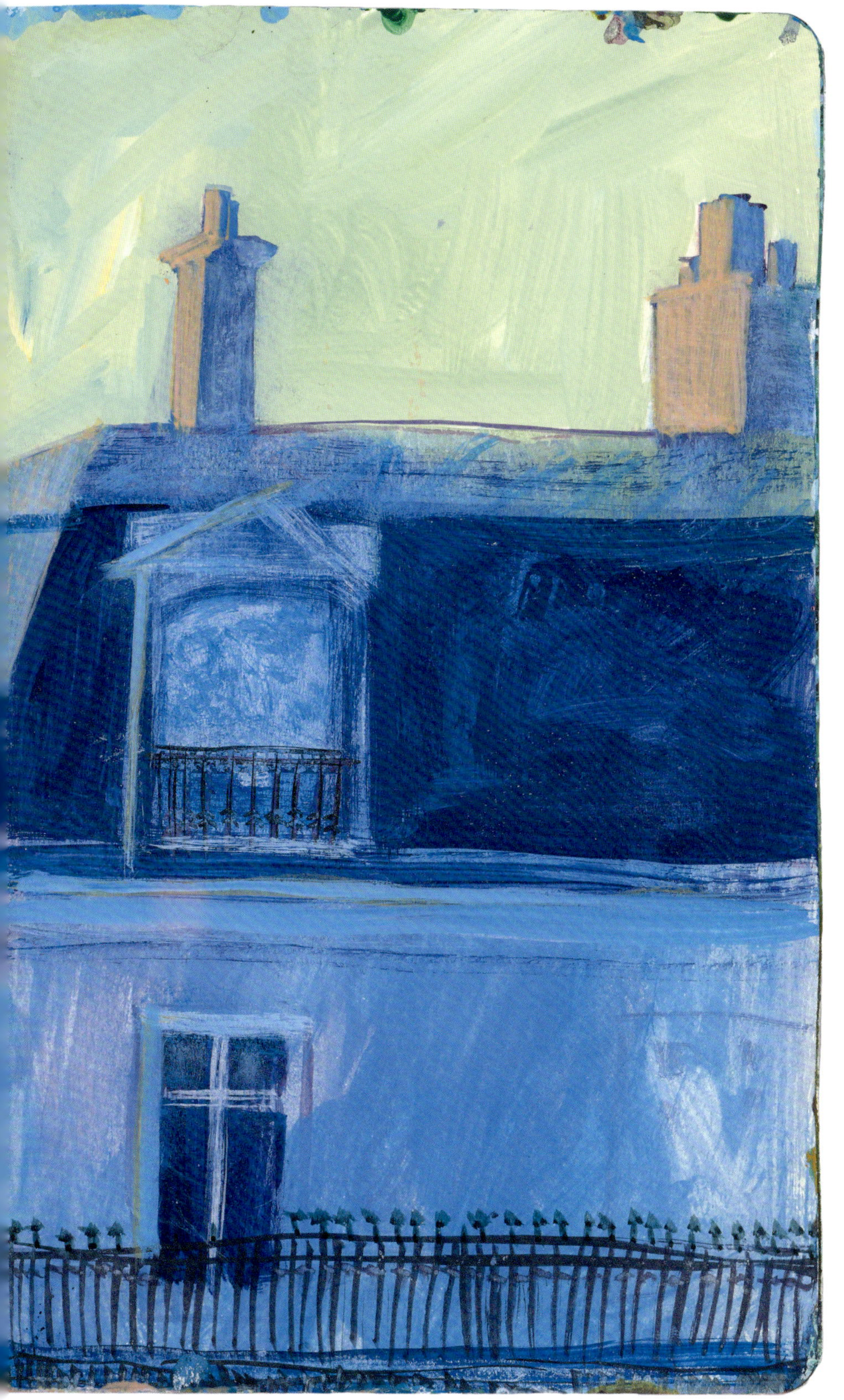

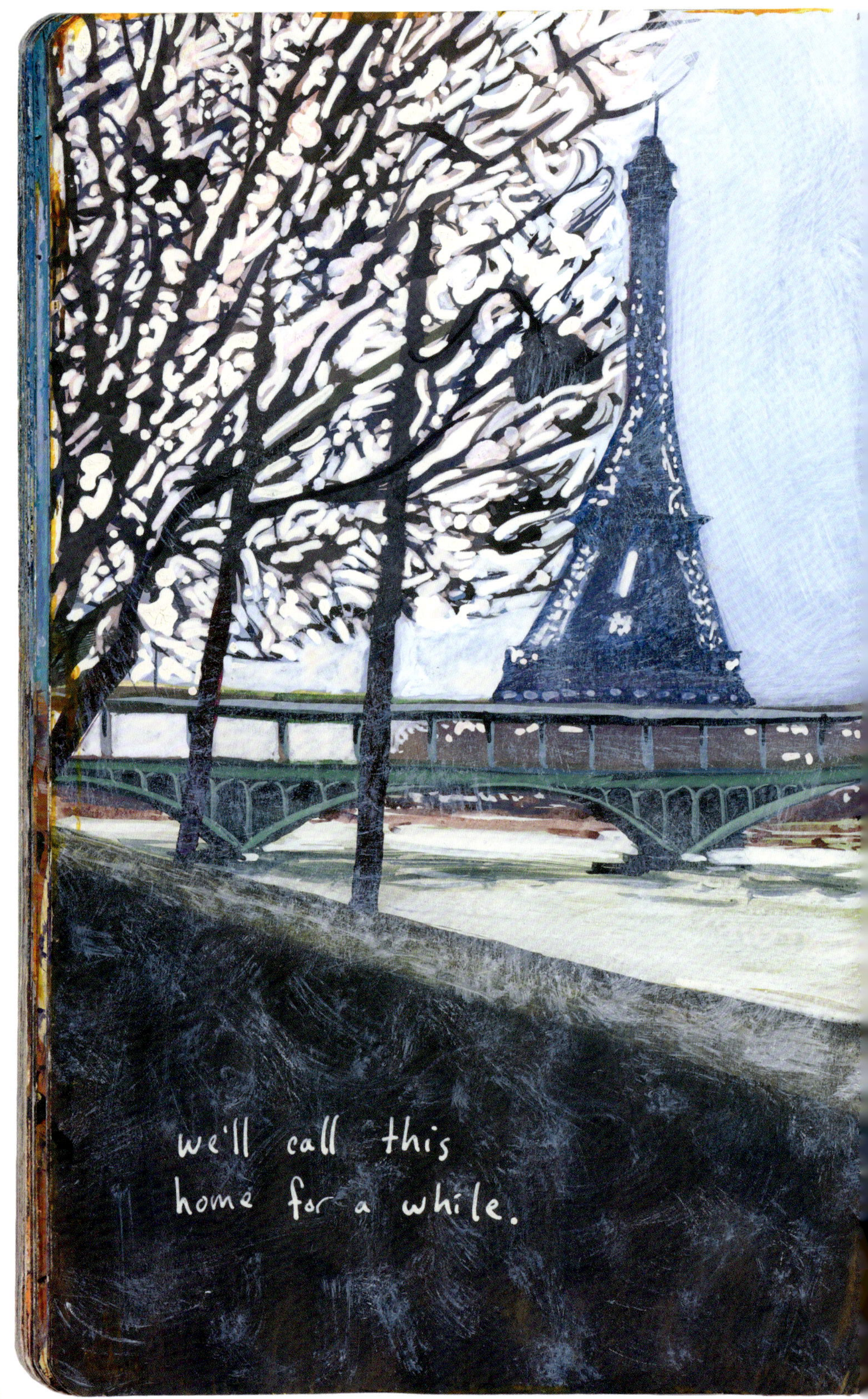
we'll call this
home for a while.

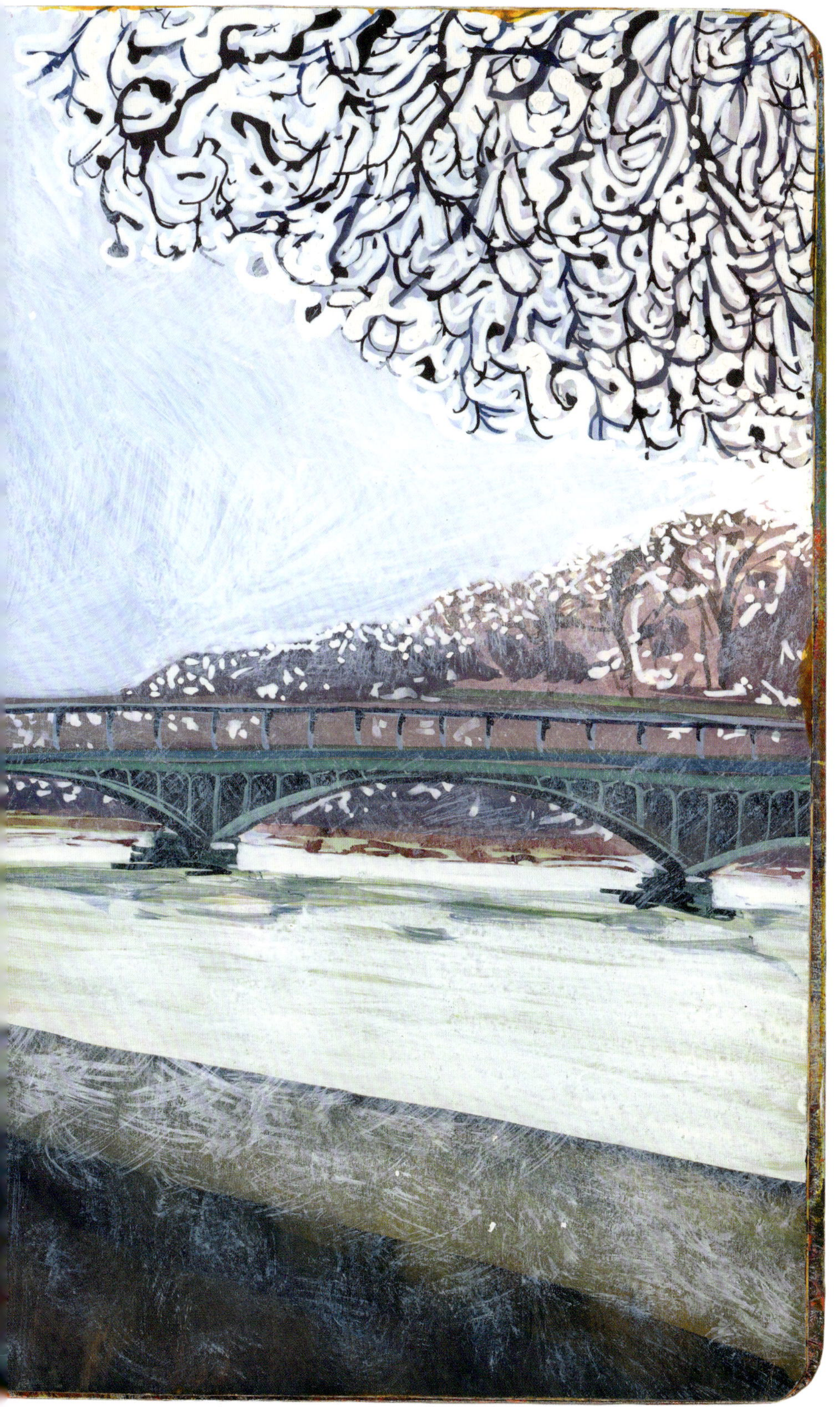

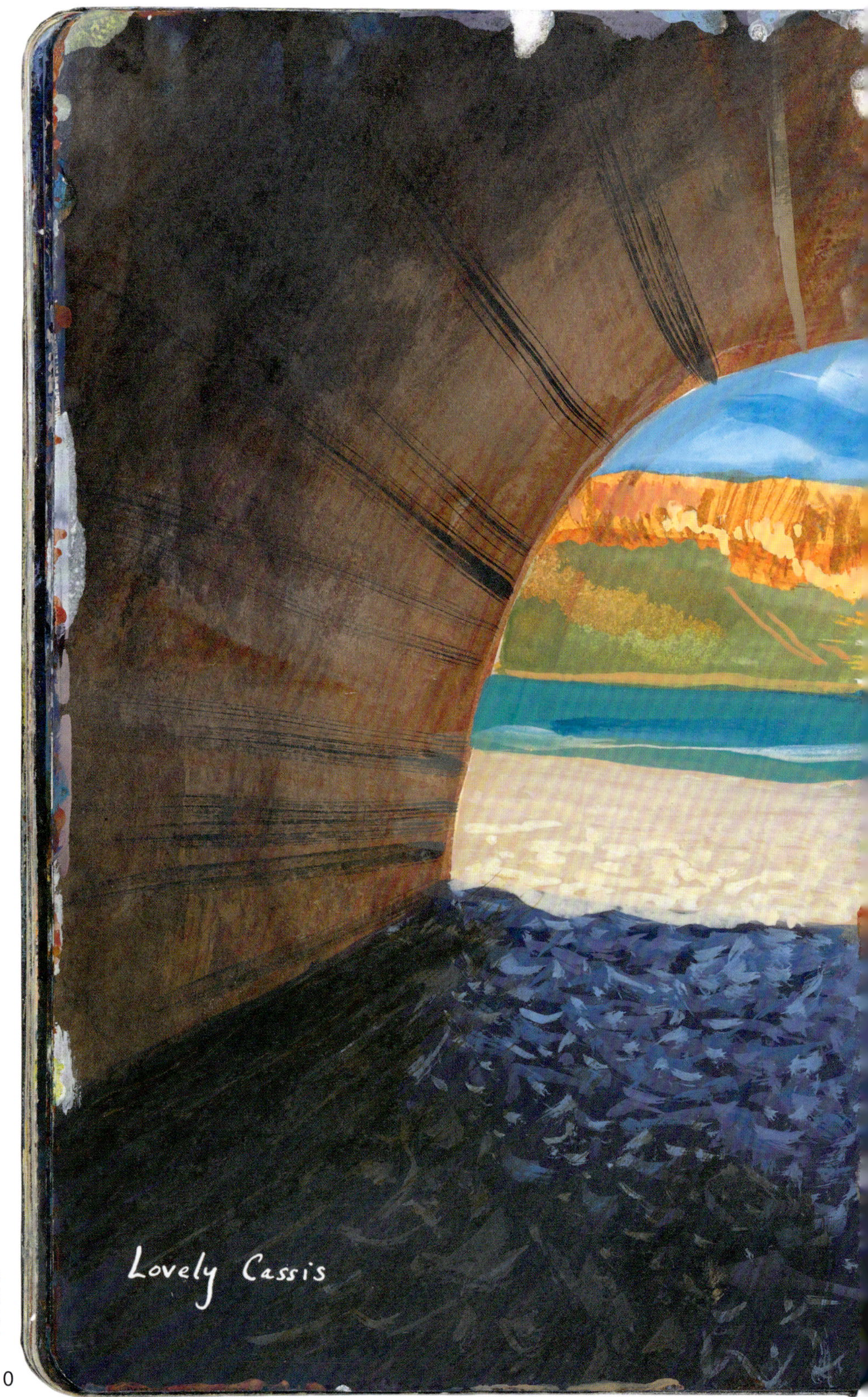

Lovely Cassis

remember this.
remember this.
remember this.

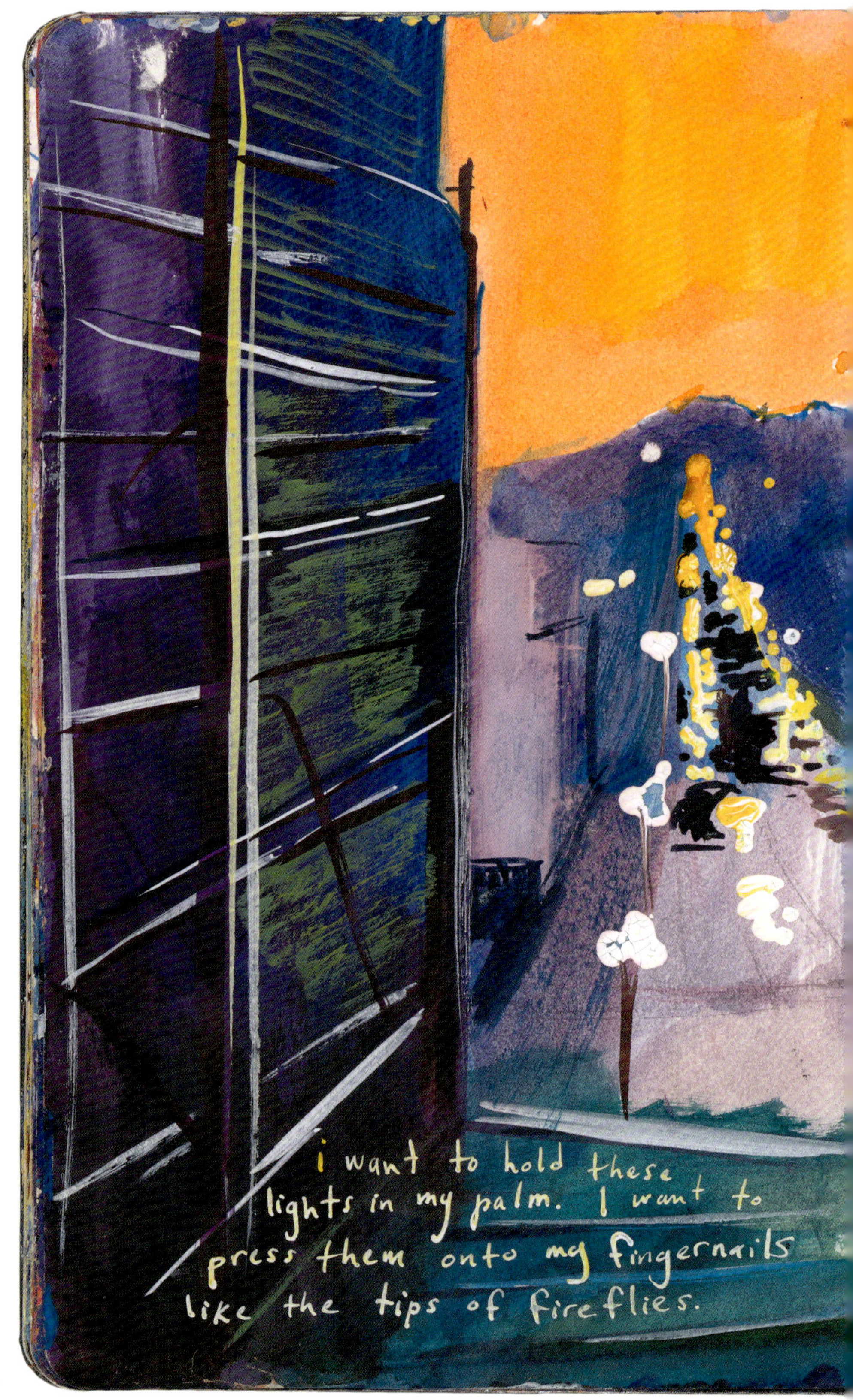

i want to hold these
lights in my palm. I want to
press them onto my fingernails
like the tips of fireflies.

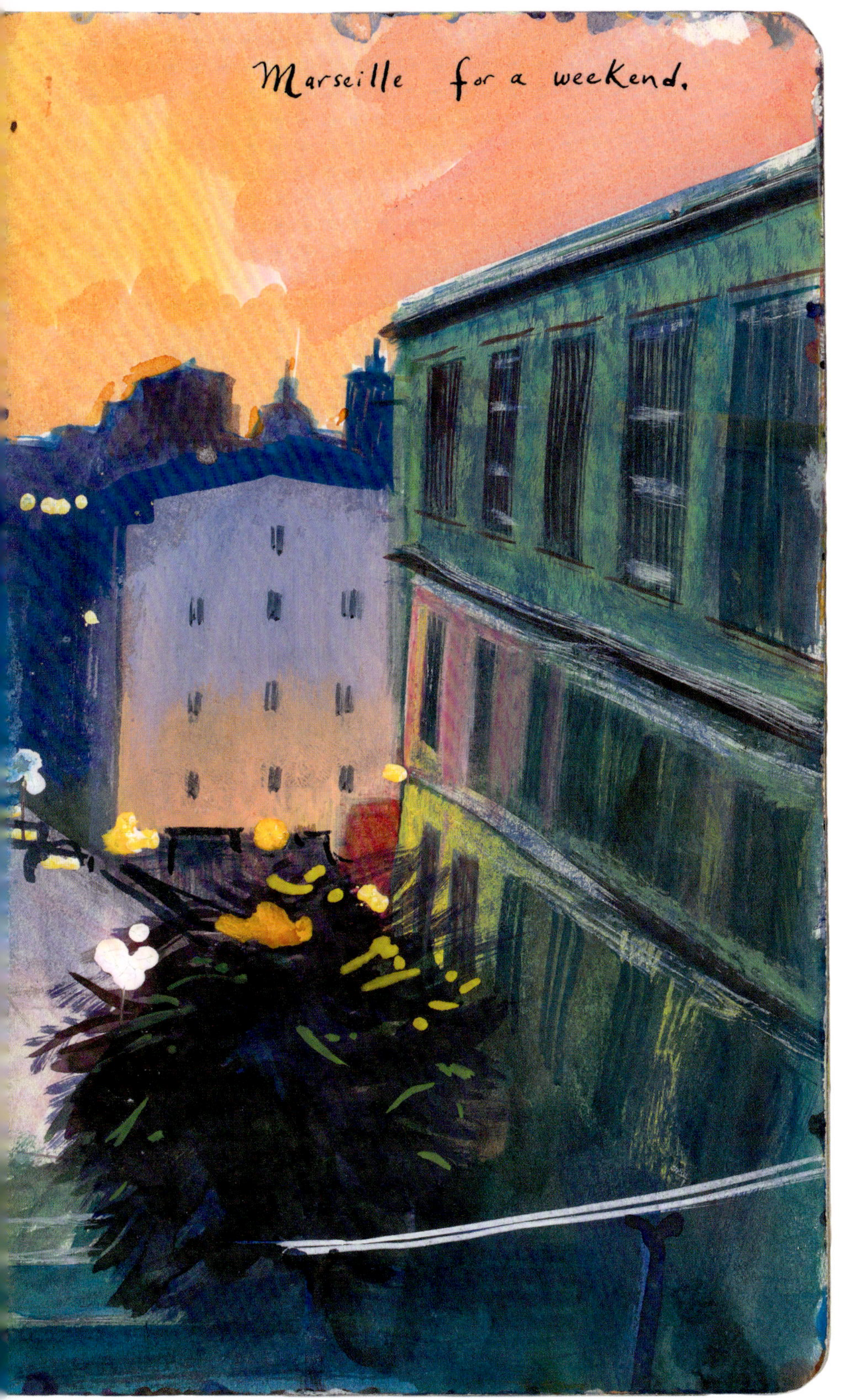
Marseille for a weekend.

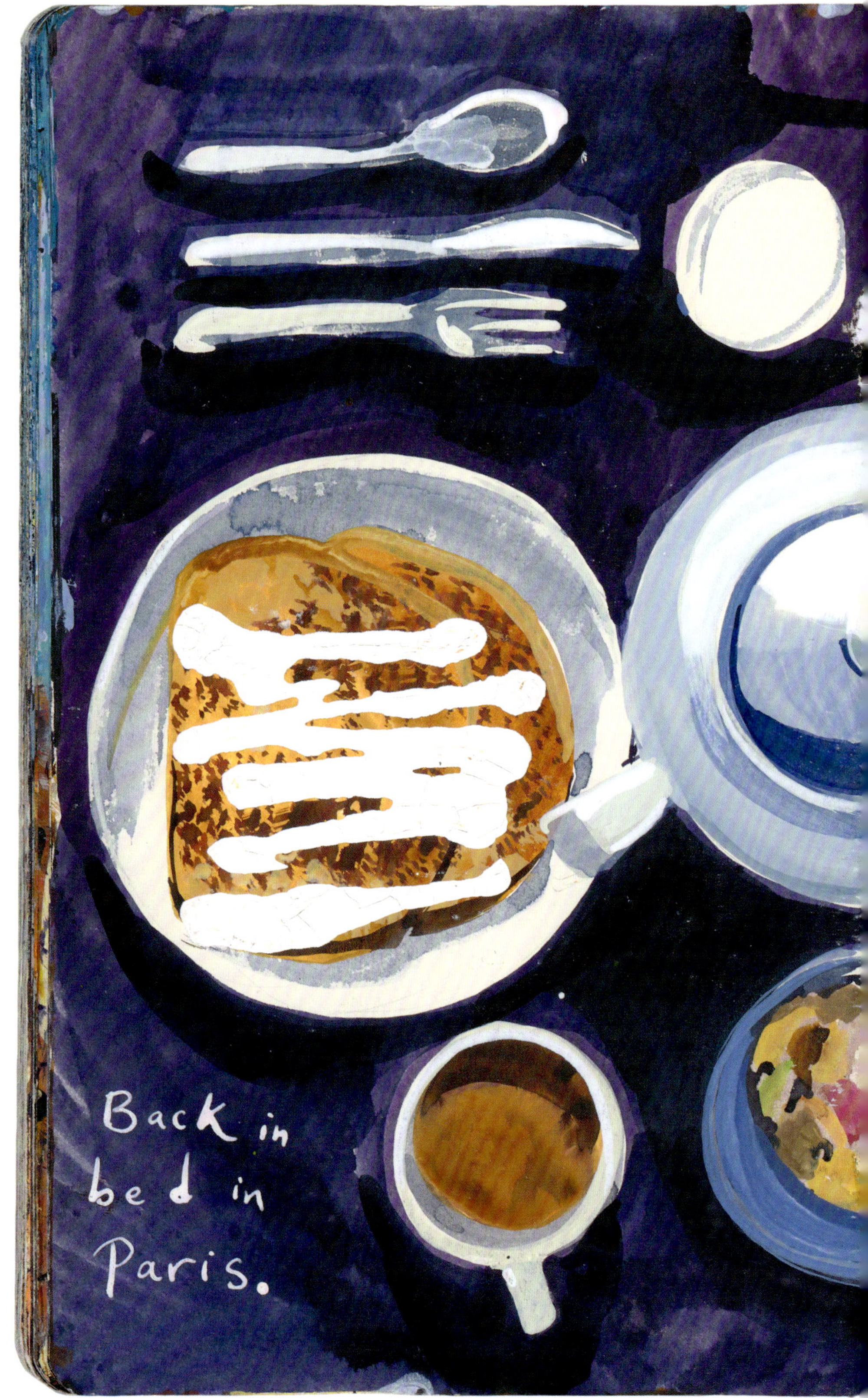

Back in
bed in
Paris.

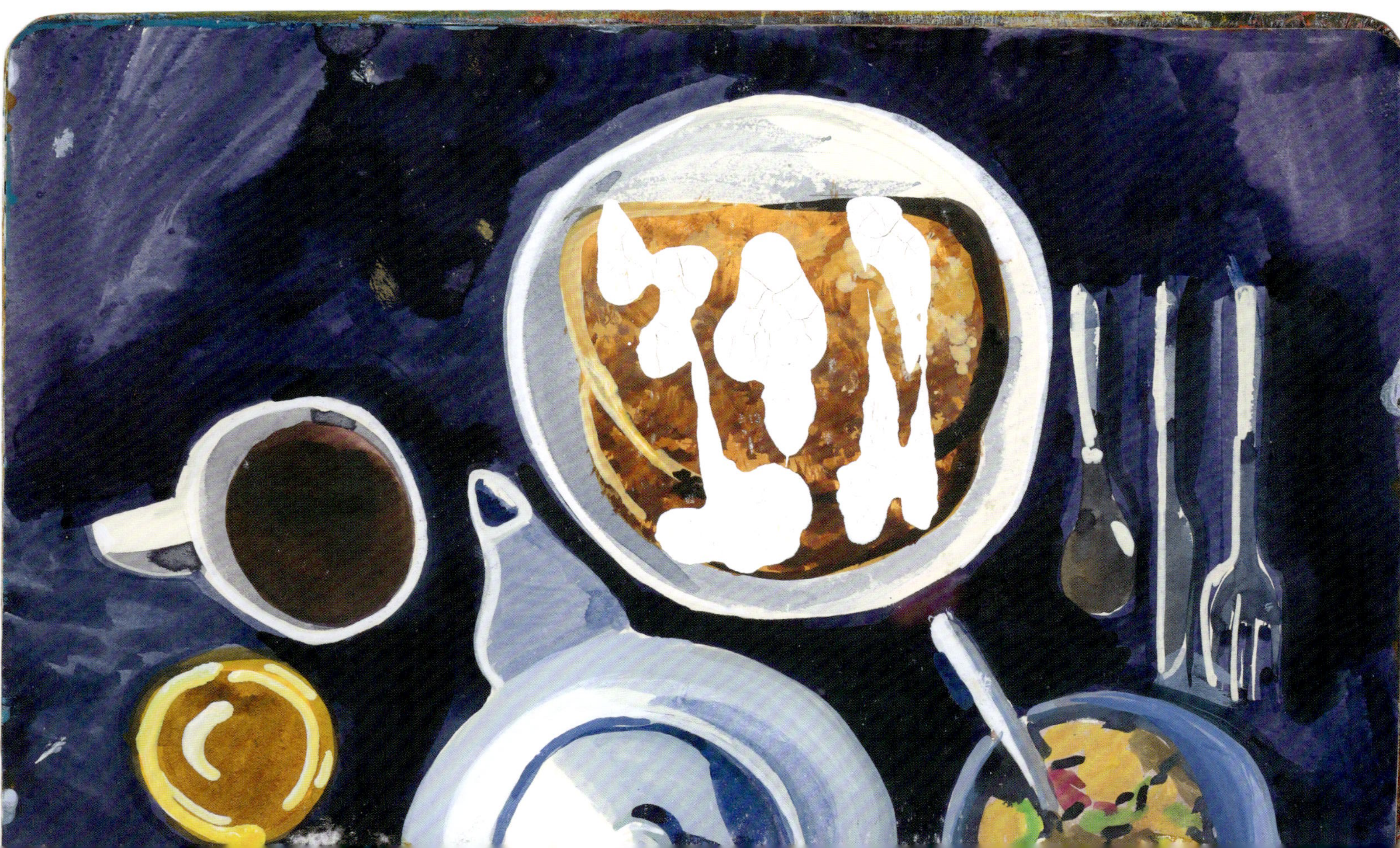

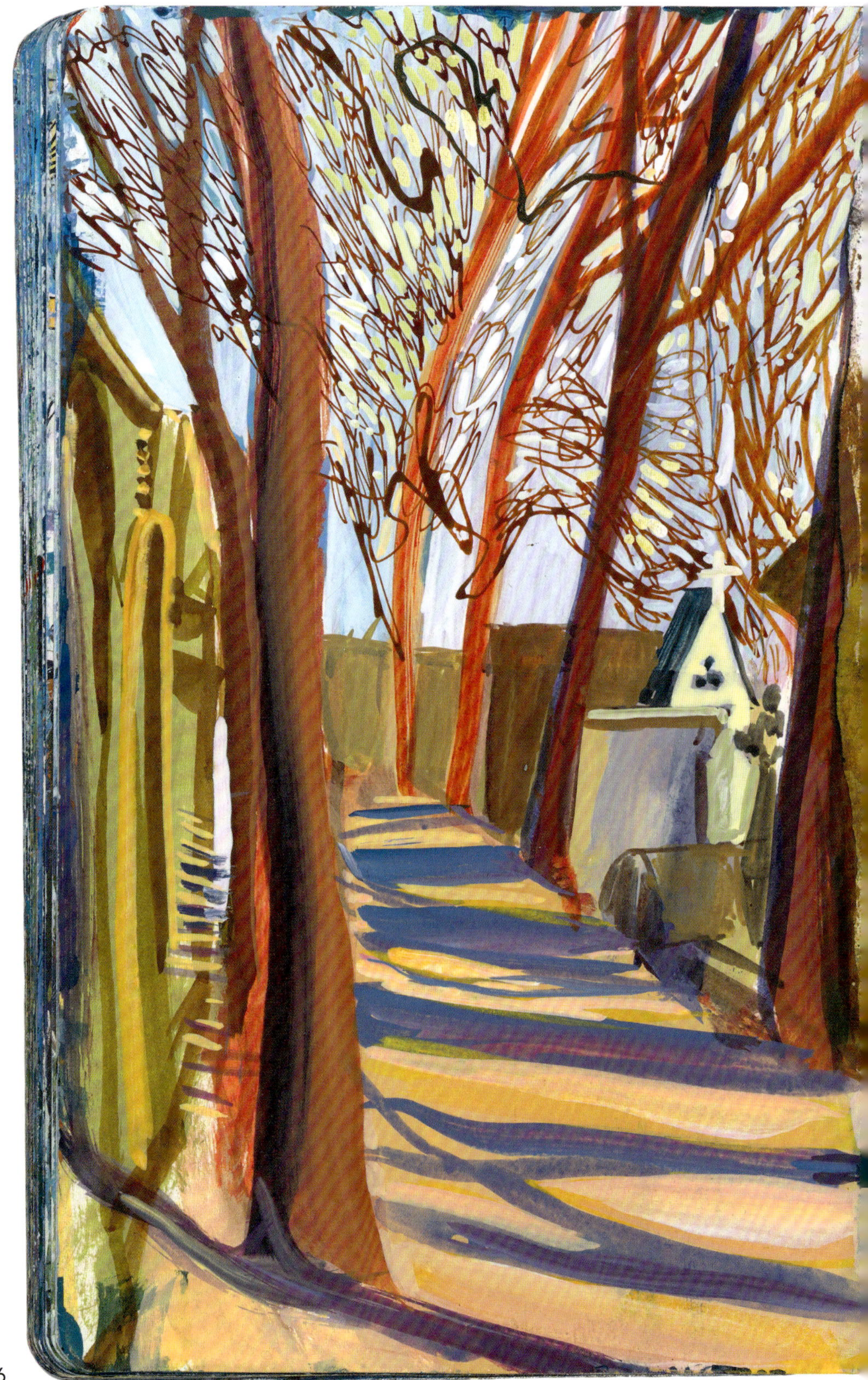

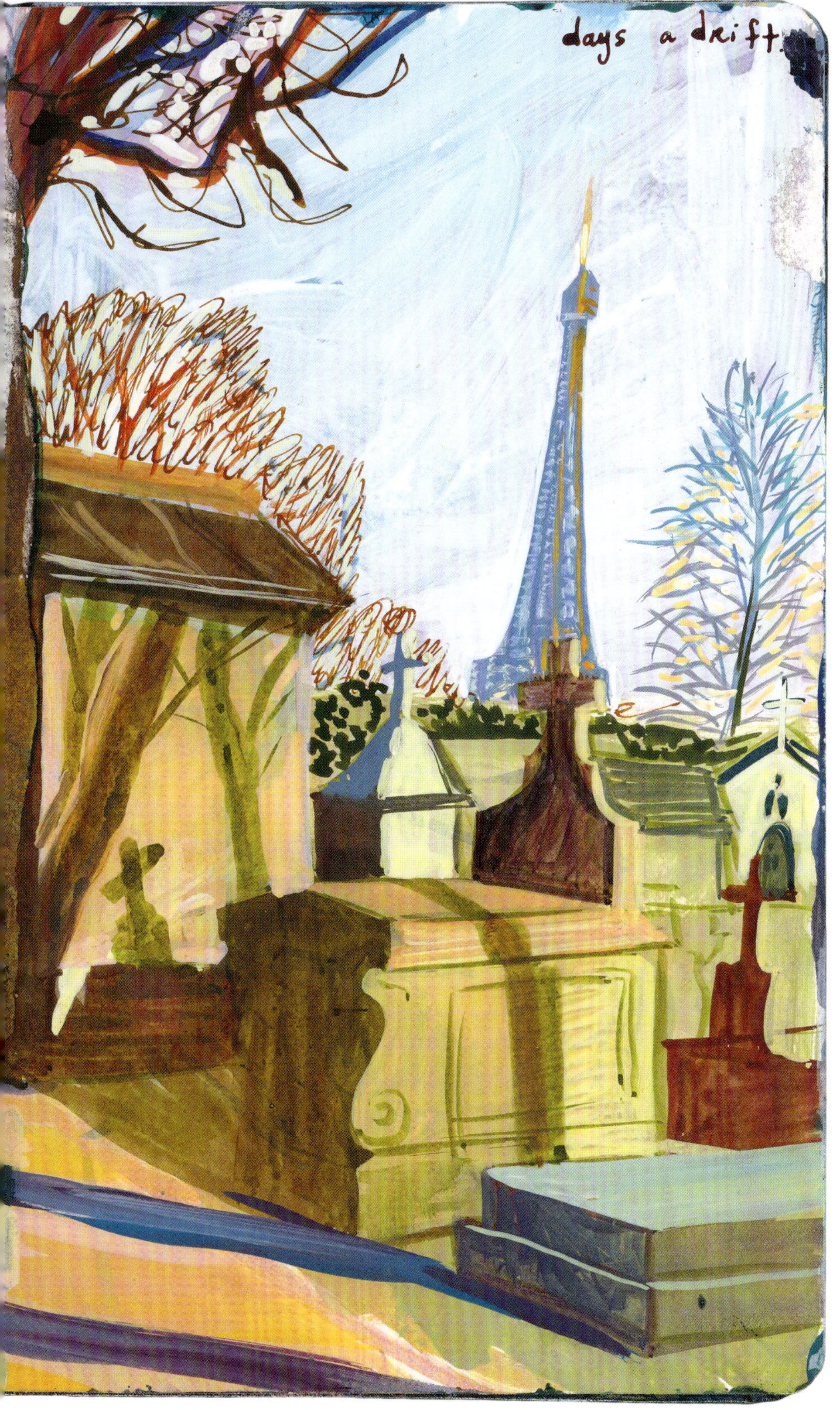
days a drift.

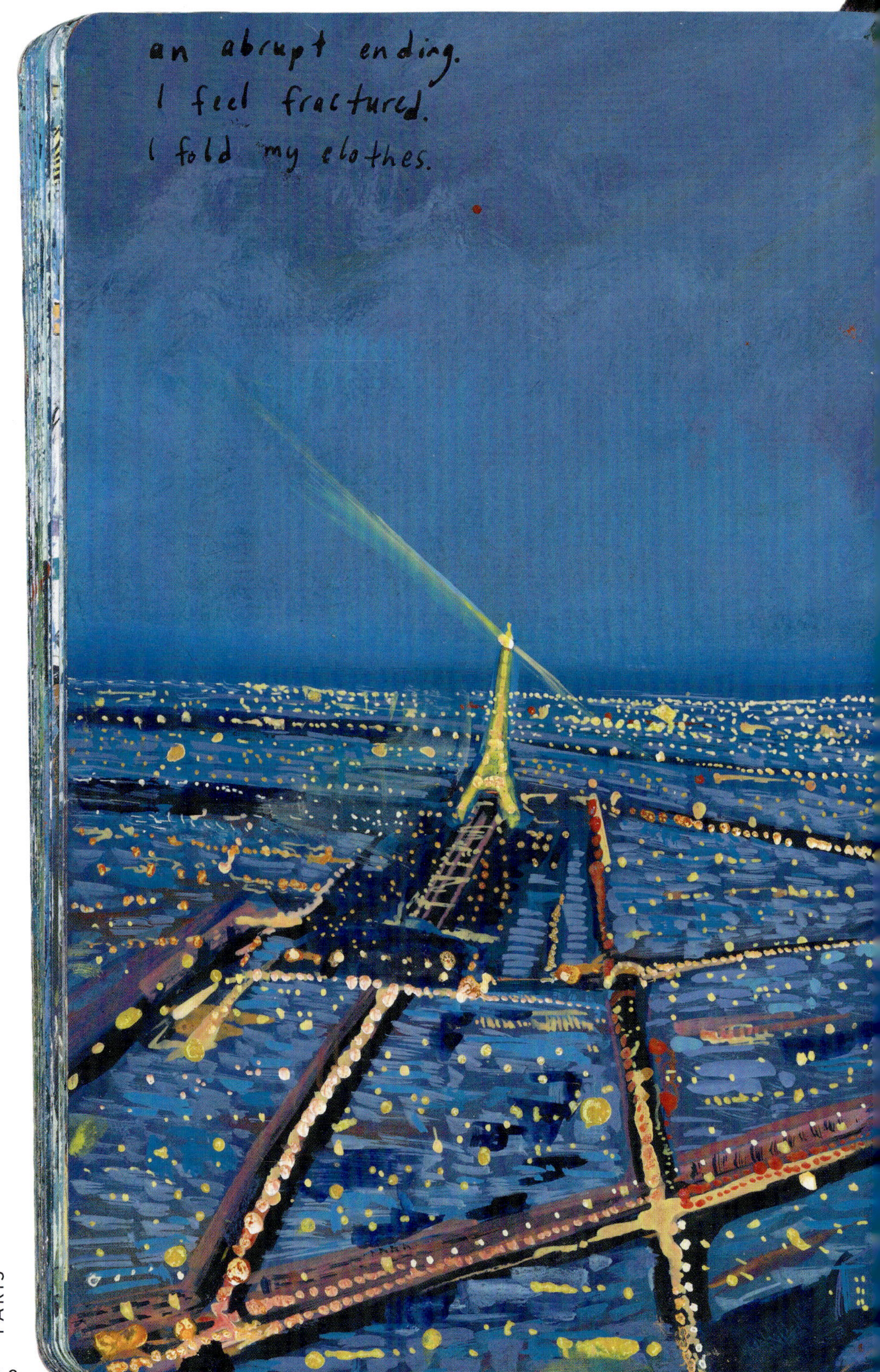

an abrupt ending.
I feel fractured.
I fold my clothes.

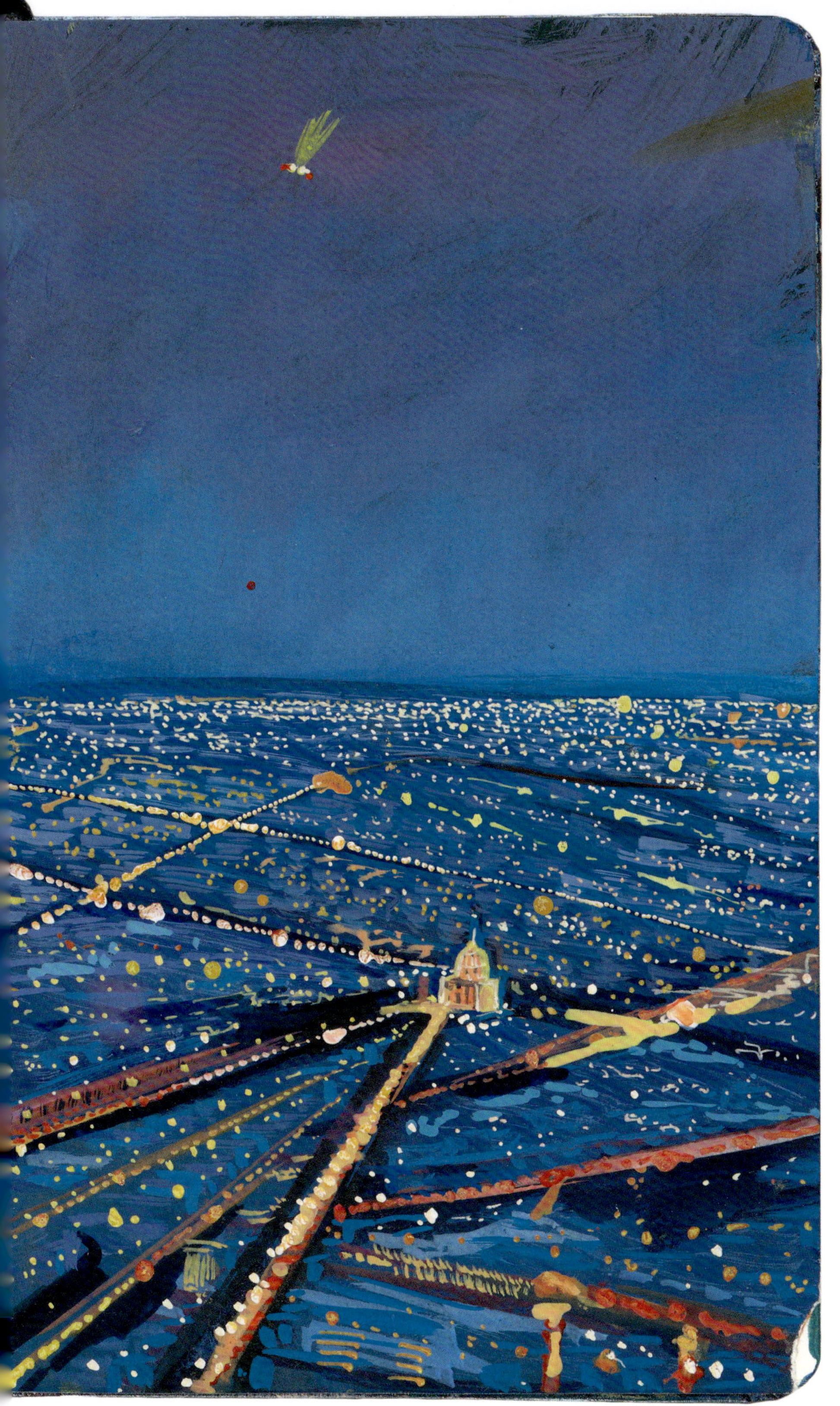

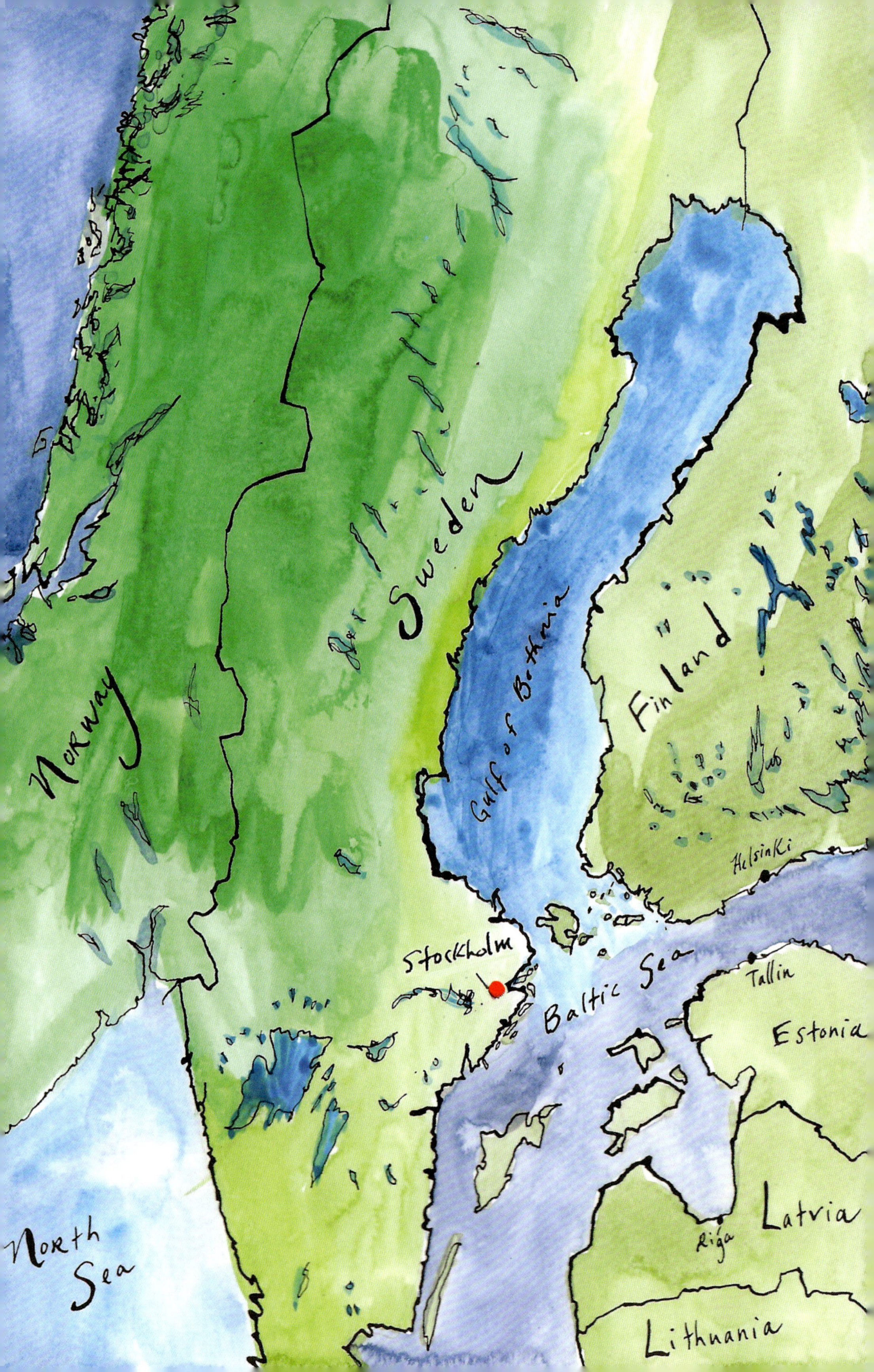

Norway
Sweden
Finland
Gulf of Bothnia
Helsinki
Stockholm
Baltic Sea
Tallin
Estonia
North Sea
Riga
Latvia
Lithuania

VI

Stockholm, Sweden

May 29th, 2016

I've given myself a week to enjoy Stockholm before continuing on to Finland. I've been infatuated with Sweden ever since befriending a Swedish girl in middle school, Matilda. I was so jealous of her house, which was decorated with magical dala horses, comforting sheepskin rugs, and colorful wool sweaters. But Stockholm is so much more than the aforementioned objects. There is also buttercup sunlight, plentiful city parks, bobbing sailboats, and a sunset that lasts for hours.

Today, I was wandering aimlessly when I heard the most enchanting chamber music drifting on a warm breeze. I had nowhere else to be, so I followed its spell and was guided to the canary-yellow Hedvig Eleonora Church. A small orchestra was practicing with the doors and windows graciously flung open. I went inside to sit in the pews for a while to rest my legs and enjoy the stillness in my mind.

colors:

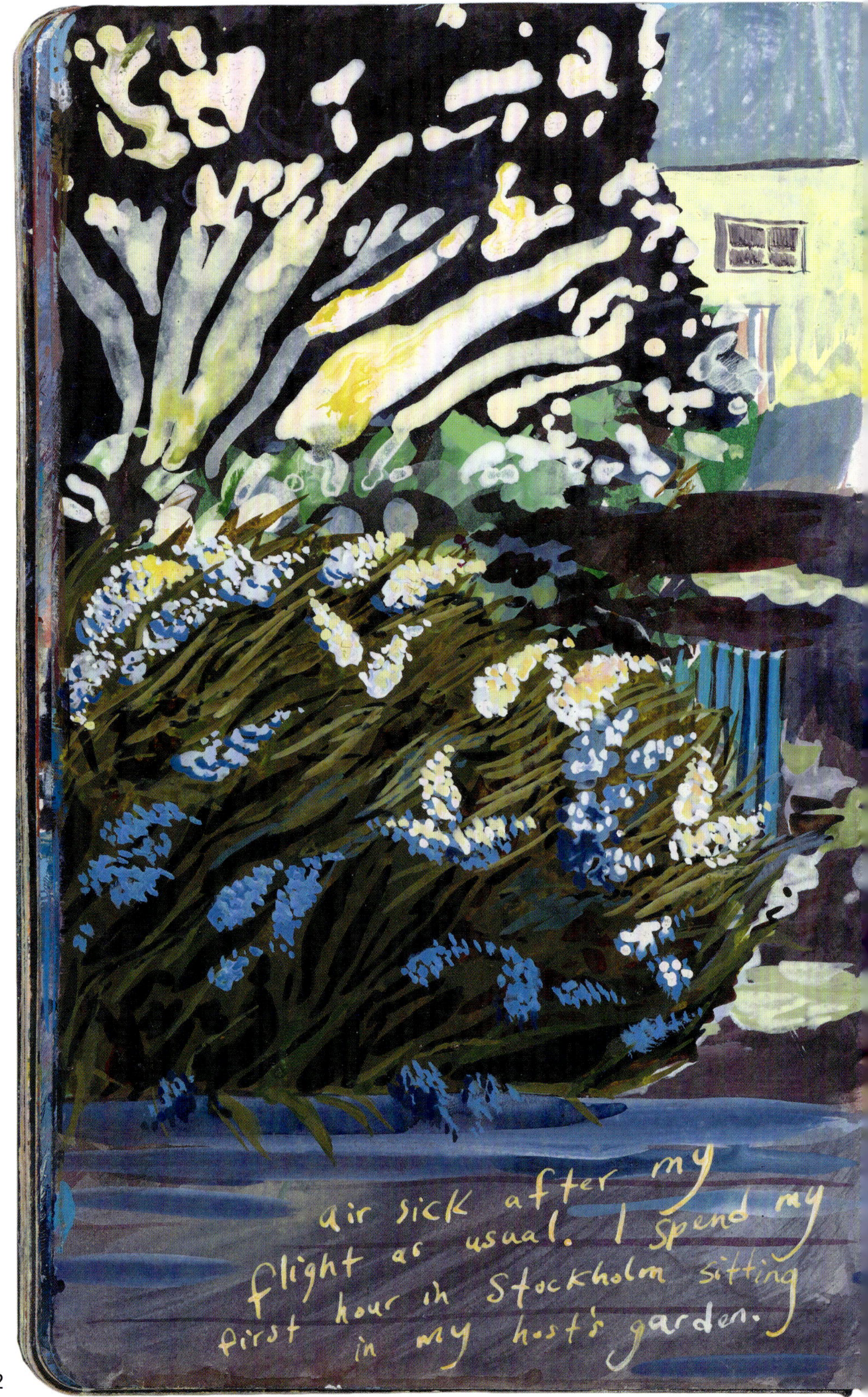

air sick after my
flight as usual. I spend my
first hour in Stockholm sitting
in my host's garden.

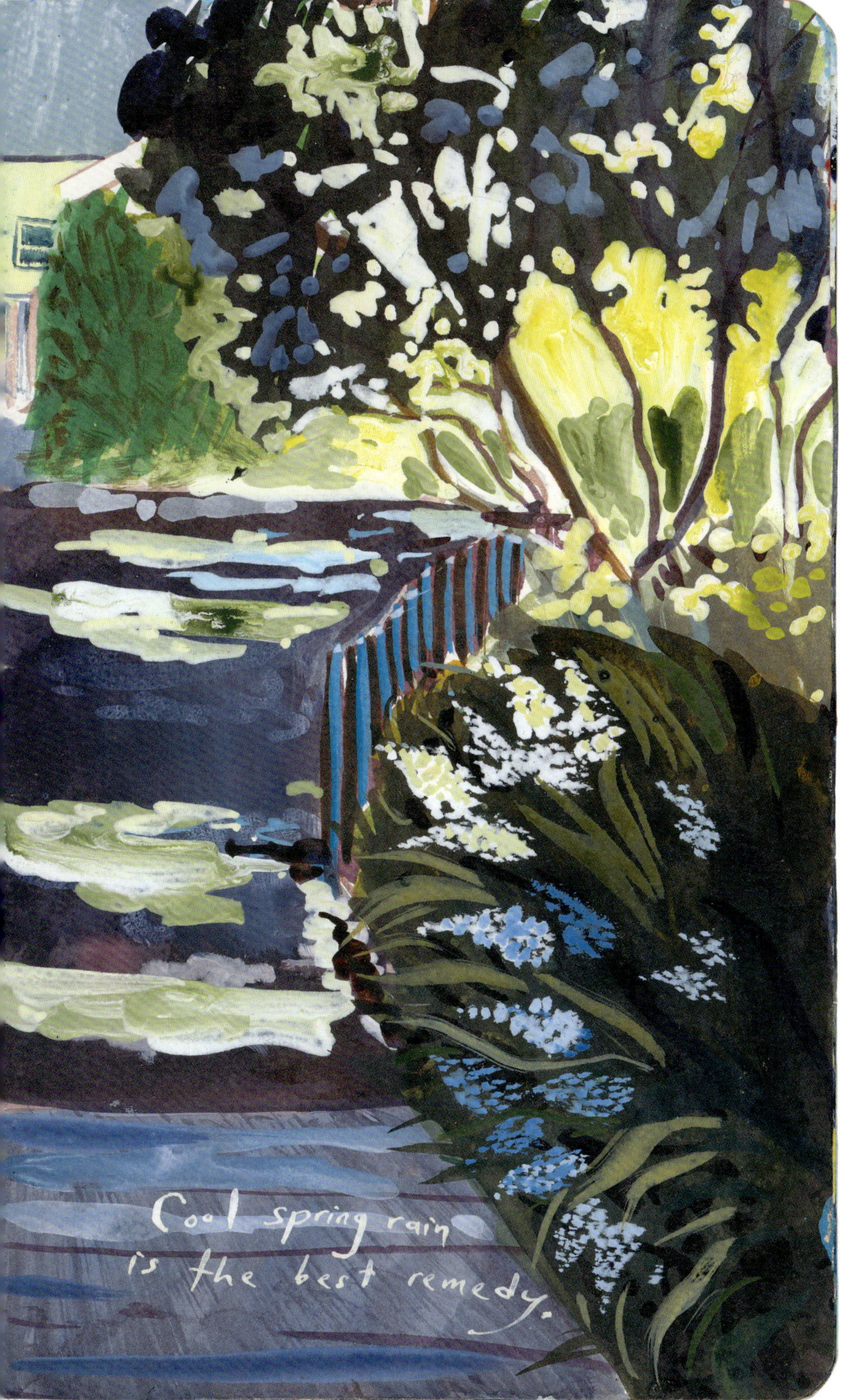
Cool spring rain
is the best remedy.

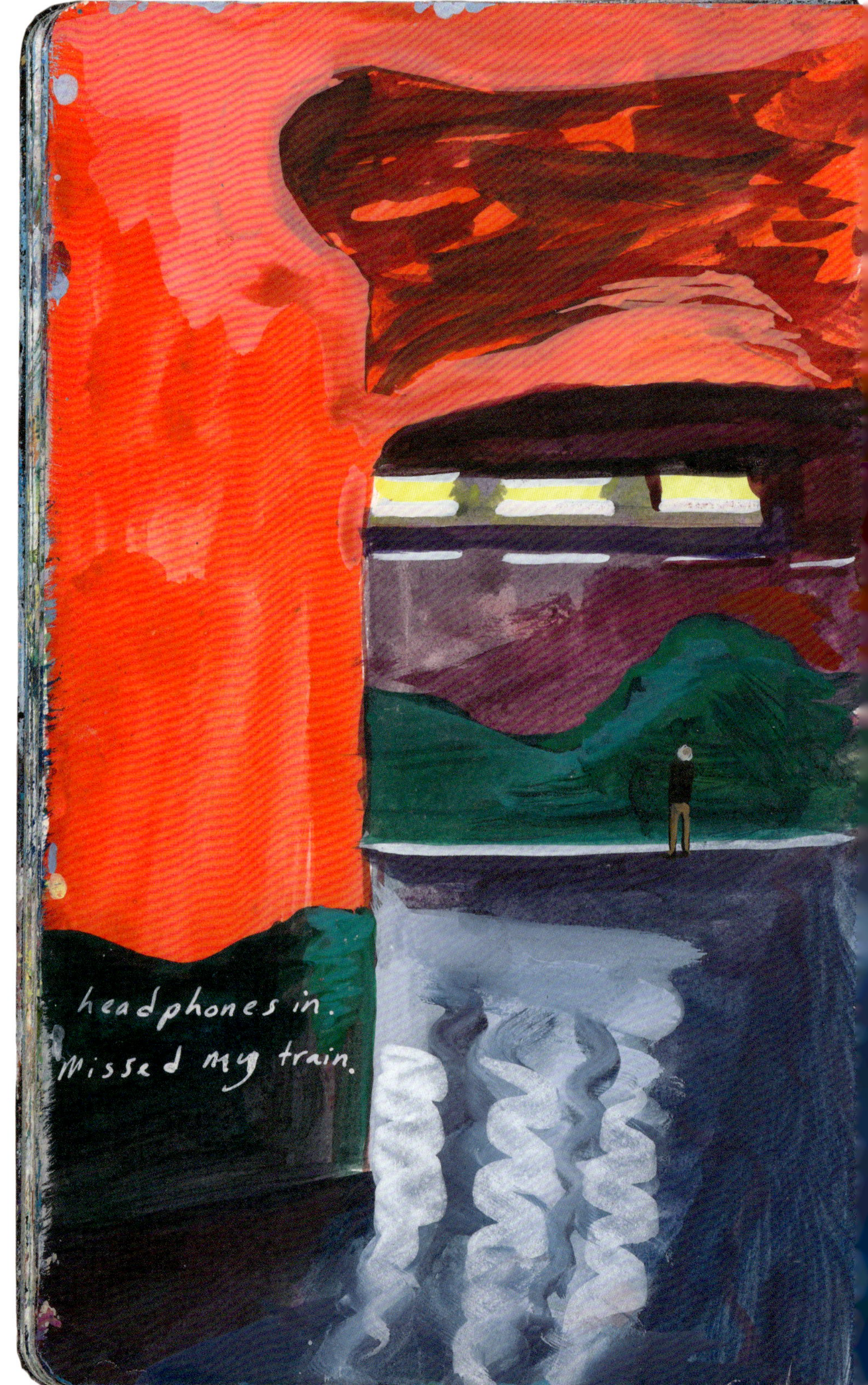

headphones in.
missed my train.

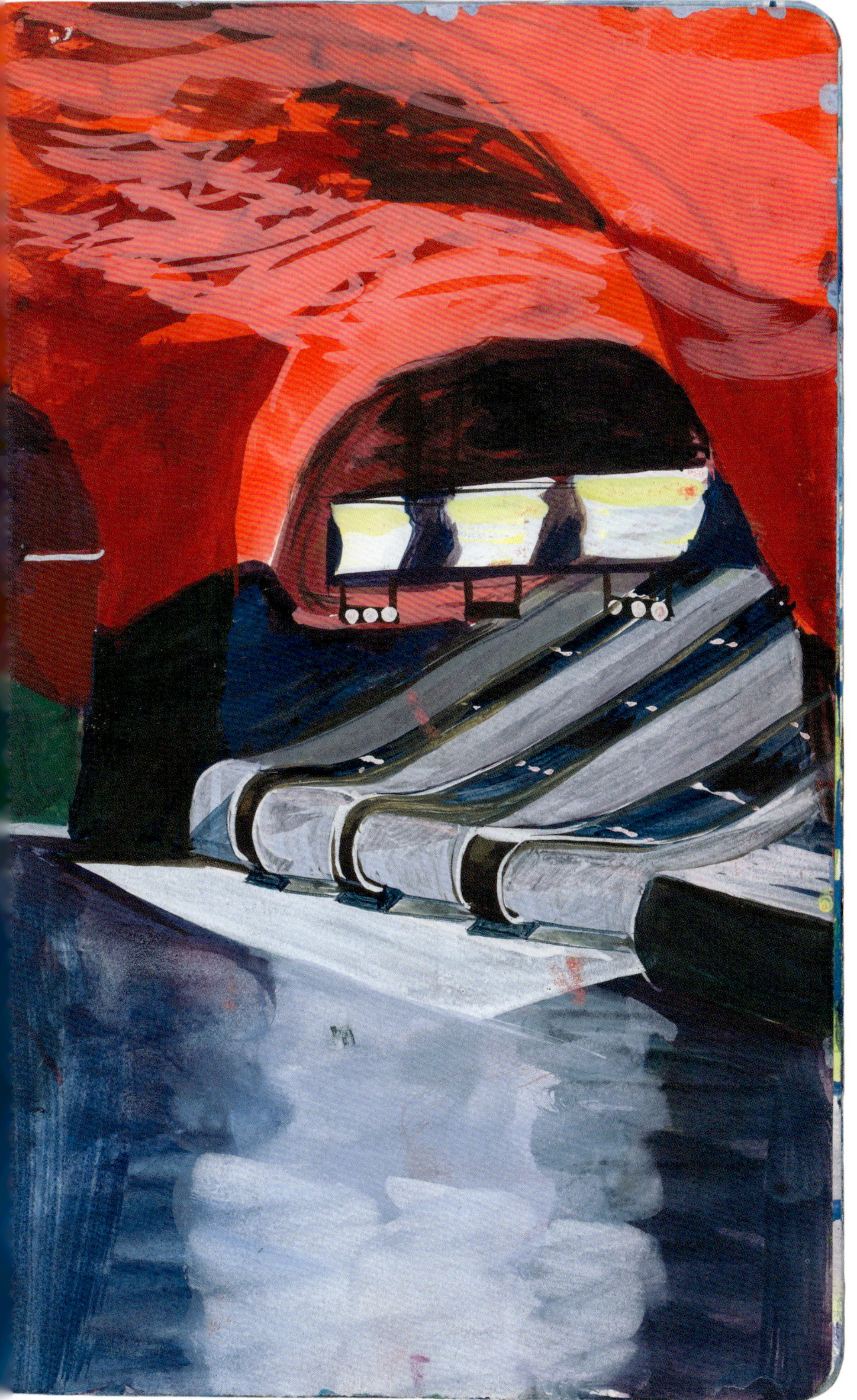

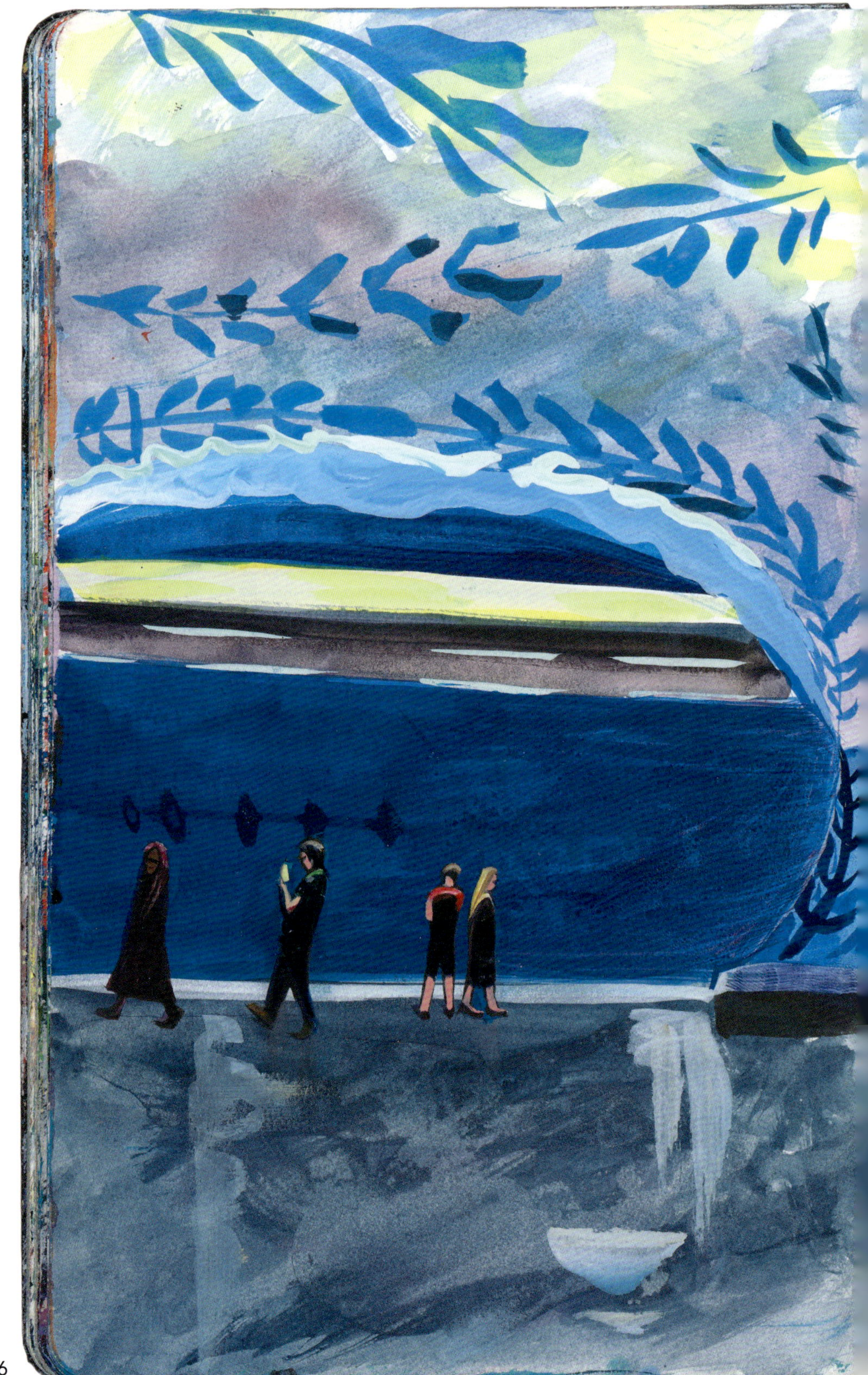

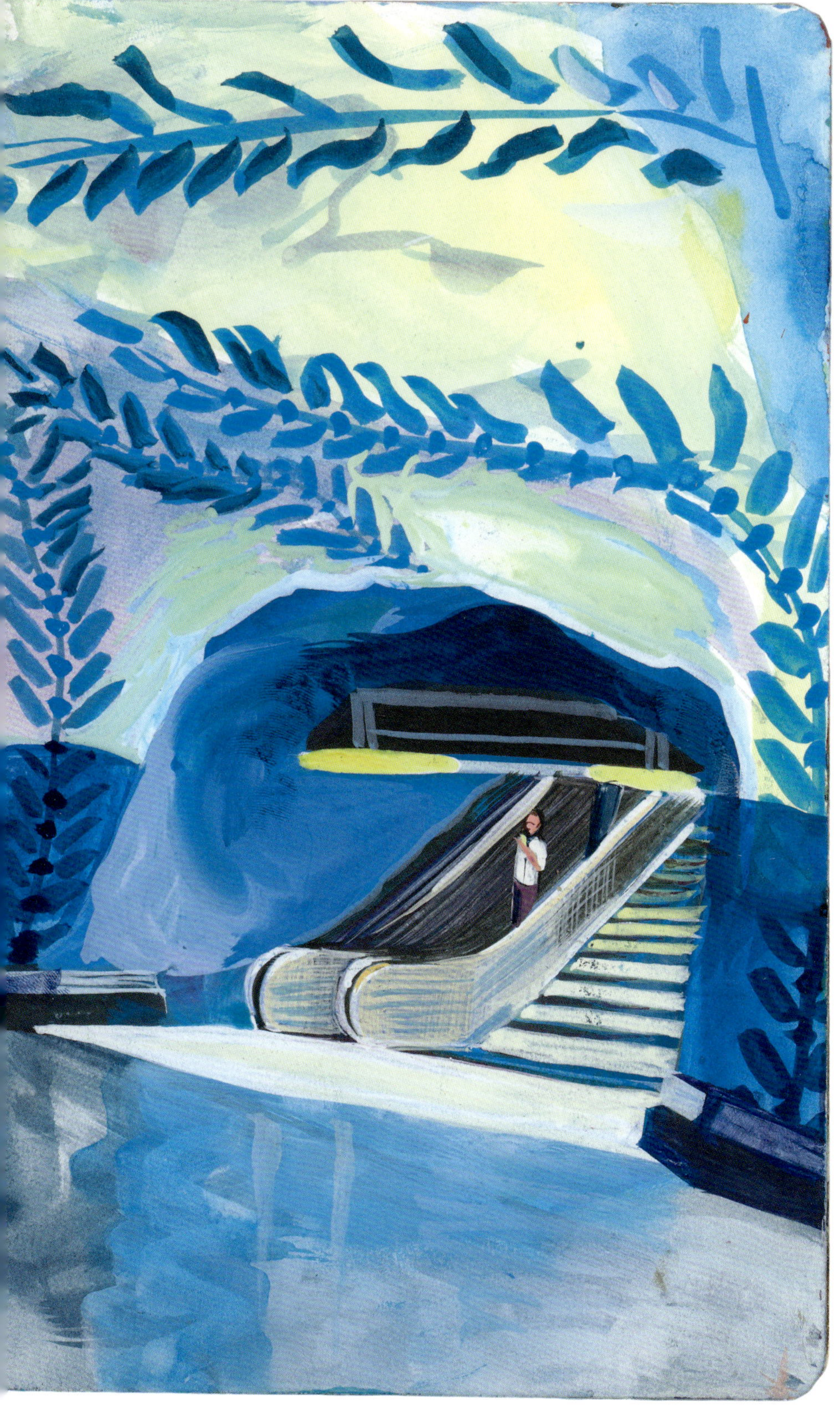

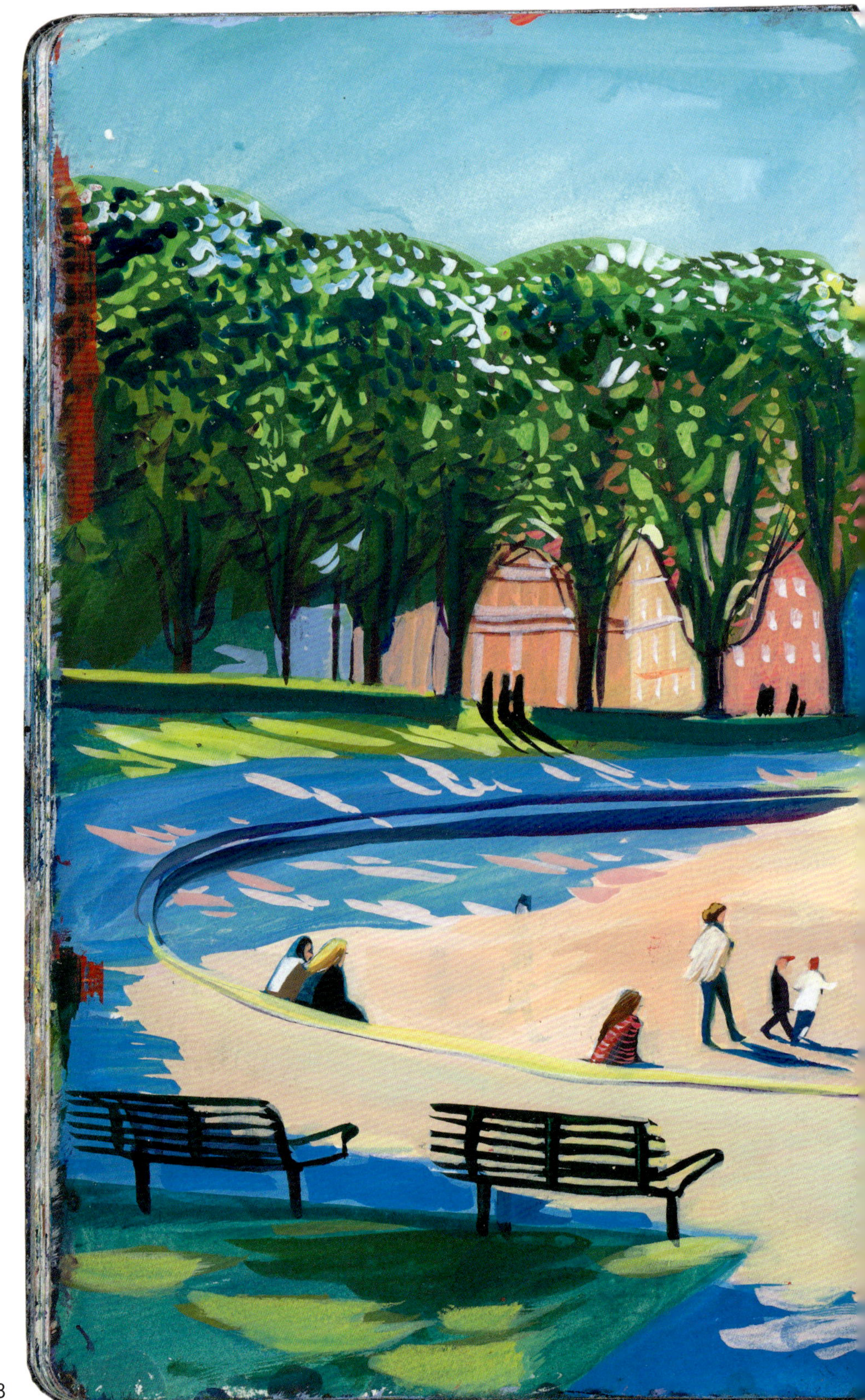

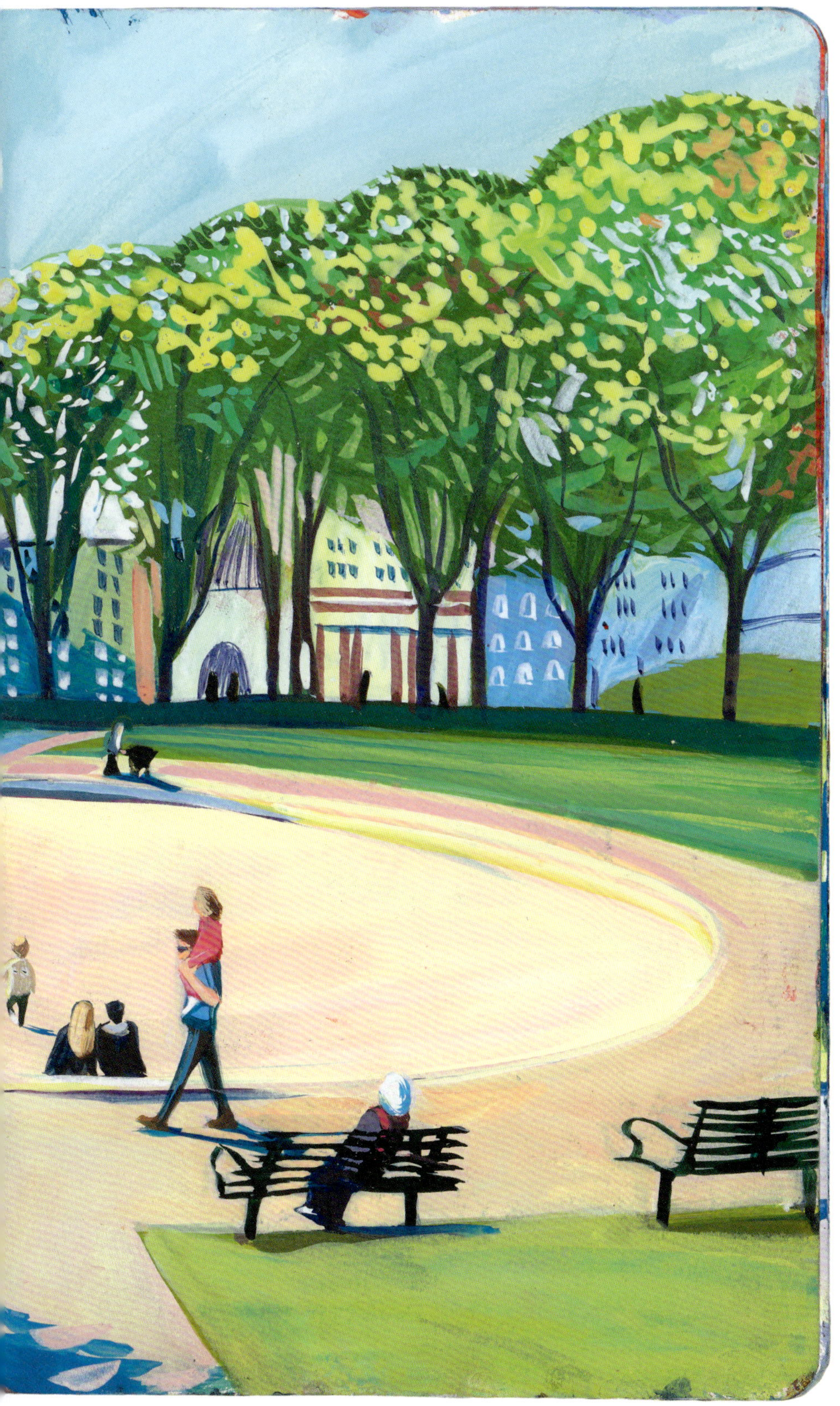

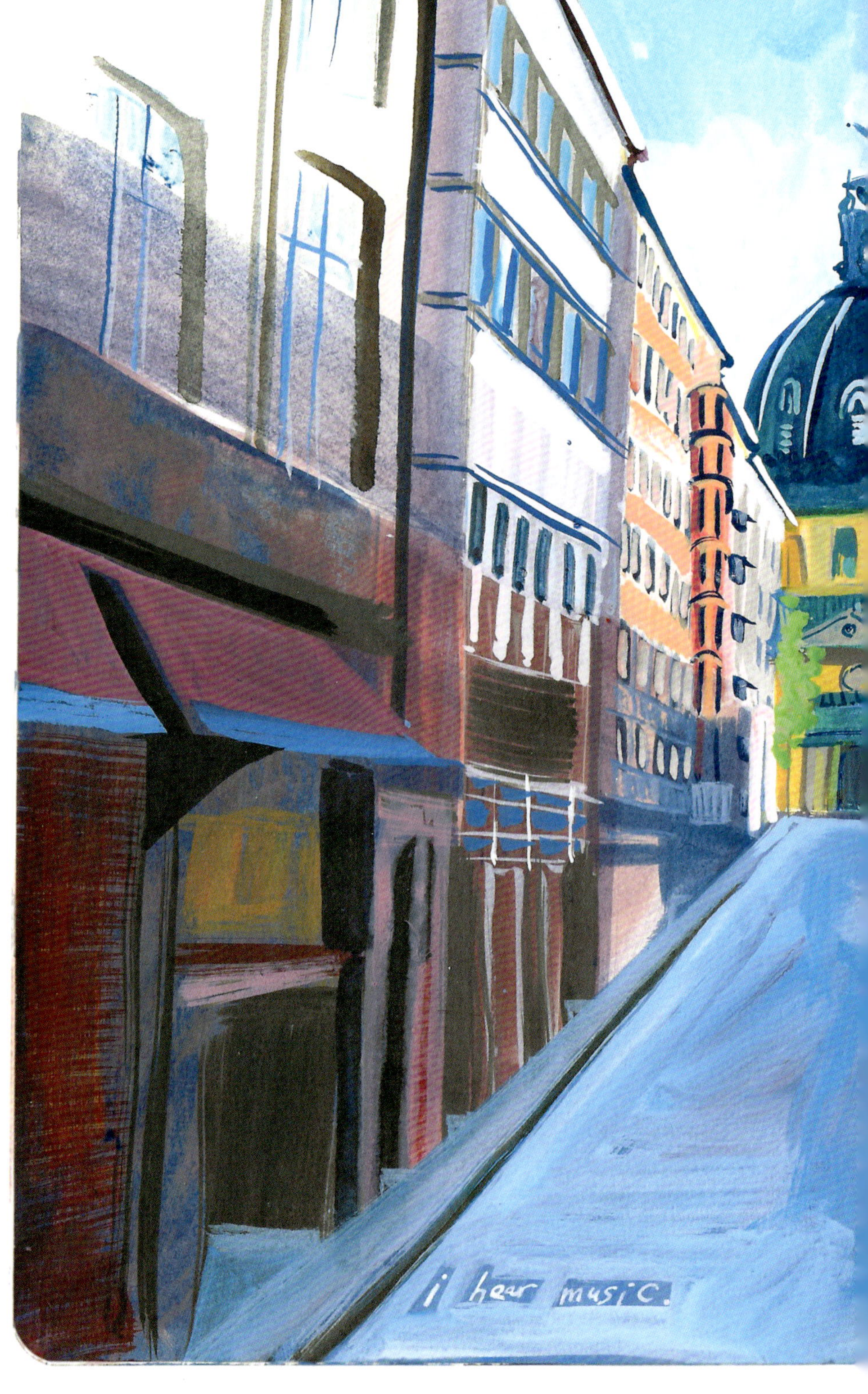
i hear music.

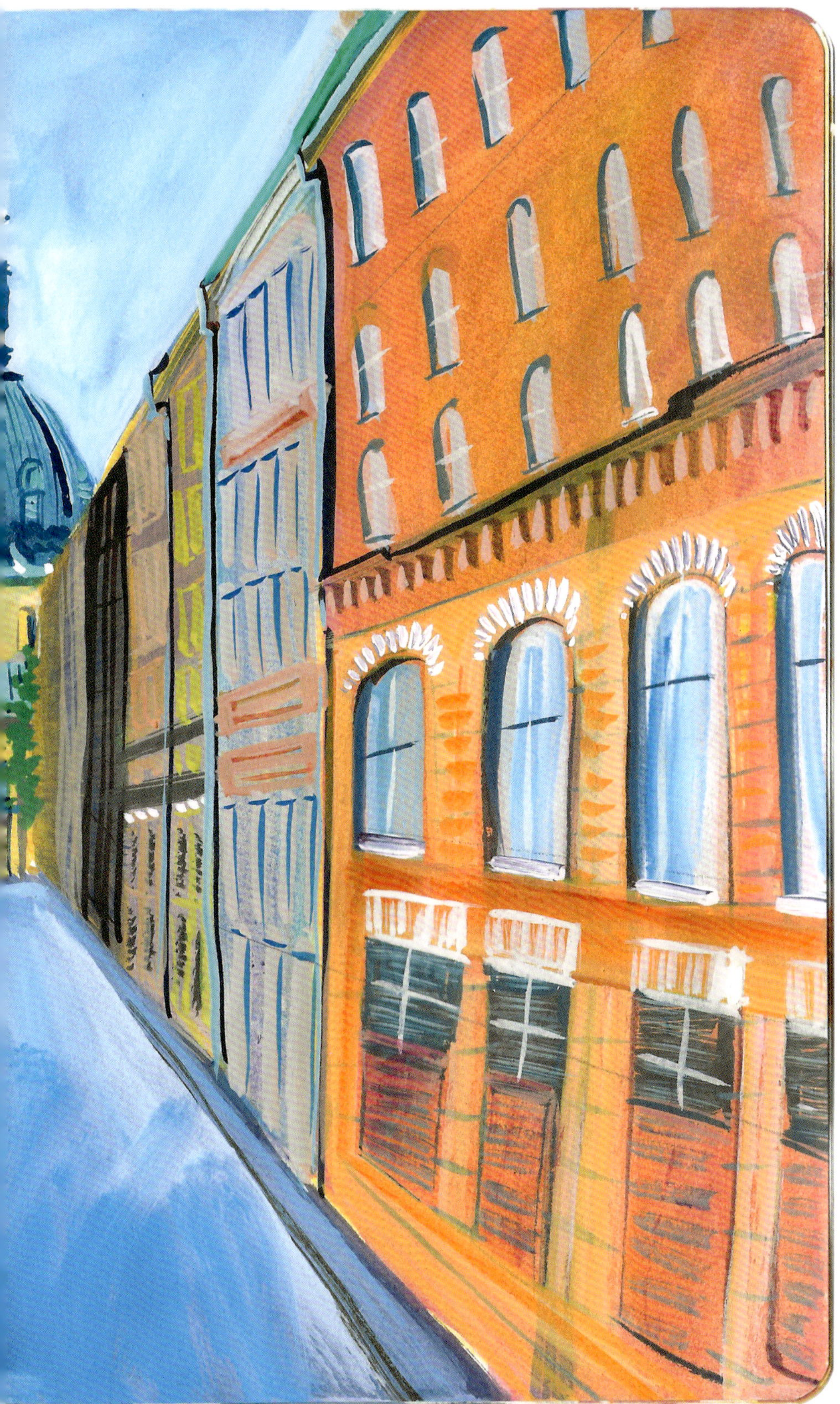

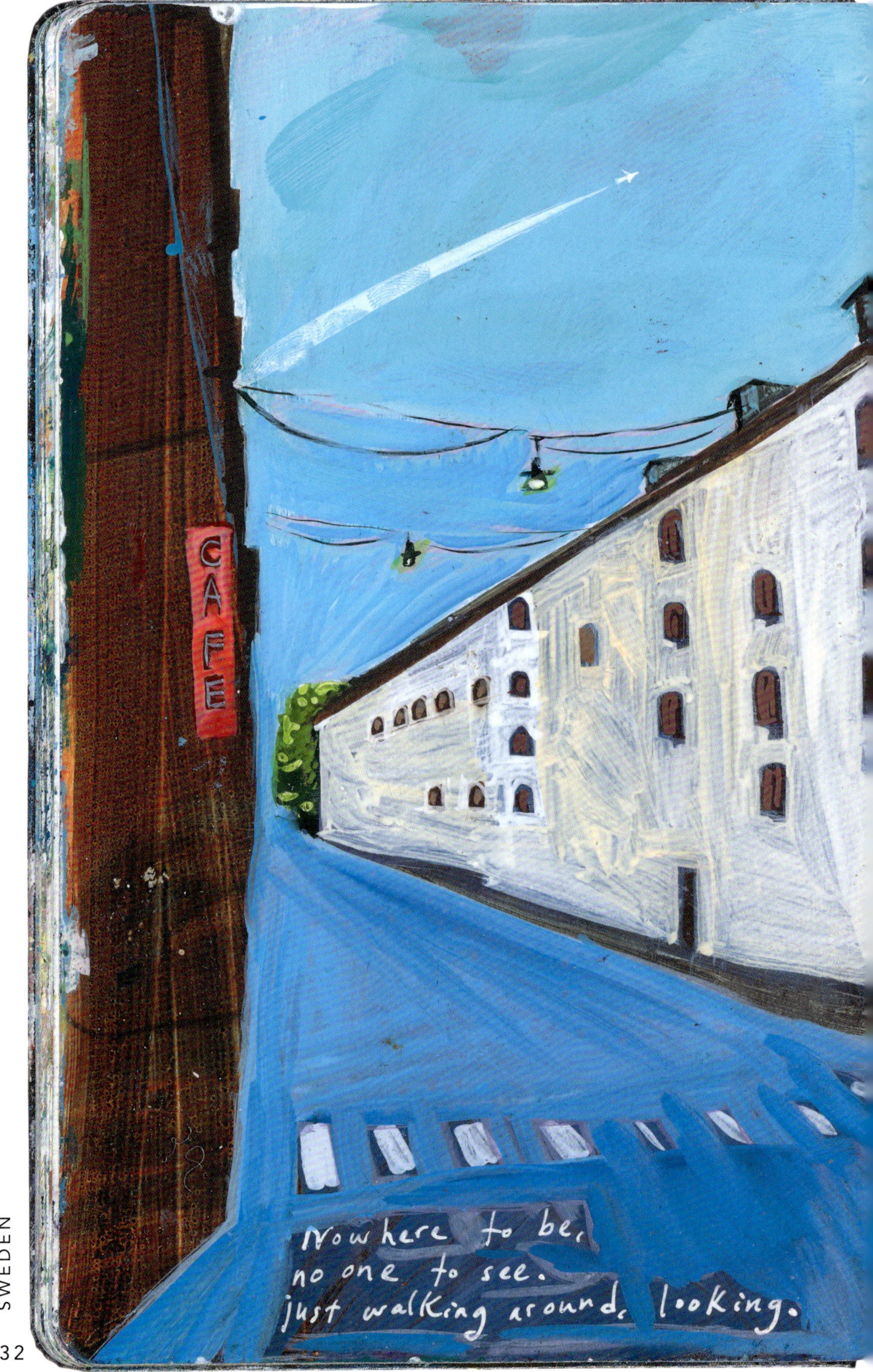

CAFE
Nowhere to be,
no one to see.
just walking around, looking.

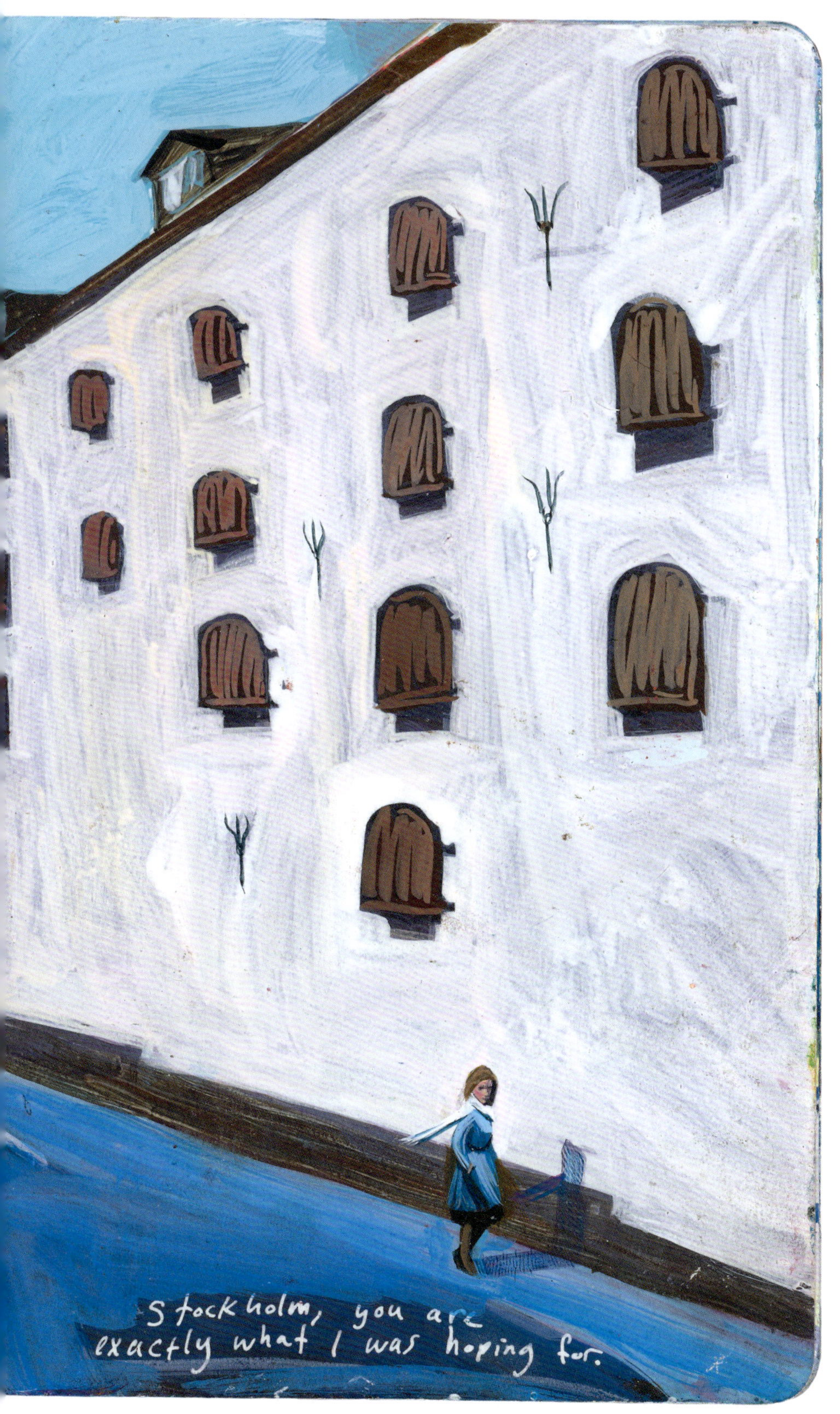
Stockholm, you are
exactly what I was hoping for.

my watch tells me it's midnight.
The sky tells me it's dawn.
My body tells me it's too early to sleep.

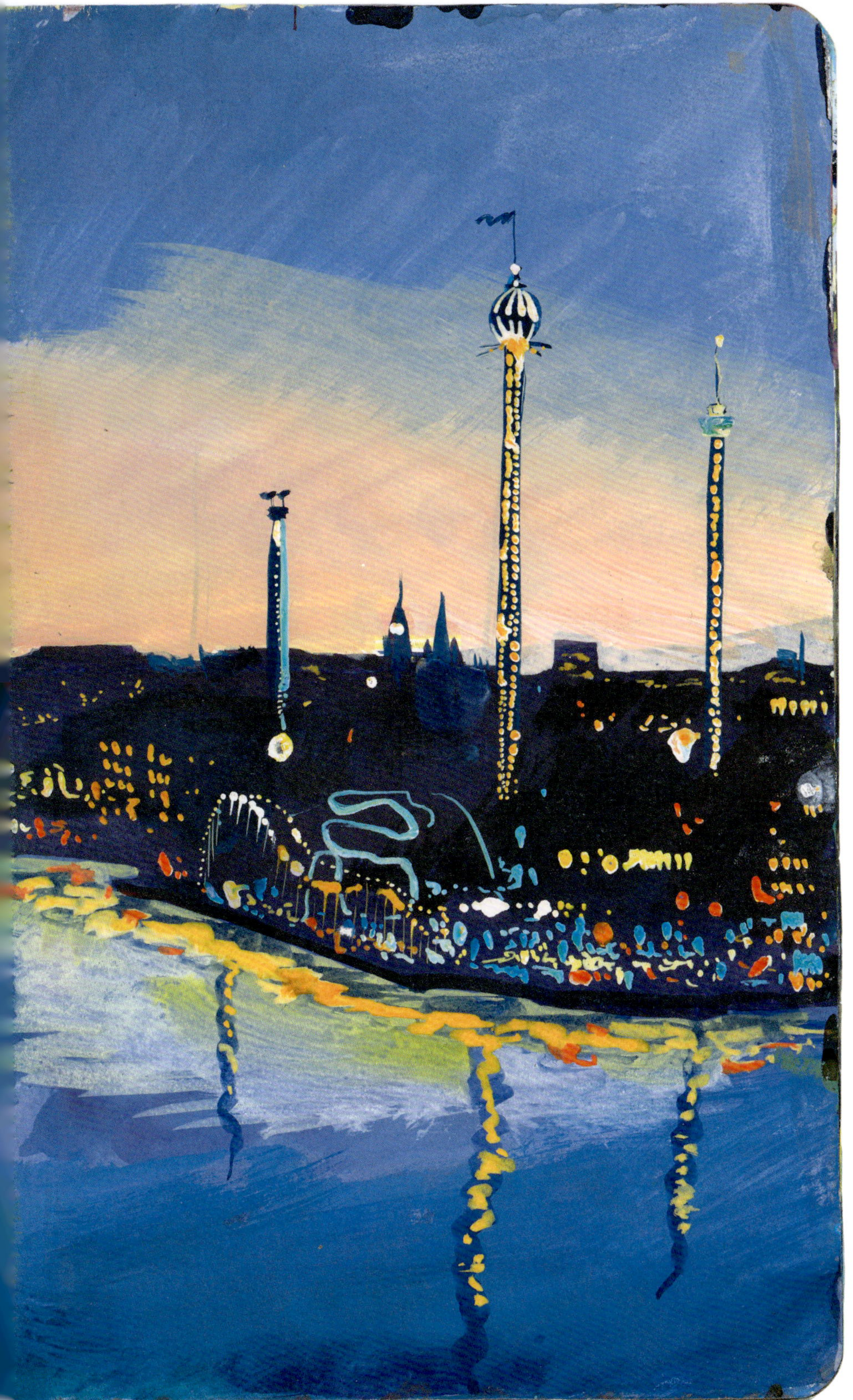

135

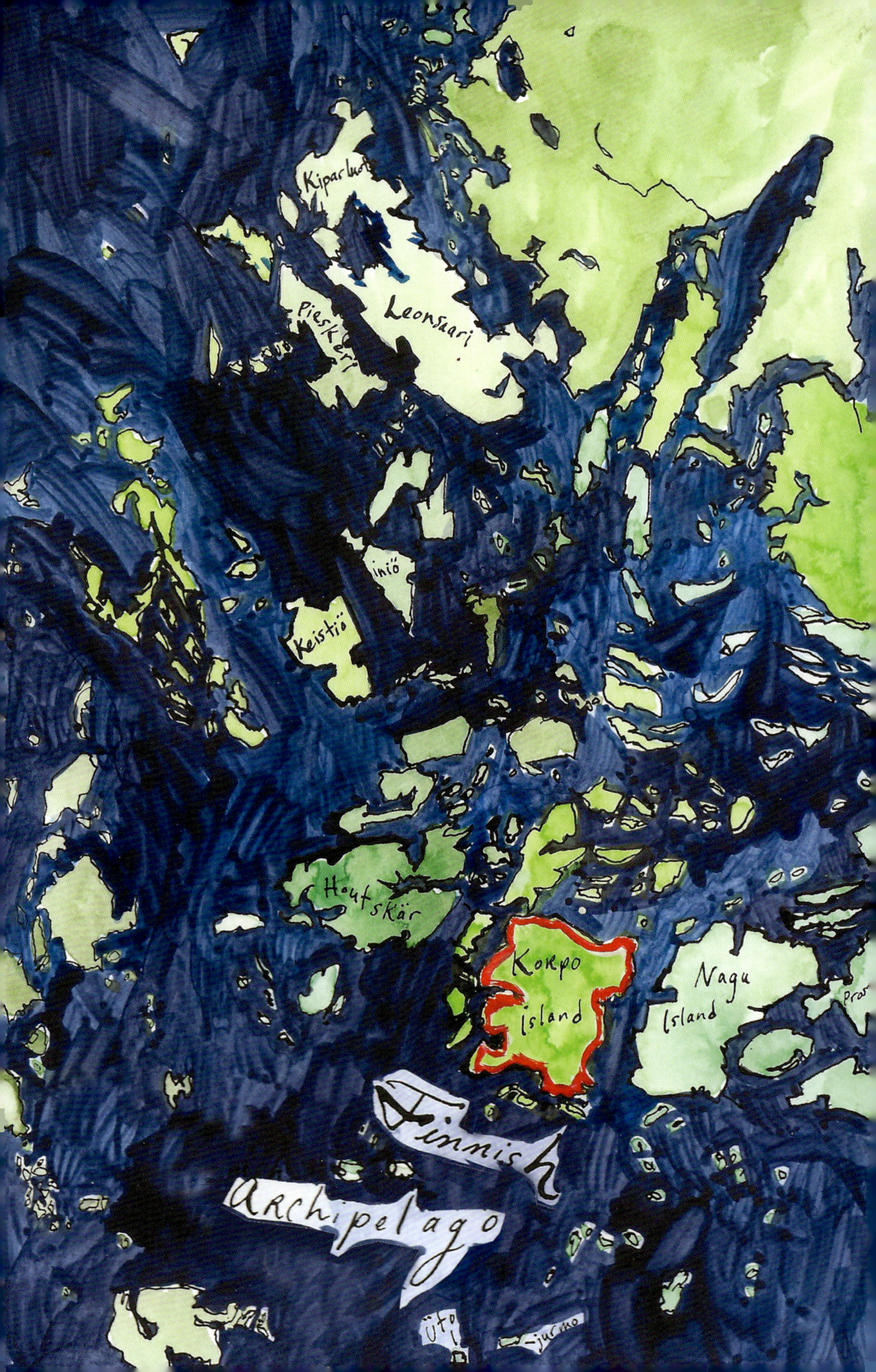

Kiparluoto
Leonsaari
Pieskeri
iniö
Keistiö
Houtskär
Korpo Island
Nagu Island
Pro...
Finnish
Archipelago
Utö
jurmo

VII

Korpo Island, Finland

June 14th, 2016

Hours I've spent on a bike before Finland: five? Hours I've spent on a bike in Finland: five every day. Cycling through pine forests and flowering meadows is my new favorite activity. If only I could ride a bike and paint at the same time.

This week, I walked around Utö Island for a few days, choosing to leave my bike behind—not my best idea. I wandered off trail onto rocky terrain to follow a warbler, when I heard a shriek from above. I looked up and saw two arctic terns preparing to plunge at my head. I froze mid-stride, and saw I was accidentally balancing on two rocks above their ground nest, as well as a large, poisonous snake. The snake wasn't too bothered, but the terns dove at my face, striking the bill of my hat. I needed a faster getaway than my legs.

colors:

i arrived at

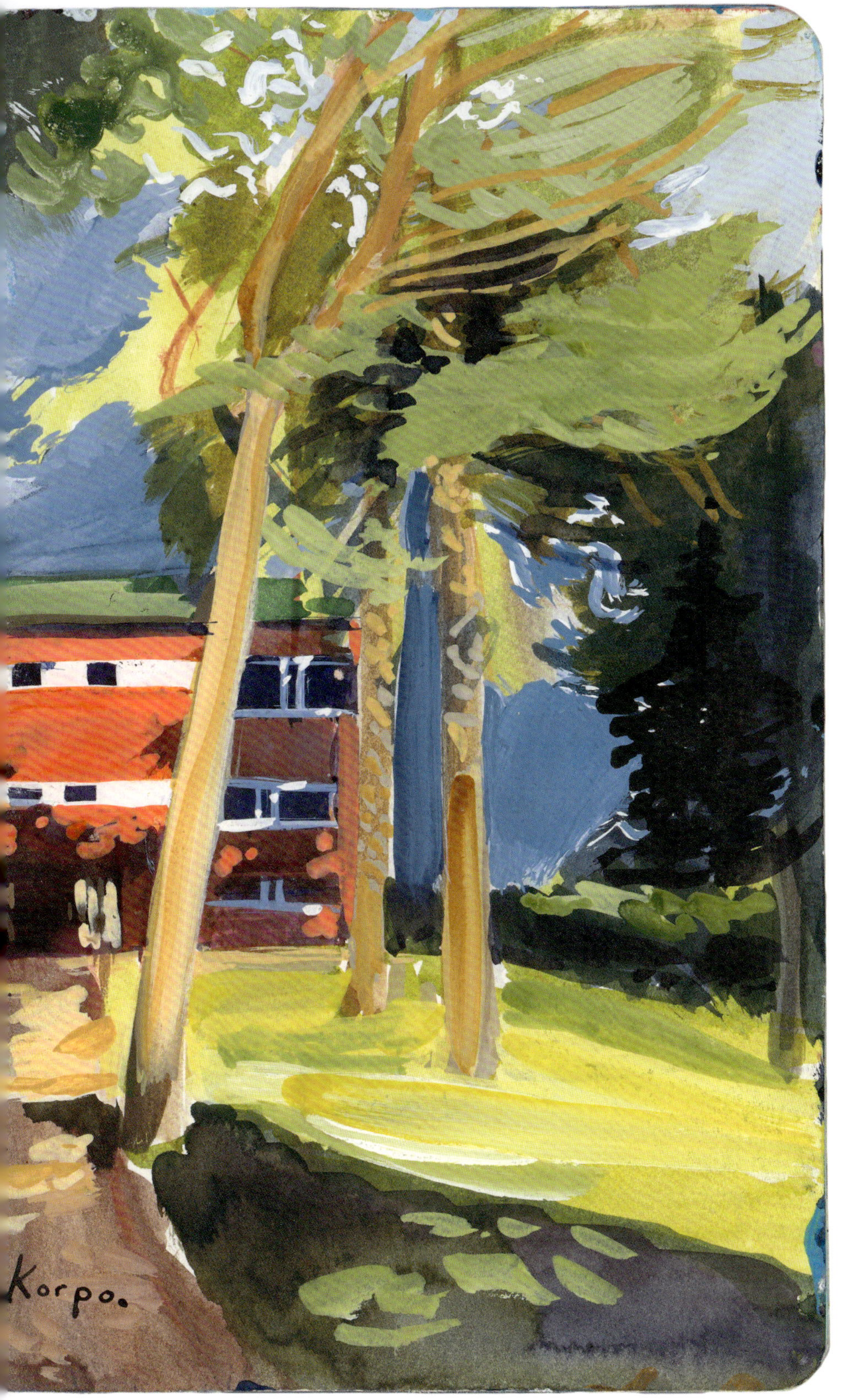

Korpo.

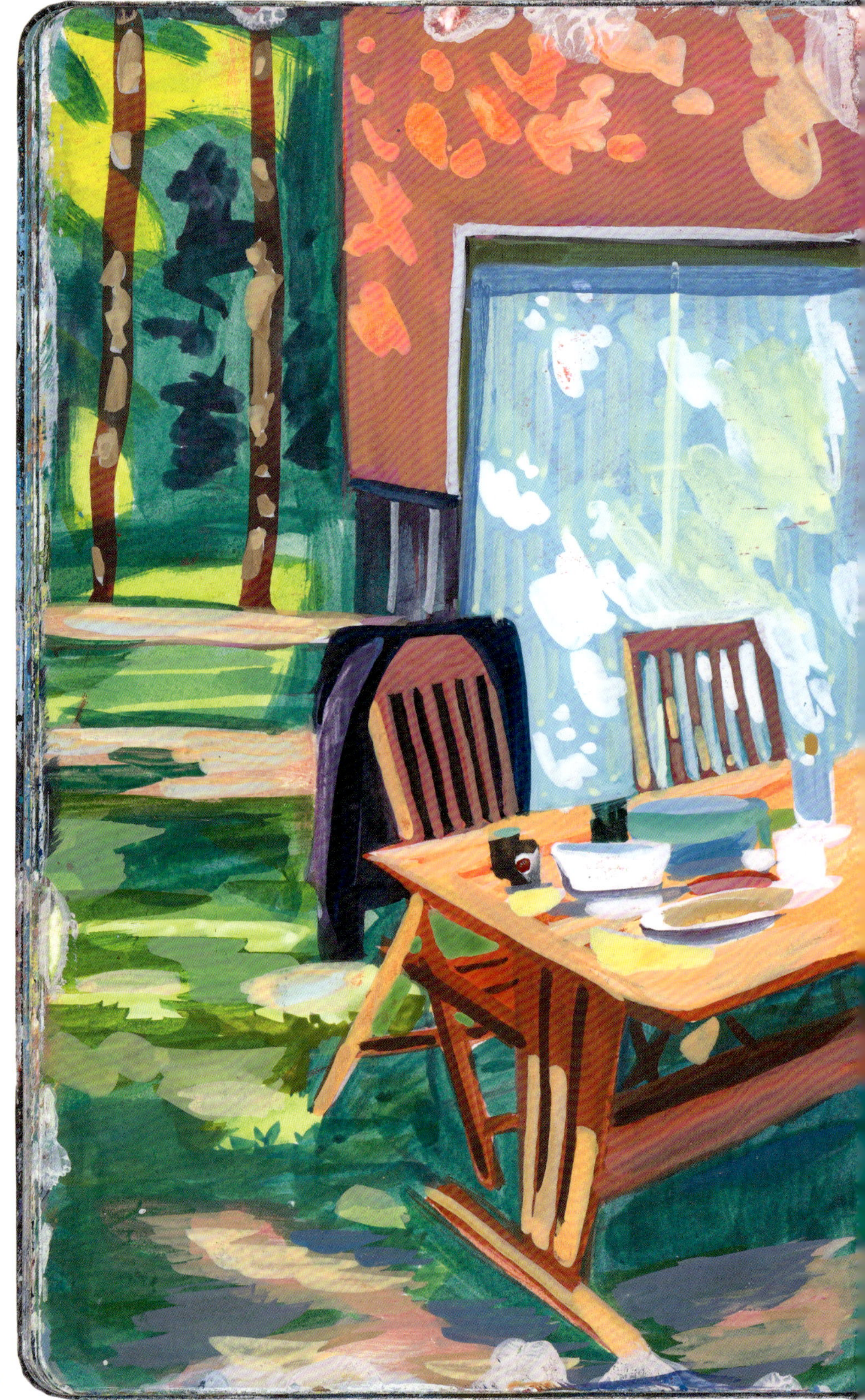

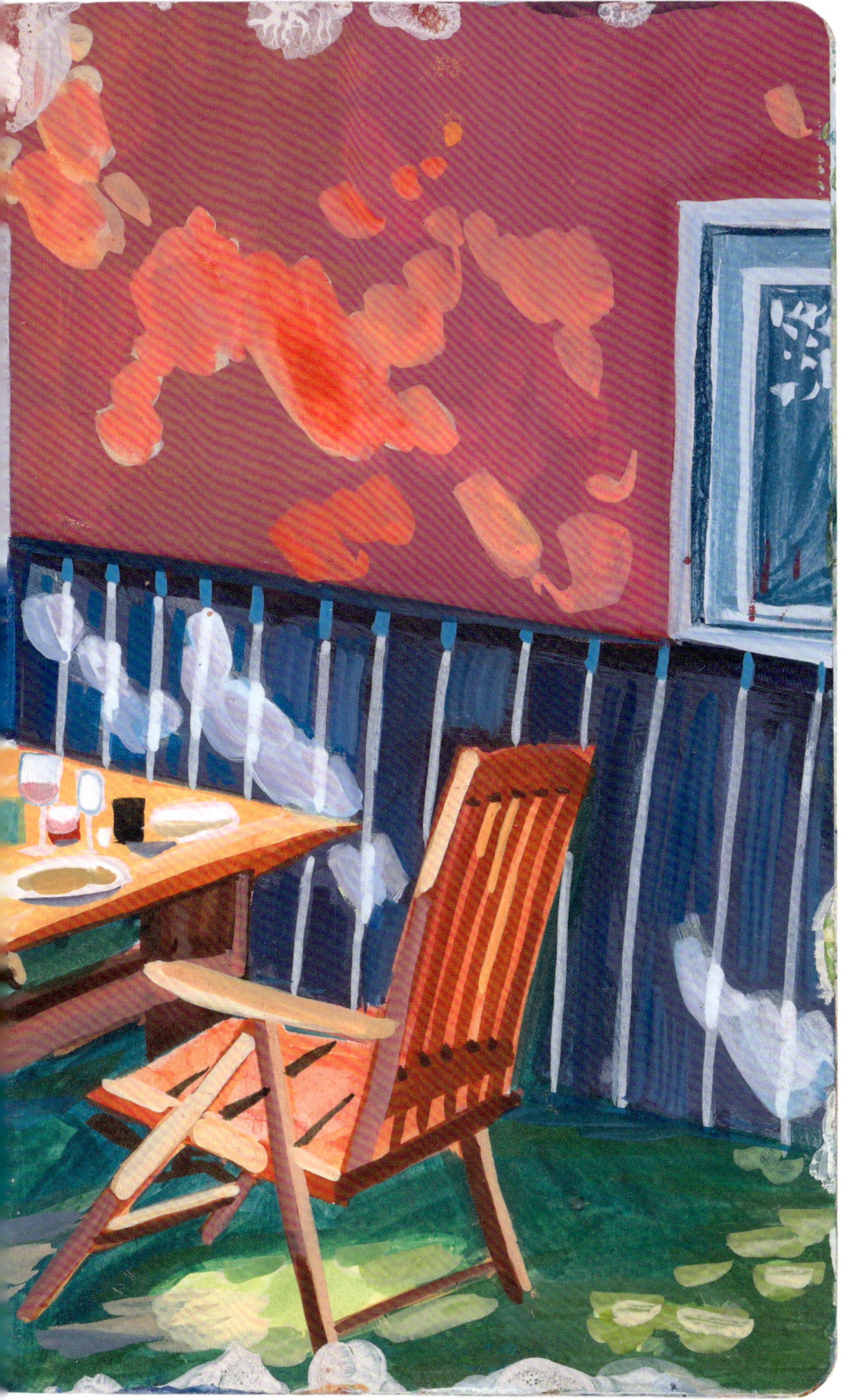

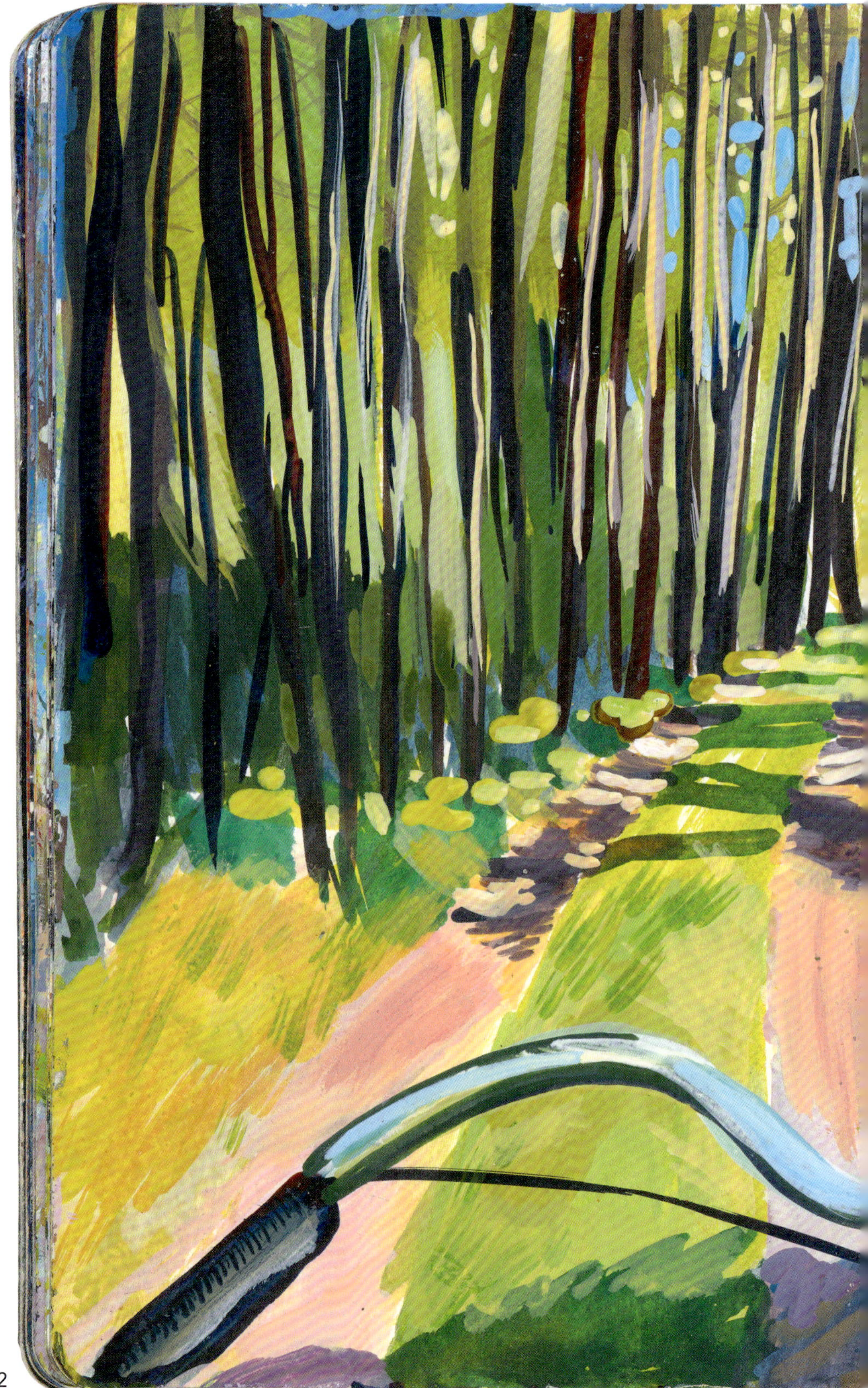

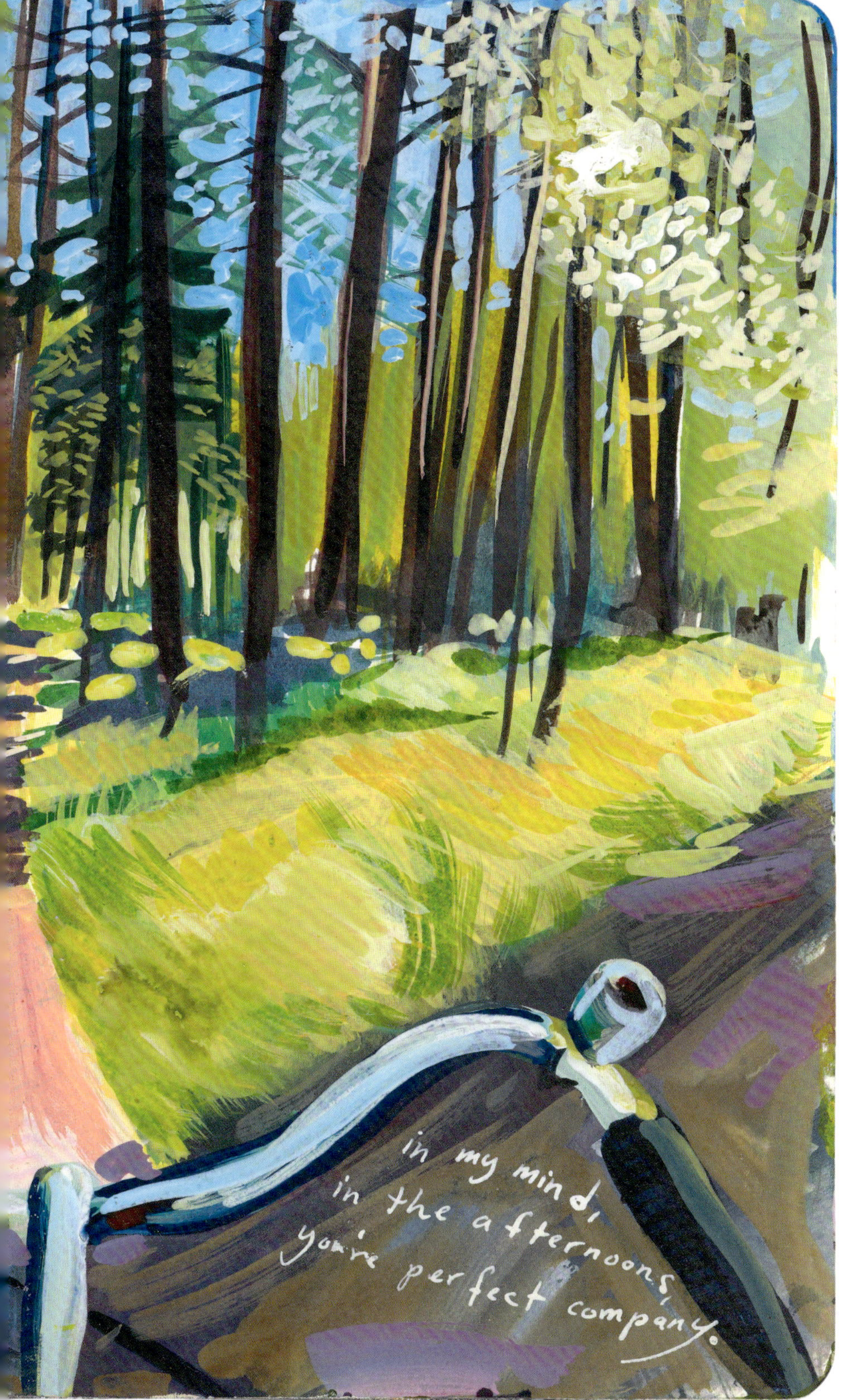

in my mind,
in the afternoons,
you're perfect company.

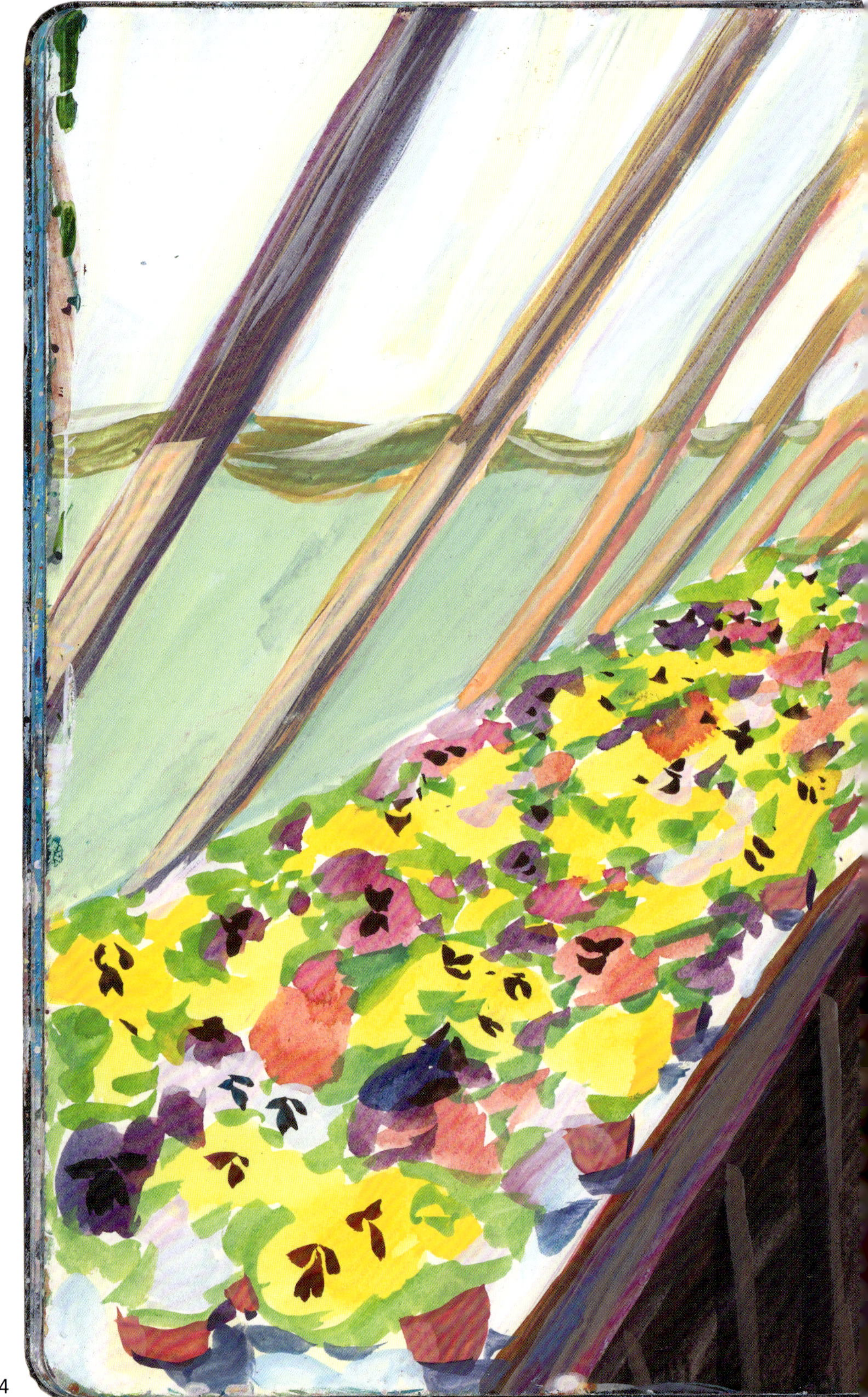

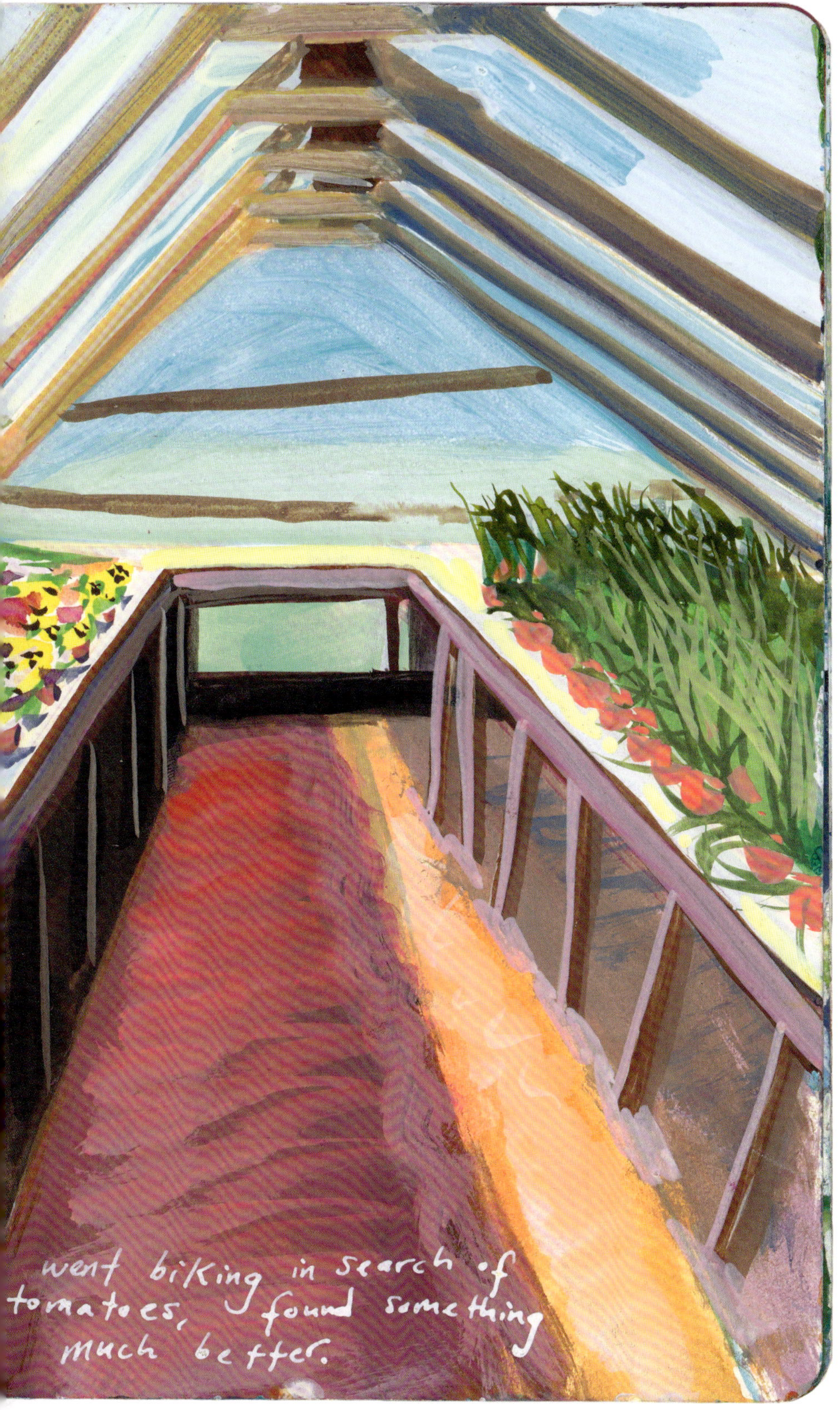

went biking in search of
tomatoes, found something
much better.

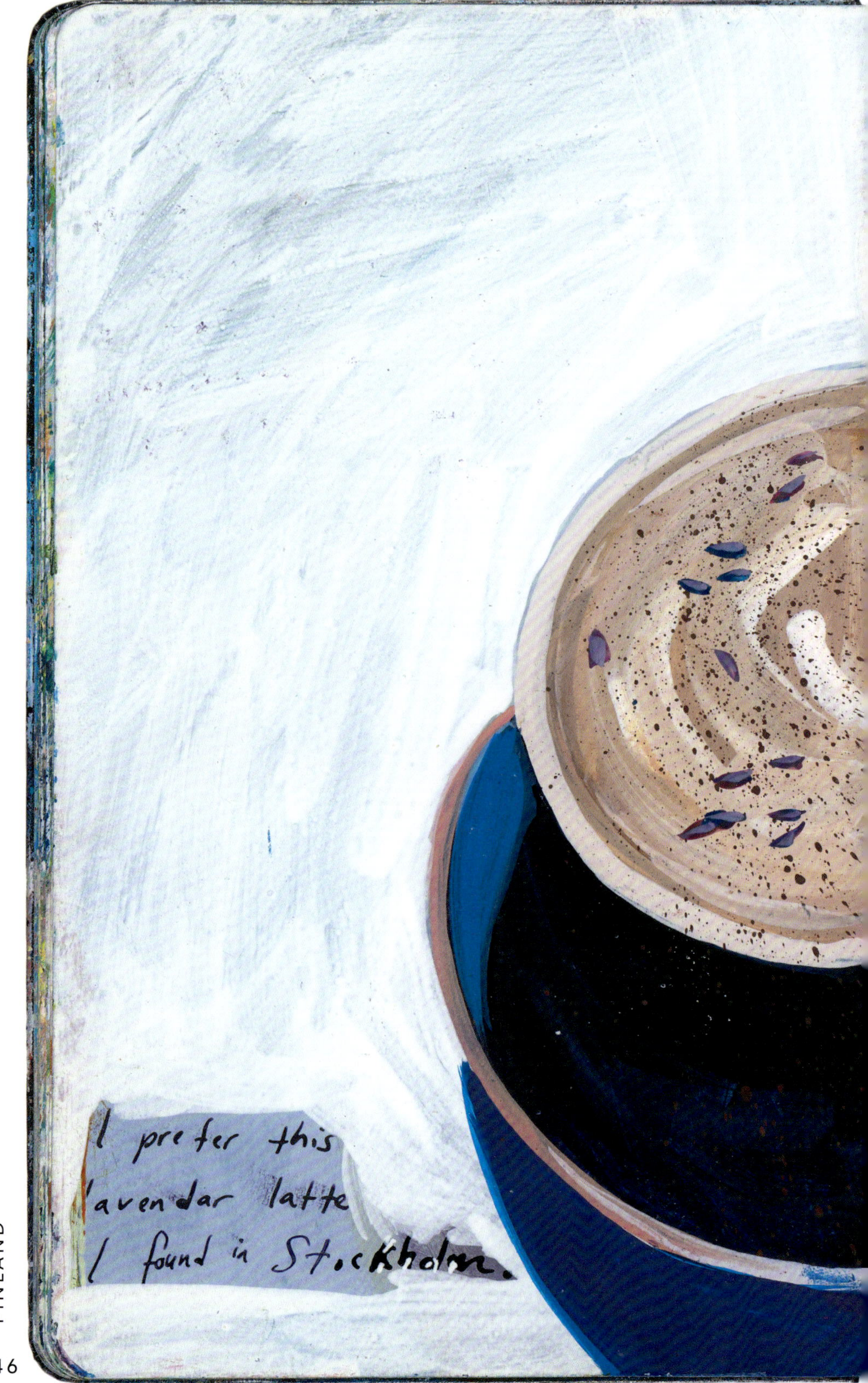
I prefer this
lavendar latte
I found in Stockholm.

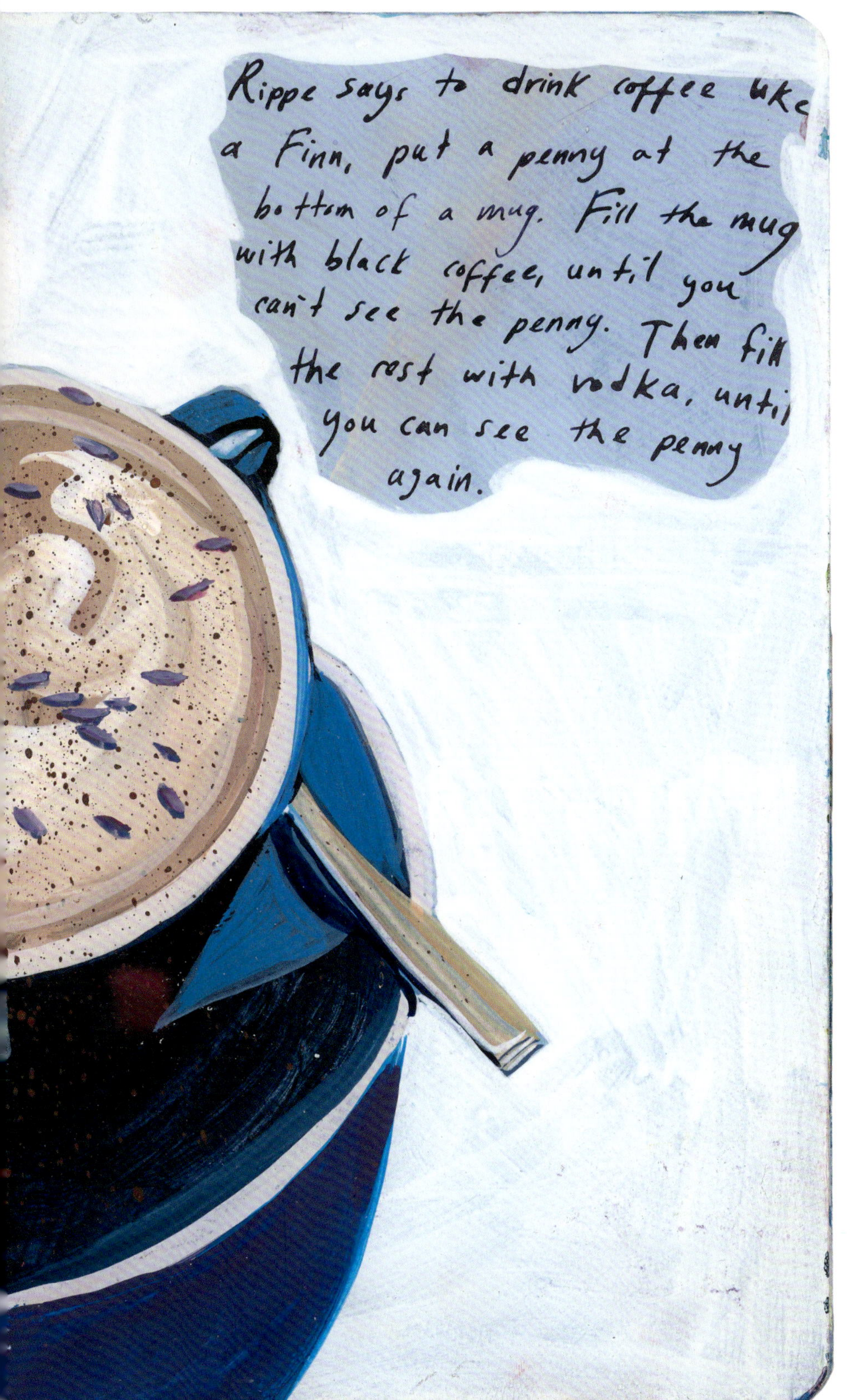

Rippe says to drink coffee like a Finn, put a penny at the bottom of a mug. Fill the mug with black coffee, until you can't see the penny. Then fill the rest with vodka, until you can see the penny again.

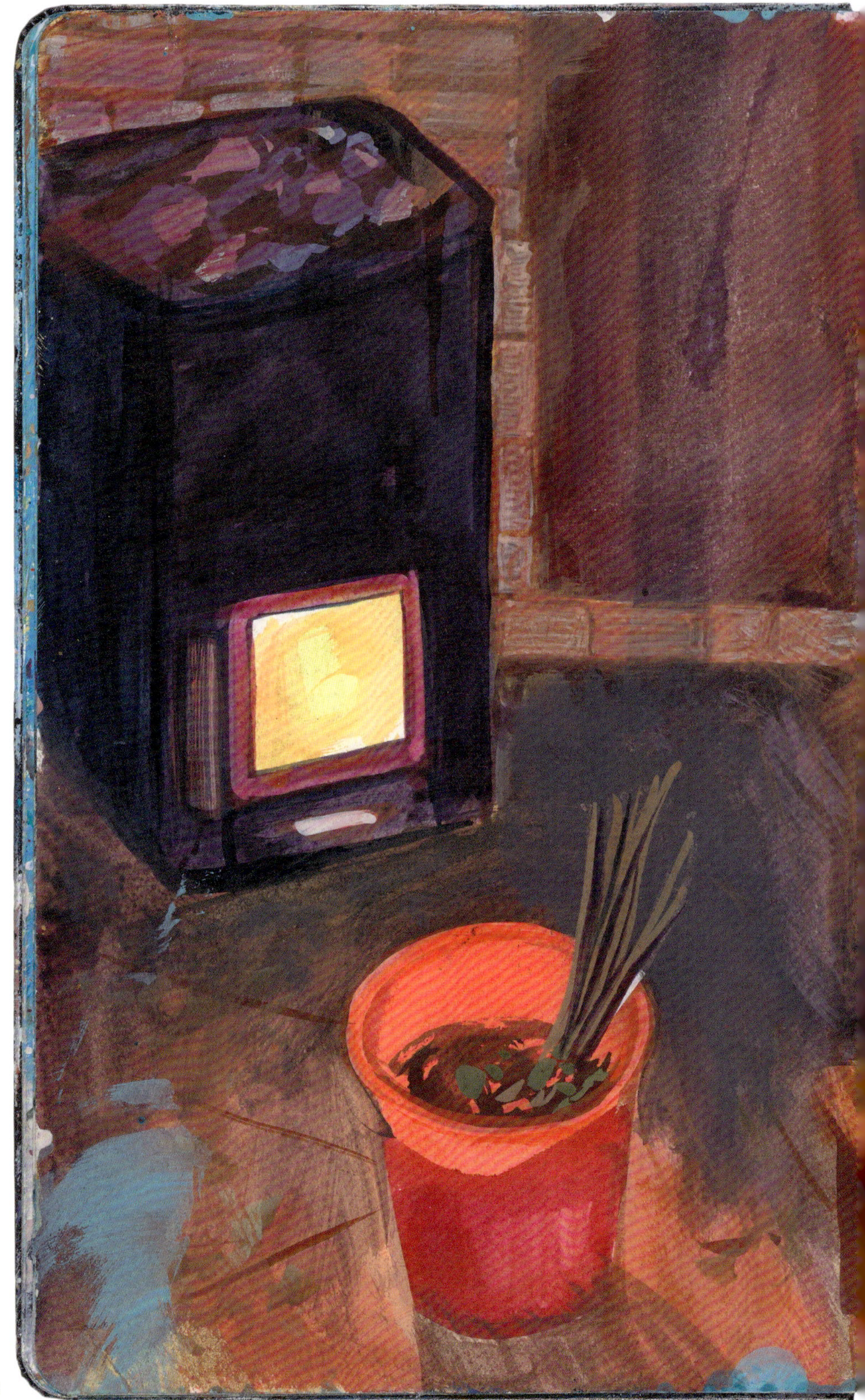

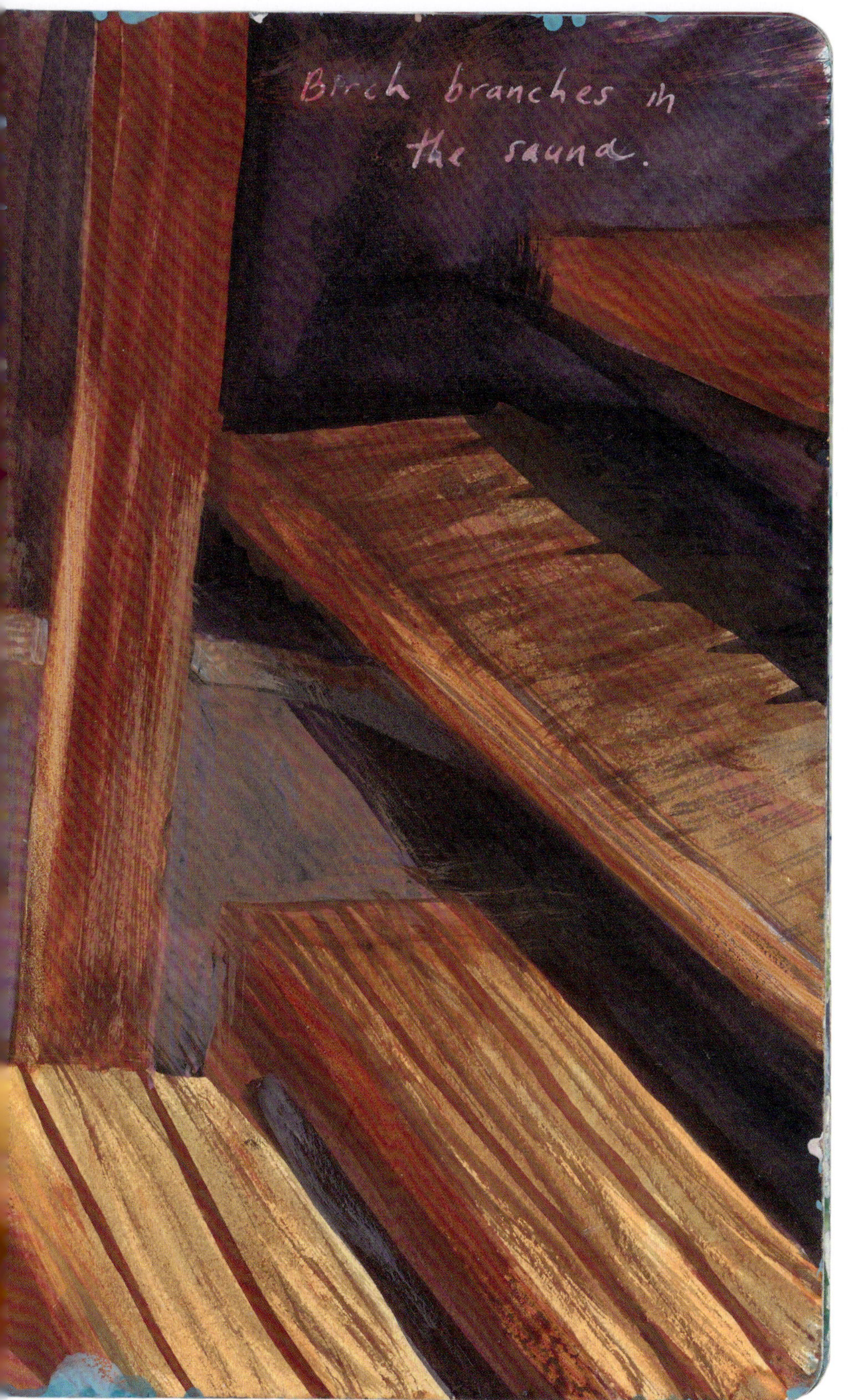
Birch branches in
the sauna.

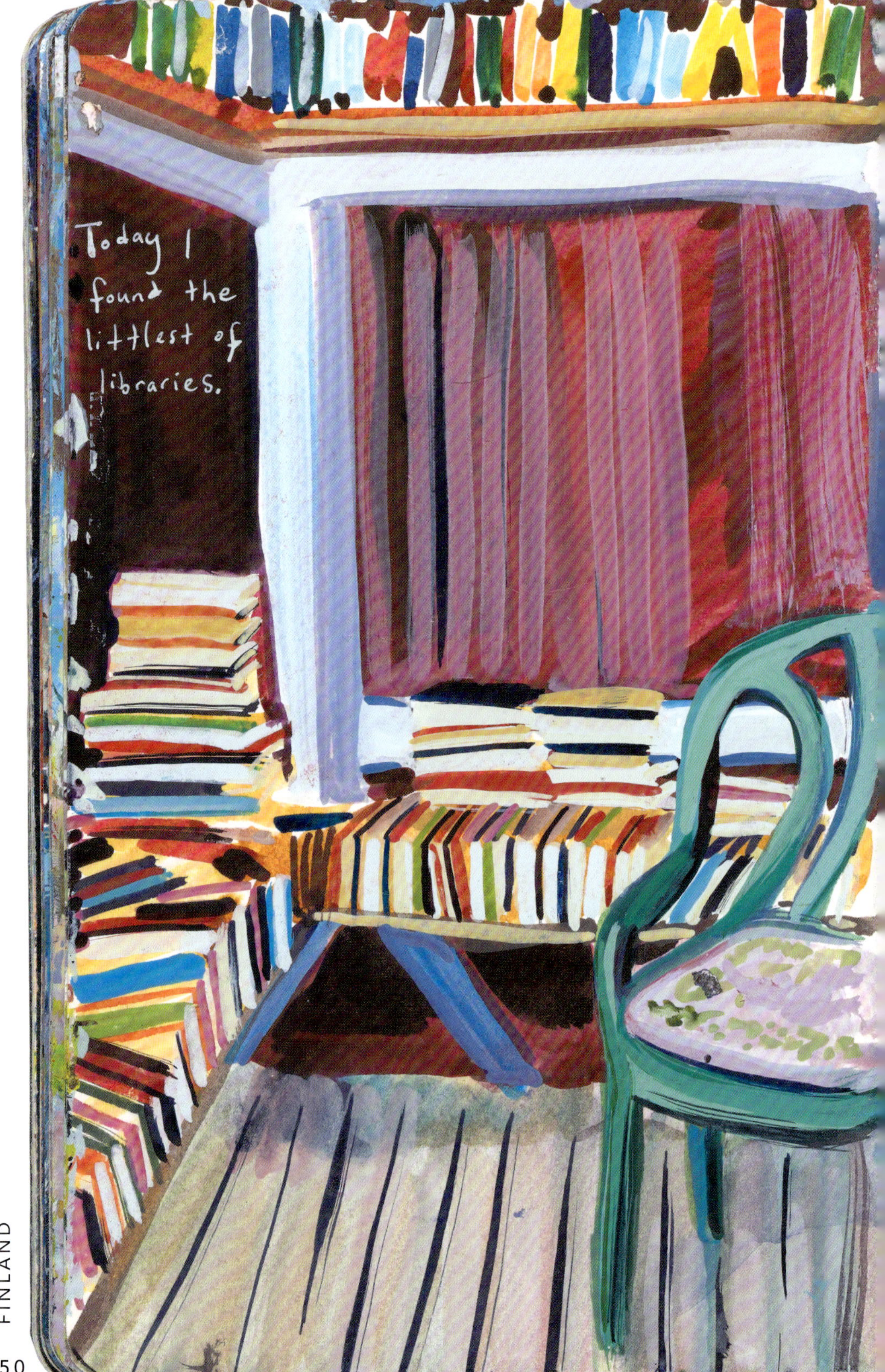

Today I
found the
littlest of
libraries.

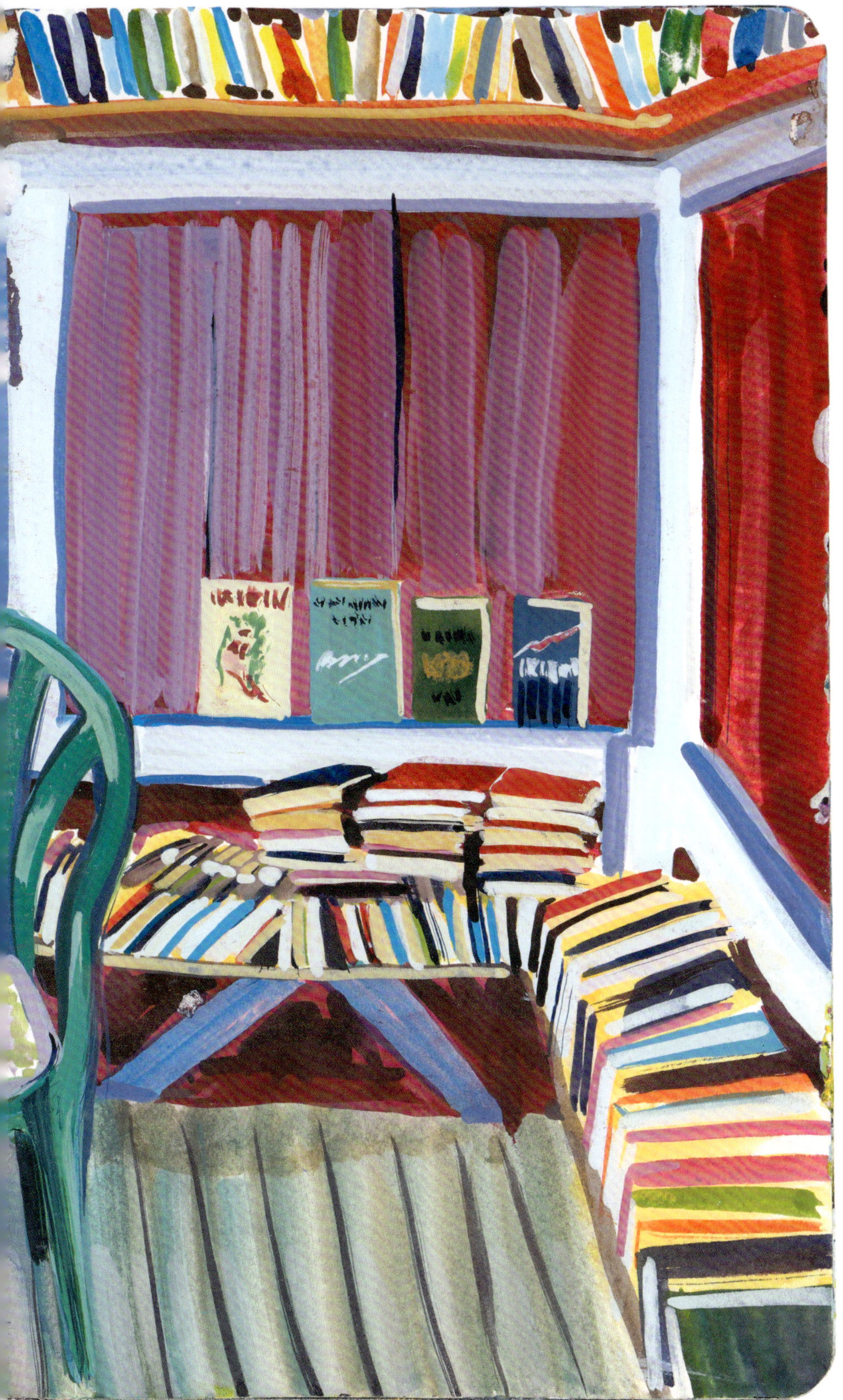

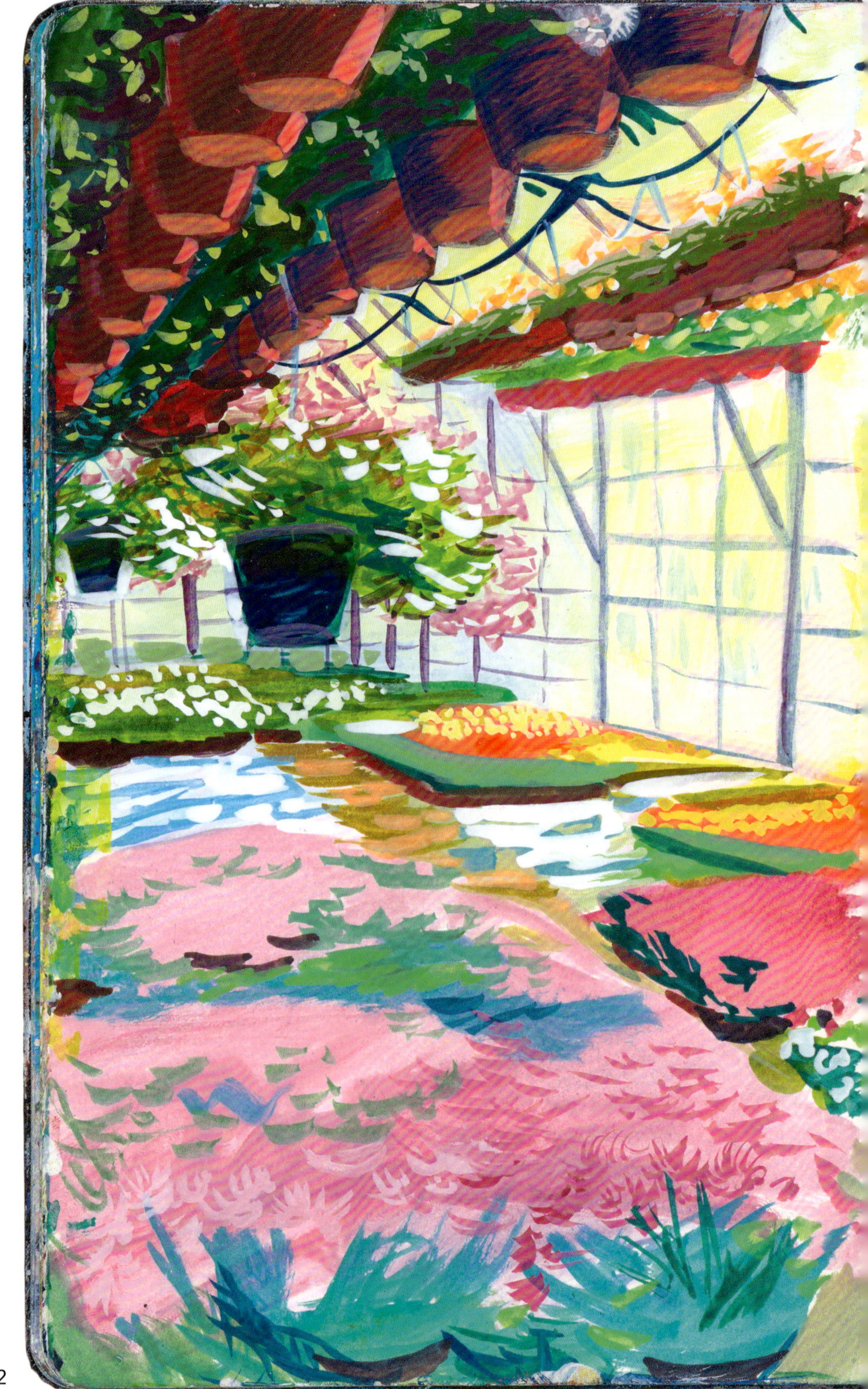

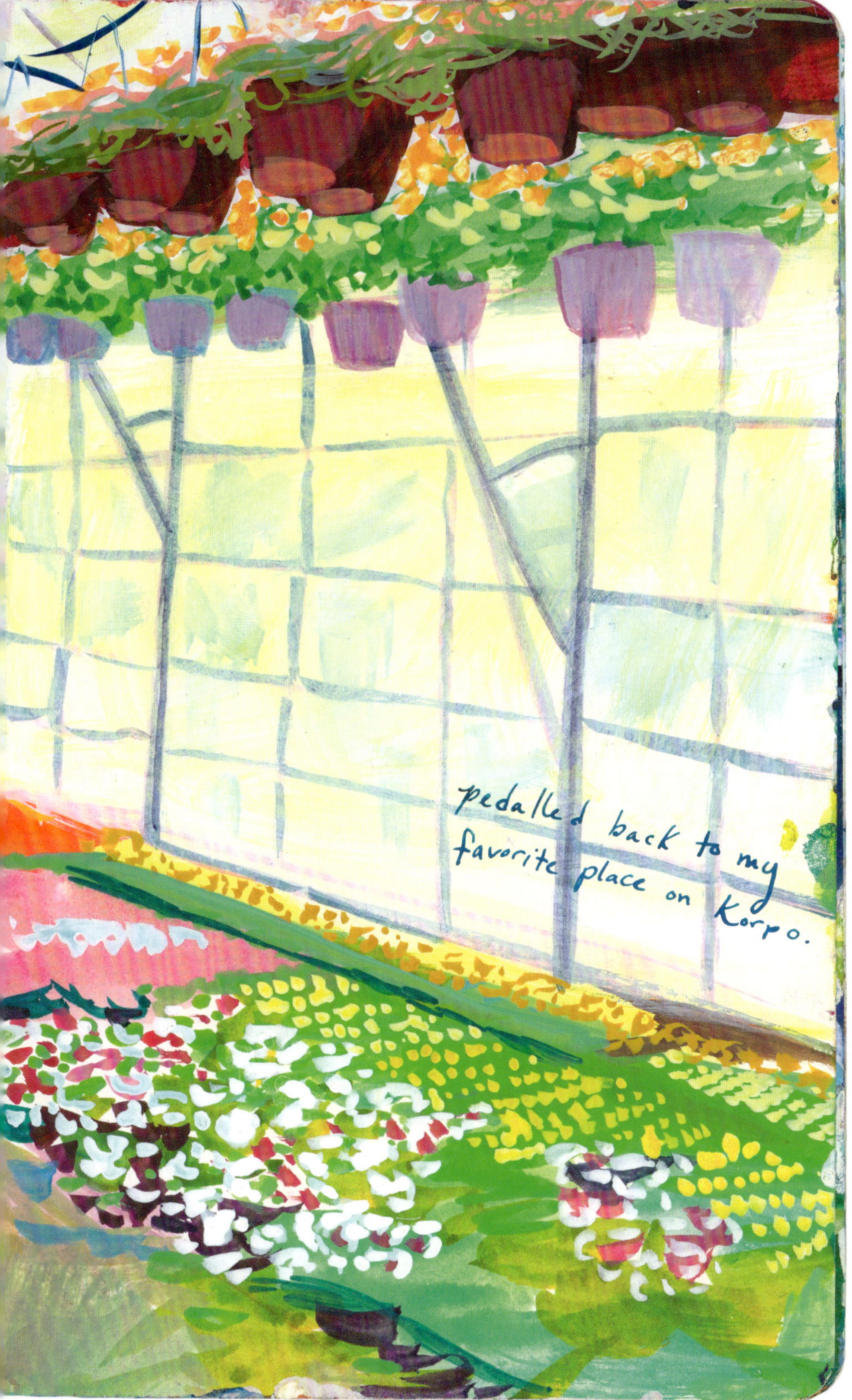
pedalled back to my
favorite place on Korpo.

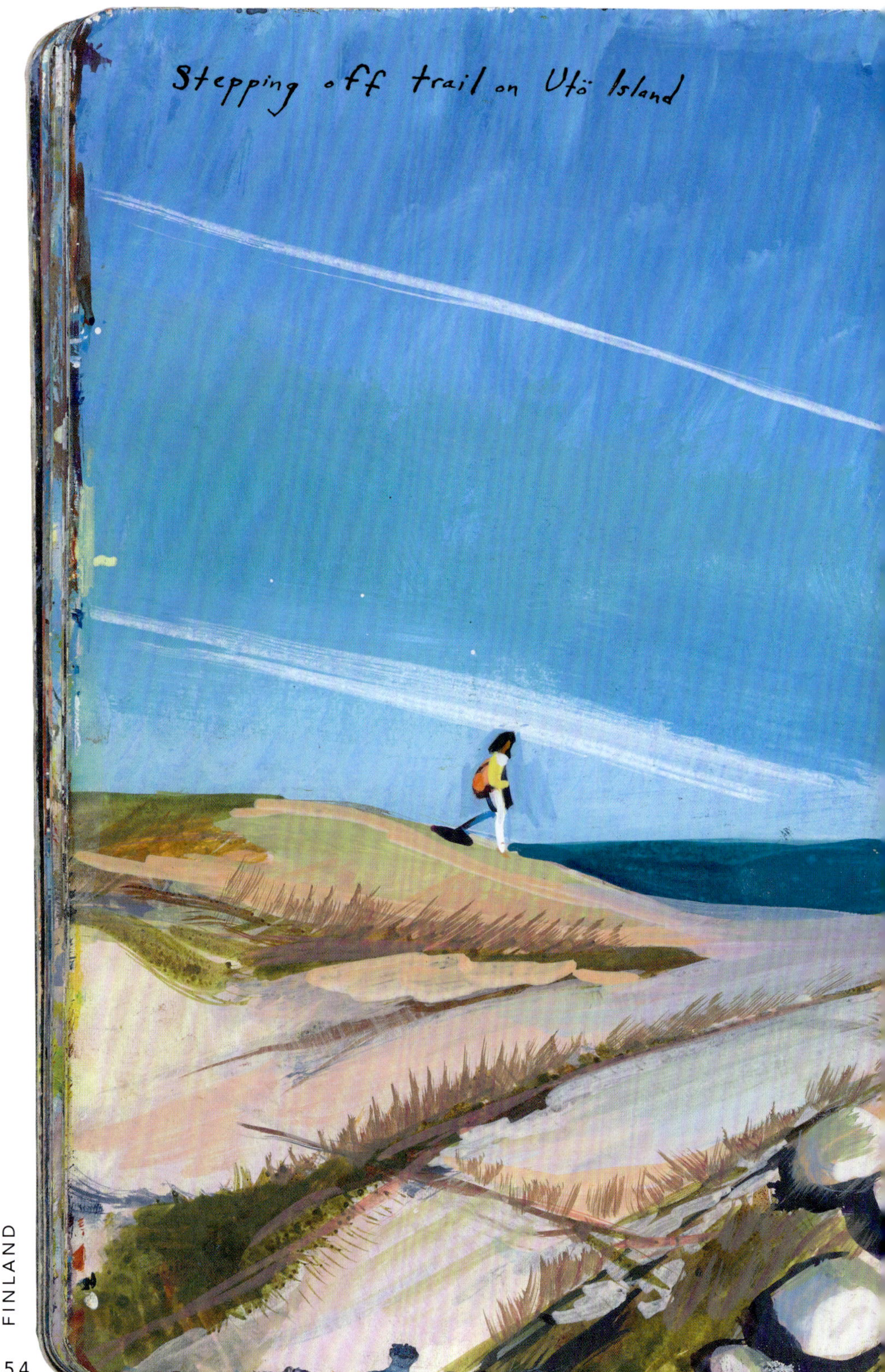

Stepping off trail on Utö Island

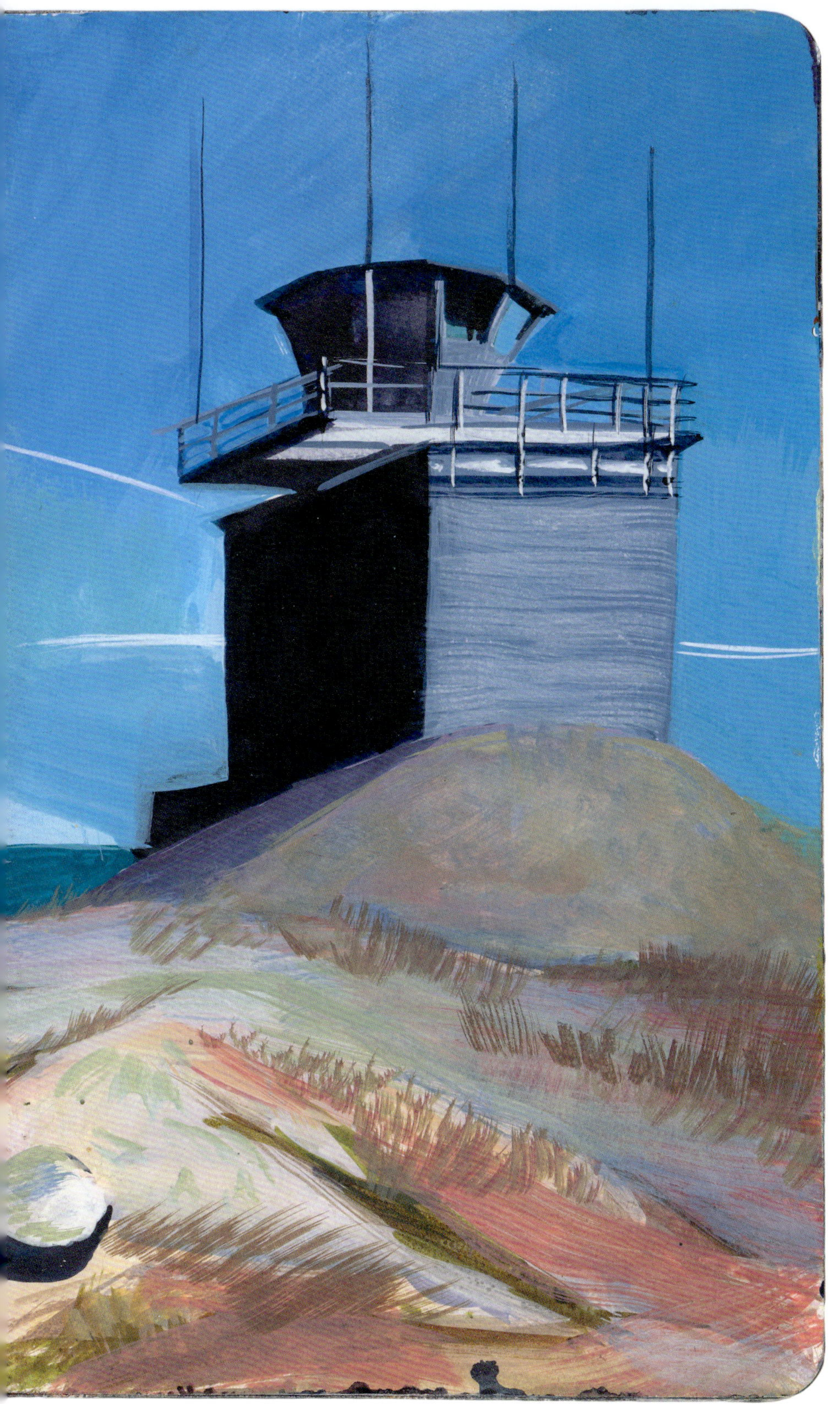

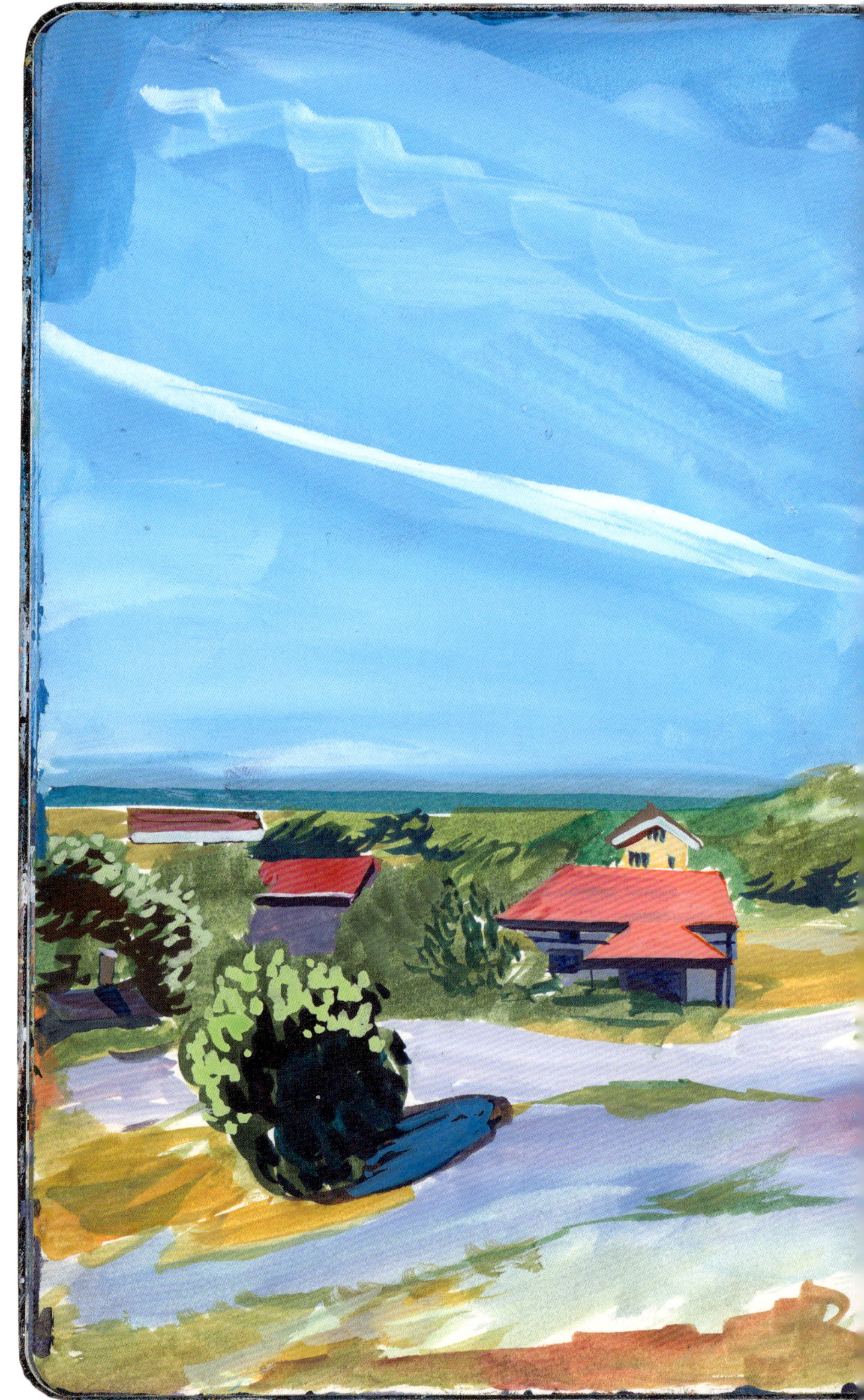

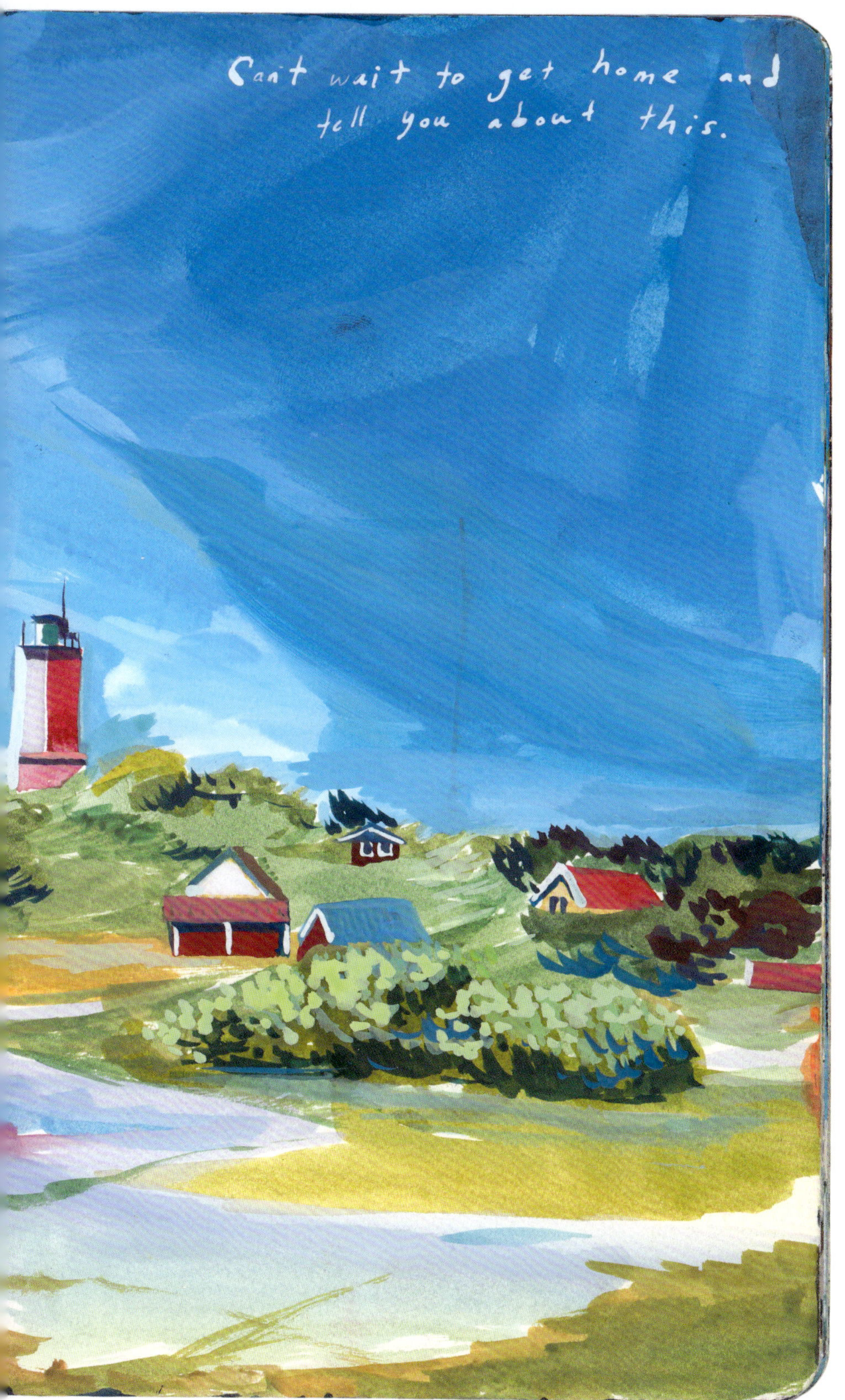

Can't wait to get home and
tell you about this.

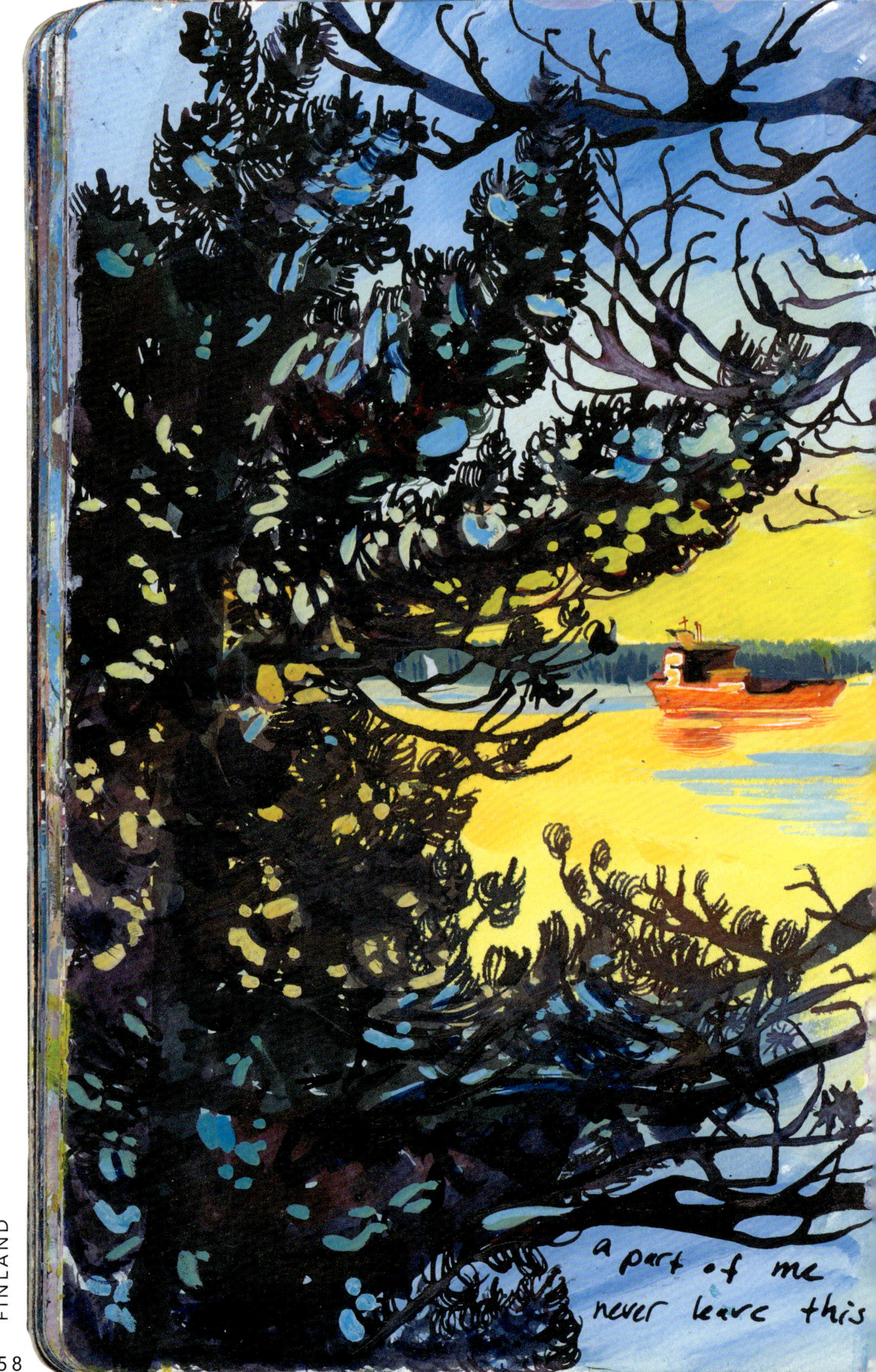
a part of me
never leave this

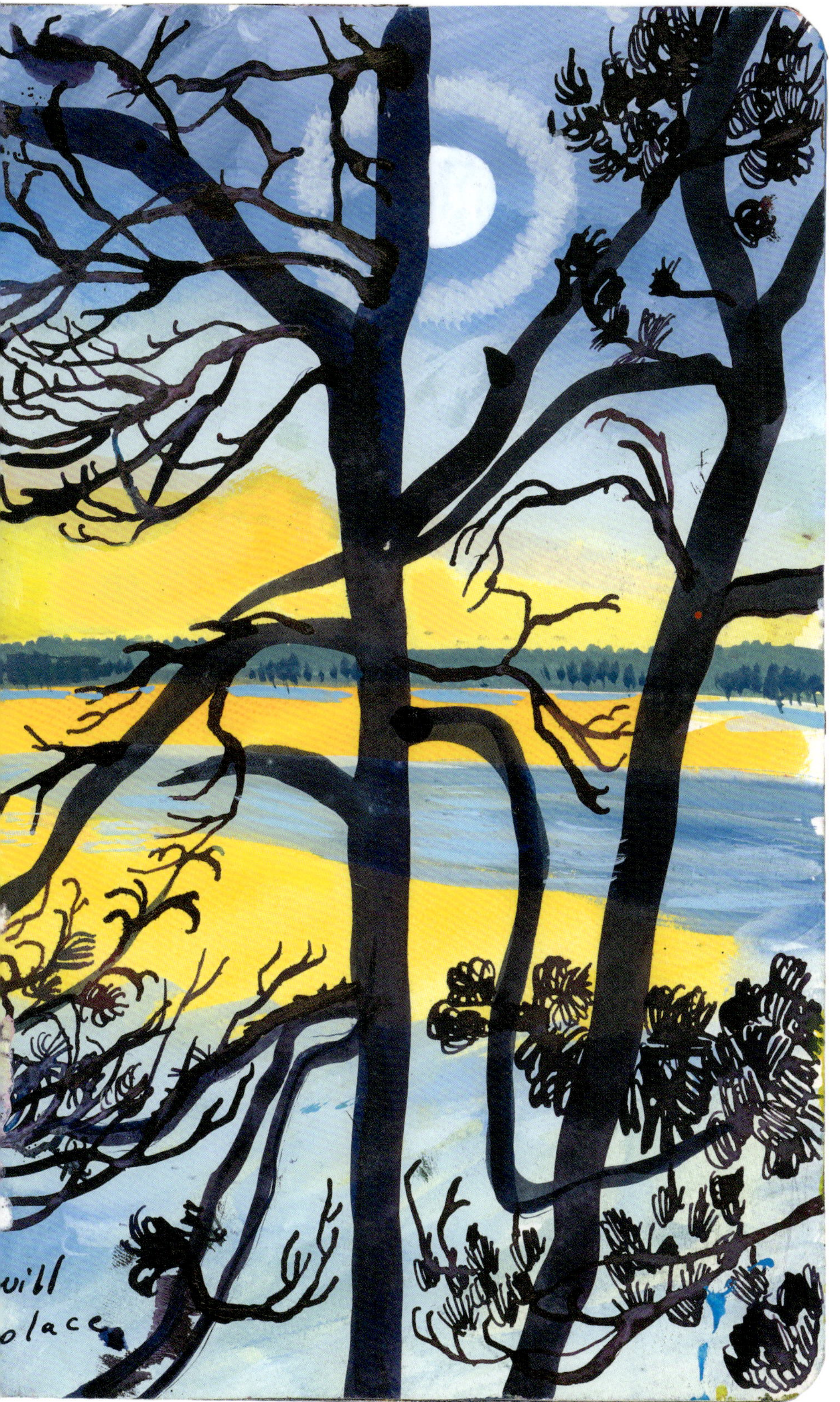

will
place

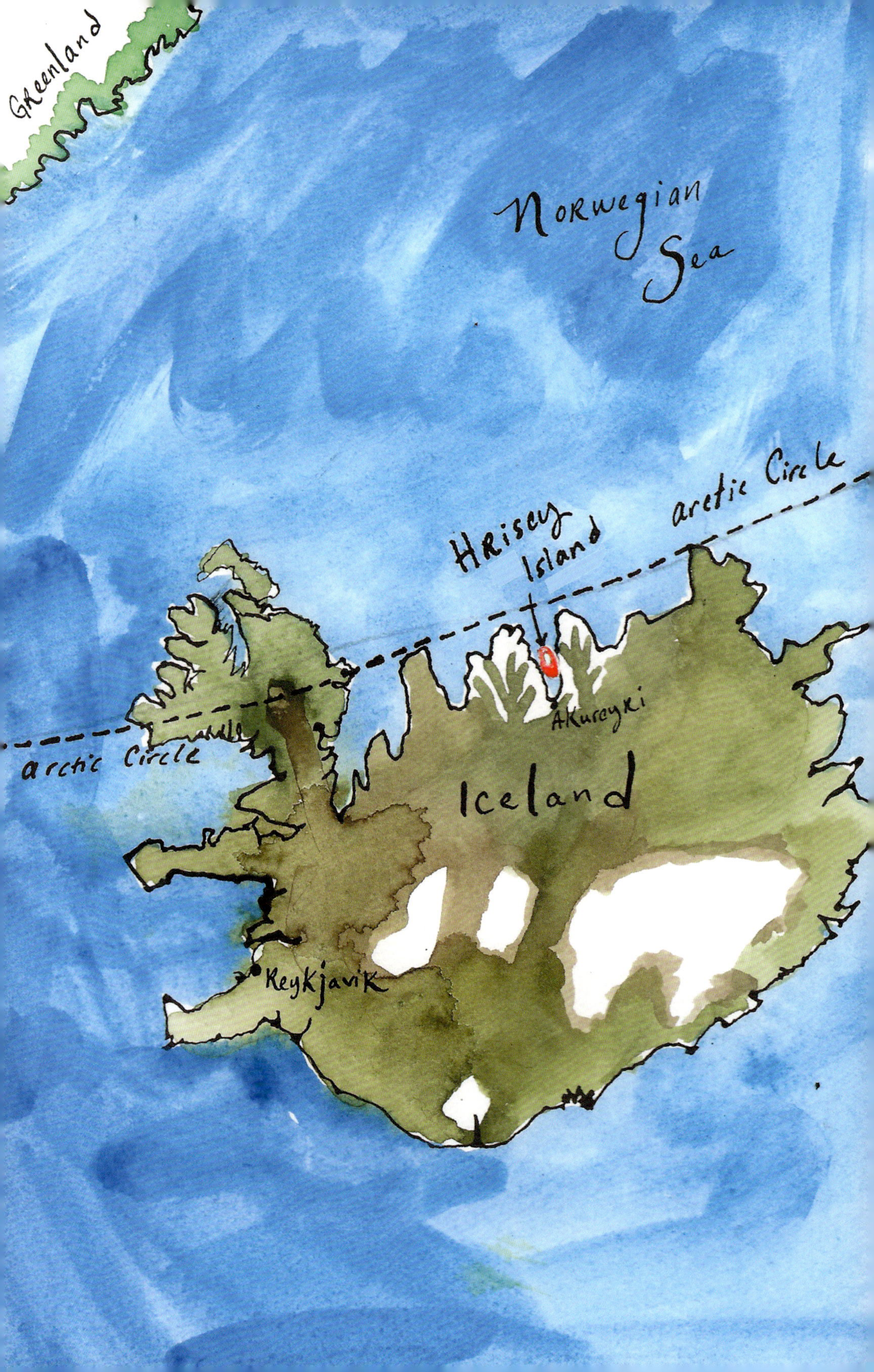

Greenland
Norwegian Sea
Hrísey Island
arctic Circle
Akureyri
arctic Circle
Iceland
Reykjavik

VIII

Hrisey Island, Iceland

October 31st, 2017

On an island off the northern coast of Iceland, I'm at my most remote residency yet. The days are getting shorter. It is so quiet, but at night the wind pummels the house. Windows rattle and doors slam shut. I hear a tapping on the desk by my bed. I'm sure it's a ghost, signaling in Morse Code.

During the day, I go for long walks to observe gyrfalcons hunt ptarmigans. Today, I sat for hours in a bed of moss, watching whales. They surfaced to feed below the fjord's tallest peak as storm clouds gathered in the distance. This has been a strange and eerie month, but today makes up for it. I don't always feel this way, but right now I have the life I dream of; I'm the woman I want to be. Happy thirtieth birthday, Missy.

colors:

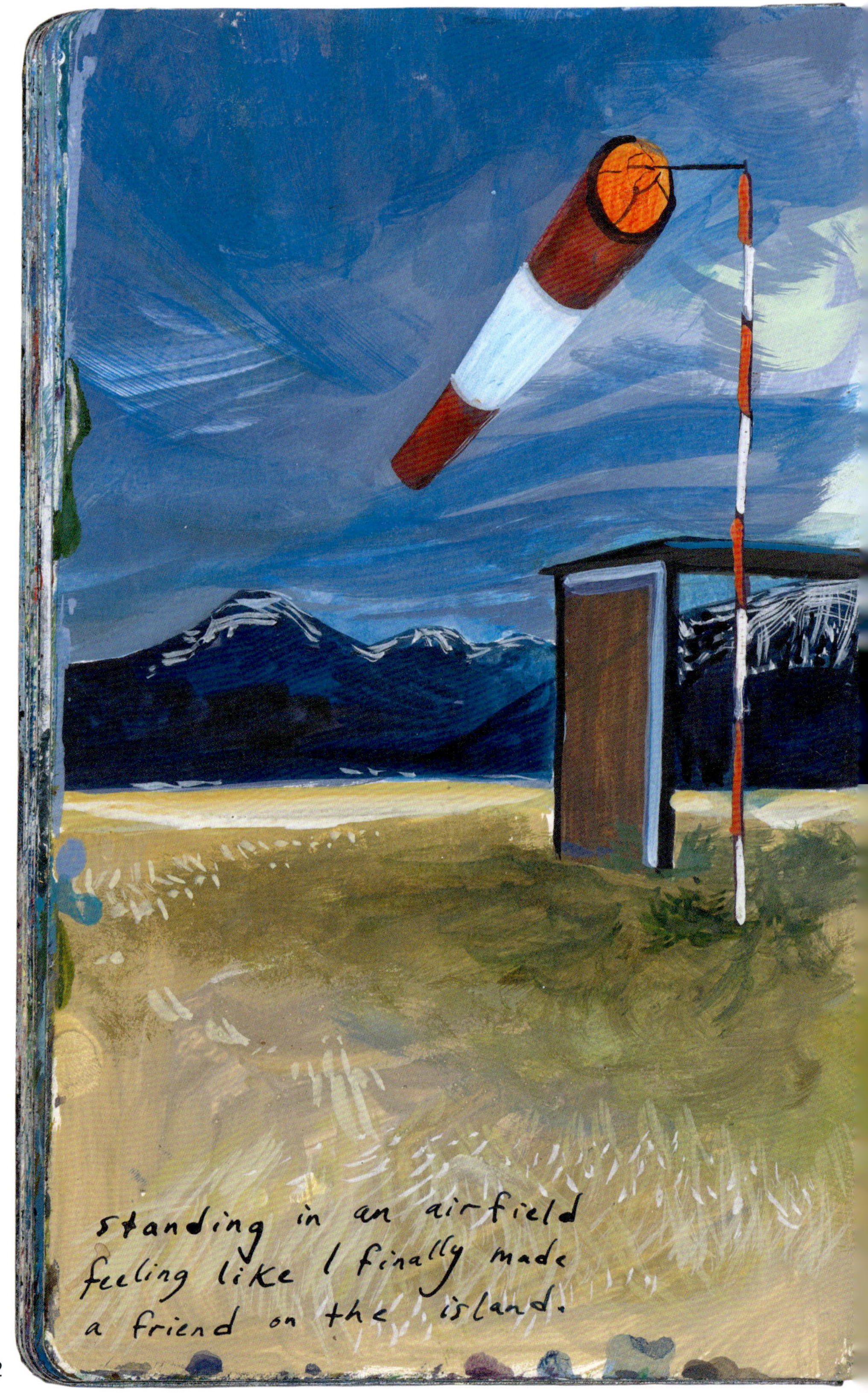
standing in an airfield
feeling like I finally made
a friend on the island.

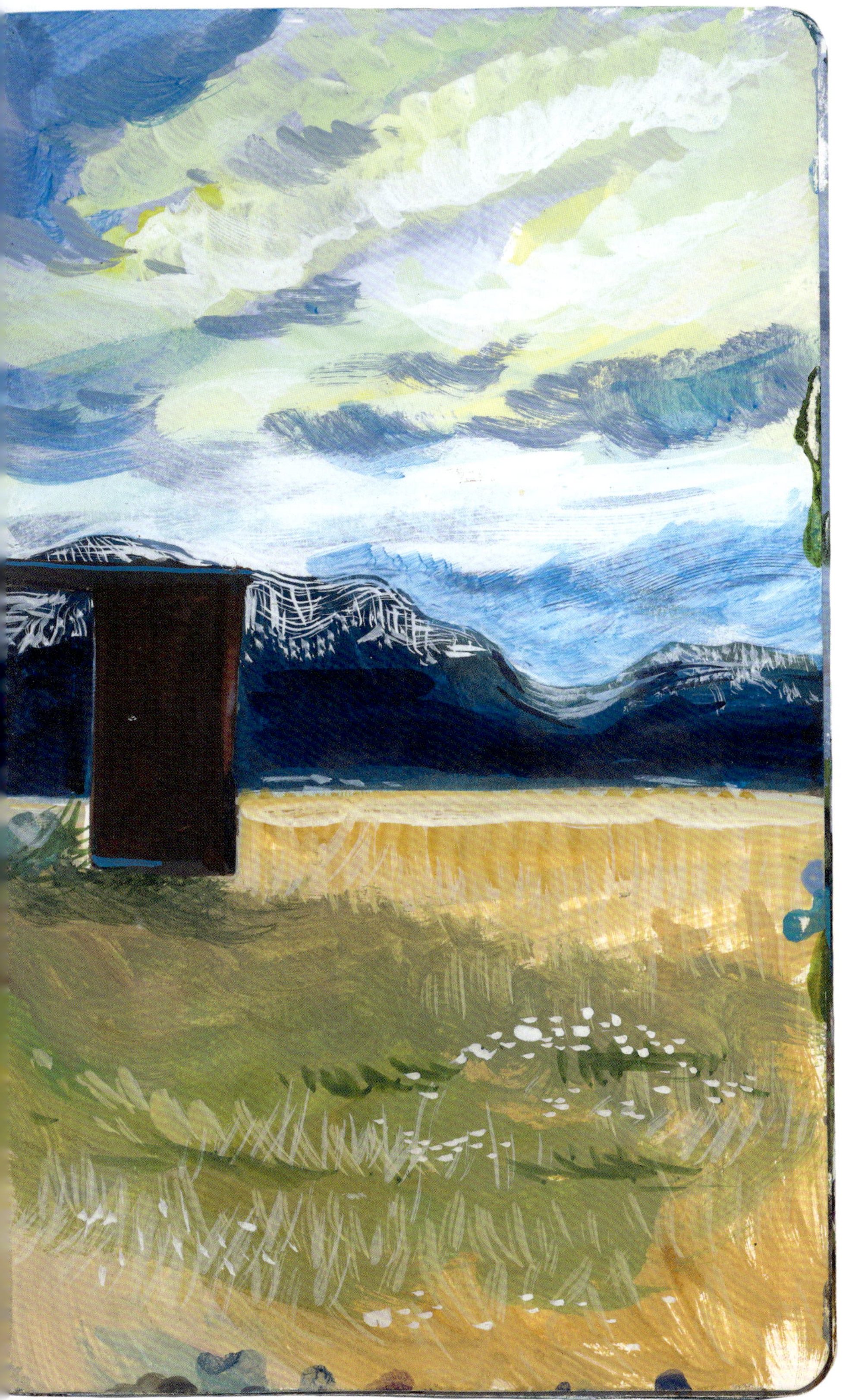

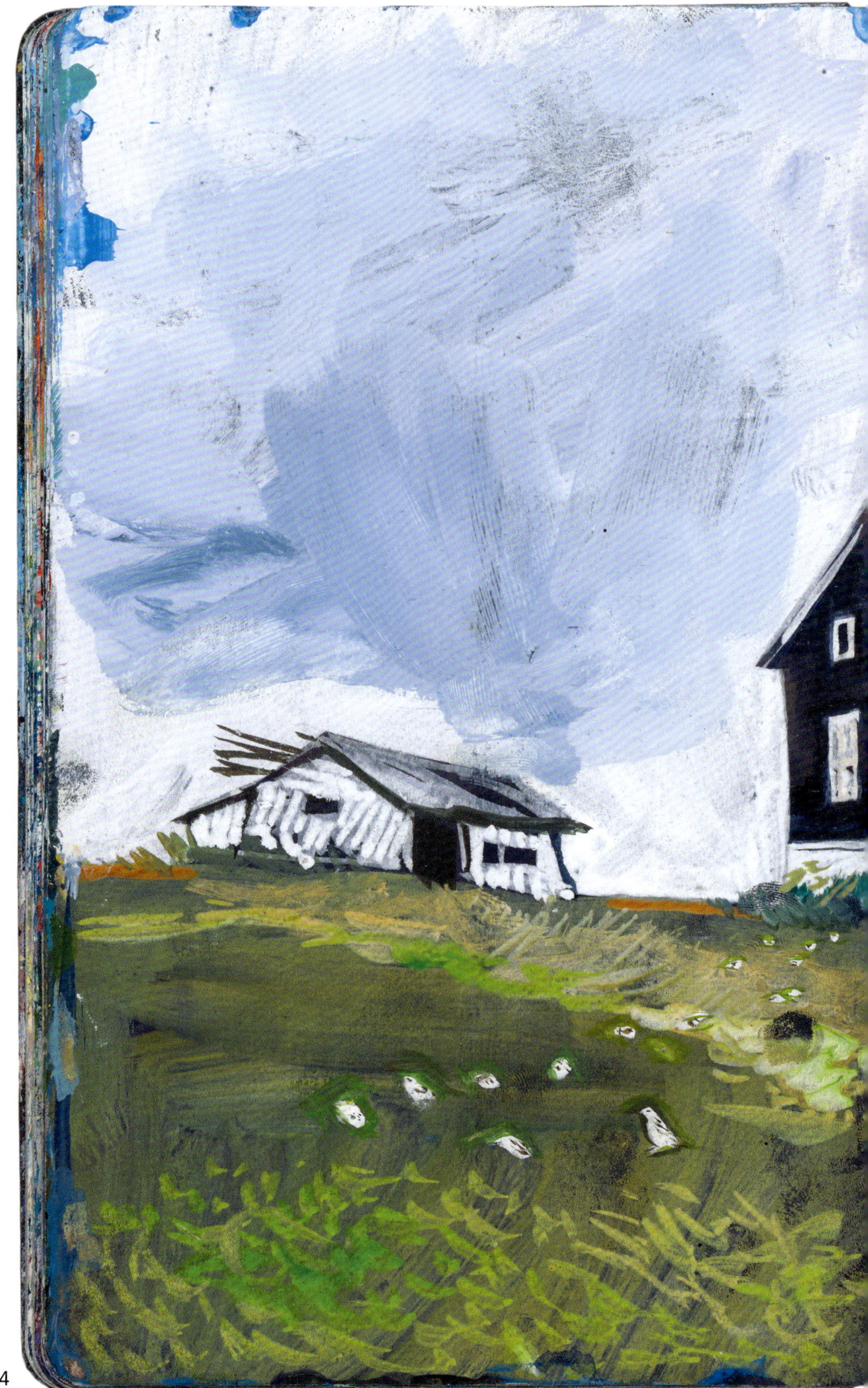

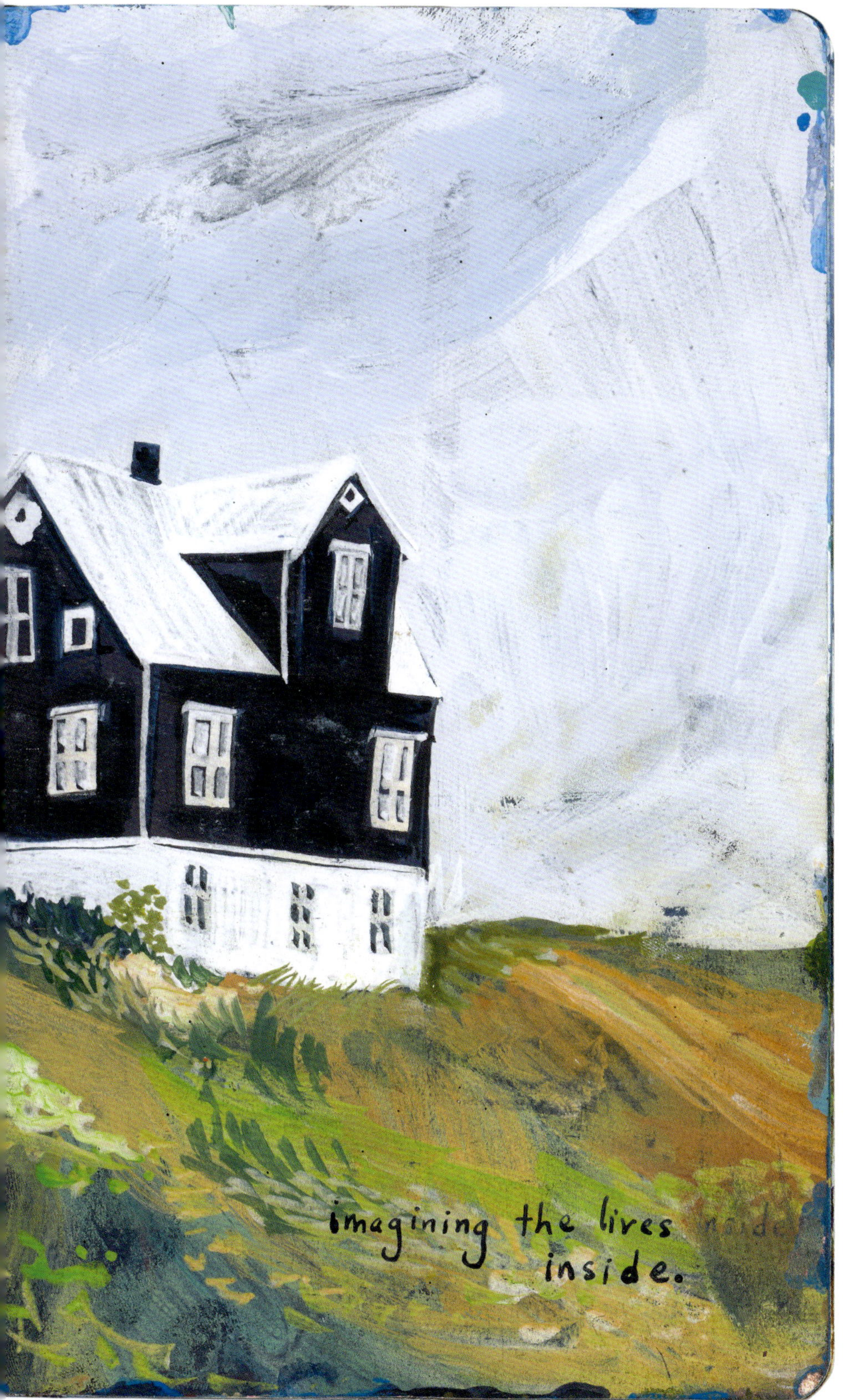

imagining the lives inside
inside.

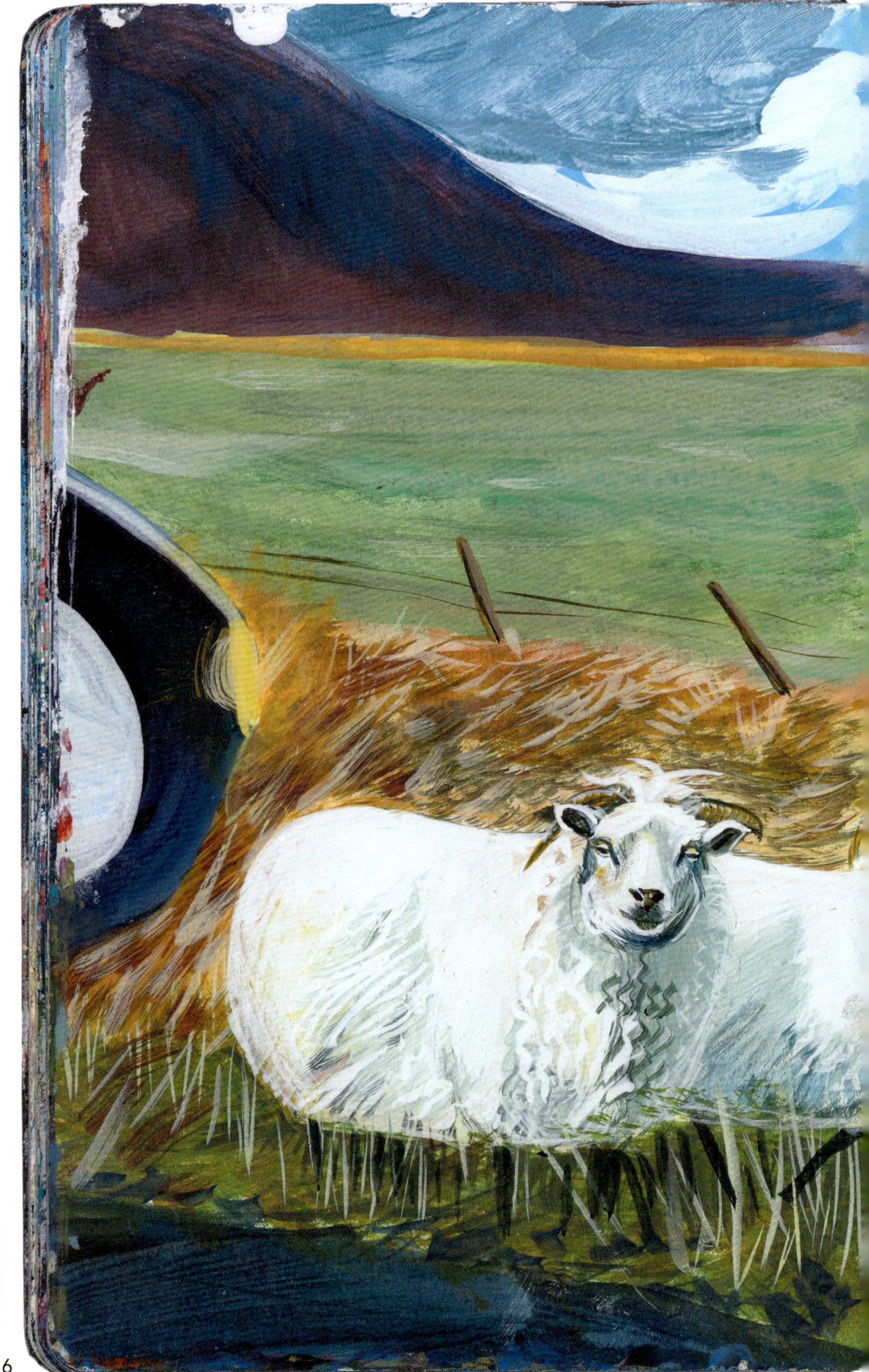

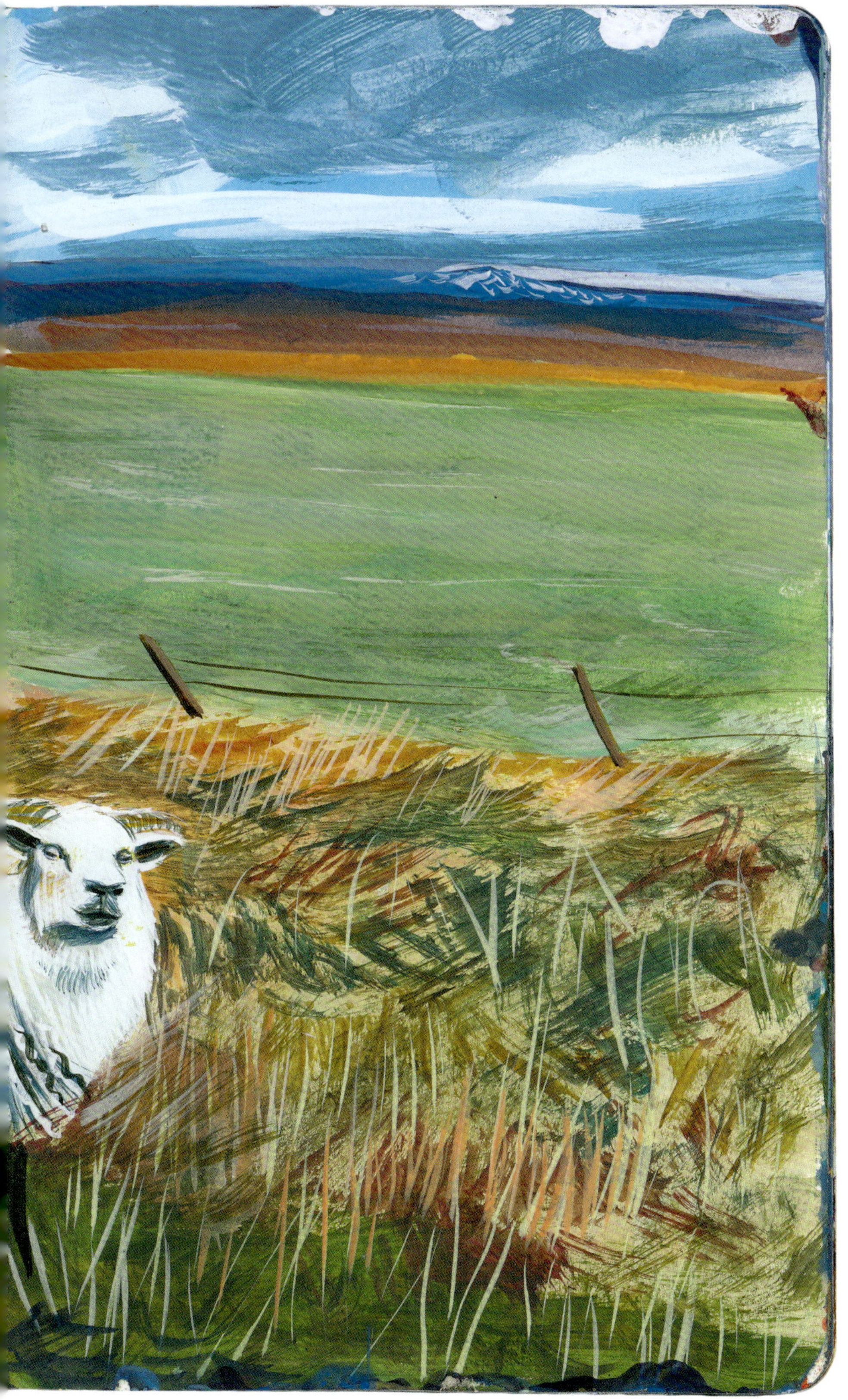

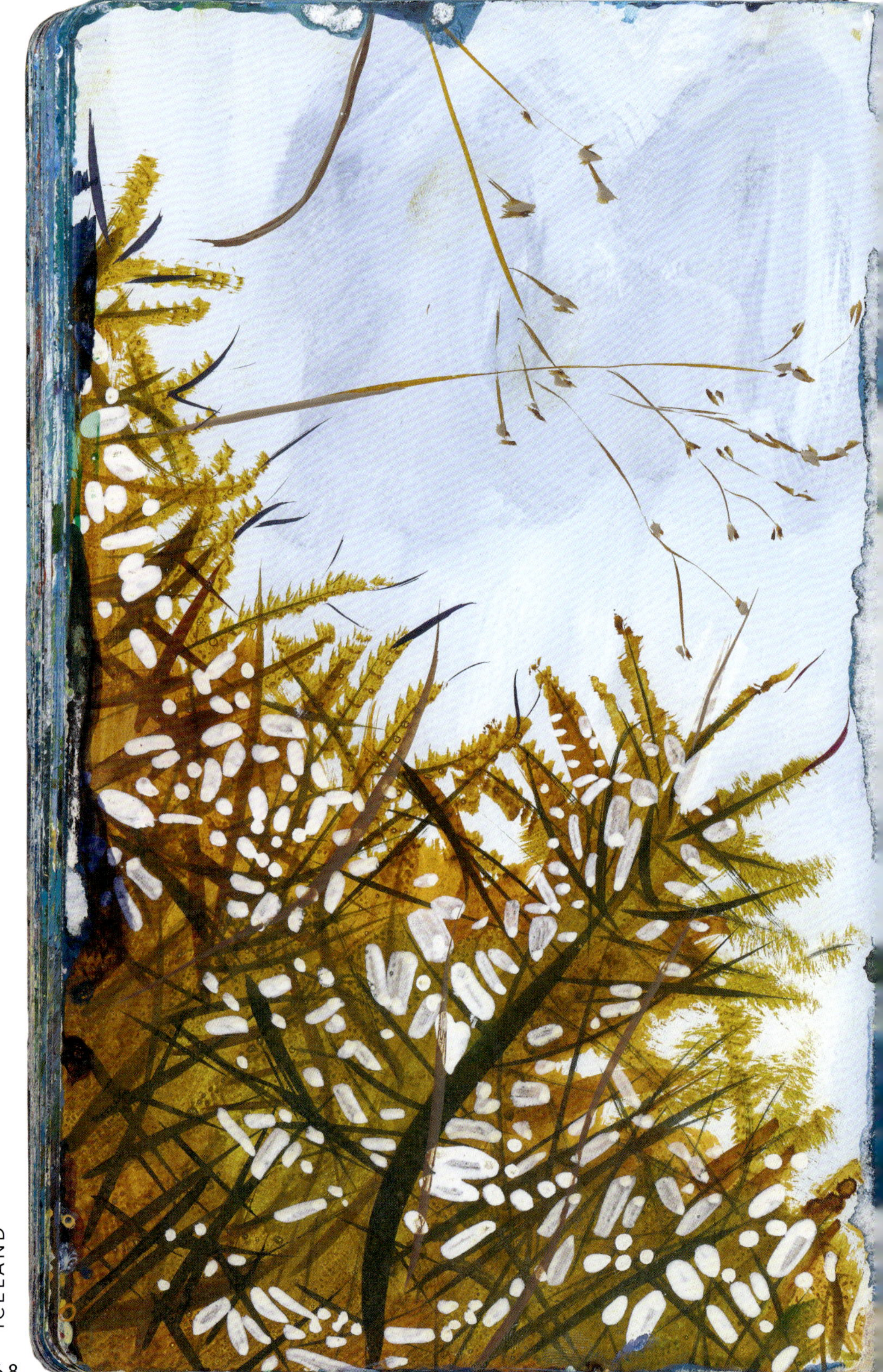

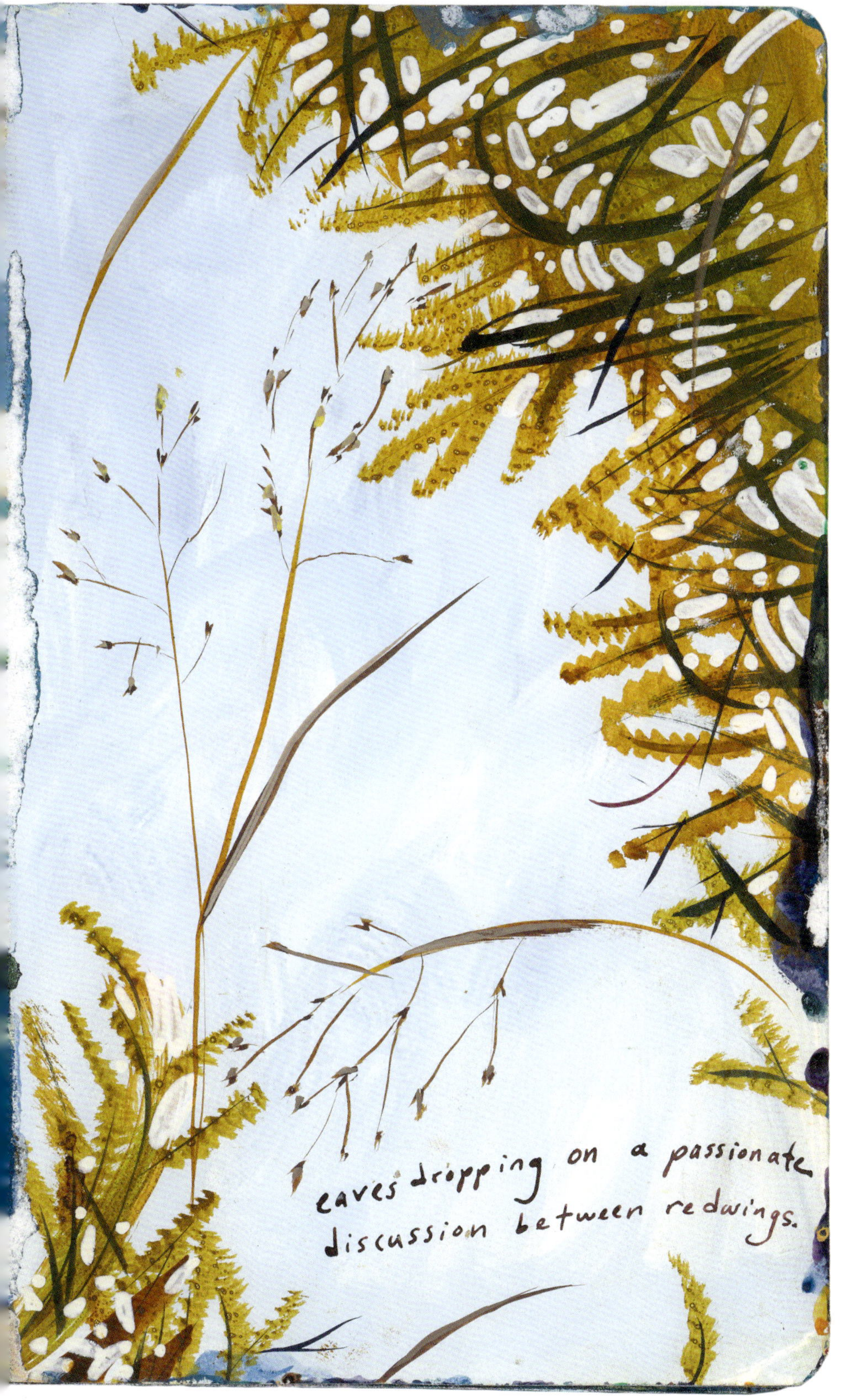

eavesdropping on a passionate
discussion between redwings.

We drove outside Akureyri and
stood at the edge of a construction site.
I had one glove, so you pulled my hand
into your pocket.
I kissed your shoulder.
You came so far to see me.

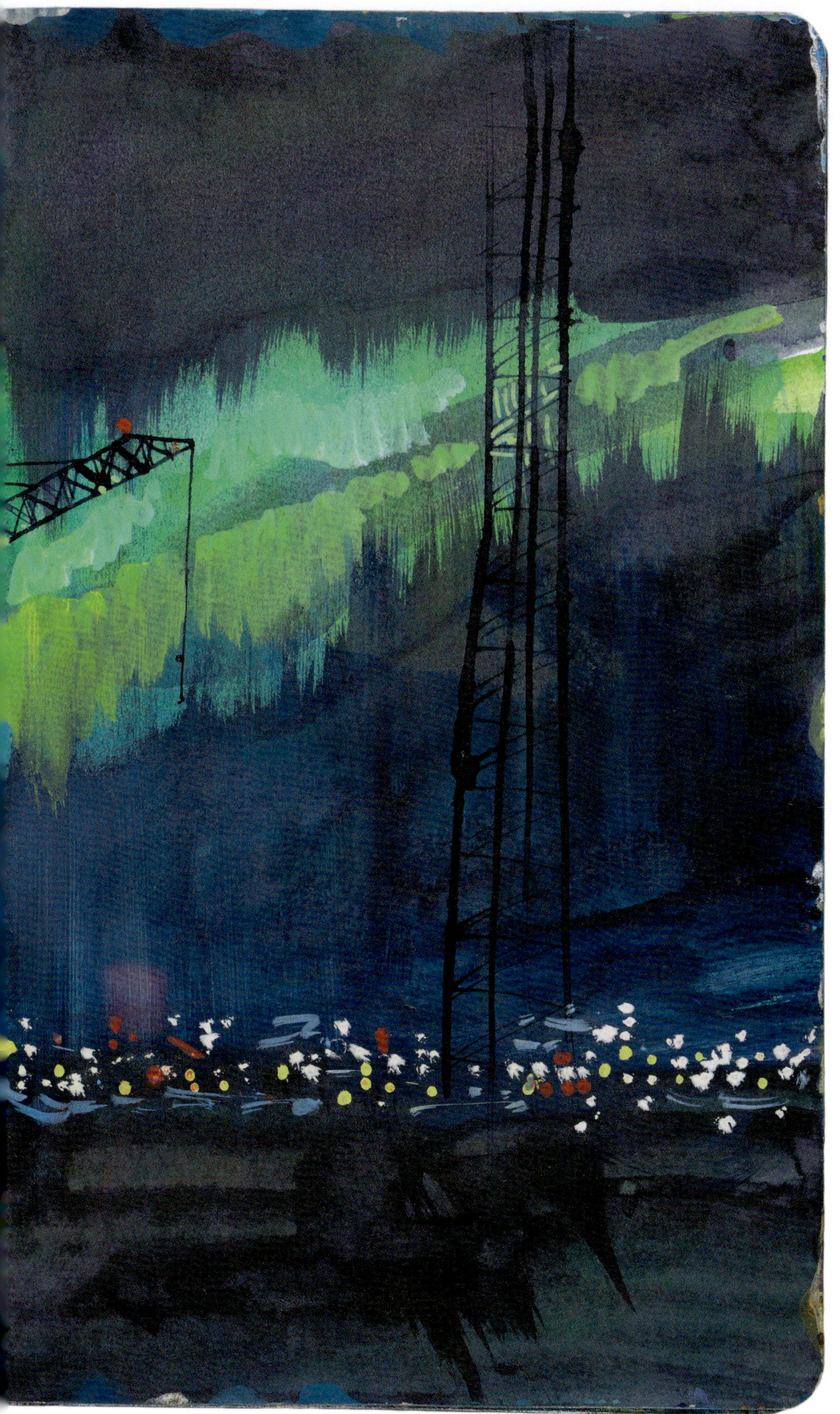

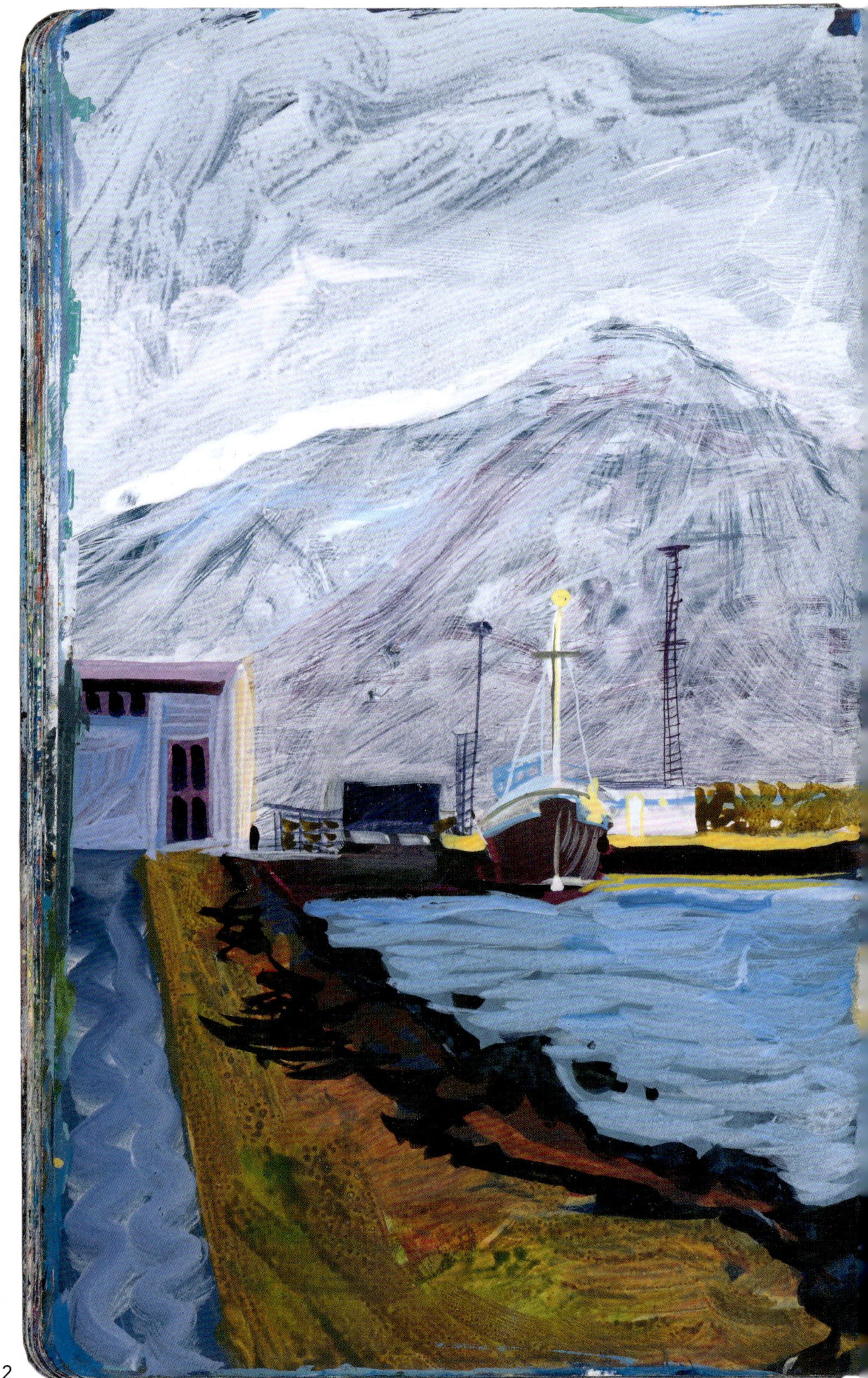

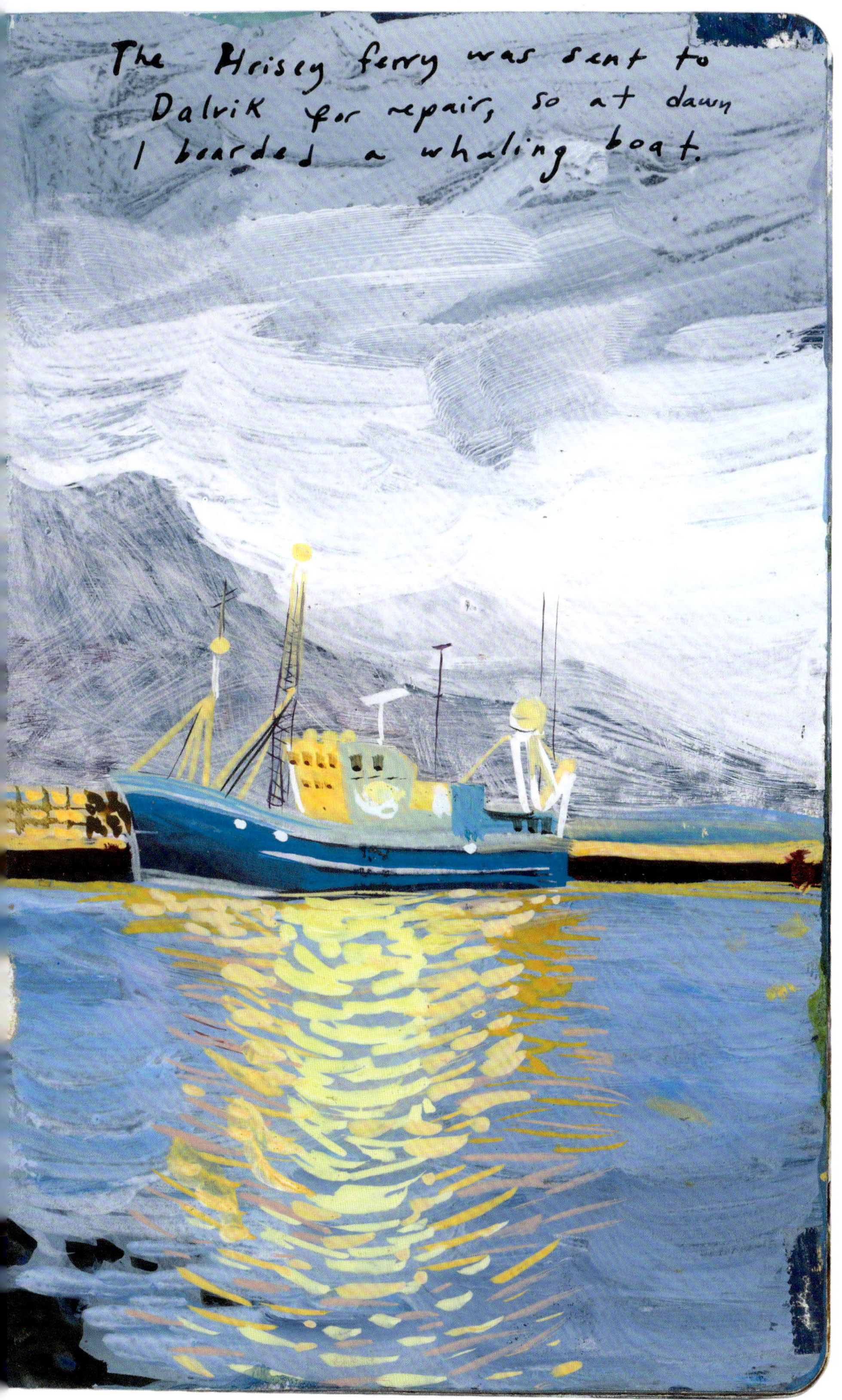

The Hrisey ferry was sent to
Dalvik for repair, so at dawn
I boarded a whaling boat.

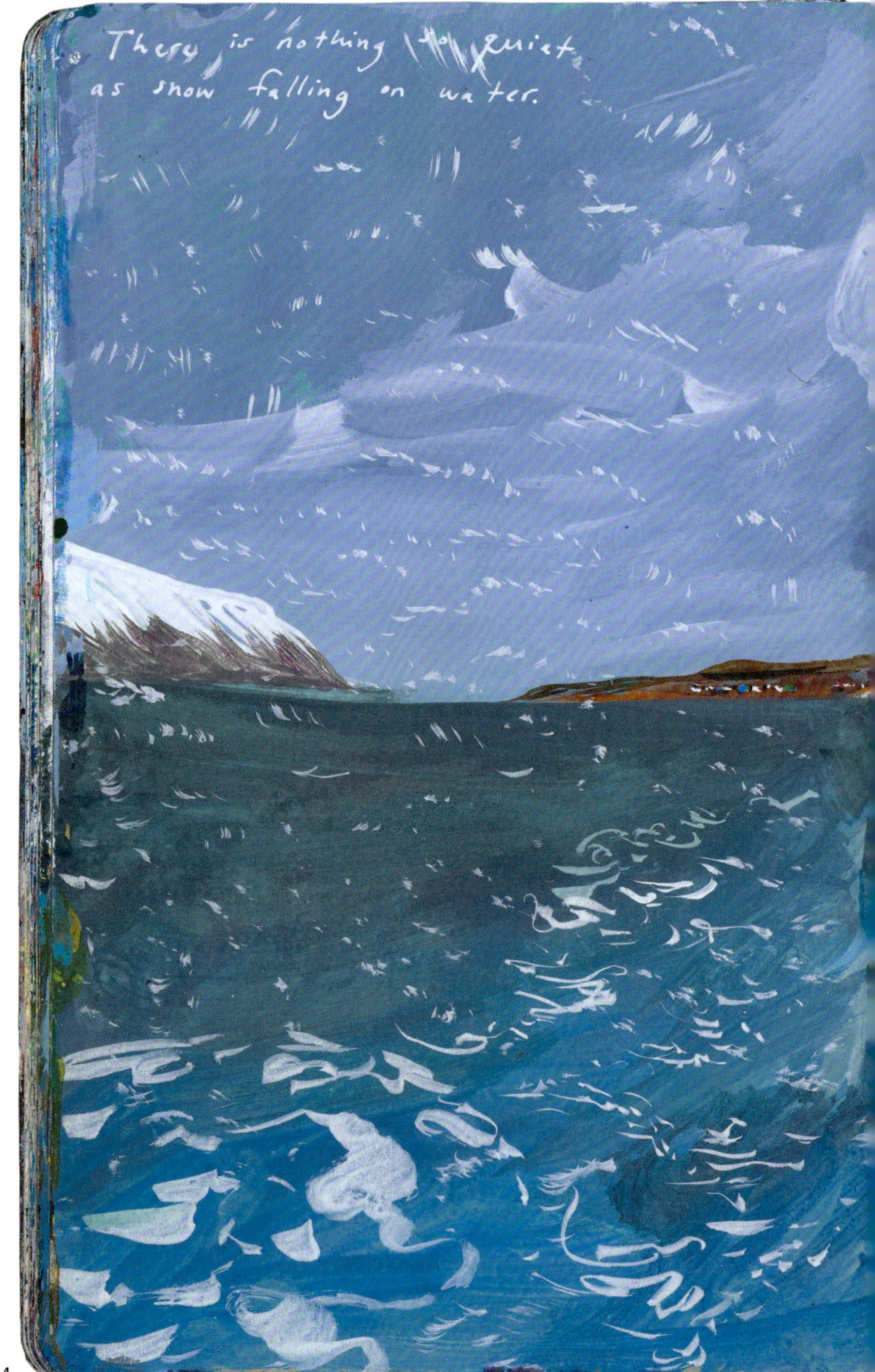
There is nothing so quiet
as snow falling on water.

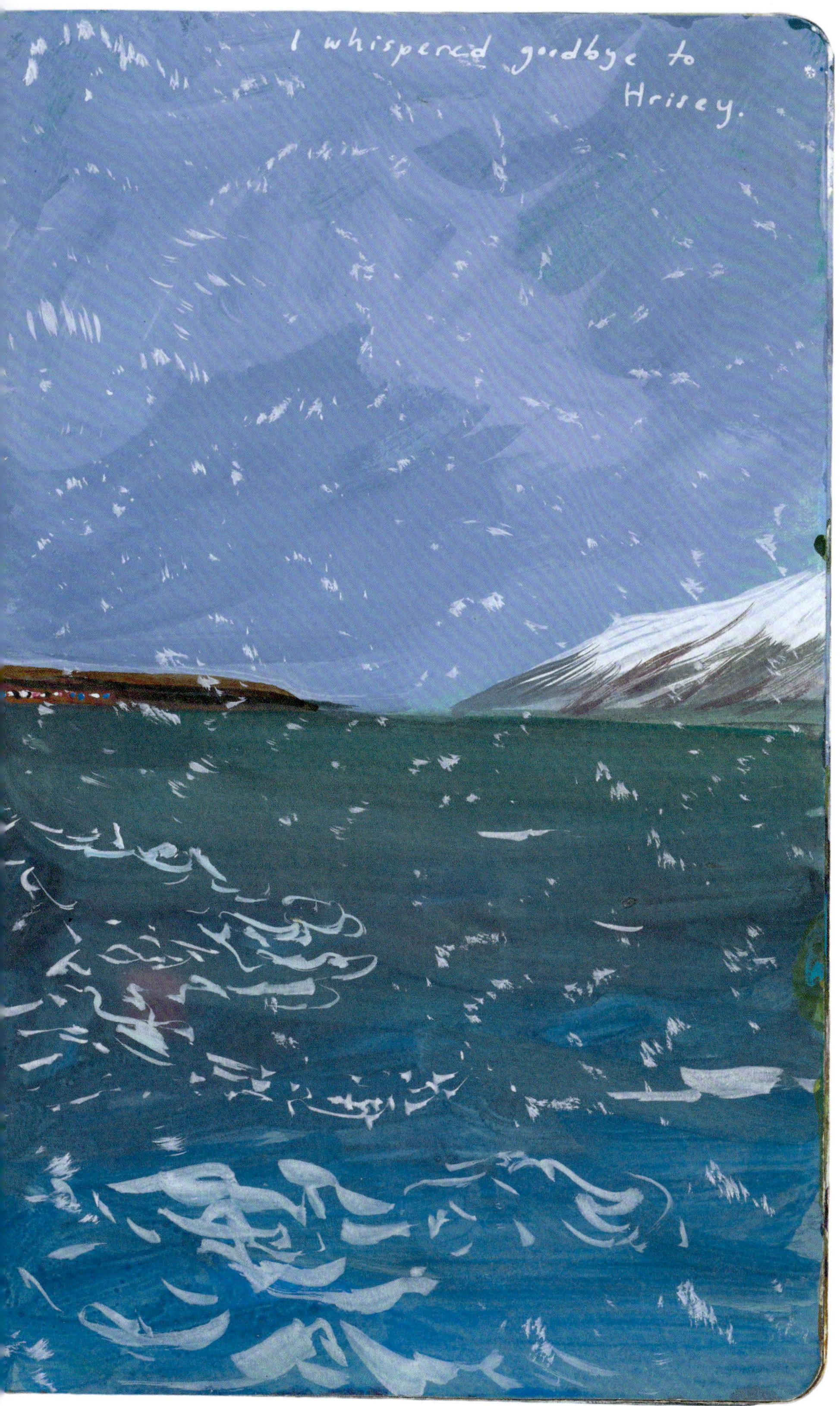
I whispered goodbye to
Hrisey.

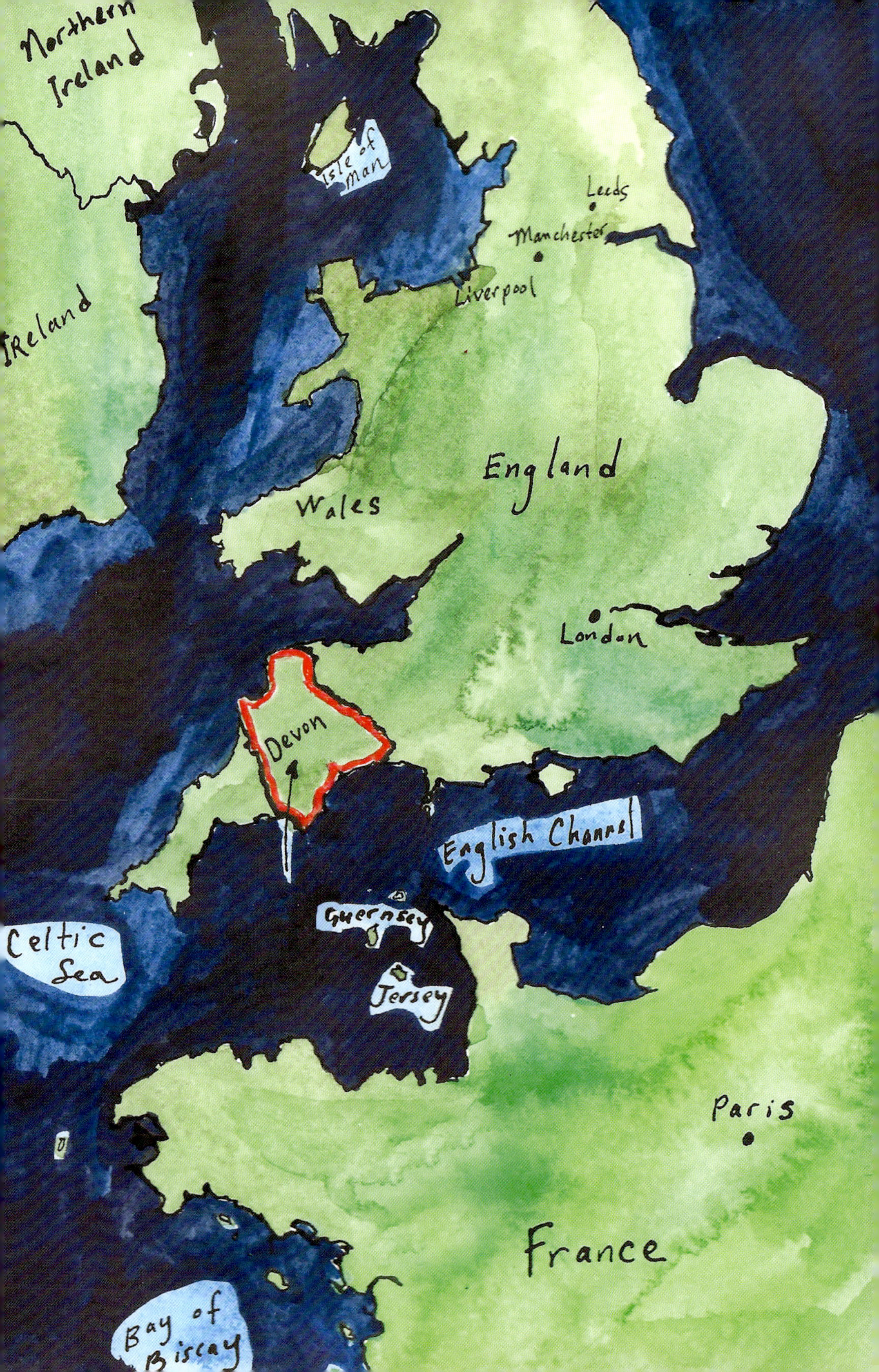

Northern Ireland
Ireland
Isle of Man
Leeds
Manchester
Liverpool
England
Wales
London
Devon
English Channel
Celtic Sea
Guernsey
Jersey
Paris
France
Bay of Biscay

IX

Devon, England

November 5th, 2017

    Harriet, a dear friend from Istanbul, invited me to her family's home in Devon. She showed me how to skin a rabbit, her father shared his collection of Jock Scott fishing flies, and her mother packed a basket of quince pies for us to enjoy atop the stony peaks of Valley of the Rocks.

    I've noticed that I have been collecting fewer and fewer souvenirs and pictures every time I travel. A few gifts from Harriet's family are all I have to take home from this trip to England. Painting has trained my mind to take mental photographs with greater clarity. I have a warmed heart, a lush record of vivid memories, and a journal full of artwork. Do I need anything more than this?

colors:

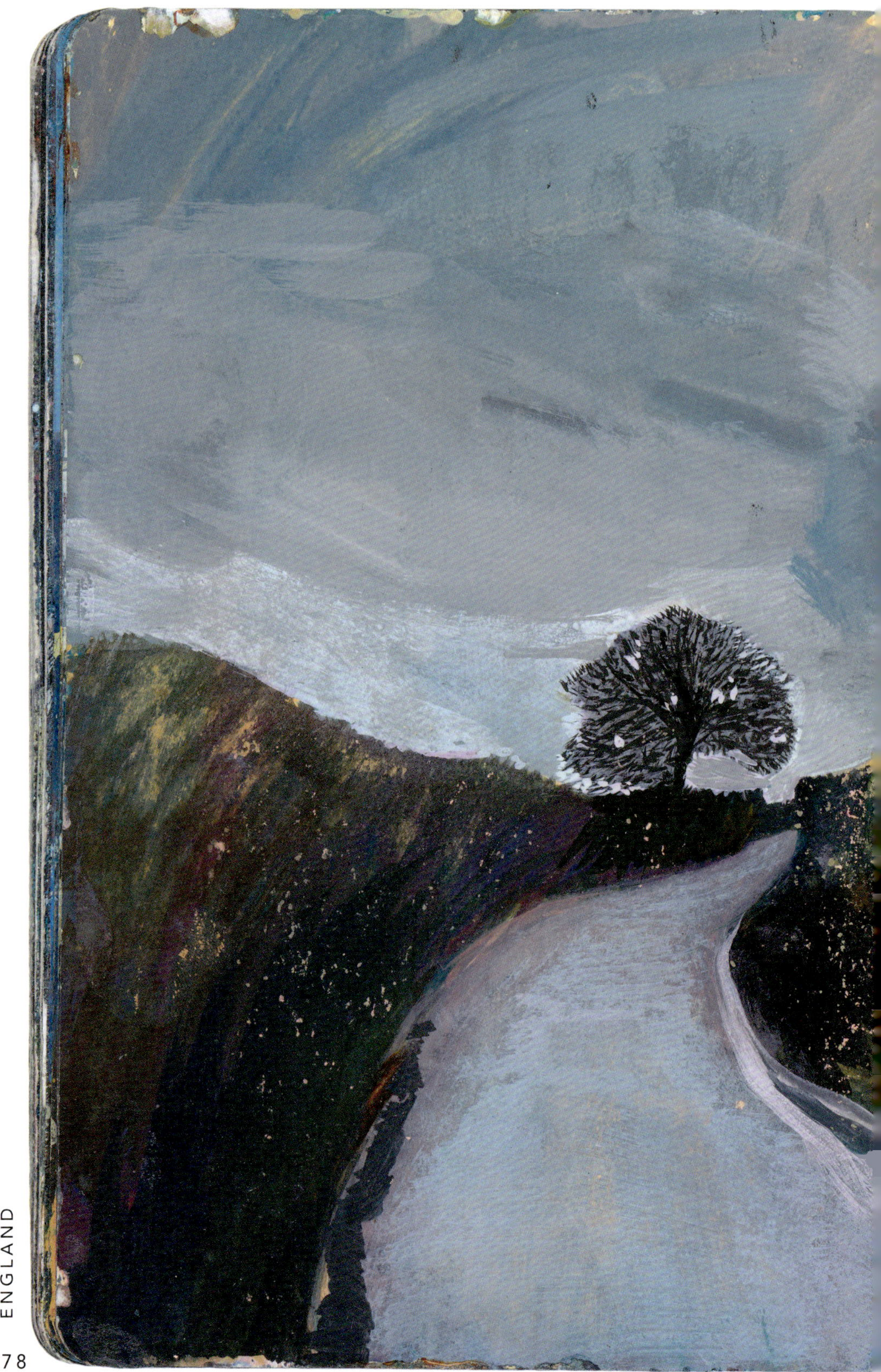

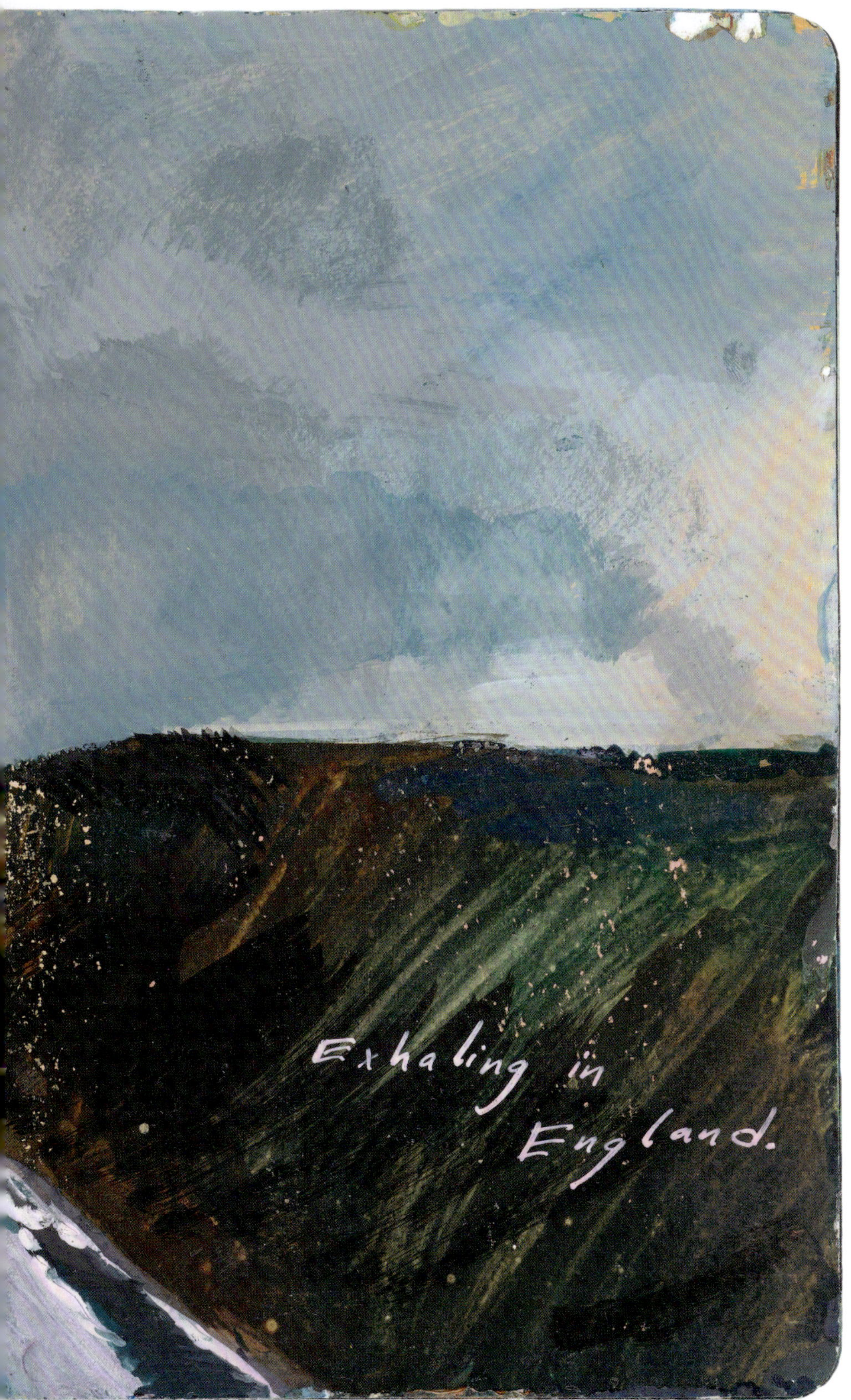

Exhaling in
England.

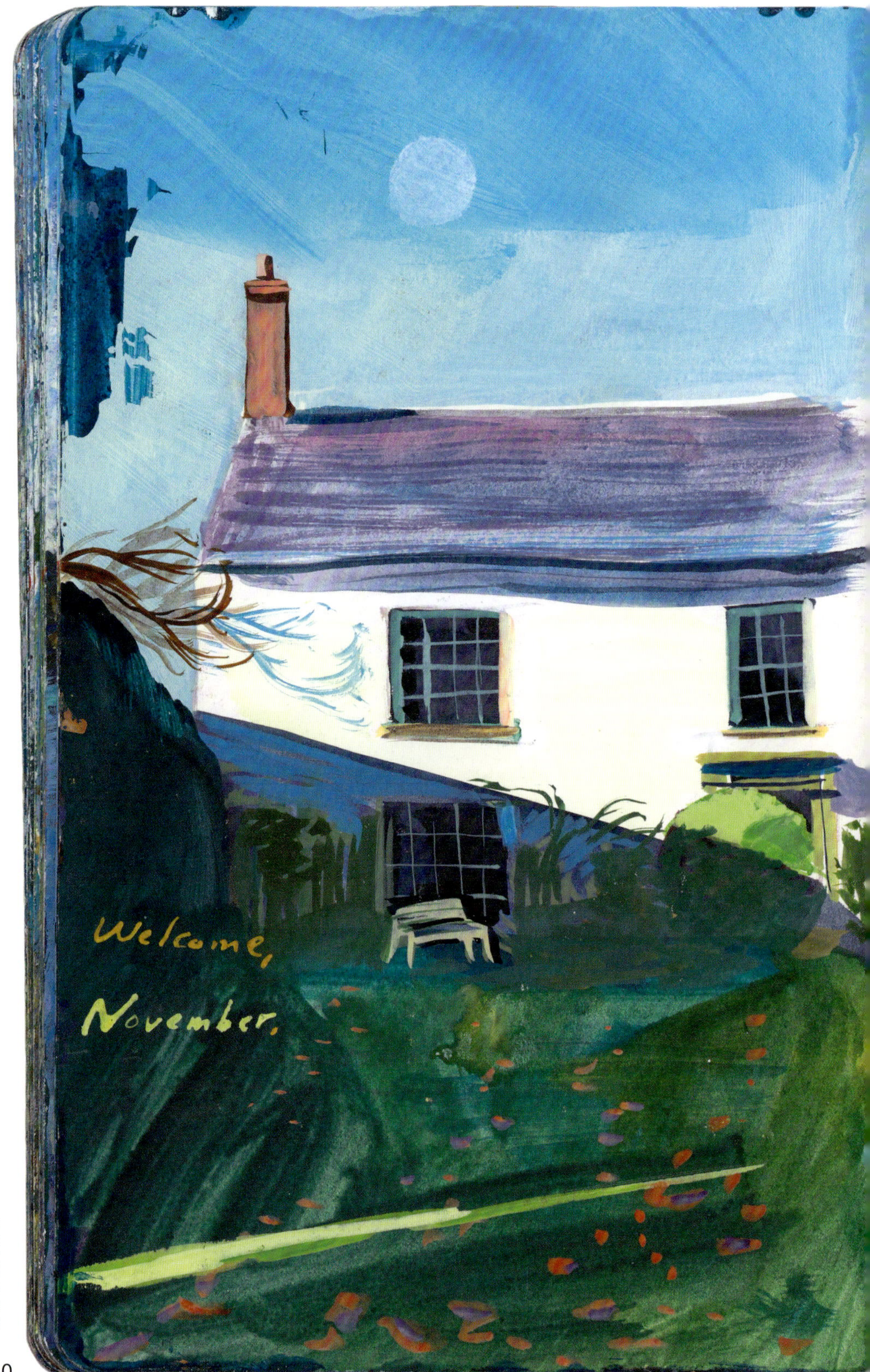

Welcome,
November.

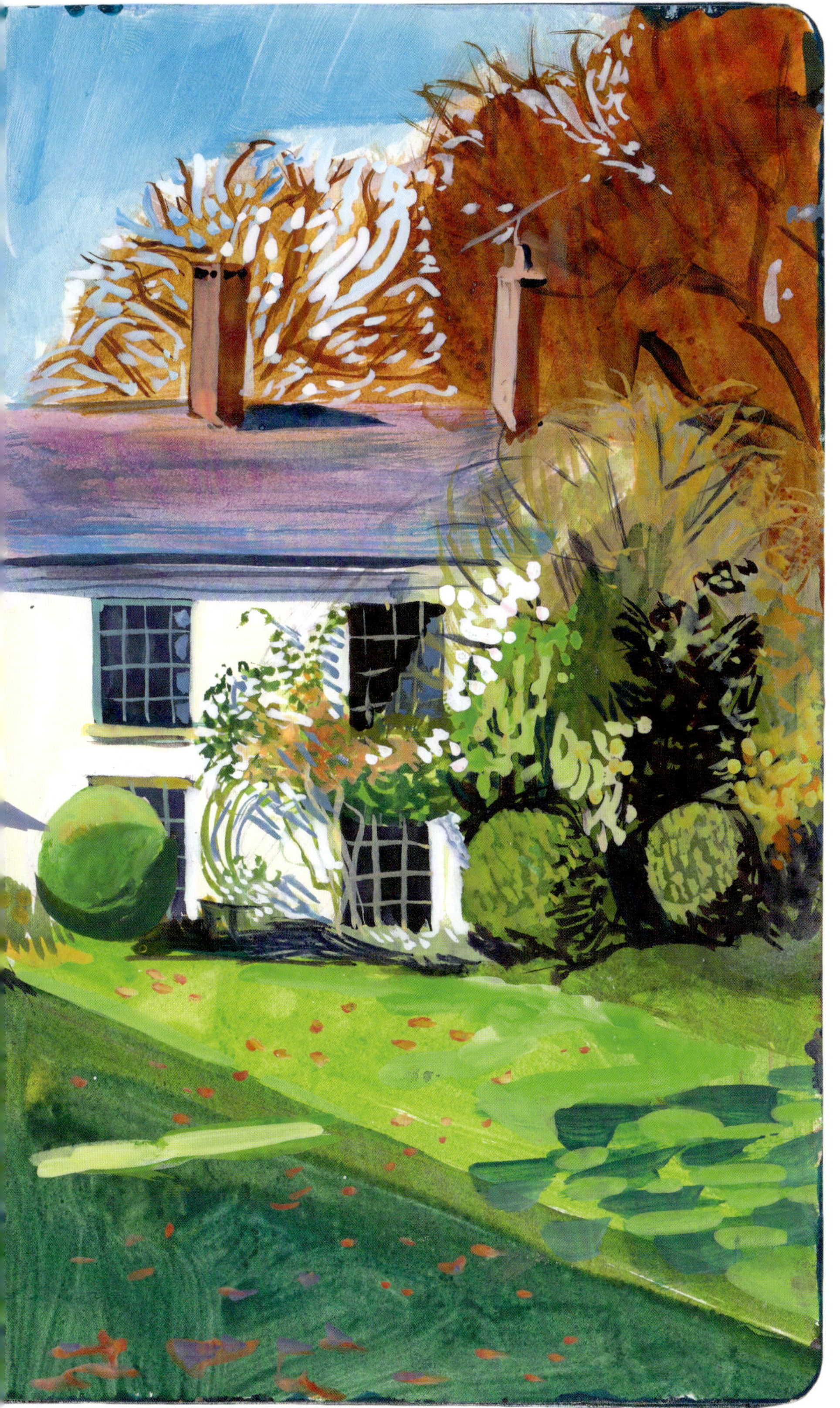

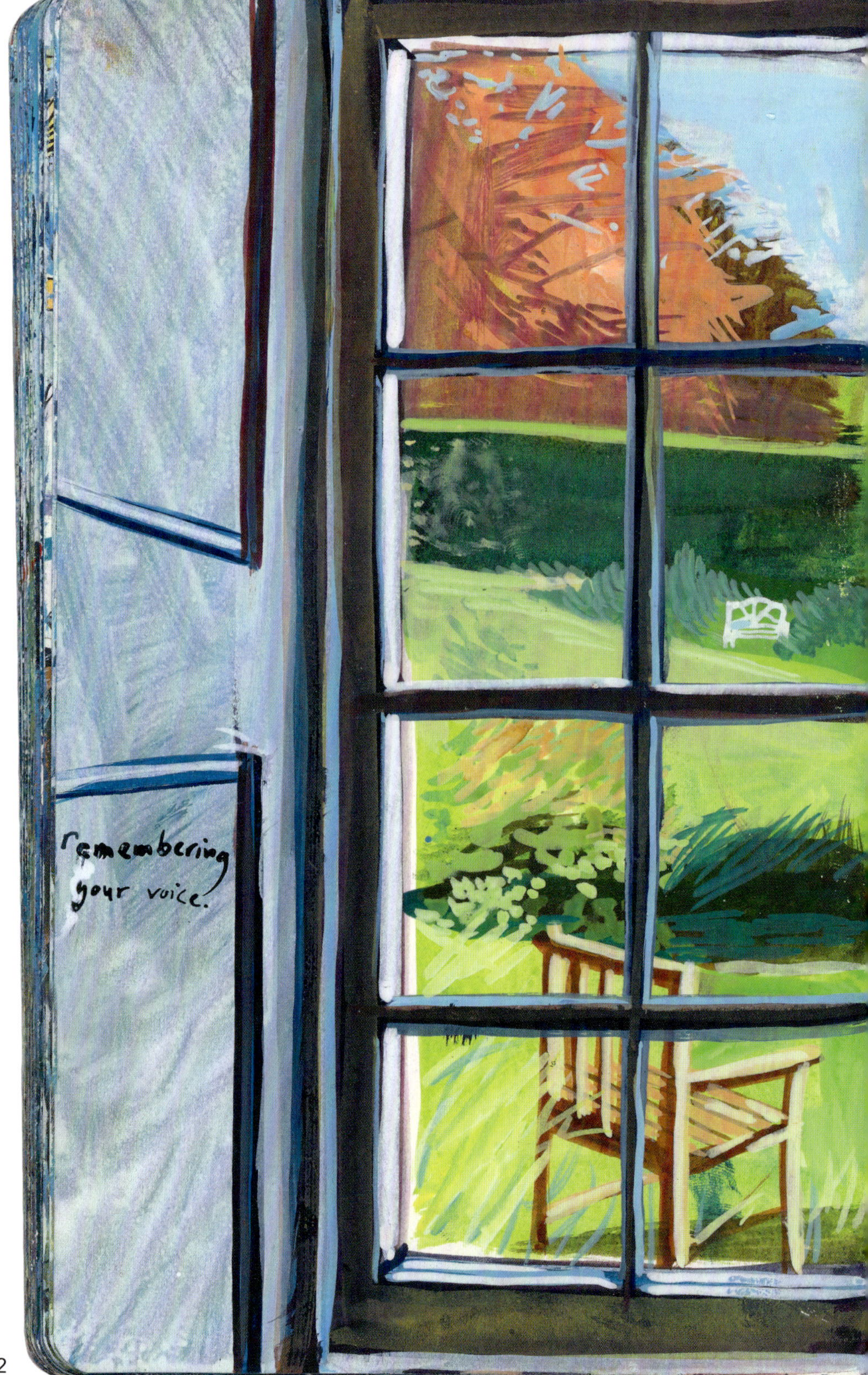

remembering
your voice.

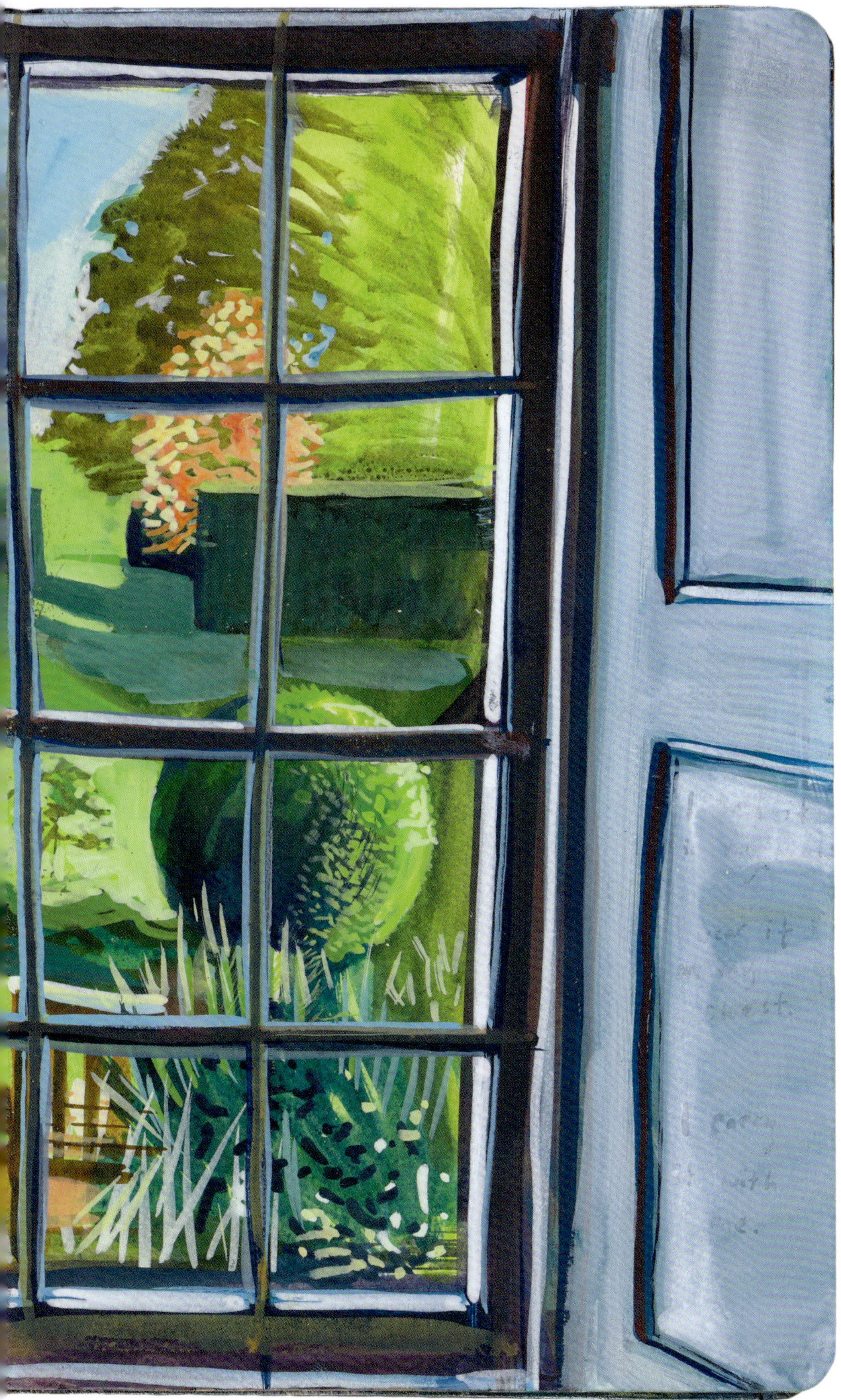

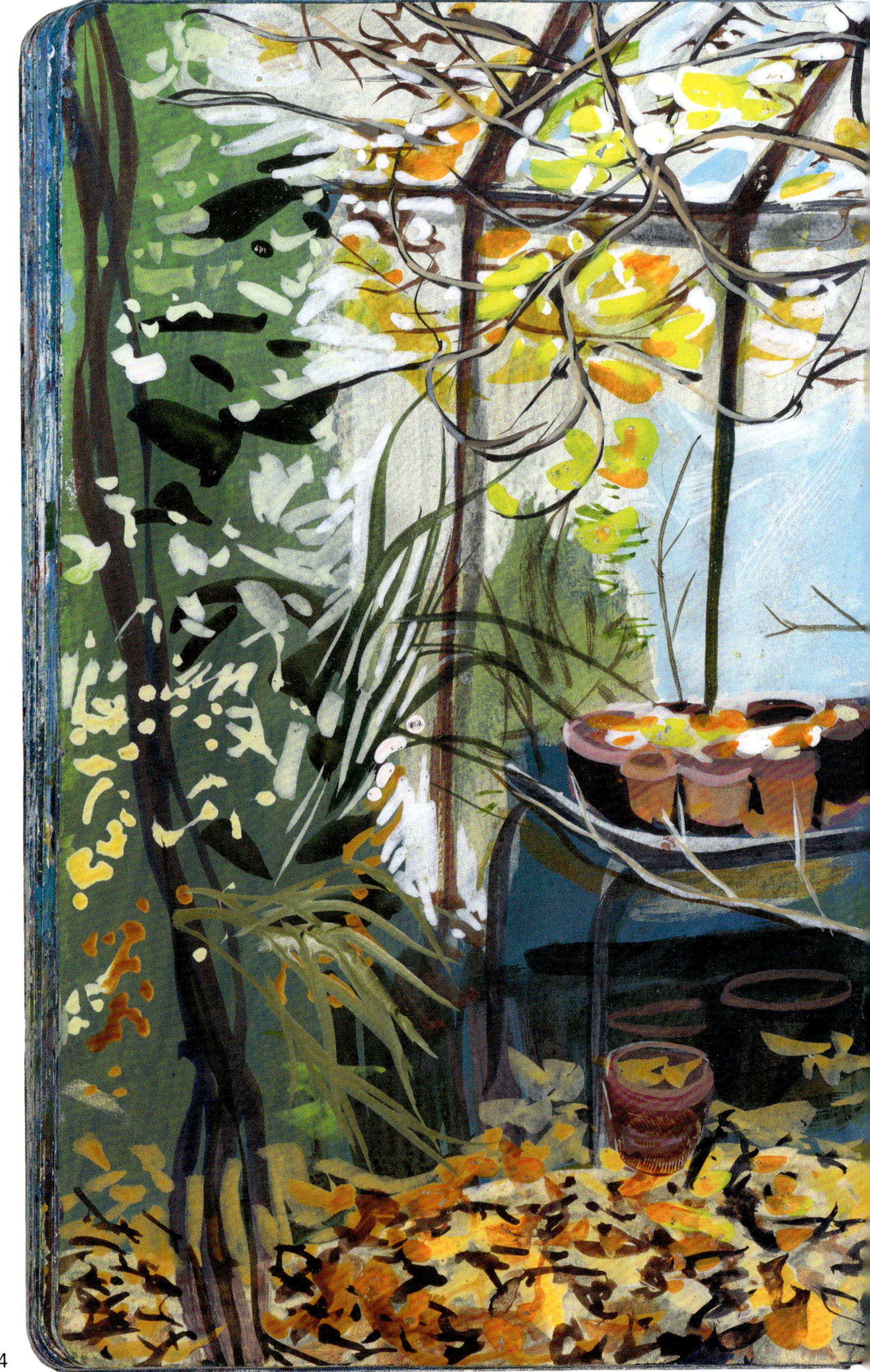

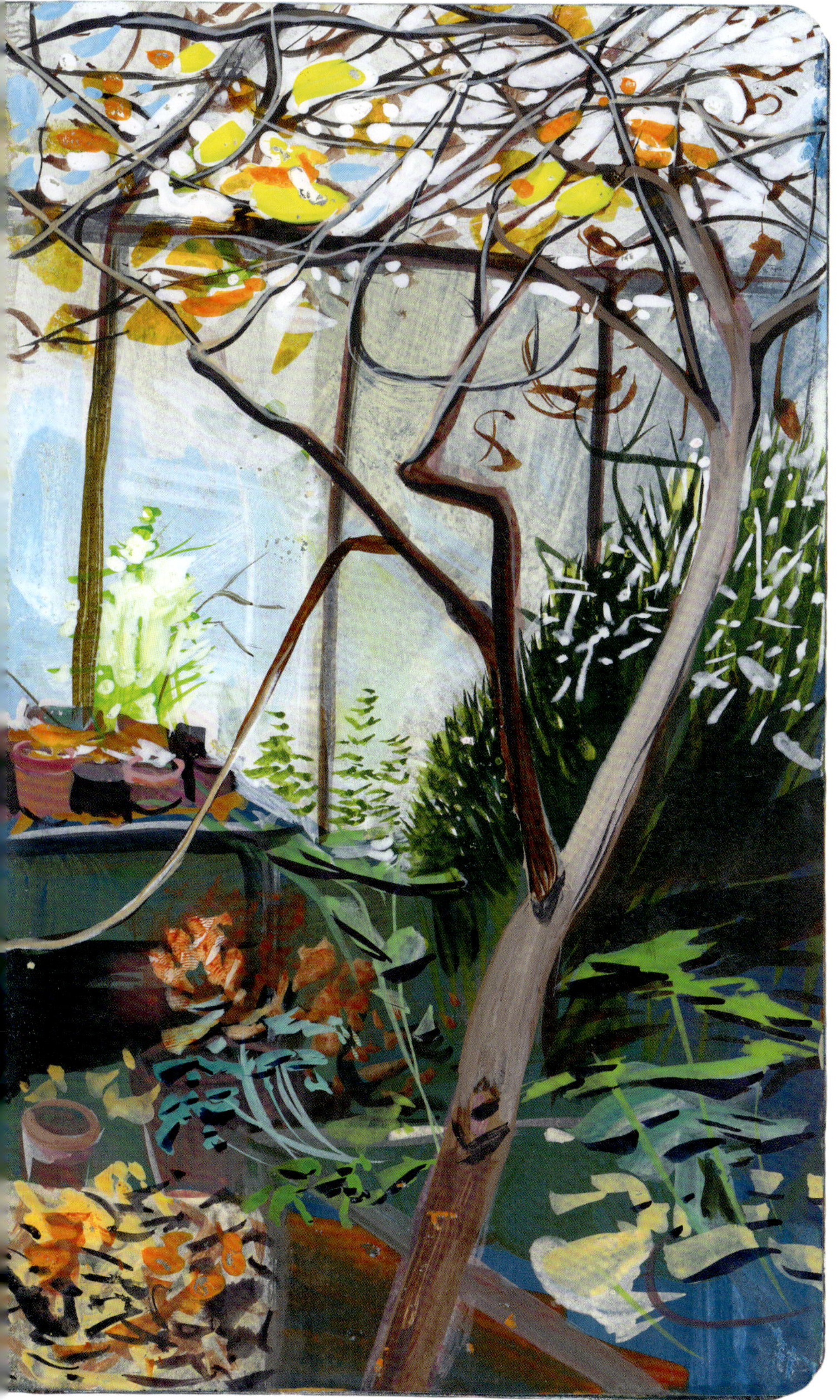

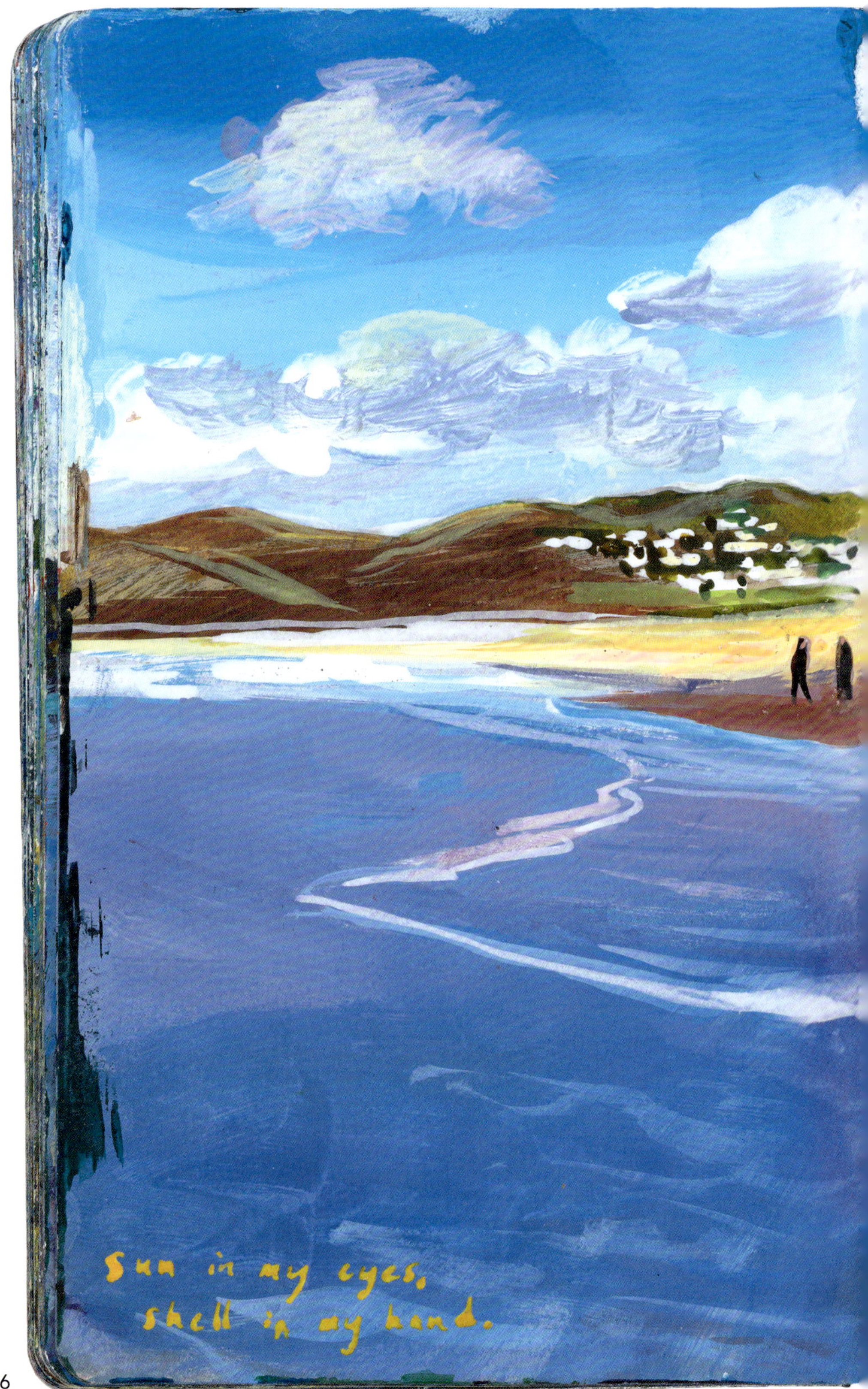
Sun in my eyes,
shell in my hand.

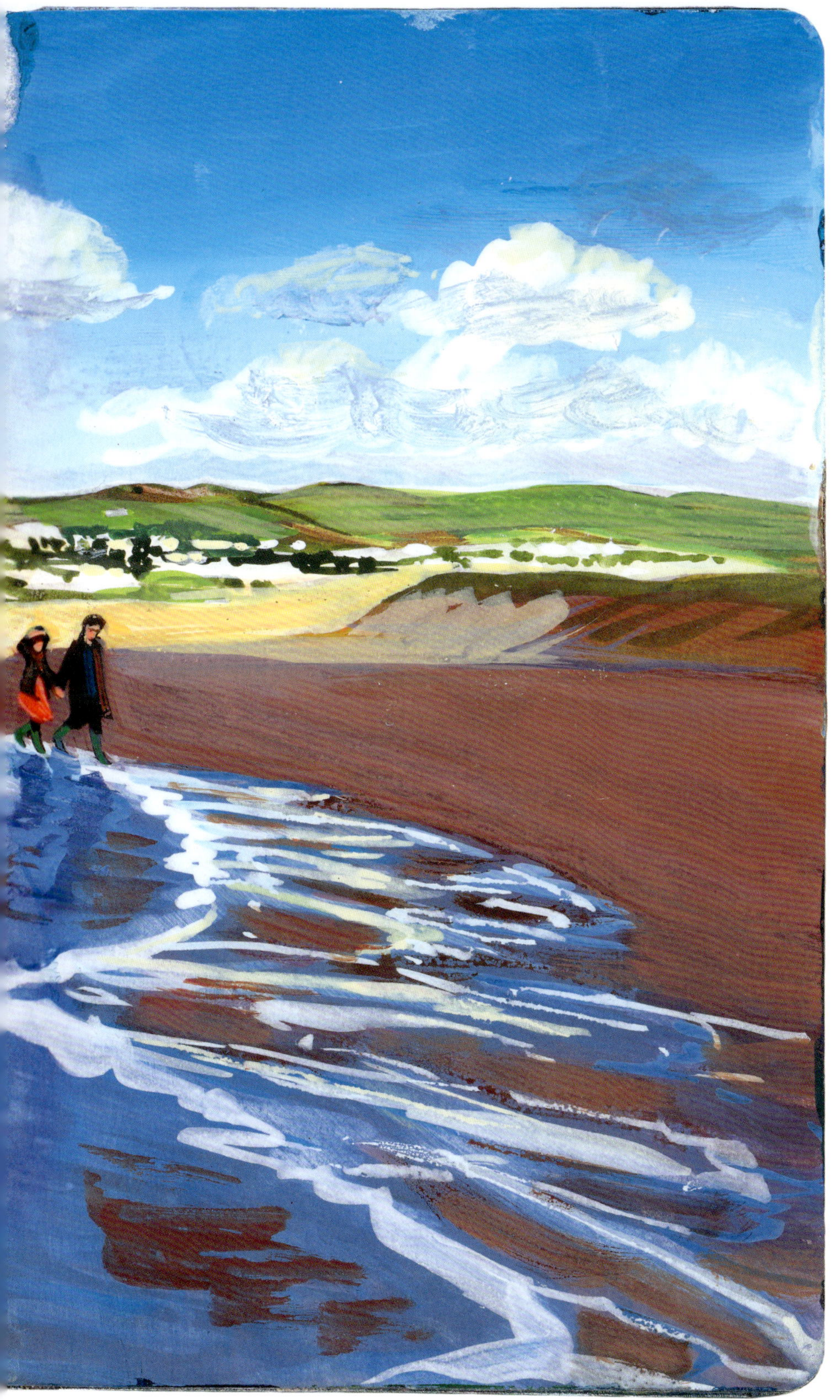

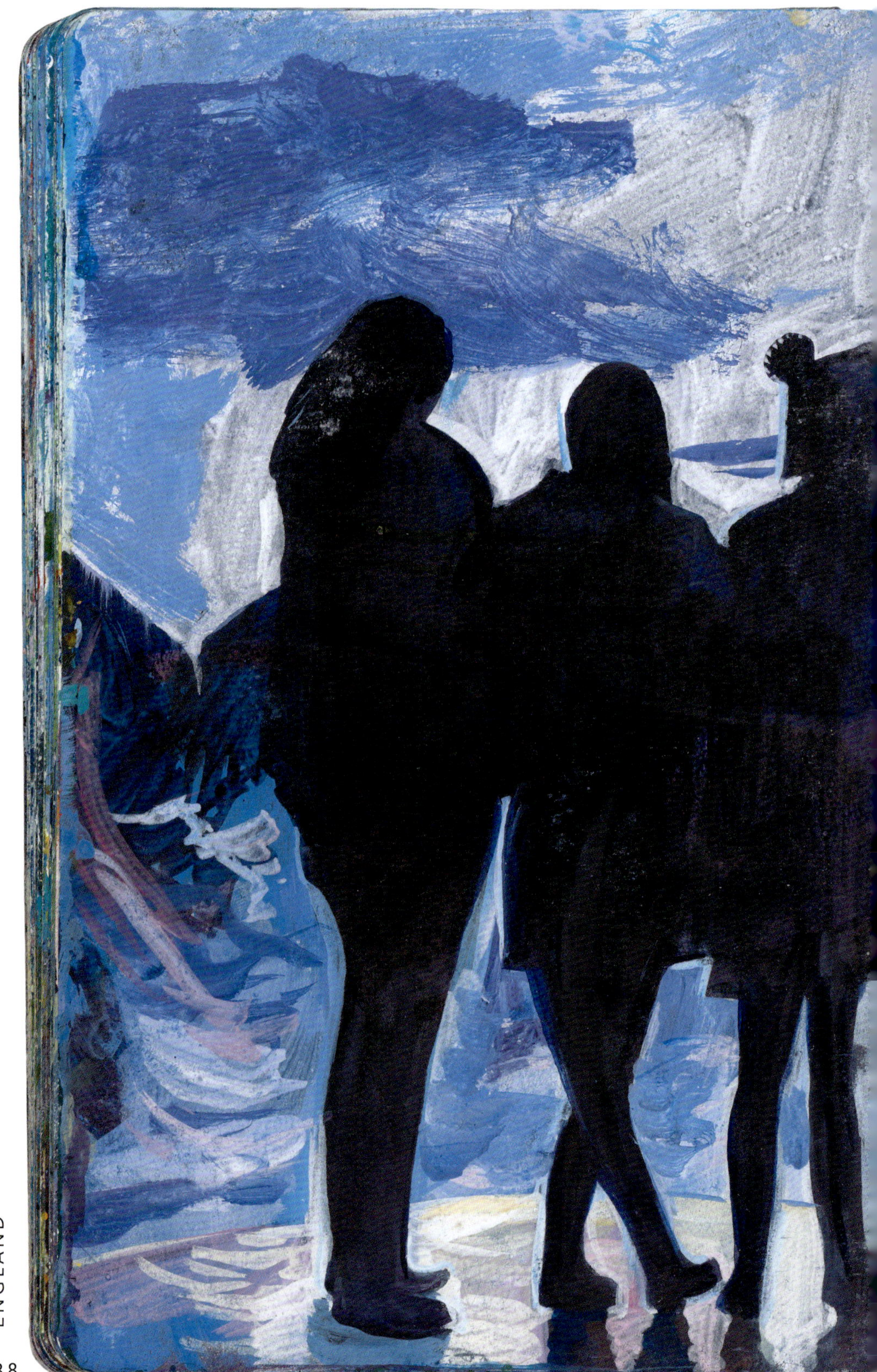

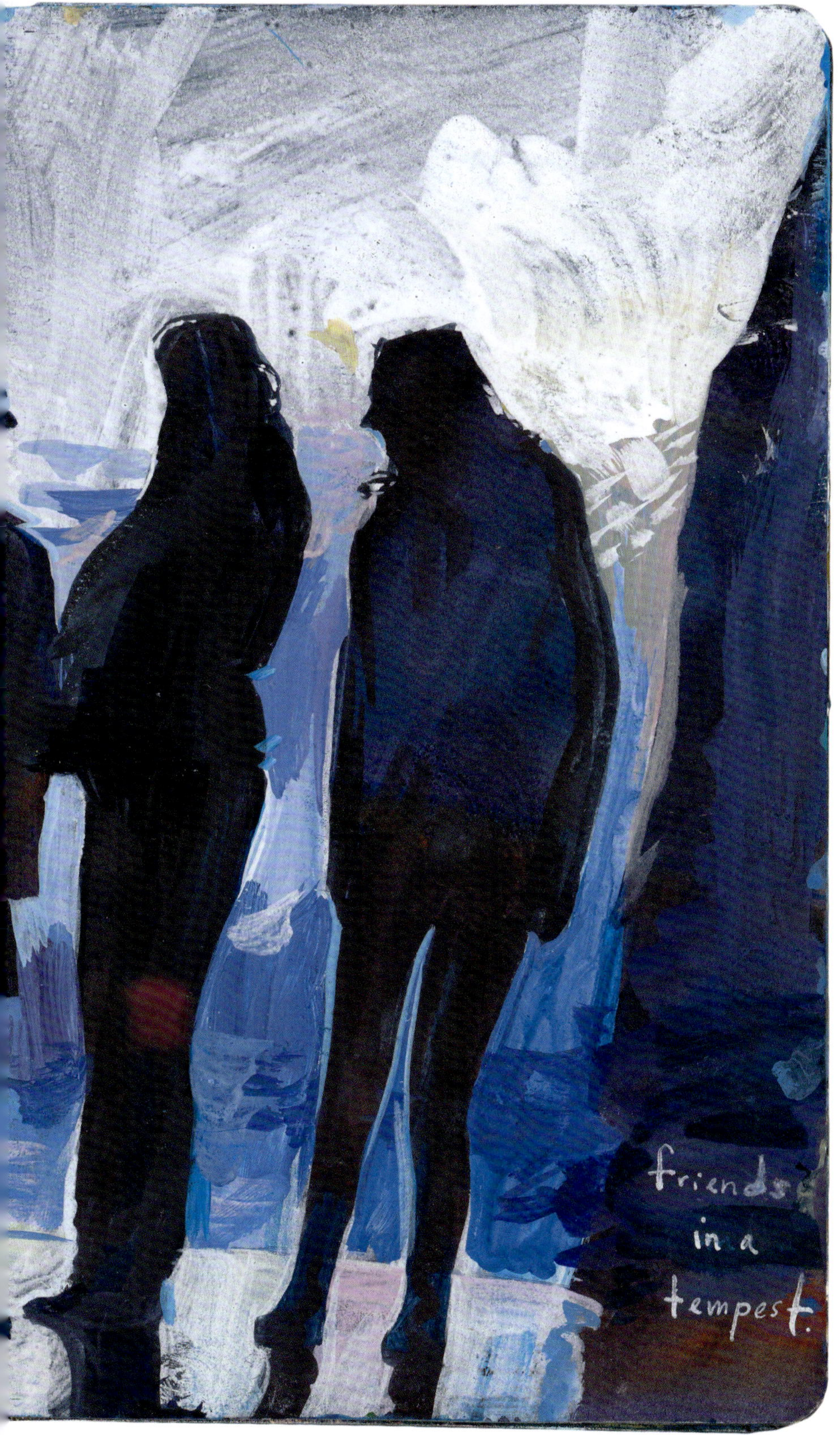

friends
in a
tempest.

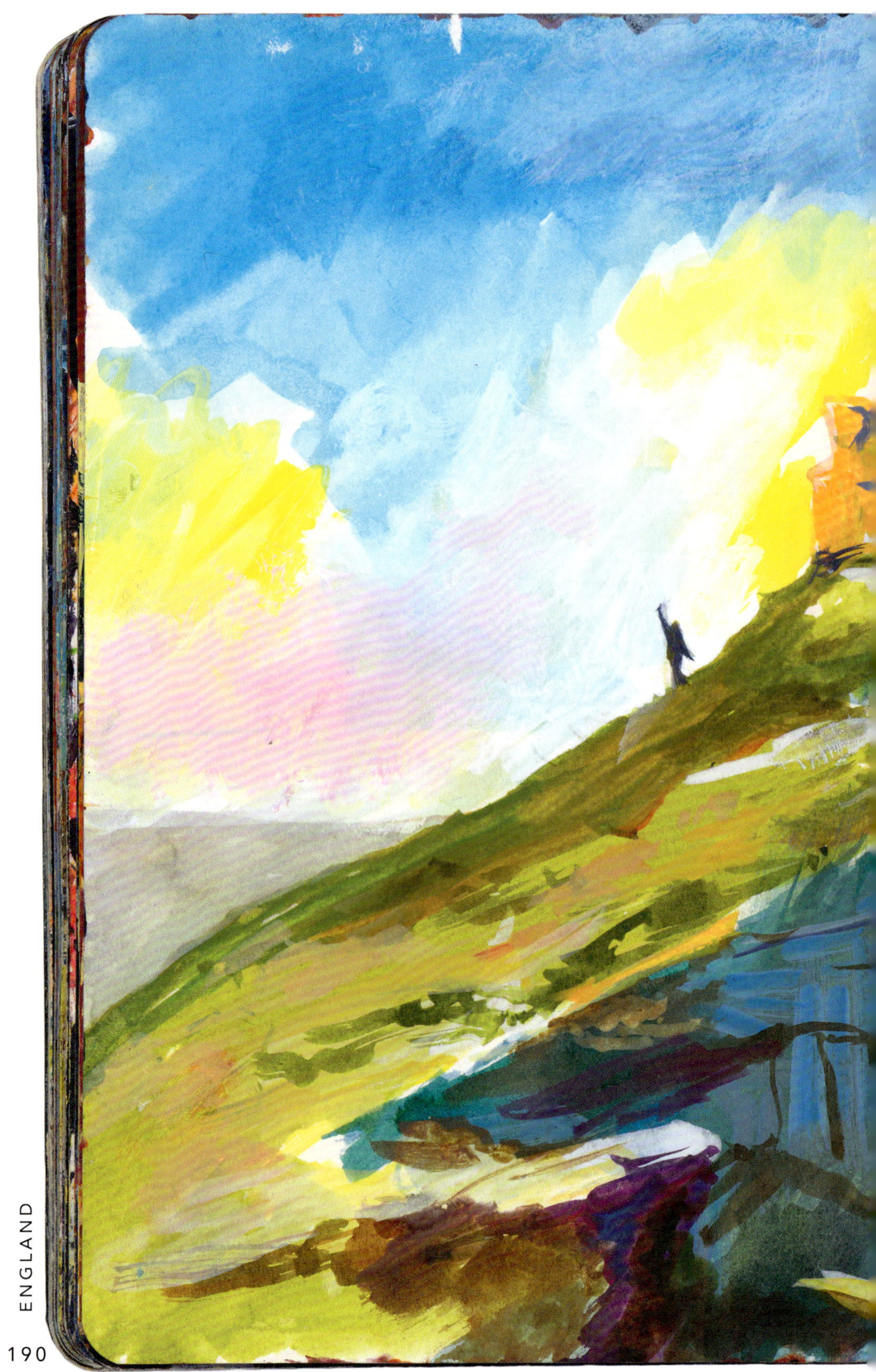

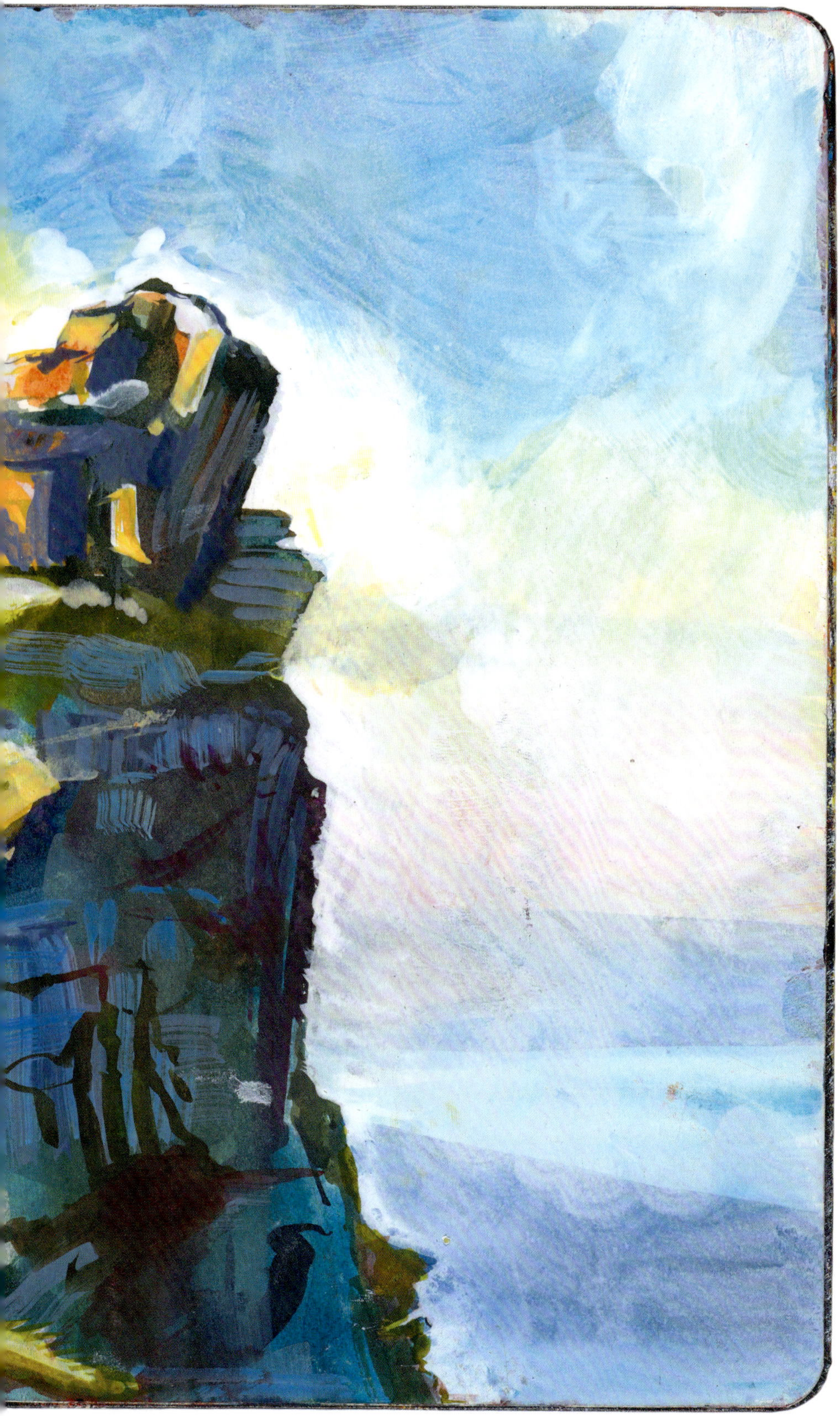

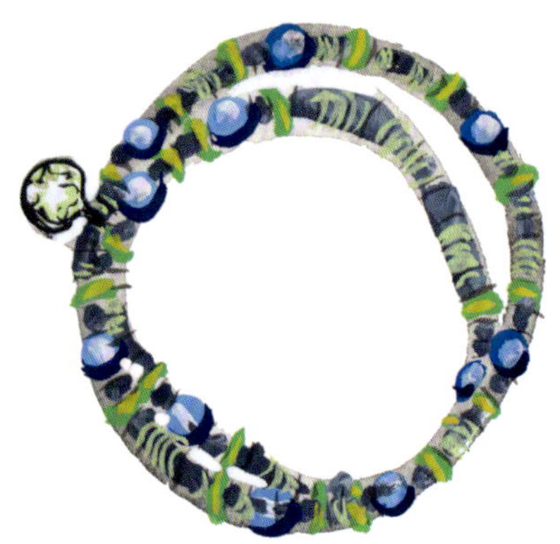

Acknowledgments

The creation of this book and the five-year journey documented in its pages were supported in part by organizations and individuals who graciously offered financial funding, travel opportunities, and professional guidance. Thank you:

Marta Hallett of G Editions; Jennifer Chen Tran of Bradford Literary Agency; The Turkish Fulbright Commission; Carnegie Mellon University Fellowships and Scholarships Office; John Anson Kittredge Fund; Babayan Culture House; Café Tissardmine, artist retreat; Archipelago Art Residency in Korpo Finland (AARK); Residency Old School/Gamli skóli run by Norðanbál art group; Western Michigan University; Courtney Cerruti; Creativebug; Dawn Devries Sokol; Kelly Marie of MEA; Portland Art Gallery; Imaging by Osher Map Library and Smith Center for Cartographic Education

A special thank you to two dear friends, travel buddies, and talented writers who assisted with revisions: Tas Anjarwalla and Malia Griggs

About the Author

Missy Dunaway is an artist and illustrator with a penchant for storytelling. Her work has been featured by Penguin Random House India, *Travel + Leisure* Magazine, Four Seasons Hotels and Resorts, The National Audubon Society, Passion Passport, and in published books including *A World of Artist Journal Pages* by Dawn Devries Sokol (Harry N. Abrams, 2015). A traveler at heart, she has been awarded seven artist-in-residence fellowships to travel and paint abroad, providing the opportunity for long visits and cultural immersion. Her artwork exhibits internationally and is displayed at institutions including Carnegie Mellon University and the Folger Shakespeare Library of Washington, DC.

Missy received her Bachelor's Degree in Humanities and Arts from Carnegie Mellon University. In 2013, she was awarded a Fulbright Research Fellowship to study Anatolian textiles in Turkey, which culminated in a series of paintings that exhibited in Istanbul, Berlin, and the US. In 2019, she was named the inaugural Four Seasons Envoy. Later that year, she was awarded a New Student Scholarship to the Academy of Realist Art in Boston, where she is currently studying.

Missy teaches online at Creativebug, where she instructs how to paint with acrylic ink and keep a travel journal. Her original artwork is available for purchase through Portland Art Gallery, located near her home studio in Cape Elizabeth, Maine.

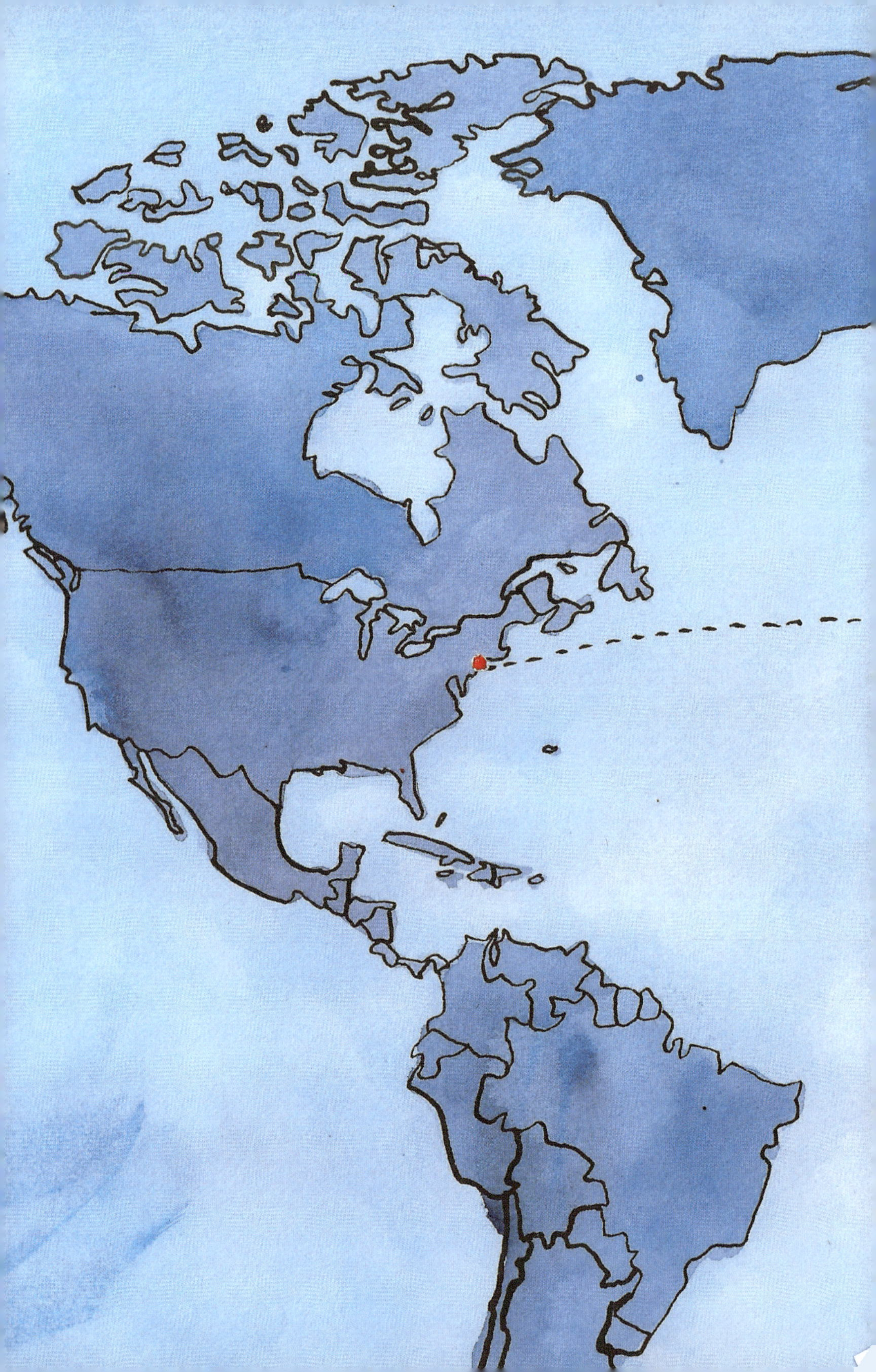